BIBLICAL INTERPRETATION AND PHILOSOPHI...

This book applies philosophical hermeneutics to biblical studies. Whereas traditional studies of the Bible limit their analysis to the exploration of the texts' original historical sense, this book discusses how to move beyond these issues to a consideration of biblical texts' existential significance for the present. In response to the rejection of biblical significance in the late nineteenth century and the accompanying crisis of nihilism, B. H. McLean argues that the philosophical thought of Heidegger, Bultmann, Gadamer, Habermas, Ricoeur, Levinas, Deleuze, and Guattari provides an alternative to historically oriented approaches to biblical interpretation. He uses basic principles drawn from these philosophers' writings to create a framework for a new "post-historical" mode of hermeneutic inquiry that transcends the subject-based epistemological structure of historical positivism.

B. H. McLean is Professor of New Testament Language and Literature at Knox College, University of Toronto. He is the author of *New Testament Greek: An Introduction* (Cambridge University Press, 2011), *An Introduction to the Study of Greek Epigraphy of the Hellenistic and Roman Periods from Alexander the Great down to the Reign of Constantine (323 BCE–337 CE)* (2002), and *Greek and Latin Inscriptions in the Konya Archaeological Museum* (2002).

To Brigid
my muse

Biblical Interpretation and Philosophical Hermeneutics

B. H. McLEAN

Knox College, University of Toronto

CAMBRIDGE
UNIVERSITY PRESS

CAMBRIDGE UNIVERSITY PRESS
Cambridge, New York, Melbourne, Madrid, Cape Town,
Singapore, São Paulo, Delhi, Mexico City

Cambridge University Press
32 Avenue of the Americas, New York, NY 10013-2473, USA

www.cambridge.org
Information on this title: www.cambridge.org/9781107683402

First published 2012

Printed in the United States of America

A catalog record for this publication is available from the British Library.

Library of Congress Cataloging in Publication data
McLean, Bradley H. (Bradley Hudson), 1957–
Biblical interpretation and philosophical hermeneutics / B. H. McLean.
p. cm.
Includes bibliographical references and index.
ISBN 978-1-107-01949-2 (hardback) – ISBN 978-1-107-68340-2 (paperback)
1. Bible – Hermeneutics. 2. Bible – Criticism, interpretation, etc. 3. Hermeneutics. I. Title.
BS476.M3477 2012
220.6–dc23   2011045032

ISBN 978-1-107-01949-2 Hardback
ISBN 978-1-107-68340-2 Paperback

Contents

Preface

Speaking as one trained as a scholar in historical methods of interpretation, I can only express my profound appreciation to scholars of past and present generations who have given us new eyes with which to view the historical dimensions of ancient Judaism and early Christianity. In no way is this book intended to be disrespectful of this grand tradition, which has accomplished so much. But, as Paul Ricoeur once observed, one of the consequences of our heightened appreciation of the historical development of Judaism and Christianity has been the loss of our "first naiveté" concerning our own existential relation to the scriptures.

No doubt, the application of these historical methods of analysis will continue to lead to exciting new insights. Nonetheless, I have written this book with the conviction that we have placed too much trust in historical methods of interpretation. I suspect that historicism and historical positivism have not taken us where previous generations of scholars had hoped it would, for it has ended in a crisis of historical meaning. This crisis has led to a loss of our second naiveté, this time a loss of naiveté concerning the possibility of historical interpretation to provide a secure historical and reasoned foundation for Christian faith. Of course, Ernst Troeltsch, a pioneer in the development of historicism in the nineteenth century, came to this same realization almost a century ago, as did Friedrich Nietzsche a generation before him.

The situation in which we find ourselves is all the more serious because with the discipline's ongoing fixation on historically based methodologies has come a corresponding dislocation with new developments in the closely related fields of study in the humanities and social sciences. For example, the impact on contemporary biblical studies of such movements as poststructuralism, psychotherapy, feminism, critical theory, neopragmatism, gender studies, New Historicism, and postcolonial criticism, to name but a few, has been modest in comparison with the continued hegemony of the discipline's traditional methodologies.

But if these new forms of scholarship have taught our world anything, it is that the human being is not a sovereign subject and that our world – and biblical texts by extension – is not a detached object of inquiry. Thus the primary question that has motivated me to write this book is, What difference would it make to the discipline of biblical studies if scholars were to disavow their "subjecthood"? And what difference would it make if scholars were to cease reading the scriptures as objects of inquiry? This book constitutes an exploration of these two basic questions.

If sovereign subjecthood is a myth of the Enlightenment (as I think it is), then the continued reliance on the subject-object epistemological model can only lead scholars more deeply into forms of alienation, from ourselves, others, and the environment. I will leave it up to my readers to assess the adequacy of my response to this crisis of historical meaning. For my part, I am sure that I have not provided a definitive answer to these questions. However, it is my hope that I have helpfully raised these two questions at a time when they need to be raised again. I believe that the process of answering these questions can lead to a renewed form of hermeneutic inquiry.

Now, it is my pleasant duty to give my sincere thanks to those who have helped make this work possible. I would like to thank Thomas Reynolds and James Olthuis, my colleagues, who provided much encouragement during the early stages of writing. I must also express my deep appreciation to Brigid Kelso and Michael Sohn, both of whom read the manuscript in draft form. Their helpful comments, criticisms, and suggestions improved the overall quality of the book. Finally, I would like to express my gratitude to Cambridge University Press for its faith in this adventurous project.

B. H. McLean
10 September 2011

Introduction

Have patience with everything unresolved in your heart
and try to love the questions themselves as if they were locked rooms or books
written in a very foreign language.
Don't search for the answers, which could not be given to you now, because you
would not be able to live them.
And the point is, to live everything.
Live the questions now.[1]

This book is intended for those who love the questions concerning the meaning of the Christian scriptures. In the face of those who believe they already possess the answers, and those who have ruled out the very possibility of there being *any* answers, those who love the questions will have an opportunity in this book to, in the words of Rainer Maria Rilke, "live the questions" of biblical interpretation. The purpose of this book is not to explain specific methods of textual interpretation but rather to explore biblical hermeneutics as a mode of questioning the meaning of biblical texts, especially as it has been carried out in the Continental (European) tradition.

One of the expected attributes of anything one calls a "text" is its meaningfulness. But what is meaning? This book focuses particularly on two kinds of meaning. The first kind of meaning I term the *"founding* sense-event," which specifies the meaning of any biblical text as understood in terms of its relation to three sets of components: its prior sociohistorical referents, its author's intentions and beliefs, and language itself. In addition to these components is a fourth component, which is that of "sense." As I discuss in Chapter 1, language always conveys something more than, or in addition to, that which is communicated through its three primary components. This "something more" is termed "sense." The second kind of textual meaning I discuss is a *"present* sense-event," which is the significance of the "founding sense-event" for us, in our own world. The present sense-event emerges from the "text-reception complex," which is the a priori role of the situated interpreter (within a changed set of "value" relations) in the disclosure of textual "sense."

---

[1] Rainer Maria Rilke, "Letter Four (16 July 1903)," in *Letters to a Young Poet,* trans. Joan M. Burnham (Novato, CA: New World Library, 2000), 35.

The present sense-event always involves a replaying, or counteractualizing, of the founding sense-event in the world of the interpreter. It involves the care of the self, and one's own purposeful engagement with others and the contemporary world in the present. One could say that this present sense-event has an existential dimension, with the understanding that the present sense-event is not anthropocentric, extending, as it does, well beyond the realm of human, intentional "meaning-making." In a very real sense, meaning is our destiny.

Over the past century, the discipline of biblical studies has almost exclusively concerned itself with the "founding sense-event" of texts, traditionally understood historically as an aggregate of their antecedent sociohistorical contexts, authorial intentions, and semantic contents. There can be no doubt that this model of interpretation has contributed greatly to our understanding of biblical texts and the sociohistorical worlds behind them. For this reason, I argue that any formulation of a renewed "post-historical" hermeneutics should continue to appreciate the insights afforded by historically focused methods of analysis. However, the interpretation of texts in terms of their respective historical contexts, authors, and semantics has often functioned as the *limit point* of interpretation, beyond which biblical scholars have been reticent to venture. In point of fact, few critical scholars dare to enter into the domain of the "present sense-event," which concerns their very selves and the world within which they live. Indeed, it has become a point of principle for many critical scholars *not* to venture there. Many hold the conviction that the role of the biblical scholar is actually to clarify the objective sense of biblical texts and dispel superstitious misconceptions.

But this conviction, which may appear laudable at first glance, is highly problematic because, as Heidegger observes, such critical scholarship "never recollects itself." In other words, this epistemological model leaves no room to examine and critique the role of the scholar, as ordering, thematizing, positing, and naming subject. As such, it overlooks a key component of the text-reception complex. Why do scholars ask some questions of texts and not others? Why do they write books on one subject rather than another? Historical positivism leaves no room to ask such questions. As such, Heidegger has argued that *many scholars grasp the phenomenon but never the thinking of the phenomenon.*

Rather than attempting to absent themselves from the process of biblical interpretation, other critical scholars have followed a different path. For example, Hans-Georg Gadamer and Paul Ricoeur have maintained that biblical interpretation necessarily requires one to venture beyond the mere recovery of a text's founding sense-event to an appreciation of a text as a present sense-event. According to this view, interpretation requires that the interpreter enter into a *dialogical* relation with biblical texts, the goal of which extends beyond that of clarifying the purported objective sense of a text to replaying or counteractualizing a text's founding sense-event as a present sense-event. This book argues that it is *only by going beyond a text's founding sense-event that the interpretive act becomes complete.*

From one perspective, this book can be read as a kind of narrative. Chapters 2 and 3 tell the story of the loss of biblical significance in the late nineteenth century: with the rapid rise of historical approaches to biblical interpretation in the nineteenth century, there also arose a growing appreciation of the cultural and social difference between the ancient worlds out of which biblical texts emerged and those of our own world. This new appreciation of historical difference caused a growing recognition that *we* are not the intended readers or recipients of the books of the Bible. With this greater appreciation of historical difference came the loss of what Ricoeur has called our "first naiveté." To read the scriptures in the present, with an historical awareness, is to experience the profound cultural distance between our own world and that of the ancient world in which the scriptures were written. The scriptures have now become for us "texts" requiring historical interpretation.

What is more, these "texts" have been transformed by historically minded scholarship into historical "sources" for reconstructing the ancient peoples and worlds behind the texts, such as the "historical Jesus" and various historical forms of early Judaism and Christianity, whose faint traces can be discerned in the texts of scripture. In the process of this transformation of scripture to texts, and texts to historical sources, it has also become clear that the beliefs and ethical teachings of Jesus, Paul, and the first Christians were culturally conditioned and historically contingent. In the nineteenth century, this heightened awareness raised a question: How can such "biblical" beliefs and ethical teachings be binding upon the modern believer, who lives in a very different cultural and social context? In other words, How can the founding sense-event of biblical texts be relevant today?

With the growing recognition of the historical relativity of all biblical texts has also come an appreciation of the historical relativity of those who interpret biblical texts in the present, for if the original authors of biblical texts were themselves conditioned by social and cultural factors within their own historical worlds, then modern-day interpreters must likewise be shaped by similar social and cultural factors. Thus, the historicization of biblical authors has brought with it the unexpected discovery that even the consciousness of biblical scholars in the present is historically conditioned. Though often ignored, this discovery has actually subverted the possibility of objective, scholarly knowledge of the Bible.

The point of this very brief overview of the recent history of the discipline of biblical studies is to demonstrate why scholarship's initial optimism over the benefits of "historicism" (historical approaches) to biblical interpretation has given way to a pervasive pessimism in the early twentieth century. Whereas the original impulse of historical analysis was to provide a secure historical and reasoned foundation for faith, many Christians and Jews later came to view it as a dehumanizing force that subverts the ethical values and truths of Christianity and Judaism. Indeed, a widespread perception arose that historicism leads to "nihilism," broadly defined as the belief that truth, meaning, and morals are socially, culturally, and historically relative. Thus, just as Friedrich Nietzsche had previously prophesied, when early Christianity is analyzed into "completely historical" knowledge, and is "resolved ... into pure knowledge," it "ceases to live" and is thereby "annihilated" by the historicizing process itself.[2]

At the very time when this crisis of historical meaning was unfolding in Europe, the First World War broke out, resulting in a magnification of the experience of nihilism. When historicism was viewed against the background of the carnage, misery, and upheaval of the war and postwar period, historicism's undistracted quest for the objective historical meaning of biblical texts and the reconstruction of the Bible's historical sources seemed to be spiritually arid and socially irrelevant. The fact that historicism (and German liberal Protestantism, which had embraced it) had no wisdom to share in the face of the bloodiest war in human history also contributed to a sense of profound disillusionment concerning the continuing relevance of purely historical approaches to the Bible.

Reflecting in our own time on this disillusionment, Emmanuel Levinas has observed that the very act of reducing the Bible to its historical foundations "calls into question, relativizes and devalues every moment."[3] Given this long-standing disillusionment with historicism, it is all the more surprising that the discipline of biblical studies in the present continues to be guided by the theoretical structure of nineteenth-century historicism, in the form of historical positivism (see Chapter 4). As a result, it has largely lost its ability to reflect on the significance of biblical texts for life in the present.

However, there is nothing new about this loss of biblical significance. As far back as the 1920s, many scholars had grown skeptical of historicism's usefulness as a way of addressing the question of biblical meaning. In part, this growing skepticism explains why Barth's ground-breaking *Commentary on Romans*, Ernst Troeltsch's classic essay "The Crisis of Historicism," and Martin Heidegger's epic *Being and Time* were all published within a few short years of each other – in 1919, 1922, and 1927, respectively. Each, in his own way, had come to view historicism, and its ideal of objectifying textual meaning according to historical categories, as an *inadequate* interpretive tool. In fact, by the time Troeltsch published his essay in 1922, the belief that a crisis had overtaken historicism had virtually become a cliché in the German academic world. Far from being the first to sense the crisis, Troeltsch's *own* admission only served to demonstrate how wide skepticism regarding historicism's continuing value had spread.[4]

[2]   Friedrich Nietzsche, *On the Advantage and Disadvantage of History for Life*, trans. Peter Preuss (Indianapolis: Hackett, 1980 [1874]), 39, 40 (§ 7).
[3]   Emmanuel Levinas, *Beyond the Verse: Talmudic Readings and Lectures*, trans. Gary D. Mole (London: Athlone Press, 1994), 17.
[4]   Jeffrey A. Barash provides a lengthy account of the emergence of the problem of historical meaning after 1850 in his *Heidegger and the Problem of Historical Meaning*, rev. and expanded ed. (New York: Fordham University Press, 1988).

For his part, Martin Heidegger set out to formulate a new foundation for *authentic,* historiological practice that could help make the "past vital again" and bring it into the future. Heidegger addressed this crisis of historicism by arguing that it is not really an epistemological problem at all but rather an *existential* phenomenon of human existence. He further argued that this crisis of meaning creates an opportunity, for if the meaning of the past concerns what it means for human beings to be historical beings, then the crisis of historicism creates an opportunity for us to explore our own human historicality. To this end, in *Being and Time* (1927) Heidegger embarked upon an ever-deepening analysis of the very structures of human historicality that constitute the hermeneutic conditions for all forms of interpretation. In fact, *Being and Time* can be read as an exploration of the "situatedness" of the interpreter, as a nonsubject, full of care, living in a particular time and place.

Heidegger reminds us that we, as interpreters, can grasp the significance of biblical texts (as founding sense-events) only by appropriating them from within our own historical lives as present sense-events. We cannot bypass the text-reception complex in the pursuit of final, scientific objectivity. This fact represents an "opportunity" rather than an obstacle, because our "historically effected consciousness" is actually the very *source* of all hermeneutical significance. Therefore, the real challenge for biblical interpreters is not to reinstate their objectivity as ahistorical, sovereign subjects but rather to reject their tacit acceptance of themselves as ahistorical subjects. This book argues that the writings of Heidegger, Bultmann, Gadamer, Habermas, Ricoeur, Levinas, and Deleuze provide alternatives to purely historical approaches of biblical interpretation. The principles they enunciate provide a kind of framework for interpreting biblical texts outside the narrow subject-object epistemological structure of traditional biblical studies.

Following the chapters dealing with Heidegger and Bultmann, this book discusses the rediscovery of Saussure's semiotic theory in the late 1950s and 1960s, and the ensuing advent of structuralism. With the so-called linguistic turn that followed in the Western philosophic tradition came the recognition that the language is more than a tool of human communication: it is also a form of codifying reality, a form that structures what is thinkable and expressible. This principle of *linguistic relativity* is officially known as the "Sapir-Whorf hypothesis" (or "Whorfianism"). According to this principle, the structures of individual languages influence the ways in which we linguistically conceptualize our world (either in speech or writing). Hans-Georg Gadamer was the first to explore how language as a form of codification informs the work of biblical hermeneutics.

After our discussion of Gadamer's *Truth and Method*, we turn our attention to Jürgen Habermas, who engaged with Gadamer in what is now widely considered to be the classic debate on the nature of hermeneutical praxis. In contrast to Gadamer, who worked within the phenomenological tradition of Husserl and Heidegger, Habermas came out of a different tradition, known as the Frankfurt school or critical theory. Whereas Gadamer deferred to the language of tradition, Habermas argued that one must also be critically reflective about the complicity of language – even in the guise of the language of tradition – in distorting communication. He insisted on the necessity of *critiquing* language as a possible carrier of ideology. Paul Ricoeur mediated in this debate by exploring the productive space of interaction between the positions of Gadamer and Habermas.

Like the work of Ricoeur and Gadamer, the hermeneutic thought of Emmanuel Levinas also originated in the phenomenological thought of Husserl and Heidegger. But whereas Heidegger argued for the priority of self-understanding over scientific explanation, Levinas exposed what is lost in Heidegger's undistracted quest for self-understanding, namely, one's individual ethical responsibility to others, which precedes self-understanding. Levinas's hermeneutical model is based on what he terms the "solicitation" and "elevation" of biblical meaning before the gaze of the other, which entreats us to ethical action.

The final chapter of this book takes up a consideration of the philosophical thought of Gilles Deleuze and Félix Guattari. Whereas previous chapters provided an overview of key figures in the canon of philosophical hermeneutics, this final chapter presents ideas that have yet to find a home within the field of biblical hermeneutics. No less a philosopher than Michel Foucault once predicted that the twentieth century would be known as the "Deleuzian" century.[5] With the benefit of hindsight, we can see that Foucault misjudged the rapidity with which the writings of Deleuze and Guattari would be received in North America. Nonetheless, their writings are now being read widely across many disciplines, including theology. Thus, the final chapter looks forward in anticipation of what may be on the horizon for biblical hermeneutics, arguing that the role of the "embodied" biblical interpreter is to enact a present sense-event within an ever-expanding global ecology of relations. In a real way, the very act of biblical interpretation both reveals and creates new relations of "sense" and bestows upon the "body" of the interpreter a "spiritual" quality that greatly exceeds its own material dimensions.

In addition to those already named, many other voices over the past century have problematized the implied scientistic mindset of the humanities and social sciences in general. After all, the crisis of historicism overlapped not only the aftermath of the First World War but also the reception of the writings of Nietzsche, Freud, and Marx, the impact of which triggered a crisis of the Enlightenment model of rationality. Their respective explorations of the "will to power," the unconscious, and ideology, respectively, challenged the epistemic status of all forms of objectifying knowledge, including the positivistic methodologies associated with biblical studies. In the present, one can still easily recognize the continuing impact of

---

[5]   Michel Foucault, "Theatrum Philosophicum," in *Language, Counter-Memory, Practice*, ed. Donald F. Bouchard, trans. Donald F. Bouchard and Sherry Simon (Ithaca, NY: Cornell University Press, 1977), 165–96, esp. 165.

their thought in such movements as poststructuralism, psychotherapy, feminism, critical theory, neopragmatism, gender studies, New Historicism, and postcolonial criticism, to name but a few.

We can likewise perceive their continuing influence in the form of the many "deaths" that have been proclaimed and celebrated over this past century, beginning with the most famous of all deaths, Nietzsche's "death of God" (i.e., the death of universal Truth). Like the collapse of the proverbial castle of cards, the "death of God" resulted in many other deaths, including Roland Barthes's "death of the author," Michel Foucault's "death of man," Theodor Adorno's "death of poetry," and Francis Fukuyama's "death of history." Against this backdrop of death upon death, this book argues that biblical studies' continued attachment to historical positivism is *more tragic than it is flawed*. It is tragic because the discipline's incapacity to conceptualize the present sense-event has allowed nihilism to take hold of it. Whether or not individual biblical scholars in their professional lives remain capable of experiencing this crisis of nihilism is irrelevant: this present crisis of nihilism is *the* dominant theme of postmodernity. Biblical studies' unwitting surrender to it simply provides yet another witness to its pervasiveness in society as a whole. What is more, the ongoing tyranny of historicism, in the form of historical positivism, within biblical studies continues to have the effect of normalizing the outmoded epistemological framework of the Enlightenment with the result that other ways of knowing continue to be marginalized and excluded.

This book not only narrates this loss of significance and the advent of the crisis of nihilism but also explores modes of biblical interpretation that return to the biblical interpreter the capacity to speak again of the significance of biblical texts, of the spiritual dimension of life, and even of revelation. In other words, this book articulates an alternative mode of hermeneutic praxis. Now, keeping this brief overview in mind, let us begin "living the questions," by exploring the meaning of meaning.

PART I

THE CRISIS OF HISTORICAL MEANING

1

∾

The Meaning of Meaning

There is no apprentice who is not "the Egyptologist" of something. One becomes a carpenter only by becoming sensitive to the signs of wood, a physician by becoming sensitive to the signs of disease. Vocation is always predestination with regard to signs. Everything that teaches us something emits signs.[1]

One of the expected attributes of anything we call a "text" is meaningfulness. In the very act of trying to read or decipher a text (fig. 1.1), one always brings the expectation of recovering something we call "meaning." But what is meaning? What are we seeking when we ask the question, What does this text *mean*? Does a text have one meaning or many? If a historian, a theologian, a psychotherapist, and a Marxist were all to read the same passage from the New Testament, each would likely find it "meaningful" but in different ways. This observation suggests that the term "meaning" is too broad for the purposes of this book.

In order to clarify the concept of meaningfulness, this chapter differentiates three components of language, as explicated by Gilles Deleuze in *The Logic of Sense*: expression and signification, denotation, and manifestation.[2] These three components concern semantic meaning, reference, and the beliefs and intentions of authors, respectively. According to Deleuze, when taken together, they form a "regime" of representation, within which culture and society are configured both materially and symbolically. Each of the three components functions with the other two in an interdependent circle. I argue that textual "sense" is an additional, fourth dimension of language that is strongly related to, but distinguishable from, these three components. In a very real way, this chapter provides the theoretical orientation for all the chapters of this book and finds its consummation in Chapter 12, which concerns the philosophy of Gilles Deleuze and Félix Guattari.

[1] Gilles Deleuze, *Proust and Signs: The Complete Text*, trans. Richard Howard (Minneapolis: University of Minnesota Press, 2008 [1964]), 5.
[2] Gilles Deleuze, *The Logic of Sense*, trans. Mark Lester, with Charles Stivale, ed. Constantin V. Boundas (New York: Columbia University Press, 1990 [1969]).

1.1. Greek inscription from Ephesus

EXPRESSION AND SIGNIFICATION

In *De trinitate*, Saint Augustine discussed the ability of words to denote things in the world (X, 1.2). Citing the archaic word *temetum* as an example, he relates the experience of hearing this word, whose meaning was unknown to him. In this very experience he recognized that the *sound* of the word *temetum* was not an "empty voice sound" (*inanem vocem*). Indeed, he knew the word was *a sign of something else*. Nevertheless, that which this linguistic sign denoted was "not fully known" to him.[3] Augustine reflected on this experience of knowing that a word is more than a mere sound (*istas tres syllabas*) but yet not knowing its meaning.[4] It was at this point that he realized that what he was actually experiencing was the very

---

[3] Augustine, *The Trinity*, trans. Stephen McKenna (Washington, DC: Catholic University of America Press, 1963), 292–93.

[4] *Temetum* actually means *vinum* (vine).

potential of words to signify. But do *all* words possess this potential to signify? The opening stanza of Lewis Carroll's wonderful poem Jabberwocky, reads as follows:

> Twas brillig, and the slithy toves
> Did gyre and gimble in the wabe:
> All mimsy were the borogoves,
> And the mome raths outgrabe.

This poem leaves the reader with a faint impression of signifying something, except for the fact that the individual words are meaningless. Although this poem's words are correctly arranged according to the rules of English syntax, it is a non-sense poem, nonetheless, because its words fail to signify.[5] This raises the question: By what means do words actually signify, and what do they signify?

In the twentieth century, the Swiss linguist Ferdinand de Saussure (1857–1913) attempted to answer these questions by developing a theory of language as a system of "signs." He named this semiotic system "language" (*langue*). According to Saussure, "language" is a semiotic structure shared by a linguistic community whereby *concepts* become associated with spoken and written words (morphemes). He termed instances of actual spoken language "speech" (*parole*).[6] Saussure emphasized the priority of the structure of "language" over any particular instantiation of this structure in actual human communication (*parole*). Like an iceberg, the great majority of which remains submerged beneath the surface of the water, Saussure's theory privileged the submerged, structural dimension of language over observable acts of human communication.

The basic linguistic unit of Saussure's semiotic model is the "sign." By definition, a "sign" is formed by the union of a "signifier" and "signified." A "signifier" is the psychological impression, or "sound-image," which a spoken sound makes upon one's consciousness. In other words, it is what one hears. The term "signified" denotes the *concept* of a thing, shared by a linguistic community, which is associated with a particular "signifier." For example, the word "tree" is a sign made up of two parts: a signifier, that is, the sound "tree" (as heard by a human ear), and a signified, which is the concept of a "tree" (i.e., a woody plant having a main trunk and leafy canopy) that comes to mind when one hears this sound. Thus, this linguistic "sign" is constituted by the *union* of a specific sound-image, "tree," and our shared concept of a tree.

The distinction between the signifier and signified is only a *modal* distinction because a sign is *indivisible*. Just as one can conceptually distinguish between the color and shape of an object, even though they are two properties of the same object,

---

Lewis Carroll, *Through the Looking-Glass and What Alice Found There* (New York: Random House, 1946), 18.

6 Saussure limited his studies to spoken language. He deemed writing to be a secondary form of language that obscured the real language system; Ferdinand de Saussure, *Course in General Linguistics* (Oxford: Duckworth, 1976 [1916]), 30.

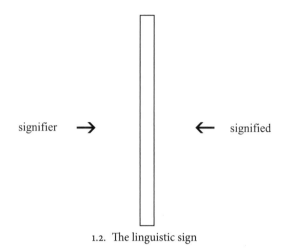

1.2. The linguistic sign

the signifier and signified likewise can be distinguished but never separated in practice. To illustrate this point, Saussure compared the linguistic sign to a piece of paper,
whose front side and back side can be distinguished but not separated (fig. 1.2).

Jacques Derrida likened a linguistic sign to a "hinge" (*la brisure*). Like a hinge,
the sign both *joins* (signifier with signified) and *breaks* (the order of signifiers from
the order of signifieds). In other words, a sign is both a joining and breaking of
two different kinds of things: sounds (or written words) and concepts. This is the
essential paradox of the sign: the unalterable difference between sounds (or written words) and concepts, even though they are joined together in a sign. Derrida's
image of a "hinge" reminds us of the impossibility of achieving a unity between the
order of the signifieds and the order of the signifiers. According to Deleuze, each
of these two orders "*is in variation* and is defined not by its constants and homo-
geneity, but, on the contrary, by a variability whose characteristics are immanent,
continuous, and regulated in a very specific mode."[7] Each order is heterogeneous
and actually changes in composition over time.

One of the implications of Saussure's theory is that words do not directly represent the sensible world or entities contained therein.[8] They merely point to the

---

[7] Gilles Deleuze and Félix Guattari, *Thousand Plateaus: Capitalism and Schizophrenia*, trans. Brian
     Massumi (Minneapolis: University of Minnesota Press, 1987 [1980]), 93–94 (emphasis added).

[8] In this respect, he was following the tradition of the Christian philosopher Boethius (475–525).
     In contrast to Augustine, who developed a theory of language that focused on individual words
     as units of meaning that refer to things in the world, Boethius developed an alternative theory of
     language that broke with Augustinian tradition. In his view, words are not individual, or compart-
     mentalized, units of meaning. Words belong to a larger significatory *system*; cf. G. R. Evans, *The
     Language and Logic of the Bible: The Earlier Middle Ages* (Cambridge: Cambridge University Press,
     1984), 72–76; Boethius, *Commentarium in librum Aristotelis "Peri hermeneias," liber primus*, ed.
     C. Meiser (Leipzig, 1877), 32; repr. Carolus Meiser (ed.), *Commentaries on Aristotle's "De interpre-
     tatione,"* 2 vols. (New York: Garland, 1987).

1.3. René Magritte, *The Treachery of Images* (*La Trahison des images*, 1928–29), Los Angeles County Museum of Art, Los Angeles, California (Digital image @ 2009 Museum Associates / LACMA / Art Resource, NY)

shared concepts we have of things. This relation between words and shared concepts was ironically demonstrated by the Belgian surrealist painter René Magritte in his painting *La Trahison des images* (fig. 1.3). In this painting, Magritte depicts a smoking pipe, under which is written "This is not a pipe" (*Ceci n'est pas une pipe*).

What is Magritte's point? This indeed is not a pipe: this is a conceptualization or representation of a pipe. To signify – whether using the medium of paint or the graphic symbols of language – is not to denote actual things in the world but to *represent* them.[9] For his part, Saussure was not interested in *how* linguistic communities establish the relations between signifiers and signifieds (e.g., why we call a tree a "tree") or in the connection between words and things. Rather, he wanted to expose the very *structurality of language* that makes all signification possible.

Saussure's theory – that words point to our shared concepts of things – may contradict your own assumptions about how language functions. You might assume

---

[9] Cf. Michel Foucault, *This Is Not a Pipe (with Illustrations and Letters by René Magritte)*, ed. J. Faubion, trans. James Harkness, enlarged edition (New York: New Press, 1998 [1968]), 187–203.

that the relation between words and things in the world is somehow natural (e.g., a tree is called a "tree" because that is its *real* name) and that language is a system of naming actual things in the world, or pointing to actual things in the world (e.g., the word "tree" points to real trees). Indeed, on the basis of Genesis 2:10 one might even presume that some sort of archaic connection exists between words and things:

So out of the ground the Lord God formed every animal of the field and every bird of the air, and brought them to Adam to see what he would call them; and whatever Adam called every living creature, that was its name. (Gen 2:10)

This story of Adam giving names to things in the world implies that at the dawn of human civilization an archaic connection was established between words and things. However, even this connection seems arbitrary, rather than natural or essential. After all, it was the all-too-human Adam, not God, who assigned names to things (fig. 1.4). In light of this mythic story, the fable of the tower of Babel (Gen 11:1–9) could be construed as God's subsequent act of confusing this archaic connection between words and things as a punishment for humanity's hubris. The story begins with the statement that "the whole earth had one language and few words (Gen 11:1). It would seem that when God "confused" or multiplied "the languages of all the earth," this archaic connection between words and things, as previously established by Adam, was forever lost.[10]

For aeons, these two mythical stories have exercised a powerful influence on the Western imagination, giving rise to the presumption that a *natural* connection does exist between words and things. But Saussurian semiotics demonstrates not only that "signifiers" (words) refer to "signifieds" (concepts), not to things, but also that the relationship between them is *arbitrary*, which is to say, it is not naturally or essentially fixed in any way.[11] For example, the concept (signified) associated with the English signifier "tree" (of a woody plant having a main trunk and leafy canopy) can be denoted by many other signifiers such as *arbre* (French), *Baum* (German), δένδρον (Greek), and *ağaç* (Turkish).

In point of fact, there are no "proper" words for things in the world. Words lack the logic of mimesis. As Gilles Deleuze observes, there are only "*inexact* words to designate" things "exactly."[12] René Magritte was fascinated by the arbitrary relation

---

[10]   Michel Foucault, *The Order of Things* (New York: Pantheon, 1970), 34–37.
[11]   There are some kinds of signs that seem less arbitrary than others. Pantomime, sign language, and gestures (what are often called natural signs) seem to have a logical relation to what they represent. But Saussure insists that all signs are arbitrary. Saussure also dismisses onomatopoeia (words that sound like what they mean, like "pop" or "buzz") as still conventional, agreed-upon approximations of certain sounds. Think, for example, about the sounds attributed to animals. While all roosters crow pretty much the same way, that sound is transcribed in English as "cock-a-doodle-do" and in Spanish as "cocorico." Interjections also differ. In English one says "Ouch!" when one bangs one's finger with a hammer; in French one says "Aïe!"
[12]   Gilles Deleuze and Claire Parnet, *Dialogues*, rev. ed., trans. Hugh Tomlinson and Barbara Habberjam (New York: Columbia University Press, 2007 [1977]), 3 (emphasis added) (cf. Chapter 12).

1.4. Theophanes the Cretan, Adam naming the animals, St. Nicholas
Anapavas Monastery Church, Meteora, Greece (fifteenth century)

between words and concepts. In his painting *The Key of the Dream* (1930), he
represented, respectively, a picture of a woman's handbag labeled with the signifier "sky" (*le ciel*), a knife labeled "bird" (*l'oiseau*), and a leaf labeled "table"
(*la table*).[13] But the picture of a sponge in the fourth box is correctly labeled
"sponge" (*l'éponge*).

The implications of the arbitrary nature of signs are profound: because *signifiers*
belong to the culturally and historically conditioned material world of specific linguistic communities, and because the linguistic "sign" is *indivisible*, then the signifier cannot be separated from the signified. By implication, *the realm of signified
(concepts) must also belong to the material world*. This means that the concepts by
which we name things in the world and construct our understanding of God, faith,
and salvation are not grounded in a metaphysical or Platonic idealism beyond
this world. Our theological signifieds (concepts) are linguistically constituted and
culturally specific, as are our signifiers (cf. Chapter 7).

Despite the fact that the connection between signifiers and signifieds is arbitrary, linguistic signs are still meaningful because of the place they hold within the
overall semiotic structure of a given language, such as English, Korean, Greek, or

---

[13] Magritte, *Der Schlüssel der Träume* (Pinakothek Museum, Munich, Inv. 1930).

Hebrew. Within this structure, the meaning of each signifier is determined by its relation to other signifiers in the semiotic structure according to a system of differences.[14] Returning to our example of the signifier "tree," the value of the sound "tree" is not the sound itself, but the *difference* between the sound "tree" and other similar signifiers such as "three," "thee," and "tea." Similarly, the signifier "cat" is meaningful to English speakers because this sound *differs* from other signifiers such as "cap," "catch," or "cut." In other words, the signifiers "tree" and "cat" have value (meaning), not because of what they sound like but because of what they do *not* sound like. *The value of any signifier is determined by its place within the whole system of signifiers, as a system of differences.* As long as people can discern the difference between the signifiers "tree," "three," "thee," and "tea," on the one hand, and "cat," "cap," and "cut," then a wide range of individual pronunciations of "tree" and "cat" is acceptable, such as in the case of people speaking with various regional accents of English. In each case, the value of the signified is based only on the fact that it does not sound exactly like any of the other signifiers in the system (except, of course, in the case of homophones). This kind of meaning is what we call "negative value."

The concept of "negative value" can be explained using real estate as an example. A house has no absolute value. Its value varies with respect to its *relation* to other houses in the same residential area and to such parameters as the number of bedrooms and bathrooms and the proportion of buyers to sellers. Thus, your house has "negative value" in the sense that its monetary value is a function of the relation of your house within the system as a whole, which interrelates it to other houses on the market in terms of a system of differences. Thus, two identical houses can have vastly different (negative) values simply because one is located in the countryside and the other in Manhattan.

Another good example of negative "value" is the system of digital bits recognized by computers. By definition, a computer byte consists of eight bits. Each bit can be either 0 (zero) or 1 (one). Neither 0 nor 1 has a positive value. Each has a negative value: the value of "0" is that it is not "1," and the value of "1" (one) is that it is not "0" (zero). Negative value occurs under the similar conditions of a network of differential relations. The individual differences between signifiers are all part of a system of differences, which accords value to each signifier in the system.[15] But,

---

[14]   Anticipating the work of Saussure, Georg Friedrich Meier argued in his *Versuch einer Allgemeinen Auslegungskunst* (Hamburg: F. Meiner, 1996 [1757]) that signs do not refer to nonsemiotic meaning or intention. Signs gain their meaning through their location in a larger linguistic whole.

[15]   What is true of sounds is also true of graphic signifiers, as printed in texts. They are also part of a *system of differences.* For example, the graphic symbol *p* is an arbitrary symbol for the sound [p]. But this sound could be represented by another symbol, such as π (as it is in Greek) or פ (as it is in Hebrew). What is important is not the symbol *p* itself but the fact that *p* can be *distinguished* from other symbols in the alphabetic system, such as *b* and *o*. Thus, the graphic symbol *p* has no positive value: it is only meaningful by virtue of the structure as a whole.

as we shall see, in contrast to computer bits, where 0 (zero) and 1 (one) have equal value, in language, one pole of the binarism is often subordinated to the other (cf. Chapters 7 and 12). (From the perspective of semiology, 1 is better than 0, because our thought privileges metaphysical presence over its absence.)

What is true of signifiers is also true of signifieds (concepts). They too can be grasped only relationally on the basis of their differences from other signifieds. In other words, signifieds are not defined positively, with a fixed content, but nega-tively according to their differences from other related concepts within the same linguistic system. For example, "dark" is what is not "light" (but "light" always has more value), "feminine" is what is not "masculine" (but "masculine" always has more value), and "Eastern" is not "Western" (but "Western" always has more value).[16] Likewise, in Hinduism, the concept of "pure" also has such negative value: one is always more pure (if you are a Brahmin), or less pure (if you are an untouchable), than other Hindus, within the shared system of Hindu purity laws. These binarisms form a kind of metaphysics, or set of cultural assumptions that lie beneath human thought processes.

Syntagmatic Assemblages

In the years following the publication of Saussure's ground-breaking lectures in 1916, his semiotic theory has been both refined and corrected. It is now recog-nized that Saussure's focus on *individual* linguistic signs is problematic because words are not compartmentalized units of meaning. Even though words do pos-sess a minimal content, they are always employed in groups in phrases, sentences, and paragraphs. Language cannot represent human thought instantly. It functions by building up ideas gradually, arranging words in extended sequences of words, ordered according to a set of shared syntagmatic practices. In fact, the minimum semantic unit is not the isolated linguistic sign but a sequence of signs, or what Deleuze terms an "assemblage": "It is always the assemblage which produces utterances."[17]

The linear relation of words to other words in such syntactical assemblages is termed a "syntagmatic" relation. In determining the meaning of any given Hebrew or Greek word in a biblical text, *the contribution of the syntagmatic assemblage is maximal,* in comparison to the contribution of each single word, which is *mini-mal.* The "general" meaning of a word is termed its "unmarked meaning." *The unmarked meaning is the minimum meaning that a sign contributes to syntag-matic assemblage.* For example, the unmarked meaning of the Greek verb *etin*

---

[16] Saussure, *Course in General Linguistics*, 115.
[17] Gilles Deleuze and Claire Parnet, *Dialogues*, rev. ed., trans. Hugh Tomlinson and Barbara Habberjam (New York: Columbia University Press, 2007 [1977]), 51.

(αἰτεῖν) is "to ask for something with the expectation of an answer."[18] But in some syntagmatic assemblages, it is appropriate to translate this verb as "to beg for alms" and in other syntagmatic assemblages to translate it as "to pray." Both meanings, "to beg" and "to pray," are determined by the syntagmatic assemblage, or semantic context. The Greek verb, *etin* does *not* mean "I beg for alms" or "I pray." These meanings are not part of its unmarked meaning. But if the syntagmatic context involves a poor man speaking, then "to beg" is an appropriate translation. If the addressee is God, then "to pray" would probably be a more appropriate translation. Thus, the contribution of semantic context to the meaning of any sign is maximal, whereas the contribution of each individual sign is minimal.

Let us look at a more interesting example. The unmarked meaning of the sign *kinarion* (κυνάριον) denotes the concept of a "small dog." But in the context of Mark 7:24–30, as a syntagmatic assemblage, this sign refers to the Syro-Phoenician woman and her daughter: Jesus declares to this woman, "It is not right to take the children's bread and throw it to the small dogs [*kinaria*]" (Mark 7:27). The contribution of the syntagmatic assemblage here is maximal and allows the sign, whose unmarked meaning indicates the concept of a "small dog," to designate Gentiles in a pejorative way. In this case, the wider informational structure of the assemblage produces an *unexpected* meaning, beyond its unmarked meaning.

The Greek sign *pnevma* (πνεῦμα), which one might mechanically translate as "(Holy) Spirit," also has *minimal meaning* apart from the syntagmatic assemblage in which it occurs. In fact, its unmarked meaning is so minimal that it can denote a surprisingly wide variety of concepts such as "blowing," "breathing," "a spiritual state of mind," a "ghost," a "wind," a "soul," "spirit as part of the human psychological faculty," and an "evil spirit," as well as the "Spirit" of God (i.e., Holy Spirit). Once again, the unmarked meaning of the sign, *pnevma*, takes on distinctly different values when it enters into different syntagmatic assemblages. Therefore, *linguistic signs are not containers of semantic meaning*. Signs refer to signs, which refer to other signs, ad infinitum, in the syntagmatic assemblages in which they occur.

The Danish linguist Louis Hjelmslev (pronounced *"yelm*-slav") revised Saussure's theory, which posited a one-to-one correspondence between signifiers and signified.[19] Recognizing that one always reads linguistic signs in the context of other signs, and that one arrives at an understanding of a sentence's overall signification (meaning) on the basis of the *interrelations between the signs*, Hjelmslev reconceptualized Saussure's signifiers as the "plane of expression" and

---

[18] All Greek words in this book will be transliterated using the historical Greek pronunciation system, as explained in B. H. McLean, *New Testament Greek: An Introduction* (Cambridge: Cambridge University Press, 2011), 7–18.

[19] Cf. Louis Hjelmslev, *Prolegomena to a Theory of Language* (Madison: University of Wisconsin Press, 1961); Louis Hjelmslev, *Language: An Introduction*, trans. Francis J. Whitfield (Madison: University of Wisconsin Press, 1970).

Saussure's signifieds as the "plane of content," or what I refer to as the "plane of signification."[20]

- **Plane of Expression**: Assemblages of audible or visible phonemes that are *expressed* as groupings of morphemes. (A *phoneme* is a perceptually distinct unit of sound in a specified language [cf. the sound of a syllable]. A *morpheme* is a meaning-unit of a language that cannot be further divided [i.e., a lexeme].)
- **Plane of Signification**: The interrelation of semiotic signs (which, from a linguistic perspective, consist of morphemes).

This necessary complication of Saussure's bilateral model (signifier ↔ signified) allowed Hjelmslev to make two further distinctions, namely the distinction between the "form" and "substance" of each plane. In the case of both the plane of expression and the plane of signification, the distinction between form and substance is a *modal* distinction: "form" and "substance" are two aspects of a single, undivided, linguistic entity.

Plane of Expression

- The "form" of the plane of expression comprises the phonemes that are *available for use* in any given language system (such as English, Korean, Greek, or Hebrew).
- The "substance" of the plane of expression comprises the morphemes (lexemes/ words) that are actually formed from these phonemes and used, in real speech and texts.
- This plane is much more the concern of linguistics than it is of hermeneutics.

Plane of Signification

- The "form" of the plane of signification comprises the "paradigmatic" associations between the concepts associated with words in the semiotic system as a whole.
- The "substance" of the plane of signification designates the actual groupings of signs chosen (from among all the available signs), and then arranged into syntagmatically correct statements, sentences, and propositions, in real speech utterances and texts.
- This plane comprises a primary focus of hermeneutics.

Paradigmatic Associations

Apart from their syntagmatic arrangements, signs have an almost unlimited potential to form associations with other signs in the semiotic system as a whole.

---

[20] Cf. Miriam Taverniers, "Hjelmslev's Semiotic Model of Language: An Exegesis," *Semiotica* 171 (2008): 367–94.

For example, we naturally associate the word "painful" with other words such as "sore," "aching," "throbbing," "bump," and "accident." Such associations are not recorded in any text. They are part of the structure of the English language itself. For example, if you were asked to list all the words you know that begin with the letter *e* you would have great difficulty because the structure of English does not organize words in this way. (Of course, the dictionary is an artificial, and relatively modern, human invention.) On the other hand, if you were asked to name the parts of a car, or all the items found in a kitchen, you would have no difficulty because these words are associated together by their "paradigmatic" associations in the structure of language itself.

In their study of the New Testament, lexicographers J. P. Louw and E. A. Nida have defined a "paradigmatic" association as an associative field of interrelated words that belong to a single conceptual category, such as words having to do with attitudes and emotions, psychological faculties, learning, knowing, thinking, household activities, power and force, time, agriculture, and building.[21] According to Louw and Nida, words are paradigmatically associated in four ways:[22]

1. According to relations of inclusion: Relations involve a hierarchical structure (e.g., canis > dog > Labrador retriever).
2. In terms of overlapping relations: Such words are often called "synonyms," which is to say words that can be used for the same meaning.
3. According to complementary relations between antonyms (e.g., high-low, hot-cold, good-bad, and male-female).
4. According to contiguous relations: These are nonhierarchical, noncomplementary relations between closely related words (e.g., water, rain, moisture, ice, snow, and hail are all natural substances under the specific heading "water").

For example, the sign *trapeza* (τράπεζα), with respect to the *form* of the plane of signification, belongs to three different paradigmatic associations. It is associated with:

1. Signs concerning "eating"
2. Signs concerning "furniture and household objects"
3. Signs concerning "institutions for the safeguarding of money"

---

[21] Louw and Nida actually use the term "semantic domains" instead of "paradigmatic associations," but I employ the latter term for simplicity and to avoid confusion; cf. J. P. Louw and E. A. Nida's *Greek-English Lexicon of the New Testament Based on Paradigmatic Associations*, 2 vols. (New York: United Bible Societies, 1988). Paradigmatic associations (or "semantic domains") should not be confused with the common occurrence of a lexeme, with an "unmarked" meaning, having multiple "contextual" meanings. The distinction being made here is between the *multiple domains* of a single lexeme, not the distinction between the unmarked and contextual meanings of a word.
[22] J. P. Louw, *Semantics of New Testament Greek* (Atlanta: Scholars Press, 1982), 60–66.

In the *substance* of the plane of signification, we can find specific examples of these three uses in the texts of the Greek New Testament, where the sign τράπεζα can signify:

1. A "meal": "He served them a *meal*" (Acts 16:34).
2. A "table": "He overturned their *tables*" (John 2:15).
3. A "bank": "You put your money in the *bank*" (Luke 19:23).

The nature of such paradigmatic associations varies from one linguistic community to another. For example, the structure of the paradigmatic associations of Hellenistic Greek, biblical Hebrew, and contemporary English are different. In the case of each of these languages, the paradigmatic associations function, as Raymond Williams notes, as a "form of codification."[23] In other words, paradigmatic associations constitute a kind of structure that establishes what is thinkable, and therefore expressible, within a given language, culture and society (cf. Chapter 7). Words exist primarily in a paradigmatic relation to one another in the system of language itself before they exist in a syntagmatic relation to one another in actual speech and texts. It is this paradigmatic relation that accords them "negative value" to one another, according to a system of differences.

Recognizing that all signs are related to other signs, paradigmatically as well as syntagmatically, Jacques Derrida famously extended the logic of Saussure's theory by arguing that his distinction between signifier and signified is itself arbitrary. Of course, a signifier "refers" or "points" to a signified, but this "referring" does not stop here. The signified, referred to by the signifier, in turn refers to other signifieds, which in turn refer to other signifieds, and so forth, within a paradigmatic system of negative differences. As Derrida astutely observes, "the signified already functions as a signifier."[24] By implication, the determination of the final signification (or presence) of any sign is indefinitely deferred or, as Derrida says, "disseminated."[25] Gilles Deleuze explains this paradigmatic associating of signs as follows:

Every sign refers to another sign, and only to another sign, *ad infinitum*. That is why, at the limit, one can forgo that notion of the sign, for what is retained is not principally the sign's relation to a state of things it denotes, or to an entity it signifies, but only the formal relation of sign to sign insofar as it defines a so-called signifying chain. The limitlessness of significance[26] replaces the sign.... All signs are signs of signs. The question

[23] Raymond Williams, *Marxism and Literature* (Oxford: Oxford University Press, 1977), 167.
[24] Jacques Derrida, *Of Grammatology*, trans. Gayatri Spivak (Baltimore: Johns Hopkins University Press, 1974 [1967]), 7.
[25] Jacques Derrida, *Dissemination*, trans. Barbara Johnson (Chicago: University of Chicago Press, 1981 [1972]).
[26] Deleuze borrows the term "signifiance" from the French linguist Émile Benveniste to designate the paradigmatic (associative) relations between words in a linguistic system as a whole. It is customary to leave the term "signifiance" untranslated.

is not yet what a given sign signifies but to what other signs it refers, or which signs add themselves to it to form a network without beginning or end.[27]

Owing to the very structure of language, the meaning of biblical texts is always open-ended. Biblical interpreters can never put the meaning of biblical texts into a straitjacket; their semiotic signs point beyond the syntagmatic assemblages in which they occur to the paradigmatic associations of the Hebrew and Greek language systems as a whole.

DENOTATION: LANGUAGE'S COMPONENT OF REFERENCE

Any text has "significance" (meaning) to a reader or interpreter, even in the absence of knowledge about the identity of the original writer, and the writer's attendant material circumstances or context. Malcolm Heath tells the story of taking a ride on a bus and overhearing someone exclaim, "Yes, then we shall all have alabaster grapes!" He immediately understood the signification arising from the subject pronoun, "we," taken with the verb "shall have," followed by the direct object, "alabaster grapes." However, he did not understand the denotation of the statement "Yes, then we shall all have alabaster grapes!"

Saussure's bilateral model (words ↔ concepts), according to which signifiers (morphemes) refer to signifieds (concepts), cannot account for the other two dimensions of language, "denotation" and "manifestation." In recognizing that words point directly to our shared concepts of things and not to things in the world, Saussure's bilateral model failed to account for the obvious fact that human beings *do* successfully employ language daily to denote actual things in the world. For example, if you were to ask your friend to buy you a "cup of coffee," you would be confident that he will not bring you a porcupine or an ironing board instead. Somehow, the semiotic assemblage "cup of coffee" does *denote* something real in our world of experience. Granted that language does *not* represent the world directly, as a kind of passive registration of the real things, but neither is it totally disconnected from the world of things.

To illustrate language's capacity to denote things in the material world, Umberto Eco relates a story, found in John Wilkin's *The Secret and Swift Messenger* (1641). This story concerns a Native American who was sent by his master on an errand, with a letter and a basket of figs in hand.[28] All that prevented the messenger from eating some of the figs was the knowledge that the accompanying letter specified the number of figs to be delivered. If he ate so much as one fig, the recipient of the basket would know this when he read the letter and counted the number of remaining figs. The ingenious messenger addressed this challenge by hiding the letter under a large stone and delivering the figs without it. Although the story

---

[27] Deleuze and Guattari, *A Thousand Plateaus*, 112.
[28] Umberto Eco, *The Limits of Interpretation* (Bloomington: Indiana University Press, 1990), 1–7.

continues, it is obvious that, should someone later discover this letter hidden under the stone, that person not only would be able to understand its "plane of signification" but would also have some basic understanding of the intended *denotation* of the letter's "substance of content" (syntagmatic relations). In other words, it would be obvious to the reader of the letter that a real person (the letter's signatory) had sent some real figs to another real person (the letter's addressee). Somehow, the semiotic signs in the letter "denoted" actual, material persons and material figs! Despite the strengths of Saussure's semiotic theory, it does not account for this fact. For this reason, it is necessary to go beyond Saussure's theoretical framework and speak of "denotation."

"Denotation" is language's domain of reference.[29] Language does not hover over the material world in some Platonic realm, as Saussure's model might seem to imply. Rather, as Monique Wittig observes, language is actually "another order of materiality."[30] For example, Greek and Hebrew possess their own materiality and historicality. This is why, for example, we cannot speak simply of "Greek," but "epichoric Greek," "Classical Greek," "Hellenistic Greek," "Byzantine Greek," and "modern Greek." Owing to the materiality of Greek, it changed and developed throughout history. In contrast to Saussure's privileging of a quasi-transcendental structure of language (*langue*) over its material manifestations (*parole*), Hjelmslev's linguistic model does not favor "form" (*langue*) over "substance" (*parole*). Both are modal aspects of language. It is this material side of language that bestows upon it the capacity to "denote" things in the world, and not only the concepts of things.

MANIFESTATION: THE INTENDING, BELIEVING, AND DESIRING AUTHOR

The third component of language is "manifestation." Saussure's bilateral model (words ↔ concepts) cannot account for this dimension of language either. Manifestation is the domain of the personal. It bestows upon language a capacity to *manifest* the conscious beliefs, ideas, and intentions of a speaker or author. The domain of manifestation also includes a writer or speaker's phenomenological "horizon" (see Chapters 3, 5, and 8), emotional investments, and moral code. Manifestation is also connected with the unconscious realm of dreams and libidinal desire.[31] Fundamental dimensions of the psychoanalytic unconscious remain not merely unknown but *unknowable*. As Foucault observes, we too quickly overlook both the role of the unconscious and unconscious desire in the determination of human identity. Thus, while being endowed with the capacity to create

[29] Cf. Deleuze, *Logic of Sense*; cf. Paul Patton, *Deleuzian Concepts: Philosophy, Colonization, Politics* (Stanford, CA: Stanford University Press, 2010), 193.
[30] Monique Wittig, "The Straight Mind," *Feminist Issues* 1/1 (1980): 108.
[31] The term "libidinal desire" refers to the energy behind all life-producing and life-destroying impulses, beyond those of desires connected with bare survival.

new knowledge, human beings remain simultaneously the never fully understood object of their own unconscious desires.[32] I return to the subject of manifestation in Chapters 2, 9, 10, and 12.

Manifestation always functions with and is conditioned by the other two components of language, signification and denotation. Of course, without signification, nothing is manifested at all. But it is equally true that there can be no full denotation without manifestation, because our beliefs, intentions, phenomenological horizons, and unconscious desires accompany all expressions of language.

༄

Each of the three components of language – signification, denotation, and manifestation – is unique and functions according to its own set of principles.[33] Because biblical texts include all three components, their meaning cannot be reduced to any single component, such as a *signified* concept, or a *denoted* thing in the world, or a *manifested* intention of an author.[34] While it is true that each of the three components of language is insufficient by itself, we must not overlook the equally important fact that *each of these three components conditions the others, in a circular fashion.* For this reason, questioning any single component, whether it be signification, denotation, or manifestation, will always lead to questioning the remaining two components. As such, Gilles Deleuze speaks of the circle in language: "From denotation to manifestation, then to signification, but also from signification to manifestation and to denotation, we are carried along a circle, which is the circle of the proposition."[35] As Deleuze explains, "How a proposition refers to something in the world [denotation] depends on how it is qualified by the moment when it is written or spoken by someone [manifestation], and this in turn depends on how its meaning is set."[36] Thus, each component of language [signification] points beyond itself.

From a practical perspective, the biblical interpreter does not have access to a text's components of denotation and manifestation without first comprehending its signification. The act of reading a Greek or Hebrew text is always the gateway into the circle. But once one has entered the circle, signification loses its primacy because the three components are not hierarchically arranged. Traditional philological analysis of biblical texts has tended to focus on the component of signification. Romanticist interpretation has focused on manifestation (see Chapter 2). Meanwhile, historicist-inspired methodologies have focused on denotation (see Chapters 3 and 4). In contrast, the post-historical interpreter must contemplate

---

32   Foucault, *The Order of Things*, 322–28.
33   Deleuze and Guattari, *A Thousand Plateaus*, 57–58.
34   Deleuze, *Logic of Sense*, 19.
35   Ibid., 17, 27.
36   James Williams, *Gilles Deleuze's Logic of Sense: A Critical Introduction and Guide* (Edinburgh: Edinburgh University Press, 2008), 40.

all three components and especially their interdependence. As James Williams explains, "neither the reference of language [denotation], nor its situation in relation to a speaker or point of writing [manifestation], nor its meaning as decipherable through the position of words in relation to one another [signification] are sufficient bases for understanding how language works. Instead, each of these must be attached to the others for its own process to be complete."[37] Perhaps the most important consequence of the heterogeneity of the three components of language, and its circularity, is the inherent flux of the system as a whole. *Each component produces its own forms of openness and instability.* Thus, when one moves through the circle, one never arrives at a point that can function as a constant or foundation for a definitive, final meaning.[38]

SENSE: THE FOURTH COMPONENT OF LANGUAGE

This circle of language is not a vicious circle because, as Gilles Deleuze observes, there is actually a way to break its circularity. This brings us to what Deleuze terms "sense," as the fourth component of language:

> From denotation to manifestation, then to signification, but also from signification to manifestation and to denotation, we are carried along a circle, which is the circle of the proposition. Whether we ought to be content with these three dimensions of the proposition, or whether we should add a *fourth – which would be sense –* is an economic or strategic question.[39]

"Sense" is more difficult to define. Negatively speaking, one can say that sense should not be identified with any of the other three components, though sense does complement each of them.

> *Sense* is inseparably *the expressible or the expressed of the proposition, and the attribute of the state of affairs.* It turns one side toward things and one side toward propositions. But it does not merge with the proposition which expresses it any more than with the state of affairs or the quality which the proposition denotes. It is exactly the boundary between propositions and things.... It is in this sense that it is an "event": *on condition that the event is not confused with its spatio-temporal effectuation in a state of affairs.*[40]

Language always conveys something more than, or in addition to, that which is communicated through its three components. "Sense" can be conceived of as a kind of value. It is the "Who cares?" factor. For example, the proposition that "the polar ice cap is melting" can be analyzed in terms of signification, denotation, and

---

[37] Ibid.
[38] Patton, *Deleuzian Concepts*, 21–24. For example, the "rules" of grammar are not objective, ahistorical, transcendental discursive laws, but sets of revisable and changing sets of relations in the syntagmatic field.
[39] Deleuze, *Logic of Sense*, 17, 27.
[40] Ibid., 22, 34.

manifestation. But none of these components captures the "value" of this proposition. Who cares? What is the significance of this statement? This statement has "sense" (value) to animal conservationists, who are committed to protecting polar bears, and to the populations of low-lying countries, such as Pakistan, which are experiencing recurrent flooding, and to multinational oil companies, which want to exploit the oil reserves under the polar ice cap. Similarly, when the various texts of the Bible were first composed, they all possessed "sense" to those for whom they were intended. I term this their "founding sense-events."

The reader of this book is invited to substitute the term "significance" for the term "sense" if this helps to clarify the meaning of this term. However, I generally employ the term "sense," because the term "significance" is laden with anthropocentric and existential connotations. In various contexts, the term "significance" can connote the humanist belief that the human race is the centerpiece of cosmic meaning, or the romanticist belief that authorial "I" is the originator of meaning (cf. Chapter 2), or even the scientistic belief that the rational "subject" is the discoverer of objective meaning, or the existential belief that every individual is a "meaning maker" (cf. Chapters 3 and 4). Over and against all such beliefs, I argue "sense" extends beyond the capacity of human beings to be meaning discoverers and meaning makers. "Sense" is something we receive, as well as something that we participate in. Because we are never entirely in control of what we find meaningful, "sense" is really our destiny.

With this clarification, let us return to the circularity of language and examine how we can break out of the circle of language by seeking out "sense." "Sense" breaks the circle of language because it is not reducible to semantic meaning (signification), or reference (denotation), or authorial beliefs and intentions (manifestation). Put simply, the fact that "sense" concerns the "value" of a speech utterance or text to a particular people in a given spatiotemporal location rescues language from its circularity. For example, the narratives of Jesus' crucifixion, as found in the four canonical Gospels, can, with some degree of precision, be analyzed in terms of their signification, denotation, and manifestation. But the only way we can escape the circularity of this undertaking is to also seek the "sense" (or "value") of these narratives for Christians. By virtue of the founding sense-event of a given passion narrative, the text meant more to early Christians than its components of signification, denotation, and manifestation allow it to mean. In the case of the first generation of Christians, the narratives of Jesus' crucifixion functioned as a "founding sense-event." In a similar fashion, the multiple interpretations of the passion narratives over the past two thousand years have constituted a "series," which connect this founding sense-event with many subsequent "present sense-events," which replay and counteractualize the "sense" of Jesus' crucifixion in various contexts over time (cf. Chapter 12). It is this ongoing repetition of the founding sense-event through an ensuing series of sense-events that possesses a destiny, which is beyond our human powers to control (fig. 1.5).

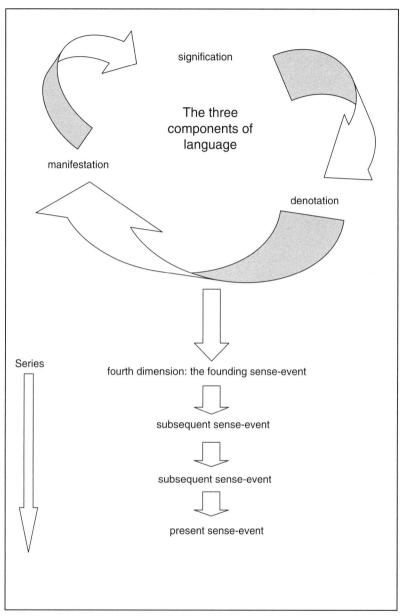

signification

The three
components of
language

manifestation

denotation

Series

fourth dimension: the founding sense-event

subsequent sense-event

subsequent sense-event

present sense-event

1.5. The hermeneutic act

THE PRESENT SENSE-EVENT: SIGNIFICANCE FOR THE NOW TIME

The founding sense-event sets in motion a series of subsequent sense-events in the history of interpretation, in which the founding event *is always implied*. Deleuze refers to this kind of telescoping of sense-events through time as their "reserve of potential happenings."[41] Owing to this inherent reserve, a biblical text is not a self-contained "well-located happening" in a spatiotemporal location but rather, as James Williams explains, more like "a distant and disembodied destiny that different [subsequent interpretive] events intermittently connect to, feed off and alter for all other events."[42] In the case of our own time, hermeneutics can be conceived of as a kind of replaying this destiny of sense at the level of the intensive relations of our own "time of the now" (Rom 8:18; 11:5; 2 Cor 8:14).

This replaying implies going beyond the original founding sense-event. This is necessary because none of the four components of a biblical text (signification, denotation, manifestation, and sense) include the present-day interpreter, the church, or the world of the twenty-first century. For this reason, the founding sense-event of a biblical text must always fail "the test of time."[43] Hans-Georg Gadamer explains this phenomenon of the failure of the historical founding sense-event:

We think we understand when we see the past from a historical standpoint, i.e., place ourselves in the historical situation and seek to reconstruct the historical horizon. In fact however, we have given up the claim to find, in the past, any truth valid and intelligible for ourselves.[44]

This failure of the historical founding sense-event in the present is an important issue because most people read biblical texts not merely to determine their original historical "sense" but also to discover their "sense" for the readers' own lives in the present. By implication, in addition to exploring the four components of a text's founding sense-event, hermeneutics must enable the potential reserve of the founding sense-event to unfold in the present as a present sense-event, within the changed set of "value" relations.

If this principle is granted, then it is strange that a great many academic interpreters of the Bible limit their focus to the three components of a biblical text and perhaps venture as far as elucidating the founding sense-event. This self-limitation is a function of an epistemological model of biblical studies that constructs the scholar as a detached *subject*, who impartially applies methods of biblical criticism

---

[41] Ibid., 184, 215.

[42] Williams, *Gilles Deleuze's Logic of Sense*, 36.

[43] James Williams, "Against Oblivion and Simple Empiricism: Gilles Deleuze's 'Immanence: A Life …,'" *Journal of Philosophy: A Cross-Disciplinary Inquiry* 5/11 (2010): 25–34; cf. James Williams, *Gilles Deleuze's Logic of Sense*, 39–76.

[44] Hans-Georg Gadamer, *Truth and Method*, 2nd rev. ed., trans. Joel Weinsheimer and Donald G. Marshall (London: Continuum, 1994 [1965]), 270.

to biblical texts, which are understood as *objects* of investigation. This "subject versus object" binarism constitutes the foundation for a validation of the objective sense of biblical texts in the discipline today. From a hermeneutic perspective, this binarism is problematic because it actually excludes the very possibility of a present sense-event.

Irrespective of the practice of scholars to treat biblical texts as objects of analysis, a review of the past two thousand years of the Christian interpretive tradition would demonstrate that biblical texts have continued to have "sense" for their readers, beyond their founding sense-events. What makes this "sense" possible is the "text-reception complex." *The text-reception complex specifies the a priori role of the situated interpreter, within a changed set of "value" relations, in the disclosure of textual "sense."*[45] By implication, biblical texts can accrue significances over time, which are beyond the intentions of their historical writers, and even beyond their founding sense-events. Gadamer observes that this bestows upon interpretation a productive aspect:

The actual meaning of a text, as it speaks to the interpreter, is not dependent on the occasion represented by the writer and his original public [as romanticists and historicists maintain]. As least it is not exhausted by it; for the meaning is also determined by the historical situation of the interpreter and thus by the whole of the objective course of history.... The meaning of a text *goes beyond* its writer, not only occasionally, *but always*. Understanding is therefore not merely reproductive, but *always productive*.[46]

Owing to the nature of the text-reception complex, biblical texts possess a latent potential of "sense" that goes beyond their founding sense-events, which can be expressed in the act of interpretation itself, resulting in an enlargement of the components of language to include the world of its later readers and their own fields of reference. Roland Barthes famously proclaimed that a text's meaning "lies not in its origins" but in its "destination," which is to say, not in its historical author but in its present-day readers. In his view, there is no text in the absence of such readers. Readers do not just decipher the semiotic signs on a page, they actually construct a text on the basis of their own particular worlds. As such, the role of biblical interpreters could even be conceived of as a kind of rewriting of the founding sense-event, within a changed set of value relations.

Taking a work of art as an analogy, consider the latent reserve of "sense" of an oil painting depicting a young man smiling. Even if the historical context behind the founding sense-event of the painting is unknown (because the historical identity of the man, the historical occasion for his smiling, and the intentions of the painter

---

[45] Roland Barthes, *Image Music Text,* trans. Stephen Heath (New York: Hill and Wang, 1977), 146, 155–64.
[46] Gadamer, *Truth and Method,* 263–64 (emphasis added).

are all unknown to the viewer of the painting), this picture nonetheless possesses a latent potential of virtual sense of happiness in the present, even after the subject of the painting and the artist are long dead. As Gilles Deleuze observes, "A young man will smile on a canvas for as long as the canvas lasts."[47] Thus, virtual sense involves an enlargement of the component of reference of the painting to include the referential world of the onlooker.

THE WIDER CONTEXTS OF BIBLICAL INTERPRETATION

Biblical interpretation never occurs in a vacuum: it is always practiced in a specific cultural context that includes one's own interpretive community – whether academic or ecclesial – and the multifaceted worlds beyond it. It is a simple fact that *all* biblical interpretation has a material, cultural, ideological, political, and institutional setting, even though, as Edward Said observes, there is a chronic tendency "to deny, suppress, or distort the cultural context of such systems of thought in order to maintain the fiction of its scholarly disinterest."[48] Said draws attention to "how the general liberal consensus that 'true' knowledge is fundamentally nonpolitical (and conversely, that overtly political knowledge is not 'true' knowledge) obscures the highly if obscurely organized political circumstances obtaining when knowledge is produced."[49] Viewed from its exteriority, the methodologies of biblical studies can be located within the broader field of discursive practices of the humanities and social sciences, and within distinct academic and ecclesia institutional locations (cf. Chapter 7).

All biblical interpretation also includes the shared phenomenological horizons of meaning of its practitioners (see Chapters 5, 7, and 8). According to Heidegger, every meaningful statement must be grounded in something unthought and unthinkable, an unconscious commonsense "horizon," which resists representation.[50] For example, within the study of "Christian origins," the grammar of historical "origins," "influence," and "development," and the progress of disciplinary knowledge, collectively function as part of this discipline's unspoken horizon of meaning, which requires no explicit validation or legitimation. This generative "grammar" constitutes the basic pretheoretical knowledge structure of the discipline of biblical studies, laying out rules for the formation of its objects in discourse – its possible subject positions, concepts, and strategies that make the creation of valid knowledge possible. In other words, *this horizon of meaning*

---

[47] Gilles Deleuze, *What Is Philosophy?*, trans. Hugh Tomlinson and Graham Burchell (New York: Columbia University Press, 1994 [1991]), 163.
[48] Edward Said, *Orientalism* (New York: Vintage Books, 1978), 345.
[49] Ibid., 10.
[50] The term "horizon" originated with the phenomenologist Edmund Husserl. In his early writings, Heidegger called this horizon the "clearing" and in his later works the "open."

determines what can be recognized as (true) disciplinary knowledge, at least to those sharing in this discursive practice. Acts of biblical interpretation relate not only to specific cultural contexts, phenomenological horizons, and the structure of disciplinary knowledge but also to the associative field of previously existing disciplinary knowledge. For example, a new book on the "historical Jesus" will not be published – never mind read – unless it meaningfully engages previous constructions of the "historical Jesus." Any new act of biblical interpretation can be granted validity only if it is locatable within an associative field of previously existing interpretations (cf. Chapter 7). On this point, Edward Said remarks that "the scholar who unearths a once-lost manuscript produces the 'found' text in a context already produced for it."[51] The articles, monographs, and commentaries written by biblical scholars are always related to other like discourses within a shared associative discursive field.[52]

All this is to say that biblical studies should not be construed as a scientific discipline, which discovers objective biblical facts. The discipline's desire for objective facts does not stem from its scientistic rigor but rather from the weight of the effective history of the Enlightenment, which now "weighs like a nightmare on the brains of the living," as Marx once said in another context.[53] In opposition to such quests for objective facts, I will argue that biblical texts possess a latent reserve of sense for our present because of the inherent openness and instability of both the circle of language and the text-reception complex.

The exploration of the present sense-event, undertaken in this book, is not based upon an appeal to mysticism, nor does it rest on piously guided intentions to recover our childlike naïveté. While it is true that a sense-event cannot be grasped scientistically through the application of a discrete set of techniques, an exploration of the present sense-event can be equally rigorous, but in different terms. In fact, Deleuze refers to this exploration of sense as a "higher empiricism" (cf. Chapter 12). But in contrast to traditional empiricism, which is based on the flawed, anthropocentric metaphysics of the subject-object binarism (cf. Chapters 3–5), this higher mode of empiricism appreciates the place of the *embodied* interpreter within a wider ecology of sense, which extends well beyond human acts of reasoning, knowing, and meaning making. All this is to say that the biblical interpreter is not the final measure and arbiter of *biblical sense-events because sense always includes an element of destiny, which our frail human bodies can never evade.* Put positively, the analysis of present sense-events opens up new possibilities for us to replay and counteractualize the sense of biblical texts in our own time

---

51 Said, *Orientalism*, 273.

52 Michel Foucault, *The Archaeology of Knowledge* (New York: Tavistok Publications/Pantheon, 1972), 79–81. Similarly, Gilles Deleuze argues that "every concept relates back to other concepts, not only in its history but in its becoming or its present connections"; cf. Deleuze, *What Is Philosophy?*, 19.

53 Karl Marx, "The Eighteenth Brumaire of Louis Bonaparte," I (New York: International Publishers, 1969 [1852]).

of the "now." I term this higher mode of interpretation "post-historical hermeneutics." We begin, in Chapter 2, with a critique of the traditional approach to
language's component of manifestation, as it manifests the intent of the author. In
Chapter 3, we critique the traditional approach to language's component of denotation, as it concerns the historical referent.

2

⌖

The Death of the Author

The analysis of biblical texts in terms of signification, denotation, and manifestation, as well as the fourth dimension of sense, functions as a limit point for most biblical scholars, with little or no attention being paid to the present sense-event of biblical texts. In this chapter I argue that this state of affairs has contributed to a crisis of nihilism. Our starting point for exploring this crisis is German romanticism, as represented by Friedrich Schleiermacher, whose equation of "sense" with "manifestation" (authorial intent) contributed to a growing crisis of historical meaning.

FRIEDRICH SCHLEIERMACHER AND AUTHORIAL INTENT

Friedrich Schleiermacher (1768–1834), the father of modern Protestant theology, served as a professor of theology at the University of Halle in Germany. In addition to being a theologian, he was also one of the greatest classicists of his time, famous for his German translation of the complete works of Plato. Schleiermacher was strongly influenced by "German romanticism," a movement known for its emphasis on the experience of strong emotions such as "strife and struggle" (*Sturm und Drang*),[1] and on the creative genius of the great individuals of the past, whose heroic acts (it was believed) dramatically transformed the world around them and history forevermore. This concept of genius was founded upon a form of Platonized idealism, which connected an author's original intent with textual meaning. From a romanticist perspective, the biographies of the great men of the past constitute the very building blocks of history, though chance and physical conditions also played a role. Thus, romanticist interpretations of the Bible tended to focus on how the lives of the Bible's great figures, its kings, prophets, saints, and especially, of course, Jesus and Paul, literally *shaped* the very course of history that followed.[2]

In Schleiermacher's hermeneutical theory, one can also detect lines of continuity with the theology of the Protestant Reformation. Schleiermacher, like theologians of the Reformation such as Martin Luther and Jean Calvin, believed that

---

[1] Literally "storm and stress."
[2] Friedrich Schleiermacher, *The Life of Jesus*, trans. S. Maclean Gilmour (Mifflintown, PA: Sigler Press, 1997).

biblical texts had an original meaning, or a literal sense (*sensus literalis*), which had become lost over time. He believed that this literal sense could be recovered through a study of the original languages of scripture and through careful philological analysis. However, in contrast to Reformation scholars, Schleiermacher broke with the concept of the theological unity of scripture. The implication of Luther's famous dictum, "Sacred scripture is its own interpreter" (*Scriptura sacra sui ipsius interpres*), and his precept of *sola scriptura,* is that each passage of scripture should be interpreted in terms of the theology of scripture as a whole.[3] The corollary of Luther's principle is that the meaning of the individual books of scripture is not ultimately determined by the intentions of their historical writers, or by their original historical contexts, but rather by the canon of scripture itself, and ultimately by God, the ultimate "author" of scripture.

The primary reference point for biblical interpretation during the Reformation was the ongoing work of God *in the present,* not the historical intentions of various writers or the original historical contexts of biblical texts. By implication, the hermeneutics of the Reformation entailed the belief that the books of scripture possessed a unified significance beyond that which was intended by their individual historical authors. This significance was identical with the intention of scripture's ultimate author, God. In theological terms, this divinely intended meaning is termed the "fuller sense" (*sensus plenior*) of scripture. This term refers to a meaning that is intended by God, though not necessarily consciously intended by the original authors of the texts of scripture. Even today, Reformed and Roman Catholic theology agree that this "fuller sense" of scripture is mediated to the church in the present by such factors as the canonical interrelatedness of the biblical writings to one another, as well as their ongoing interpretation in light of the Christian tradition that followed.

In contrast to this hermeneutic tradition of the Reformation, Schleiermacher argued that the goal of interpretation is to discover what the individual human authors intended to say in their acts of writing, and to interpret their writings in terms of their particular literary and historical contexts. In his view, the purpose of hermeneutics is to bring to light the intent of these authors. Thus, in terms of the theoretical structure laid out in Chapter 1, we could say that Schleiermacher emphasized the language's component of "manifestation," particularly in its aspect of the *conscious* beliefs and intentions of scriptures' authors. In his view, the goal of hermeneutics was to understand the inner mind of the authors of scripture and

---

³ Richard A. Muller and John Thompson, "The Significance of Precritical Exegesis," in *Biblical Interpretation in the Era of the Reformation*, ed. Richard A. Muller and John Thompson (Grand Rapids, MI: Wm. B. Eerdmans, 1996), 335–42, esp. 340; Gerhard Ebeling, "Wort Gottes und Hermeneutik," *ZThK* 56 (1959): 288ff.; Gerhard Ebeling, "Die Anfange von Luthers Hermeneutik," *ZThK* 48 (1951): 174–230; Bernard Ramm, *Protestant Biblical Interpretation*, 3rd rev. ed. (Grand Rapids, MI: Baker Book House, 1970), 107; A. Berkley Mickelsen, *Interpreting the Bible* (Grand Rapids, MI: Wm. B. Eerdmans, 1963), 38.

to see the ancient world through their eyes. Thus, for Schleiermacher, "authorial intent" constituted the truth of a text.[4] Schleiermacher's emphasis on the intentions of historical authors actually undermined the Reformation concept of the theological unity of scripture. The effect of his focus on the heroic individual, who shaped the world around him, was to emphasize the *historical particularity and difference* of biblical texts – not their theological unity.

The fact that many contemporary readers of scripture now take the historical particularity and difference of the books of the Bible for granted owes much to the legacy of Schleiermacher. Moreover, with the knowledge that the intended recipients of the books of the Bible were contemporaneous with the authors of these texts came the recognition that we are not the intended readers of these texts. Here we can begin to glimpse how a *historical* understanding of the Bible had the potential to challenge a theological reading of scripture.

HERMENEUTICS AS A UNIVERSAL PROBLEM

Before Schleiermacher, the practice of hermeneutics was regionalized according to the type of literature being studied. In fact, in his early years, even Schleiermacher's own hermeneutic theory began with a course on biblical interpretation entitled "*Sacred* Hermeneutics" (1805). But his elaboration of the field of hermeneutics soon extended well beyond scripture. Schleiermacher set out to develop a coherent set of "universal" (i.e., general) rules that could be applied to all types of texts, secular as well as sacred.[5] Schleiermacher maintained that scripture does not require an interpretive method that is unique to itself. Texts are texts. Thus, as Paul Ricoeur observes, by developing a "universal" set of principles that could be applied to the interpretation of *all types* of texts – secular as well as sacred – Schleiermacher "de-regionalized" the field of hermeneutics.[6] Thus, in 1809–10 Schleiermacher taught a new course, Universal Hermeneutics, in which he argued that the problem of hermeneutics does not arise solely in the field of sacred texts: hermeneutics

---

[4] Though this truth may not be true in any other sense, that is, as correspondence (a proposition is true when it corresponds to the facts as they really are).

[5] The influence of Schleiermacher's contribution to the field of hermeneutics is almost entirely due to the efforts of his student Friedrich Lücke, who published Schleiermacher's writings after his death, including his handwritten manuscripts and lecture notes. From Schleiermacher himself, we have only "On the Concept of Hermeneutics with Reference to F. A. Wolf's Remarks and Ast's Handbook" (1829). Schleiermacher developed his hermeneutical theory in debate with his contemporaries Friedrich August Wolf (1759–1824) and Friedrich Ast (1778–1841), both of whom studied hermeneutics from a philological perspective. For example, Ast did not focus on the genius of historical authors but rather contextualized ancient texts within world history. Similarly, Wolf combined a dual focus on both the cultural framework and the peculiarities of individual authors. As their concept of the world-historical spirit (*welthistoriche Geist*) suggests, both were more interested in what was typical of the spirit of an age than what was novel.

[6] Paul Ricoeur, *Hermeneutics and the Human Sciences: Essays on Language, Action and Interpretation*, trans. John B. Thompson (Cambridge: Cambridge University Press, 1981), 45–48.

is relevant to the reading of all kinds of texts and even to our daily interactions with others. In fact, the problem of hermeneutics arises every time two human beings attempt to communicate with each other. Schleiermacher famously defined hermeneutics as "the art of understanding [*Verstehen*] another person's utterance correctly."[7] In other words, hermeneutics concerns the interpreter's attempt to reach an understanding about something that has been communicated by somebody else. This is why he termed his theory "universal." The interpretation of scripture does not require a method that is unique to itself because the fundamental principles of interpretation operate within the universal phenomenon of human communication and understanding.

We should not overlook the fact that Schleiermacher was also famous for his translation of the works of Plato, whose surviving writings consist almost entirely of dialogues between his teacher, Socrates, and his various interlocutors. In these writings, truth is worked out in the dialogical process itself. On the basis of his interest in the Platonic dialogues, it is not surprising that Schleiermacher modeled all hermeneutic practice on the *dialogic process*, as did Hans-Georg Gadamer in the twentieth century (see Chapter 8). From this perspective, hermeneutics is really about engaging in an ongoing dialogue of question and answer with biblical texts and, ultimately, with their historical authors. The goal of this dialogue is to achieve mutual understanding. As such, we could compare Schleiermacher's model of interpretation to a conversation in which two people arrive at a shared understanding through a "dialogical search for knowledge."[8]

Schleiermacher also emphasized the very real possibility of misunderstanding, especially when the texts involved are rooted in contexts and cultures very different from one's own. In fact, it is highly probable that an interpreter living in the twenty-first century will misunderstand that which is culturally foreign and alien within a biblical text. Moreover, the philological problems posed by interpreting Hellenistic Greek or biblical Hebrew should not be minimized. Schleiermacher was particularly interested in those cases in which one realizes that a breakdown of communication has occurred: these cases provide an opportunity not only to reconsider the content of that which is misunderstood but also to examine *how and why* the misunderstanding occurred. In other words, these instances of misunderstanding provide the chance to explore what went wrong. Because we are normally *unaware* of how we interpret the world and texts around us, such events of misunderstanding provide significant opportunities to reflect deeply on how our acts of understanding and misunderstanding actually take place.

---

[7]   Friedrich Schleiermacher, *Hermeneutics and Criticism and Other Writings*, trans. and ed. Andrew Bowie, Cambridge Texts in the History of Philosophy (Cambridge: Cambridge University Press, 1998), 5.

[8]   Wolfgang H. Pleger, *Schleiermacher's Philosophie* (Berlin: Walter de Gruyter, 1988), 10.

This brings us to Schleiermacher's concept of the laxer practice of hermeneutics. Schleiermacher famously distinguished between a "laxer" and "stricter" practice. In the laxer practice, which is aimed at avoiding misunderstanding, one must scrutinize one's own preunderstandings and presuppositions so as not to interpret a biblical text through one's own cultural and theological biases. The stricter practice aims at understanding the meaning of a text by reconstructing the viewpoint of its author. Schleiermacher famously divided this stricter practice of interpretation into two parts: "grammatical interpretation"; and "technical" or, as he later renamed it (and as we adopt in this chapter), "psychological interpretation."

These two parts of interpretation are closely connected: one cannot understand the psychology of an ancient author without first understanding the grammatical side of a text. Likewise, in Schleiermacher's view, a greater appreciation of the grammatical side of a text is made possible by a nuanced understanding of an author's own inner psychology. On this basis, Schleiermacher argued that these two parts of interpretation – the grammatical and psychological – must be accomplished in a coordinated fashion: "Correct interpretation requires a relationship of the grammatical and psychological interpretation, since new concepts can arise out of new emotional experiences."[9] In other words, it is necessary to grasp the points of interaction between the language employed by an author (language's component of "signification") and the actual mind of the author (language's component of "manifestation").

THE GRAMMATICAL AND PSYCHOLOGICAL SIDES OF INTERPRETATION

The grammatical side of interpretation is the general side of hermeneutics.[10] For any text to possess signification, it must follow the prescribed grammar and syntax of a particular linguistic community. For this reason interpretation must begin with grammatical interpretation; "the grammatical interpretation leads the way," with the psychological interpretation only supplementing the grammatical interpretation.[11] In the case of the Bible, this would require a knowledge of biblical Hebrew and Hellenistic Greek, as well as Aramaic.

As previously noted, Reformation scholarship stressed the importance of reading biblical texts in their *original* languages. In many ways, the Renaissance's revival of the study of the classical languages served as the foundation for theologians

---

[9] Friedrich D. E. Schleiermacher, "The Hermeneutics: Outline of the 1819 Lectures," in *The Hermeneutic Tradition from Ast to Ricoeur*, ed. Gayle L. Ormiston and Alan D. Schrift (Albany: State University of New York Press, 1990), 85–100, 89 (§ 13.1).

[10] This section breaks down into three subsections: determination of the material elements, determination of the formal elements, and the quantitative understanding of these material and formal elements.

[11] Schleiermacher, "Hermeneutics: Outline of the 1819 Lectures," 96 (§ 23.4).

such as Erasmus, Luther, Melanchthon, and Calvin, all of whom emphasized the importance of reading biblical texts in their original languages, as opposed to reading them in the Vulgate (Latin) translation, as was the practice in the medieval period. The Dutch scholar Desiderius Erasmus (1466/9–1536) lamented the neglect of Greek grammar among the medieval scholastics of the previous era: "While mere knowledge of [Greek] grammar does not make a theologian; still less does ignorance of it; and certainly some scholarship conduces to knowledge of theology, while want of it impedes such knowledge."[12] From this vantage point, Schleiermacher's emphasis on reading biblical texts in their original languages represents a continuation of some of the basic tenets of Renaissance and Reformation scholarship. In Schleiermacher's view, the grammatical side of interpretation includes what he referred to as the *"outer* form" of a "discourse" (*Rede*).[13] He employs the term "discourse" to designate the grammatical dimension of a text. An examination of this "outer form" includes a text's genre, structure, style, and the relation of the parts of a text to the whole, all of which would be interpreted with respect to the literary norms of culture in which the text was written. As Schleiermacher observes,

First, one must consider the prior development of the genre of the work at the time when it was written; second, one must consider the use made of the genre typically in the place where the writer worked and in adjacent areas; finally, no exact understanding of the development and usage is possible without a knowledge of the related contemporary literature and especially the works the author might have used as a model.... With these contextualizations [*Vorkenntnissen*] in hand one can gain an excellent perception of the essential characteristics of a work upon a first reading.[14]

On the other hand, Schleiermacher termed the idiomatic, or idiosyncratic, dimensions of a given text, as they occur in the writings of particular authors, as "language" (*Spruche*). He argues that, besides a *general* knowledge of Greek and Hebrew grammar, one must also attain a *specific* "knowledge of the language as the author used it" because authors often employ language in idiosyncratic ways and exhibit individual styles.

Though the importance of Schleiermacher's grammatical and psychological principles may seem self-evident to us, we must not lose sight of the revolutionary nature of his hermeneutics from the perspective of the Reformation. Calvin, for instance, was interested in neither authorial intent nor the idiosyncrasies of a text's structure and style. He interpreted the Old Testament in the context of the *literary*

---

[12] Marjorie O'Rourke Boyle, *Erasmus on Language and Method in Theology* (Toronto: University of Toronto Press, 1977), 22, n. 69; cf. 36, n. 26, 22, n. 69.

[13] "One finds the purpose [*Wille*] of the work most precisely in its peculiar or characteristic development of its material. Often the characteristic motif has only a limited influence on certain sections of a work, but nonetheless shapes the character of the work by its influence on others" (Schleiermacher, "Hermeneutics: Outline of the 1819 Lectures," 98 [Part II, § 7]).

[14] Ibid., 97–98 (Part II, § 5).

norms of classical Greek and Latin literature, and he even employed the categories of classical Latin rhetoric (especially those of Cicero) to interpret forms of expression in Hebrew texts.[15] In so doing, his primary purpose was always to demonstrate that the true meaning of scripture does not conflict with the understanding of the world as explicated in the (venerated) ancient Greek and Latin authors.[16]

In contrast, Schleiermacher argued that one must compare biblical texts to other texts written by the same author, and to texts written in the same language and during the same historical period. One must have knowledge of "the vocabulary and the history of the period" in which an author lived.[17] But Schleiermacher did not conceive of hermeneutics on a purely grammatical level. As previously noted, the second part of Schleiermacher's hermeneutics was psychological in nature.[18]

In fact, Schleiermacher's hermeneutical theory emphasized the psychological side of interpretation over the grammatical side. He conceived of texts as imperfect exteriorizations of the inner minds of their authors. If grammatical interpretation represents the general side of hermeneutics (in the sense that it focuses on the general grammatical system shared by a linguistic community), then "psychological" interpretation represents the specific side, because it involves trying to understand the particular idiosyncrasies of a particular historical author. In Schleiermacher's view, the meaning of a text is not identical with the explicit grammatical sense of a text: the interpreter must always probe further to discover what the author *intended* to say but may not have stated fully or explicitly. The interpreter must attempt to discern, on the basis of a text's outer grammatical form, an author's inner motivation for writing. Thus, Schleiermacher argued that the outer grammatical form of a text has the power to disclose an inner form, namely the author's motivating principle.[19] In this light, "the task of hermeneutics consists in responding, as completely as possible, to the entire *inner discourse* of the writer's activity in composing."[20] Schleiermacher's term for this process of coming to understand these inner motivations is "divination." A "divinatory" method (being psychological in nature) complements the comparative, grammatical method:

The whole task requires the use of two methods, the divinatory and the comparative, which, however, as they constantly refer back to each other, must not be separated. Using the divinatory, one seeks to understand the writer intimately to the point that

[15] For example, hyperbole, hypotyposis, personification, following the example of Melanchthon before him. See Olivier Millet, *Calvin et la dynamic de la parole* (Geneva: Editions Slatkine, 1992).
[16] Randall C. Zachman, "Gathering Meaning from the Context: Calvin's Exegetical Method," *JRel* 82/1 (2002): 1–26, esp. 10–11; Randall C. Zachman, "'Do You Understand What You Are Reading?' Calvin's Guidance for the Reading of Scripture," *Scottish Journal of Theology* 59/1 (2001): 1–20.
[17] Schleiermacher, "Hermeneutics: Outline of the 1819 Lectures," 94 (§ 19.1, § 20).
[18] F. Schleiermacher, "General Hermeneutics [1810]: Psychological Explication," in *Hermeneutics and Criticism and Other Writings*, 90–157.
[19] Schleiermacher, "Hermeneutics: Outline of the 1819 Lectures," 96 (Part II, § 1).
[20] Schleiermacher, "Über den Begriff der Hermeneutik," *Hermeneutik und Kritik*, ed. M. Frank (Frankfurt am Main: Suhrkamp, 1977), 321.

one transforms oneself into the other. Using the comparative, one seeks to understand a work as a characteristic of a type, viewing the work, in other words, in the light of others like it.... Both refer back to each other. The first depends on the fact that every person has a susceptibility to intuiting others, in addition to his sharing many human characteristics. This itself appears to depend on the fact that everyone shares certain universal traits; divination consequently is inspired as the reader compares himself with the author.[21]

For Schleiermacher, the ultimate goal of the grammatical side of interpretation is to move past the outer form of a text – past its words, sentences, and paragraphs – to grasp its true inner origin, which lies in the originating spirit, or presence, of its author.[22] Indeed, he believed that texts exist "like miracles, only to direct our attention toward the [individual human] spirit that playfully generates them."[23]

At this point, we must emphasize that Schleiermacher's term "divination" does not denote some kind of mystical communion with a deceased author. By divination he meant a kind of intuiting or "read(ing) between the lines" of the text and making temporary hypotheses with a view to appreciating the inner origin of a text in the mind of its author.[24] Schleiermacher did not want to hypostasize an author or to recover an actual authorial presence, which is more real than the text itself. Rather, for Schleiermacher, this intuiting always bestows upon the hermeneutic act a creative or reconstructive dimension.

Schleiermacher conceived of the act of exegesis as a kind of *reversal* of the original act of composition: because every speech depends on earlier thought, the "act of understanding is the *inverse of an act of speaking*, in that the thought underlying the speech must enter consciousness."[25] In other words, hermeneutics is the art of moving backward from the exteriority of a text to the fuller presence of the authorial voice and then, reaching beyond this voice, to the full presence of the actual "language of the heart" (*verbum cordis*) of the historical author himself.

Put simply, in Schleiermacher's view, a text means what its author intended it to mean, as opposed to what is explicitly preserved on the grammatical surface of a text. By implication, the true meaning of a text is not to be found in its sentences

---

[21] Schleiermacher, "Hermeneutics: Outline of the 1819 Lectures," 98 (Part II, § 6). According to Schleiermacher, not all texts will have the same balance between the grammatical and the technical side. Schleiermacher remarks: "A minimum of grammatical [interpretation] accompanies a maximum of psychological [interpretation] in the exposition of personal letters, especially when they transmit didactic advice or historical information." Ibid., 89 (§ 12.2).

[22] F. Schleiermacher, *Werke Schleiermachers*, ed. Hermann Mulert (Berlin: Prophläen Verlag, 1924), III/3, 355, 358, 364.

[23] F. Schleiermacher, as quoted by Wilhelm Dilthey, in *Das Leben Schleiermachers*, 2 vols. in 4 (Berlin: Walter de Gruyter, 1970), appendix, 117.

[24] Schleiermacher, *Werke*, III/3, 355, 358, 364; Manfred Frank, *Das individuelle Allgemeine. Textstrukturierung und –interpretation nach Schleiermacher* (Frankfurt am Main: Suhrkamp, 1977), 313ff.; Wolfgang H. Pleger, *Schleiermachers Philosophie* (Berlin: Walter de Gruyter, 1988), 10.

[25] Schleiermacher, *Hermeneutik und Kritik*, 76 (emphasis added).

and paragraphs but rather *behind* the text, "in the reconstructed viewpoint of the author," which lay beyond the text itself.[26] This theoretical perspective requires that an interpreter go beyond the mere words of text to disclose all that its biblical author consciously intended, and hoped and wished to say. Thus, romanticist exegesis ultimately situates the meaning of a text *beyond the text* itself in the inner motivations of its original, historical author. Schleiermacher even believed that it is possible for the interpreter to understand a historical author better than he understood himself.[27] Through the benefit of hindsight, he believed that an interpreter can view the subsequent consequences of a particular historical life and thus appreciate the wider importance of that life of an author better than the person himself.[28]

SCHLEIERMACHER'S HERMENEUTIC CIRCLE

Schleiermacher recognized that this process of interpretation confronts the interpreter with a problem: if a particular passage of scripture can be correctly understood only by way of understanding the *whole* of the text, how can one understand this greater whole without first understanding the text's particular parts? The implication of this question is that the interpretive process must be circular:

An individual element can only be understood in the light of its place in the whole text; and therefore, a cursory reading for an overview of the whole must precede the exact exposition. Understanding appears to go in endless circles, for a preliminary understanding of even the individuals themselves comes from a general knowledge of the language.[29]

According to the circularity of the interpretive process, our general understanding of the whole of a text shapes how we interpret its individual parts within it; but our understanding of these parts, in turn, shapes our general understanding of the text as a whole. So for Schleiermacher, the hermeneutic process is a "circle":

The vocabulary and the history of the period in which an author works constitutes the whole within which his texts must be understood, with all their peculiarities. 1) This complete knowledge is contained within an apparent circle, so that every extraordinary thing can only be understood in the context of the general of which it is a part, and *vice versa*. And all knowledge can only be scientific to the extent that it is complete. 2) This circle makes possible an identification with the author, and thus it follows that, first, the more complete the knowledge we possess, the better bolstered we are for

---

[26] Jean Grondin, *Introduction to Philosophical Hermeneutics* (New Haven: Yale University Press, 1994), 71.

[27] Schleiermacher, *Hermeneutik und Kritik*, 104, 325; F. Schleiermacher, "Allgemeine Hermeneutik von 1809–10," ed. W. Virmond, *Schleiermacher-Archiv* 1 (1985): 1269–1310, esp. 1308.

[28] Schleiermacher, "Hermeneutics: Outline of the 1819 Lectures," 93 (§ 18.3).

[29] Ibid., 95 (§ 23.1).

exposition, and, second, no material for exposition can be understood in isolation; rather, every reading makes us better suited for understanding by enriching our previous knowledge.[30]

The conceptualization of the process of biblical interpretation as a circle implies that, when we interpret a biblical text, we must always move back and forth between the general (the whole of the grammatical, of the genre, of the historical period, etc.) and the specific (an author's specific intentions, particularities and idiosyncrasies). These two dimensions of interpretation complete each other: our understanding of the whole increasingly becomes more complete through understanding particular parts, and the particular parts each become more completely understood as one achieves an overview of the whole.

Given the circular nature of interpretation, Schleiermacher considered hermeneutics to be more of an "art" than a science. It is an "art" in the sense of the Greek term *tekhni* (τέχνη), that is, it requires the skill of a loving craftsman. For this reason, he argued that interpretation cannot be reduced to a set technique that can be followed mechanically to achieve objective results. A genuine understanding of any biblical text will always require the exercise of patience, sound judgment, and even imagination. This insight remains as true today as it was in Schleiermacher's time.

SCHLEIERMACHER'S LEGACY

Now imagine for a moment that you traveled to Israel on holiday and, while strolling through the shop of an antiquities dealer in east Jerusalem, you came across a brittle little papyrus scroll, on which were written about twenty lines of Greek text. On the reverse side, you decipher from faded characters the words ΠΡΟΣ ΛΑΟΔΙΚΕΙΑΣ (to the Laodiceans). Your heart leaps with joy when you remember that in Paul's letter to Philemon 4:16, Paul requested that his "Letter to the Laodiceans" be read in the church of Colossae. You also recall that Marcion's "canon" lists Paul's "Letter to the Laodiceans" as one of the original canonical books of the New Testament. On this basis, you conclude that this fragile papyrus fragment must be a copy of Paul's long lost letter to the Laodiceans. With this realization, you vow to purchase this scroll at any price.

But when the shopkeeper tells you the high price he is charging for the little scroll, you decide to reexamine the inscription one more time. Now you begin to have second thoughts, for what you first supposed to be faded Greek characters now seem to be mere unintelligible marks or indecipherable letters. Suddenly, the value of the scroll seems doubtful to you, and you put your credit card back in your wallet. Once you concluded that Paul was likely *not* the author, the scroll, which

---

[30] Ibid., 94 (§ 20.1–2).

you were at one time prepared to pay almost any price for, now seems almost worthless.

The strong desire which you *first* felt to purchase this scroll is evidence of the continuing legacy of Schleiermacher. Your attribution of the apostle Paul as its author functioned on more levels than mere historical antiquarianism. Your attribution of Paul as author also functioned at the level of your beliefs and assumptions. It governed both your classification and valuation of this manuscript. In effect, your assertion of "Paul-as-author" functioned by validating the truth of the scroll's words. To assert Paul-as-author seemed to assert that the message on this scroll was consistent with the theological teachings of Paul, as attested in his other authentic letters.[31] For within a romanticist paradigm, a writer as "author" is the source or origin of meaning. Thus, when authorship is determined, a text's meaning is also stabilized.

This helps explain why biblical scholars continuously debate the authenticity of such letters attributed to Paul as Ephesians, Colossians, 1 Timothy, 2 Timothy, and Titus. What is really at stake is not the historical identity of the authors of these books per se, but rather the overall contours of Paul's theology. For example, it matters a great deal to many scholars whether Paul, or someone else, commanded "Let a woman learn in silence with all submissiveness" (1 Tim 2:11). In other words, the assertion and denial of authorship are always ways of controlling the "sense" (significance) of a text.

Jacques Derrida has observed how scholars routinely appeal to authorial presence as a strategy to stabilize the interrelation of textual elements within a text, and thereby to stabilize what I have termed the founding sense-event. In philosophical terms, the concept of an "author" often functions as the center of a text's system of meaning: when an author is found, the text is explained, and the play of disseminated signification is minimized or eliminated altogether. For example, the attribution that Paul is the author of Galatians imposes a limit on the meaning of the text and requires that apparent contradictions between this text and other texts (such as Romans and 1 Corinthians) concerning the Torah observance, or the role of women in church, be explained and neutralized rather than ignored. Similarly, the attribution of Paul as the author of 1 Timothy necessitates that the admonition for women to "keep silent" in church (1 Tim 2:11–15, 4:7) be held in tension with the seemingly contradictory teachings in Galatians 3:28, which presuppose gender equality for all who are "in Christ" ("neither male nor female"), and 1 Corinthians 11:5, where Paul assumes that women will be vocal participants in worship and therefore not keep silent.

---

[31] Michel Foucault, "What Is an Author?" in *Language, Counter-Memory, Practice*, ed. Donald F. Bouchard, trans. Donald F. Bouchard and Sherry Simon (Ithaca, NY: Cornell University Press, 1977), 113–38, 121.

All this is to say that the romanticist concept of how authors *determine* textual meaning continues to guide our own commonsense approaches to the interpretation of biblical texts. Schleiermacher's exploration of the general phenomenon of human understanding and his exposition of the grammatical and psychological sides of interpretation have provided a theoretical foundation that continues to inform the contemporary practice of some biblical interpretation. The imprint of Schleiermacher's thought is particularly evident in the field of Pauline studies. Scholars routinely attempt to go beyond what Paul's letters "grammatically" say to speculate upon Paul's inner psychological being. It is difficult to pick up a book about Paul that does not make such conjectures. By way of example, consider the writings of C. H. Dodd, who described Paul's "affliction in Asia" (2 Cor 1:8–10) as "a sort of second conversion."[32] He describes this near-death experience in Paul's life as a psychological watershed that may have served as a catalyst for his development of a theology of the cross:[33]

But when he [Paul] accepted his limitations he was liberated afresh.… When he wrote again (2 Cor 1–9), it was in a strangely chastened mood.… He also makes it plain that he has gone to the depths and made terms with the last realities. There is nothing in earlier letters like the quiet self-abandonment of 2 Cor 4–5. Whether or not I am right in isolating this particular spiritual crisis as a sort of second conversion, it is at any rate plain that in the later epistles there is a change of temper. The traces of fanaticism and intolerance disappear, almost if not quite completely, along with all that anxious insistence on his own dignity.[34]

C. H. Dodd, like Schleiermacher, goes beyond what Paul's words *grammatically* say to disclose Paul's inner spiritual turmoil, his hidden thoughts, and even his unconscious motivations. Dodd's interest in Paul's inner feelings and spiritual crises is in no way unique in scholarship. This theme appears routinely in the works of many contemporary scholars.[35] This is not surprising because, to one degree or another, we are all children of romanticism. Our commonsense assumption is

---

[32]   However, before he had a chance to depart from Ephesus, Paul was detained. He suffered what he calls his "affliction in Asia" (2 Cor 1:8–10). Paul writes: "We do not want you to be unaware, brothers, of the affliction we experienced in Asia; for we were so utterly, unbearably crushed that we despaired of life itself. But we felt that we had received the sentence of death; but that was to make us rely not on ourselves but on God who raises the dead. He who rescued us from so deadly a peril will continue to rescue us" (2 Cor 1:8–10).

[33]   C. H. Dodd, "The Mind of Paul: I," in *New Testament Studies* (Manchester: Manchester University Press, 1953), 67–82.

[34]   Ibid., 81.

[35]   F. F. Bruce, *Paul, Apostle of the Heart Set Free* (Grand Rapids, MI: Wm. B. Eerdmans, 1977); Terence L. Donaldson, "Zealot and Convert: The Origin of Paul's Christ-Torah Antithesis," *CBQ* 51 (1989): 655–82, esp. 656; James D. G. Dunn, *The Theology of Paul the Apostle* (Grand Rapids, MI: Wm. B. Eerdmans, 1998); Ben Witherington III, *Grace in Galatia: A Commentary on Paul's Letter to the Galatians* (Grand Rapids, MI: Wm. B. Eerdmans, 1998), 102–3.

that the meaning of a biblical text is the meaning intended, or "put there," by its historical author.

This hermeneutic principle may seem self-evidently true in light of our everyday experience of reading a personal letter, an email, or even a grocery list. In such cases, we are most interested in what the writer intended to communicate to us. For example, if you found a list on your kitchen table one morning, on which were written the words "bread, eggs, tea, milk," you would intuitively recognize the *intention* of the "author" (your spouse) that somebody (you?) should purchase these grocery items.

However, ascertaining the intent of the author of a biblical text is more complicated than deciphering a grocery list. Biblical authors, and the intended recipients of their texts, were ancient peoples who communicated in, what are to us, foreign languages (Hebrew, Aramaic, Greek). They lived in cultures and societies vastly different from our own. Moreover, in most cases, the actual historical identities of the writers of biblical texts are unknown to us, in contrast to my example concerning the apostle Paul. For example, all critical scholars would agree that Moses was not the author of the Pentateuch. In fact, each of the five books of the Pentateuch had multiple authors, who successively wrote and redacted these texts over a period of centuries. Similarly, the identities of the writers of the four canonical gospels and the book of Acts are likewise unknown. The Gospels are all anonymous. The pastoral epistles (1 and 2 Tim, Titus), the Epistle to the Hebrews, 1 and 2 Peter, and 1, 2, 3 John are all pseudonymous writings. But why do we even care about authors? We care because of the legacy of romanticism. In some manner, we assume that the author anchors the truth of a text.

However, besides the fact that it is not possible to determine the historical authorship of most biblical writings, there is also a theological problem. Let us begin with the most obvious objection, one that Calvin and Luther would have made, if given the chance: namely, that the theorization of textual meaning solely in terms of authorial intent overlooks the "fuller sense" (*sensus plenior*) of scripture, not to mention its continuing significance in the present, which I have termed the present sense-event.

The construal of textual meaning as residing "behind" the text, in the hidden motivations of the original historical authors of the Bible, is rooted in two misunderstandings. The first of these misunderstandings is the belief that texts can be collapsed into, or elided with, human speech. In effect, this belief conceives of a text as frozen speech. This confusion is based on the false logic that a text is orality transposed into graphic symbols. In his book *Of Grammatology*, Jacques Derrida argued that, from Aristotle onward, writing has always been conceived of as a representation of speech, that is, as a "sign of a sign,"[36] and therefore as derivative of

---

[36] Supposing speech itself as a sign of an author's actual inner thoughts.

speech.[37] The second misunderstanding is the related romanticist conviction that speech (from which a text is thought to have been derived) is relatively transparent and can be directly traced back to a speaker's silent intentions.

According to Derrida these two misunderstandings are based on the concept of "phonocentrism." Phonocentrism is rooted in the binary opposites of "presence" versus "absence" and "original" versus "copy." In the case of presence-absence binarism, the physical absence of an author (when reading a text) is subordinated to the full physical presence of the author in speech. In the case of the original-copy binarism, the text, as a copy of speech, is subordinated to original founding intention or speech act. In both of these aspects of phonocentrism, speech is privileged over writing, which, in turn, privileges the interiority of authorial presence (intentionality) over speech. This metaphysics of presence undergirds the romanticist strategy of tracing textual meaning back to a prior original authorial presence. For if a text is conceived of as an expression of the intentions and feelings of its author, then the purpose of interpretation must surely be to reproduce the original intentions and feelings that gave rise to the text.

The phenomenon of phonocentrism is even evident in the case of the tradition of interpreting the sayings of Jesus, who, of course, was not an author (as far as we know). Even though Jesus was not an author, he has been transformed into an author through the practice of treating the "sayings of Jesus," as recorded in the canonical gospels, as if they were the "very words of Jesus" (*ipsissima verba Jesu*). This practice ignores the very real contributions of the redactors of the Gospels (i.e., the "authors" of Matthew, Mark, Luke, John) and the complex oral and written prehistory of the Gospels. These many contributions to the "sayings of Jesus" tradition are ignored when these synoptic and Johannine texts are conceived of as a representations of Jesus' actual speech, and then this "speech" is confused with Jesus' actual presence. By confusing the final form of the canonical sayings attributed to Jesus with the sayings of the historical Jesus, the canonical sayings can be traced back one further step to authorial, dominical presence, thereby converting Jesus into an "author." This practice represents another face of phonocentrism. It provides further evidence of the continuing influence of romanticism in contemporary biblical interpretation.

By treating the material papyri and vellum manuscripts of the canonical Gospels as "sources" of the historical Jesus' authorial voice, which is itself an expression of Jesus' prior intentions, we subordinate what we actually possess, namely the material manuscripts of the four canonical Gospels, to what we positively lack, that is, the physical sound of Jesus' speech and access to his actual intentions. But

---

[37] Jacques Derrida, *Of Grammatology*, trans. G. C. Spivak (Baltimore: Johns Hopkins University Press, 1974 [1967]), 27–73. Note how Saussurian semiology begins with the "spoken word" (*vox*) as the primary linguistic signifier. In effect, Saussure reduces writing to the status of recording a prior oral communication, with the result that speech becomes associated with the immediacy of personal presence while texts are understood in terms of absence.

the material manuscripts of the canonical Gospels should be respected as distinct forms of communication: they are distinct because they consist of "assemblages" of written graphic signs. This fact bestows on them properties that differ from the physical sounds of human speech, as well as, of course, from the psychological intentions of the historical Jesus of Nazareth.

In his critique of phonocentrism, Derrida argues that a text is not a human voice reduced to the silence of graphic symbols. A text is not "frozen speech." In fact, texts and speech have very different properties: for example, a text, unlike speech, presumes the absence – not presence – of its author.[38] This fact of the authorial absence of biblical texts renders them *open-ended* because they can always be read and understood in multiple contexts over time, within the text-reception complex. The text-reception complex itself becomes a kind of performance, replaying, or counteractualizing of textual "sense," bestowing upon interpretation a productive dimension. Owing to the flux of the circularity of language's three components (signification, denotation, and manifestation), a text, once dispatched by its author, refuses to be controlled and funneled into single meanings. The theological concept of the "fuller sense" (*sensus plenior*) of scripture is implicitly based on this principle.

The "fuller sense" of scripture is perhaps most evident in the practice of reading the Bible according to a lectionary. The lectionary reading of biblical texts in churches, Sunday by Sunday, is one example of reading of biblical texts *outside* their original contexts. Not only do biblical texts have historical contexts that differ from *our* contexts, but their individual historical contexts differ *from one another.* Typically, lectionaries specify three historically disconnected biblical texts to be read in the worship on a given Sunday of the year.[39] The very act of reading the Bible by means of a lectionary involves reading historically unrelated texts side by side. The weekly churchgoer is taken from one discontinuous block of three texts to another, knowing that the intervening historical and cultural gaps will never be filled in. Like childhood memory, the lectionary creates dramatic shifts in time, profound breaks in narrative sequences, and ruptures in historical causality. When reading texts according to a lectionary, time can run backward, as well as forward. When the Bible is read this way, it is almost inevitable that it will be interpreted in light of our own modern contexts, apart from any historical knowledge of the

---

[38] Jacques Derrida, "Signature Event Context" [1971], in *Limited Inc*, trans. Samuel Weber (Evanston, IL: Northwestern University Press, 1990), 1–24, esp. 3, 7–8; cf. Derrida's two essays on speech-act theory: "Signature Event Context" [1971] and "Limited Inc a b c" [1977], also in his *Limited Inc*, 29–110.

[39] The Revised Common Lectionary specifies for each Sunday of the year one reading from the Old Testament, Psalms, the epistles, and the Gospels, respectively, in a three-year cycle. The Revised Common Lectionary was created in 1983. The revision was the product of a collaboration between the North American Consultation on Common Texts (CCT) and the International English Language Liturgical Consultation.

original writers.⁴⁰ Perhaps authorship is not as determinative of meaning as we sometimes assume.

THE DEATH OF THE AUTHOR

The romanticist concept of an author has been problematized in the past fifty years – so much so that in 1967 the literary critic Roland Barthes famously proclaimed the "death of the author." With this proclamation, he challenged the conventional romanticist appeal to authors as a way of imposing a limit on the meaning of texts, a practice that he termed "interpretive tyranny." In Barthes's view, an author is actually an *effect* of the text itself: when one reads a text, the sense one experiences of being in the author's presence is actually an effect of language of the text itself. For example, Barthes would say that our sense of Jeremiah-as-author, Isaiah-as-author, Paul-as-author, and John-(of Patmos)-as-author is actually a product of textuality. After all, it is language's component of signification that creates the very grammatical position and possibility for a writer to say "I" in text.

This grammatical function is known as "deixis."⁴¹ Pronouns, such as English "I" and Greek *ego* (ἐγώ), do not refer to any determinate subject through relation. If you picked up a note lying on the ground and read the words "I am going to the beach," you would have no idea who the subject was because the pronoun "I" can be defined only with respect to its place in the wider discourse in which it occurs.⁴² In other words, the pronouns "I" and "you," "she" and "he," function within the very "taking place" of language. The use of the pronoun "I" by any biblical "author" creates the *effect* of an authorial presence within the significatory structure of language. Of course, part of the delight of reading a story is the feeling of being told a story *by* someone, even in the case of such authorially layered texts as Genesis and Exodus. We, as readers of biblical texts, may feel that we experience the presence of a real author, even though this experience is actually an *effect* generated by the text's own components of "signification" and "manifestation."

---

⁴⁰ Derrida, "Signature Event Context," 9.
⁴¹ The Greek Stoic philosophers termed this grammatical concept "deixis" (δεῖξις). Deixis is the ability of language to refer only to itself. For example, demonstratives such as "there" and "here" and pronouns such as "I" and "you" have no determinate essence. Unlike nouns, they do not refer to any determinate object through relation. In the absence of a relation to a noun, they are empty signs that rely on the here and now. Roman Jakobson (1896–1982), co-founder of the Moscow Linguistic Circle (1915), refers to such words as "shifters." Rather they refer to the pure taking place, or instance, of language. When one identifies oneself as "I," who speaks or writes, these pronouns refer to the instance of discourse itself. They cannot be defined outside their relation to the discourse. As such, the shifter "I" actually erases the psychosomatic individual; cf. Giorgio Agamben, *Language and Death: The Place of Negativity*, trans. Karen E. Pinkus with Michael Hardt (Minneapolis: University of Minnesota Press, 1991), 19, 21–31.
⁴² Giorgio Agamben, *Remnants of Auschwitz: The Witness and the Archive*, trans. Daniel Heller-Roazen (New York: Zone Books, 2002), 117.

Let me hasten to add that, with his famous proclamation of the death of the author, Barthes was not refuting the everyday fact that human beings compose texts. Rather, his announcement of the "death of the author" represents his attempt to displace the historical author as the origin and foundation of textual meaning in favor of a more sophisticated understanding of the sense-event, both past and present. After all, for all practical purposes, *the destination of all texts is always the text-reception complex*. On the basis of this observation, Roland Barthes argued that a text's sense lies not in its author but in its readers and interpreters: its meaning "lies not in its origins" but in its "destination," which is us.[43]

In the estimation of Michel Foucault, Roland Barthes did not fully resolve the problem of the author. By confining his concept of an "author" to an event within textuality, Barthes overlooked the *exterior deployment* of authors in academic discourse and in the interpretive tradition. Taking up the problem afresh, Foucault asks why the concept of historical authorship continues to be regarded as "solid" and "fundamental" for the determination of textual meaning.[44] Indeed, the authors to which interpreters refer no longer exist as historical facts that can be investigated: biblical authors must always be constructed by scholarly discourses.[45] By selecting some authorial attributes and dismissing others, scholars construct the very authors to which they refer. For example, in constructing "Herman Melville" as the author of *Moby Dick*, scholars routinely select the attribute that Melville actually did embark upon on a whaling voyage, while they routinely ignore the fact that he also worked in a bowling alley in Hawaii. Although both of these attributes are historically true, scholars have chosen one attribute and dismissed the other in their cultural construction of "Melville-as-author."

The same point could be made of authors of scripture, such as Paul, who is undoubtedly the most historical of all biblical authors. The construction of Paul as author is routinely carried out on the basis of an attribute that Paul never mentions, namely his conversion on the road to Damascus (Acts 9, 22, 26). All Paul says about his conversion is that God "was pleased to reveal his Son" either "in him" (implying an inner mystical experience) or "in his case" (Gal 1:16).[46] Over the centuries, scholars have constructed the effect of Paul-as-author on the basis of the letters attributed to him and the book of Acts. Over the centuries, this constructed effect has accumulated an illusory "effect of the real" personal presence of Paul.[47] But Paul's life and mind are available to us only through textualized traces. In the

---

[43] Roland Barthes, "The Death of the Author," in his *Image Music Text*, trans. Stephen Heath (New York: Hill and Wang, 1977), 142–48, esp. 148.
[44] Foucault, "What Is an Author?" 113–38.
[45] Ibid., 128.
[46] In the phrase ἀποκαλύψαι τὸν υἱὸν αὐτοῦ ἐν ἐμοί, the preposition ἐν may mean "in" (referring to an inward ecstatic experience), or "in my case."
[47] I here borrow the phrase "effect of the real" from Roland Barthes, "From History to Reality" [1984], in *The Rustle of Language* (New York: Blackwell, 1986), 127–56, esp. 141–48.

case of pseudonymous (as opposed to anonymous) Pauline and Petrine texts, the authors associated with Colossians, Ephesians, the Pastoral letters, and 1 and 2 Peter have actually *inserted themselves into the author function* of Paul and Peter, respectively. By claiming Paul's and Peter's authorial identities, later generations of Christians managed to achieve automatic authorization of the "truth" of their own discourses, proving that even ancient Christians understood how the author function works.

In his discussion of the Christian practice of constructing authors, Foucault cites Saint Jerome's four criteria for maintaining a single authorship of multiple texts. These criteria constitute a list of the external constraints (in contrast to Barthes's internal textual effect) that determine what he terms the "author function":

1. *The principle of quality*: Texts are eliminated from the list of an oeuvre of an author if they are deemed to be markedly superior, or inferior, to other supposedly authentic texts.[48] In this case, the author function operates as an external guarantee of a certain standard of quality (of inspiration/truth/ revelation).

2. *The criterion of coherence*: A text is eliminated from the list of works belonging to an author when the ideas found in the text are deemed to significantly contradict, or conflict with, ideas found in other authentic texts. For example, because the requirement that "women learn in silence with all submissiveness" and "have no authority over men" in 1 Timothy 2:12–15 contradicts Paul's tacit permission for women to function as prophets in the Corinthian church, praying and prophesying alongside men (1 Cor 11:2–6), most scholars eliminate 1 Timothy from the list of Paul's authentic letters. Thus, the author function denotes a field of conceptual coherence that is constructed by interpreters.

3. *The criterion of stylistic unity*: A text is eliminated from belonging to a particular author when the text's style differs significantly from that of other texts belonging to that author. In other words, the author function requires a degree of stylistic uniformity with other authentic texts.

4. *The historical criterion*: Texts are also eliminated that refer to events that took place after the death of the author. For example, the narrative of the death of Moses in Deuteronomy 34:5–6 implies that Moses could not have authored this text. In this case, the author function requires a definite

---

[48] In Pauline studies the term *Hauptbriefe* designates the letters in the New Testament that are universally accepted as being written by Paul the apostle, namely Romans, Galatians, 1 Corinthians, 2 Corinthians; the "pastoral epistles," namely 1, 2 Timothy and Titus, are generally considered pseudonymous. On 2 Cor 6:14–7, see Hans-Dieter Betz, "2 Cor 6:14–7:1: An Anti-Pauline Fragment?" *JBL* 92 (1973): 88–108.

historical figure in which a series of historical events converge as a continuous narrative.[49]

Thus, to designate "Paul-as-author" means much more than to attribute a particular historical person as the originator of a text. Paul-as-author is a cultural
construction, fabricated by scholars, connoting a degree of quality, coherence, and
stylistic uniformity, in addition to some historical limitations. From this perspective, "Paul" is not the name of a historical person but rather the name of a relatively
homogeneous group of texts, formed through the elimination and selection of
texts, based on the preceding four criteria. Thus, the name "Paul" functions in the
same way as the names "Plato" and "Shakespeare" do. These names are routinely
used to designate a coherent group of texts and the ideas found within them (i.e.,
the dialogues of Plato, the plays and sonnets of Shakespeare, the letters of Paul).[50]
From this perspective, Paul-as-author is neither a historical person nor even just
an internal signifying effect of the text (as Barthes would have it) but rather a possible "subject position," which any pseudonymous writer could insert himself into
and inhabit, within the structure of textual signification and say "I."

There is more to say. Whereas, according to the romanticist view, authors are
understood as the sources and origin of meaning, this "author function" actually decenters the historical author as the source of meaning. This is not to say
that Foucault disputes the commonplace fact that historical persons composed
texts. But he does challenge the romanticist practice of appealing to such historical persons as a way of *controlling and limiting textual meaning*. Foucault's point
is not that we should dispense with the materiality of human authors in favor of
free-floating textuality, or that we should invert the romanticist author-text hierarchy as a text-author hierarchy. Rather, he is saying that we have outgrown the
romanticist tradition and it is time to move on. We now recognize that all appeals
to biblical authors are rooted in a metaphysics of presence, or what Derrida terms
"phonocentrism," which is really an effect of the text and the scholarly construction of authors. In most cases, such appeals to historical authors thinly conceal an
interpreter's attempt to impose a limit on textual meaning.

In reality, biblical authors are not psychic presences concealed beneath the semiotic surface of a text. *Authors are zones of indiscernibility.* Biblical authors always
remain both distinct and obscure at the same time in texts. Framed in terms of
the previous chapter, one could say that language's component of manifestation
(which is the domain of the personal, of conscious beliefs, ideas, and intentions)
is always in flux because it points beyond itself, in a circular fashion, to the components of signification and denotation. Moreover, the plane of manifestation
encompasses more than the conscious beliefs, ideas, and intentions of a writer: it

[49] Foucault, "What Is an Author?" 128.
[50] Michel Foucault, *The Archaeology of Knowledge* (New York: Tavistok Publications/Pantheon, 1972
      [1969]), 15, 16, 93–96, 209.

also includes the author's phenomenological preunderstanding and unconscious libidinal desires as well. And because the present sense-event of a text will always be distinct from the founding (authorial) sense-event, the concept of "authorial intent" should not be allowed to function hermeneutically as a way of limiting and controlling textual sense. Moreover, from a theological perspective, the doctrine of the inspiration of the whole of scripture does not require that we resuscitate historical authors to guarantee the truth of its message.

In many ways, the writings of Martin Heidegger, Karl Barth, Hans-Georg Gadamer, Paul Ricoeur, and Rudolph Bultmann all challenge and correct fundamental aspects of the romanticist paradigm. Not only does a romanticist interpretation exclude the concept of the fuller significance of scripture, but, when combined with historicism, it also ends in nihilism. I return to this issue in the following chapter, where we study the work of Wilhelm Dilthey, who championed Schleiermacher's concept of authorial intent in the nineteenth century.

3

The Crisis of Historical Meaning

The painting *Wanderer above a Sea of Mists* (1818), by the German artist David Caspar Friedrich (fig. 3.1), portrays a cultured European man, holding a walking stick. He faces away from us, standing on a mountain summit, as he surveys a vast sea of mist stretching to the horizon. This "wanderer" is an isolated, solitary figure, a single point of consciousness, who observes the world around him from afar. His elevation implies a relation to the world of domination.

I would suggest that this image presents us with the Enlightenment ideal of the modern, rational subject. His divinely ordained mission is to tame the world by analyzing it, standardizing it through measurement and classification, explaining its meaning through linguistic representation, and, finally, by gaining control and mastery over it. In many ways this painting also gives us a glimpse of the nineteenth-century ideal of the historian. In the nineteenth century, a movement known as "historicism" arose, within which we can observe the growing awareness of the *distance* between the historian as "subject" and history as an "object" of inquiry. Nineteenth-century historicism understood the historian as a detached subject, whose task was to survey the past from a great height. Through a careful sorting and reading of historical documents, his task was to objectively reassemble the dusty facts of the past into a unified whole, which is to say, into a historical narrative of what actually happened.

In part, the rise of historicism can be traced back to the Enlightenment project. Its theoretical moorings grew out of the Enlightenment ideal of human rationality as the basis for all knowledge. As such, historicism epitomizes the three dreams of rationalism: the development of rational methods of inquiry, the development of a unified science, and the development of a technically precise language by which to express universal knowledge.[1] As Hans Frei observes, the execution of this program had consequences that would soon call into question traditional aspects of Christian belief. Biblical scholars began to question the historical truth, or accuracy, of key events narrated in the Bible. They soon recognized that the Bible does not constitute even a *single* narrative of God's dealings with humanity but rather consists of many separate texts, which, in totality, lack a clear and linear narrative.

---

[1] Stephen Toulmin, *Cosmopolis: The Hidden Agenda of Modernity* (New York: Free Press, 1990), 104.

3.1. David Caspar Friedrich, *Wanderer above a Sea of Mists* (*Der Wanderer über dem Nebelmeer,* 1818), Hamburger Kunsthall, Hamburg, Germany (bpk, Berlin / Hamburger Kunsthalle / Art Resource, NY)

Under the influence of Baruch de Spinoza, Friedrich Schleiermacher, and others, a new generation of biblical interpreters argued that the Bible is not a unified book but rather a collection of diverse historical documents. They also argued that these historical documents should be interpreted using the *same* methods of interpretation as are applied to other historical documents. In so doing, they reversed the direction of critique, evaluating the Bible in terms of the dictates of current methodologies rather than evaluating the contemporary age in light of the biblical witness, as the reformers had previously done.[2] Thus, in carrying out this historicizing program on the Bible, it quickly became evident that the emerging historical foundations of biblical texts would, in many ways, conflict with the tenets of traditional Christian piety.

The rise of historicism can be traced back even beyond the Enlightenment to the Protestant Reformation. Historicism, as a movement, arose primarily within Protestant Christianity, as a response to this breakdown of authority. Its original impulse was not to subvert Christian faith but to provide a secure historical and reasoned foundation for faith. Protestantism attempted to repudiate the authority of the Roman Catholic Church by asserting the primacy of scripture as the sole rule of faith (*regula fidei*). The resulting schism brought about two conflicting ecclesiastical systems, both of which – Catholic and Protestant – turned to the humanistic tradition to establish a new approach for the interpretation of scripture. The Protestant emphasis on the authority of scripture, over and against Catholic religious dogma, can also be viewed as an intensification of the Renaissance's ongoing commitment to the study of classical literature in its original languages, and its skeptical critique of ecclesiastical authority.[3] However, far from resolving the problem of authority in the church, Protestantism's appeal to scripture, in effect, replaced the unified ecclesial authority of the Roman Catholic Church with countless new authorities – growing numbers of biblical interpreters – each claiming to interpret scripture correctly.[4] This conflict was much more than a theological debate. The appeal to the "true" meaning of scripture, which Protestants hoped would release the church from medieval superstition, ecclesial abuses, and oppressive religious authoritarianism, actually resulted in an intensification of oppression and suffering. With this religious conflict also came bloodshed, malnutrition, and human suffering.[5] As a result, the Reformation resulted in a crisis of the authority of scripture that continues to the present day.

THE THEORETICAL FOUNDATIONS OF HISTORICISM

The various forms of historicism can claim the same theoretical foundations.[6] First, as its name implies, historicism limited its object of study to *historical* entities,

---

[2]   Hans W. Frei, *The Eclipse of Biblical Narrative: A Study of Eighteenth and Nineteenth Century Hermeneutics* (New Haven: Yale University Press, 1980).

[3]   Toulmin, *Cosmopolis*, x.

[4]   Jeffrey Stout, *The Flight from Authority: Religion, Morality, and the Quest for Autonomy* (Notre Dame, IN: University of Notre Dame Press, 1981), 41.

[5]   Ibid., 13.

[6]   Calvin G. Rand, "The Two Meanings of Historicism in the Writings of Dilthey, Troeltsch, and Meinecke," *Journal of the History of Ideas* 25 (1964): 503–18.

excluding such ideal or transcendental principles as God, providence, or the Hegelian progress of the "spirit" (*Geist*). Historicism viewed the biblical narratives as a historical phenomenon, composed of unique, unrepeatable acts, arising from mundane material causes. Under the growing influence of the natural sciences, the biblical world was viewed as an "interconnected nexus of causes, a self-contained and autonomous whole, whose laws had the lucidity and validity of mathematical axioms, thus emptying the world of the need for special interventions of the divine (i.e., miracles)."[7]

Second, historicism asserted the irreducible *uniqueness* of each historical entity, situating each person, event, institution, and society within its own specific historical context. For example, Johann Gottfried von Herder stressed the uniqueness of all historical people and nations, with unique characteristics and distinctive values.[8] This historical understanding can be traced back to Baruch de Spinoza, who, in chapter 7 of his *Tractatus theologico-politicus* (1670), contended that, in order to interpret the most difficult scriptural passages, the interpreter must establish the *historical* environment of each book (e.g., author, occasion, historical context) and the subsequent editorial history of each book. In following the precepts of Spinoza, historicism reconfigured the Reformation hermeneutical principle of understanding the parts in terms of the larger whole by redefining the "whole." The whole was no longer the whole theological unity of scripture but the whole *of history*.[9] As a result, a close study of biblical texts revealed, as Thomas Reynolds observes, "not infallible and verbally inspired truths, but *contingent* religious worldviews, representative of the varied circumstances in which they were written."[10]

Third, historicism presumed that the historical relations between these historical entities exist *as facts*, independent of the mind of the historian, who orders, classifies, posits, and thematizes them. On this basis, it was concluded that the primary duty of the historian is to *recover* these facts and use them to reconstruct a connected narrative of history. Leopold von Ranke, the so-called father of historicism, conceived of history as existing "there," awaiting discovery in documents of the past. He understood historical documents as "sources," that is, as the means of laying hold of the historical reality that resides *behind* the text. According to Ranke, the primary duty of the historian is to reconstruct the past "as it essentially

---

[7]   Thomas E. Reynolds, *The Broken Whole: Philosophical Steps toward a Theology of Global Solidarity* (Albany: State University of New York Press, 2006), 22.

[8]   Johann Gottfried von Herder, *Against Pure Reason: Writings on Religion, Language, and History*, trans. and ed. Marcia Bunge (Minneapolis: Fortress, 1993), 40–45.

[9]   Benedictus de Spinoza, *Spinoza Opera*, ed. Konrad Blumenstock (Darmstadt: Wissenschaftliche Buchgesellschaft, 1967–); B. de Spinoza, *Theological-Political Treatise*, ed. Carl Gebhardt, trans. Samuel Shirley (Indianapolis: Hackett, 2001).

[10] Reynolds, *Broken Whole*, 32 (emphasis added). For a survey of historicism in Germany and America, see Sheila Greeve Davaney's excellent overview, *Historicism: The Once and Future Challenge for Theology* (Minneapolis: Fortress, 2006).

happened" (*Wie es eigentlich gewesen*).[11] In other words, the responsibility of the historian extends beyond the mere recording of the bare, antiquarian facts of history to their reconstruction into a *unified*, coherent, meaningful historical narrative.[12]

Fourth, historicism asserted that all historical entities ought to be interpreted in their own terms and that no universal system of values exists by which they may be critically assessed. For example, Herder argued that each culture and nation ought to be evaluated on its *own* terms, not according to the contemporary ideals of European Christendom: "The universal, philosophical, philanthropic tone of our century readily applies 'our own ideal' of virtue and happiness to each distant nation, to each remote period in history. But can one such single ideal be the sole standard for judging, condemning, or praising the customs of other nations or periods?"[13] By implication, biblical interpreters must break free from their own values and become submerged in the worldview (*Weltanschauung*) of the ancient world.

Fifth, the term historicism also referred to a tradition of scholarship that values the past for its own sake without reference to the concerns or questions of the present. In other words, historicism concerns itself with the four components of texts – signification, denotation, manifestation, and sense – not with their present sense-event. According to Ranke, the "supreme law" of history is to put forward an unbiased presentation of historical facts for their own sake, without any reference to or interference from the interpreting subject. This ideal of historical practice was antiquarian in spirit. As Hayden White explains,

The "historical method" … consisted of a willingness to go to the archives without any preconceptions whatsoever, to study the documents found there, and then to write a story about the events attested by the documents in such a way as to make the story itself the explanation of "what had happened" in the past. The idea was to let the explanation emerge naturally from the documents themselves, and then to figure its meaning in story form.[14]

Last, historicism is committed to the notion of *methodological* access to truth. This commitment reflects the growing importance of methodology in the natural sciences in nineteenth-century Europe. It contended that access to the "facts" of history must be achieved through the correct application of approved, scientific methods to the literary and archaeological evidence of the past. Obviously, this

[11] Leopold von Ranke, *Geschichten der romanischen und germanischen Völker von 1494 bis 1514*, 3rd ed. (Leipzig: Duncker & Humblot, 1885), vii.
[12] Leopold von Ranke, *Der Weltgeschichte* (Duncker & Humblot, 1921), vol. IX, part 2, xliii; quoted by Hans-Georg Gadamer in *Truth and Method,* 2nd rev. ed., trans. Joel Weinsheimer and Donald G. Marshall (London: Continuum, 1994 [1965]), 202.
[13] Herder, *Against Pure Reason*, 40–44.
[14] Hayden White, *Metahistory: The Historical Imagination in Nineteenth-Century Europe* (Baltimore: Johns Hopkins University Press, 1973), 141.

commitment to methodological access to historical truth continues in biblical studies to the present day. In fact, the notion of *methodological access to truth* is the most notable and consistent feature of all contemporary forms of biblical interpretation.

As already noted, the emergence of historicism can be viewed as an extension of the rationality of the Enlightenment project. Descartes famously attempted to develop a philosophical method founded solely upon the autonomous, rational interpreter, without appeal to scripture or religious authority. Thomas Reynolds describes three key themes of the Enlightenment project: its emancipatory thrust over and against normalizing tendencies of religious doctrine; its reflexivity or capacity for self-critique; and its belief in the possibility of progress toward the discovery of objective, universal truths, through dispassionate application of reason.[15] Thus, when considered against the background of the Renaissance and Reformation, the dawn of historicism represented a new mode of inquiry, one that continues to guide the practice of the historical study of the Bible even in the present day.

HISTORICISM IN CONTEMPORARY NEW TESTAMENT STUDIES

In recent decades, the field of biblical studies has explored many new methodologies, including literary criticism, reader-response criticism, narrative criticism, canonical criticism, feminist criticism, and postcolonial criticism.[16] Without diminishing the importance of these new developments, it remains true that a great many contemporary biblical scholars continue to employ methodologies that are grounded in the theoretical framework of nineteenth-century historicism. This extension of historicism in the present is termed "historical positivism." We can find the imprint of historicism in present-day scholarship, not only in the continued use of the four classical historicocritical methods[17] but also in the sociocultural criticism of the 1980s and in the methods employed by the Westar Institute's "Jesus Seminar" and by the "International Q Project." Moreover, even a cursory review of the journals affiliated with academic societies, such as the *Journal of Biblical Literature* and *New Testament Studies,* reveals that much of the current discipline remains rooted in the theoretical foundation of historicism. The continued influence of historicism in New Testament studies is evident in a number of significant features.

First, the practice of the discipline continues to be dominated by the reconstruction of early Christian history and by the search for the historical relations between

---

[15] Reynolds, *Broken Whole,* 48.
[16] For example, in the field of the Hebrew Bible, see John J. Collins's overview of alternative approaches in *The Bible after Babel: Historical Criticism in the Postmodern Age* (Grand Rapids, MI: Wm. B. Eerdmans, 2005).
[17] Namely, textual criticism, form criticism, source criticism, and redaction criticism.

a limited set of variables: namely, the genealogical relation between biblical texts and their literary "sources" (e.g., synoptic problem), their historical authors, and their antecedent historical contexts. The appeal to both authorial intent and historical context in the determination of the meaning of New Testament texts continues to function as a mainstay of much contemporary exegetical interpretation, especially in denominationally affiliated institutions. To a greater or lesser extent, the explication of this limited set of relations functions as the normative paradigm, while other interpretive practices are subordinated to a supplementary, or ancillary, status. As such, in many ways nineteenth-century historicism, in the contemporary form of historical positivism, continues to serve a gate-keeping role within the discipline.[18]

Second, a major thrust of New Testament studies in North America has been the tracing of the historical development of phenomena attested in the New Testament back to their "origins" in, for example, Second Temple Judaism, Jewish apocalypticism, Hellenistic culture, Essenism, protognosticism, and a supposed "Q community," according to a pattern of influence and development. Thus, Ranke's mandate to connect the writings, events, and characters of history, together within a single, historical narrative, continues to function as a primary goal of the discipline. The most striking example of this phenomenon is the labeling of the discipline of New Testament Studies in North American universities as "Christian origins." This simple substitution of "Christian origins" for "New Testament studies," in effect, recasts the traditional theological questions concerning the meaning of the New Testament in terms of a quest for Christianity's lost beginnings and a mapping out of subsequent developments. This change accords a privileged status to a circumscribed set of key concepts – namely, historical contexts, origins, and the narrative of their development.

Yet experience has taught us that all quests for origins have the structure of a *regressus in infinitum*. They inevitably lead through the most dubious and tentative chronologies to an ever-receding past and *multiple* origins, which must, by their very nature, elude final determination. Indeed, in view of the tremendous outpouring of scholarly effort over the past fifty years, it is notable that the continued application of the methods of historicism to the New Testament has not resulted in the production of a continuous historical account of the life of the historical Jesus or of Paul, or of the emergence of early Christianity, which is convincing to the majority of its practitioners. In part, one can hold the nature of the New Testament documents themselves responsible: these documents abound in discontinuities, dislocations, temporal gaps, inconsistencies, contradictions, and stubborn silences, all of which collectively *resist* the scholar's efforts to unify them within a single historical narrative.

---

[18]   Collins, *The Bible after Babel,* 4.

But this failure of historicism is not merely the fault of the documents themselves. Actual history is not a linear narrative: history is naturally *polycentric*. In
truth, the historical past is more like a series of interconnected worlds than it is
like a linear succession of events. The construction of historical narratives always
requires the selection and deselection of historical facts. But any resulting totalizing narrative will always oversimplify the complexity of history.

Third, notwithstanding these setbacks, many scholars continue to believe that the
narrative of early Christianity's lost origins and subsequent developments exist as
objective facts, independent of the work of scholars as subjects in the construction
of history (historiology). In short, they suppose that early Christian history, which
they themselves have created, is itself a *factum brutum*. But, as Jürgen Habermas
observes, the construction of a historical narrative from what are deemed to be
historical facts (including what can be known of facts of the lives of the historical Jesus and Paul) is always "organized backward from a projected endpoint [of
the interpreter] into a story."[19] This explains how it is possible for scholars to have
constructed such diverse and contradictory portraits of the historical Jesus. For
example, Ben Witherington III's "Jesus, as the genius who founded Christianity,"
and John Dominic Crossan's "Jesus, as a radical revolutionary and anti-dogmatic
Cynic philosopher, who did *not* found Christianity," and David Flusser's "Jesus, as
Jewish genius, who *accidentally* caused Christianity," all employ historical methodologies and have access to the same historical data.[20] How can this bizarre state
of affairs be explained? Ironically, it is the competing and contradictory constructions of the "historical Jesus" scholars (such as those of Witherington, Flusser, and
Crossan) that create the comforting illusion that the facts of the historical life of
Jesus can actually be known.

Because the possible historical contexts for New Testament texts are almost
inexhaustible, and biblical scholars themselves cannot agree on how to distinguish
between the "facts" and "pious tradition" in New Testament texts, the selection and
deselection of the evidence, and its subsequent organization into a linear narrative,
always involve a subjective factor and even an element of arbitrariness or guesswork. Just as historians connect isolated historical facts to form coherent stories
with the aid of modern categories (e.g., the Thirty Years' War), so also the life of

---

[19] Jürgen Habermas, *On Logic of the Social Sciences*, trans. Sherry Weber Nicholsen and Jerry A. Stark
      (Cambridge: Polity Press, 1988 [1967]), 162.
[20] Ben Witherington III, *The Jesus Quest: The Third Search for the Jew of Nazareth*, 2nd ed. (Downers
      Grove, IL: InterVarsity Press, 1997); John Dominic Crossan, *The Historical Jesus: The Life of a
      Mediterranean Jewish Peasant* (San Francisco: Harper San Francisco, 1991); John Dominic Crossan,
      Jesus: A Revolutionary Biography (San Francisco: Harper San Francisco, 1994); David Flusser, *Jesus*,
      3rd ed., corrected and augmented, in collaboration with R. Steven Notley (Jerusalem: Magnes Press,
      Hebrew University of Jerusalem, 2001); David Flusser, *Judaism and the Origins of Christianity*
      (Jerusalem: Magnes Press, Hebrew University of Jerusalem, 1988). Michel de Certeau notes that
      historians, like psychoanalysts, can attend to "a return to the past" only through the discourse of the
      present ("Histoire et mystique," *Revue de l'histoire de spiritualité* 48 [1972]: 74).

the "historical Jesus" and the formation of "early Christian history" are always *constructed backward* on the basis of the retrojection of the schemas of a later era.[21] For example, the Tübingen school (especially F. C. Baur) adopted Hegel's "thesis/antithesis/synthesis" model in its interpretation of Jewish Christianity (as thesis), Gentile Christianity (as antithesis), and Catholic Christianity (as final synthesis).[22] Without such constructive work, we would have no recourse to biblical "history." Such "histories" are always bound up with the transcendental framework of those who reconstruct them. Thus, as Habermas observes: "As soon as the historian acts at all, he produces new relationships that combine into a further story from a new perspective."[23] In the act of interpretation, the historian's transcendental framework is never extinguished but always put to work through the coordination of historical facts into what appears to be a continual process of historical transformation.

Fourth, the discipline remains committed to the conviction that New Testament documents must be studied for their own sake and on their own terms. The corollary to this commitment is that the challenges, questions, and issues confronting the contemporary reader, believer, and scholar must not be allowed to influence the interpreter's detached antiquarian quest for the immutable historical facts of "primitive" Christianity. In other words, the archival quest for the founding sense-event is deemed to be sufficient. Bultmann once opined that history and philology have bred what he colorfully termed "a kind of pathology of the necrophiliac theological archivist."[24] If Bultmann's language seems extreme, his insight that the discipline of New Testament studies has largely lost interest in questions of significance is still defensible.

Last, most New Testament scholars remain committed to the belief that the correct manner of access to these objective historical facts is through the rigorous application of a discrete set of methods that have been authorized by the discipline. Through a strict adherence to such methods, scholars assume that the influence of their own subjectivity, bias, and social location on the production of objective

---

[21] On this point, Habermas states, "Two successive historical events can be understood as the relation of a past-event to a past-future only by retrospectively applying the reference system of acting subjects who assess the present conditions with a view to anticipated future conditions" ("Review of Gadamer's *Truth and Method,*" in *The Hermeneutic Tradition from Ast to Ricoeur*, ed. Gayle L. Ormiston and Alan D. Schrift [Albany: State University of New York Press, 1990], 226); "A series of events acquires the unity of a story only from the point of view that cannot be taken from those events themselves. The actors are caught up in their histories; even for them – if they tell their own stories – the point of view from which the events can take coherence of a story arises only subsequently.... As long as new points of view arise, the same events can enter into other stories and acquire new significations" (227).

[22] Cf. Ferdinand Christian Baur, *Paul, the Apostle of Jesus Christ*, 2 vols. (London: Williams & Norgate, 1873–75); F. C. Baur, *The Church History of the First Three Centuries*, 2 vols. (London: Williams & Norgate, 1878–79).

[23] Habermas, "Review of Gadamer's *Truth and Method,*" 229.

[24] Friedrich Wilhelm Graf, "Die 'antihistorische Revolution' in der protestantischen Theologie der zwanziger Jahre," in *Vernunft des Glaubens: Wissenschaftliche Theologie und kirchliche Lehre*, ed. Jan Rohls and Gunter Wenz (Göttingen: Vandenhoeck & Ruprecht, 1988), 377–405, esp. 387, 390.

knowledge can be minimized, if not eliminated. But the problem raised by their trust in their research methodologies is that these methodologies fail to recognize the role of the constructive knower (the interpreter/scholar) within their own epistemological structure. The very concept of Western scholarship is founded upon the principles of critique and the construction of new knowledge, not simply the accumulation, repetition, and commentary on the knowledge of past generations of scholars. But few of the methodologies of biblical studies leave room for an examination and critique of the scholars themselves, as ordering, thematizing, positing, and naming subjects. Why do scholars ask some questions of the historical data and not others? When a new scholarly monograph is published, why are we more likely to ask, "Is it factual?" rather than, "Why was this factual book written, instead of any number of other possible factual books, at this time?"

THE GROWING CRISIS OF HISTORICAL CONSCIOUSNESS IN THE NINETEENTH CENTURY

Perhaps the most surprising fact about historicism is that it continues to be popular (in the form of historical positivism), even though it fell into crisis more than a century ago. One can catch a glimpse of the emerging generational anxiety over the implications of historicism as far back as Friedrich Nietzsche's *The Use and Abuse of History* (*Vom Nutzen und Nachteil der Historie*), published in 1874. In this tract, Nietzsche disparaged historicism as the "historical sickness" of his time. He attacked its deadening effects on religious faith and argued that the prevailing culture of historicism had ceased to serve life and now instead causes one's life forces to "wither": "[W]e require history for life and action, … but there is a degree of doing history and an estimation of it which brings with it a withering and degenerating life."[25] Nietzsche also critiqued the use of human rationality as the sole measure by which truth is validated. He observed that, when knowledge is defined as an "object" that is produced through the exercise of human rationality, then rationality has, de facto, taken the place of the concept of "God" as the ultimate foundation of truth. This substitution of human rationality for God is what Nietzsche's madman meant by his famous announcement of the "death of God": "'Whither is God?' he cried; 'I will tell you. *We have killed him* – you and I. All of us are his murderers.'"[26] According to Gianni Vattimo, humanism is "a perspective that places humanity in the centre of the universe and makes it the master of Being.… There is no humanism without the bringing into play of a metaphysics in which the human subject determines a role for itself which is necessarily central or

---

[25] Friedrich Nietzsche, *On the Advantage and Disadvantage of History for Life*, trans. Peter Preuss (Indianapolis: Hackett, 1980 [1874]), 7.

[26] Friedrich Nietzsche, "The Gay Science" [*Fröhliche Wissenschaft*, 1882], in *The Portable Nietzsche*, ed. and trans. Walter Kaufmann (New York: Viking Penguin, 1982), 95 (§ 125).

exclusive."²⁷ It was the Enlightenment's substitution of human rationality in place of "God," as the foundation of truth, that prompted Nietzsche's madman to accuse humanity of "killing God." When the determination of truth is made to be dependent on the perspective of the historical subject, then it is no longer possible to privilege any perspective as *the* perspective, and therefore, any truth as *the* Truth, which guarantees all other truths. In short, with the reduction of truth to a product of human reason, reason has replaced God as the final arbiter of all truths.

This reduction of truth to a commodity that is repeatedly surpassed and replaced by better truths, through the exercise of human reason, is what Nietzsche terms "European nihilism." Nietzsche's assessment of nihilism is summarized in the section of *Twilight of the Idols* (1888) titled "How the 'True World' Finally Became a Fable."²⁸ In his view, the overall effect of the Enlightenment program has been to empty human existence of any essential meaning, purpose, truth, or value.²⁹ Nietzsche, opining the loss of an unchanging foundation for Truth, once declared, "What have we done, in unchaining this earth from its sun? Whence is it rolling now? ... Have we not thrown ourselves into a continuous fall? ... Are we not straying across an infinite nothingness? Do we not feel the breath of the void?"³⁰

Because the epistemological structure of knowledge is now based on the subversion of any permanent ground for knowledge, historicist-guided biblical interpretation can never express any knowledge that is itself not already historically conditioned. Thus, we might join with Nietzsche in his lament. By establishing human rationality as the *arbiter for what counts as knowledge*, historicism's subject-object epistemological model has actually abolished the possibility of there being an unchanging foundation for historical knowledge.³¹ For this reason, the so-called progress of historicism has been accompanied by a corresponding *loss* of any permanence of truth, values, and ethics. In words that now seem prophetic, Nietzsche proclaimed that any religion that "under the rule of pure justice" is "transformed into historical knowledge" and is "thoroughly known in a scientific way" will "at the end of this path ... *also be annihilated*."³² Indeed, in Nietzsche's view, the attempt to understand the *true essence* of Christianity through a purely historical study is doomed to failure:

²⁷ Gianni Vattimo, *End of Modernity*, trans. Jon R. Snyder (Baltimore: Johns Hopkins University Press, 1991 [1985]), 32.
²⁸ Friedrich Nietzsche, "Twilight of the Idols," in *The Portable Nietzsche*, trans. Walter Kaufmann (New York: Viking Penguin, 1982), 463–563, esp. 485–86.
²⁹ Friedrich Nietzsche, *Will to Power*, trans. Walter Kaufman and R. J. Hollingdale (New York: Random House, 1968), 7–82; Philip R. Fandozzi, *Nihilism and Technology: A Heideggerian Investigation* (Washington, DC: University Press of America, 1982), 5; Laurence Lampert, "Heidegger's Nietzsche Interpretation," *Man and World* 7 (1974): 363.
³⁰ Friedrich Nietzsche, *The Joyful Wisdom*, trans. Thomas Common, in Harold J. Blackham, *Reality, Man, and Existence: Essential Works of Existentialism* (New York: Bantam Books, 1965), 66–67.
³¹ Martin Heidegger, *Nietzsche V: Nihilism*, ed. David Farrell Krell, trans. Frank A. Capuzzi (San Francisco: Harper Collins, 1991), 205.
³² Nietzsche, *On the Advantage and Disadvantage*, 39 (§ 7) (emphasis added).

What one can learn from Christianity, [is] that as a result of historicizing treatment it has become blasé and unnatural, until finally a completely historical, that is, a just treatment has resolved it into pure knowledge about Christianity and so has annihilated it.... It ceases to live when it has been dissected completely and lives painfully and has become sick once one begins to practice historical dissection on it.[33]

By reducing biblical texts to their prior histories, according to its own categories of development, cause, and effect, historicism has reduced all spiritual experience to historical phenomena arising from mundane historical causes. For example, in the case of the Ten Commandments, David Clines asserts that these commandments are not timeless, ethical maxims: when considered in terms of their original *historical* context, it is clear that they were intended to serve the interests of married, male, elite Israelite property owners.[34] In other words, the Ten Commandments functioned, historically, as part of a structure of oppression. If this is true, then how can such historically contingent commandments be binding upon modern believers?

According to Emmanuel Levinas, the very act of interpreting the meaning of biblical texts in terms of purely historical categories "calls into question, relativizes and devalues every moment."[35] But Levinas also challenges historicism's presumed right to critique all prior historical moments in its own terms:

[E]verything in history ... does not count as history. Every moment counts, but everything is not a moment.... The West professes the historical relativity of values and their questioning, but perhaps it takes every moment seriously, calls them all historical too quickly, and leaves this history the right both to judge the values and to sink into relativity. Hence the incessant re-evaluation of values, an incessant collapse of values, an incessant genealogy of morals. A history without permanence or a history without holiness.[36]

Levinas also recognizes that human values and ethics *are* historically contingent. Nonetheless, he argues that a permanence of holiness is possible through a sublimation of biblical values, which elevates the possibilities lying latent within them for the future (see Chapter 11).

My point is not that historicism is wrong per se. However, one of the consequences of the continued dominance of historicist-based methods of interpretation is a *crisis of significance*. For, as Thomas Reynolds explains, when "all human events, traditions, and texts are historical, subject to the limiting conditions of time and space, ... the reverse follows suit: there is no fixed and final center of truth

---

[33]   Ibid., 39, 40 (§ 7).
[34]   David Clines, *Interested Parties: The Ideology of Writers and Readers of the Hebrew Bible,* JSOPSup 205 (Sheffield: Sheffield Academic, 2005), 33.
[35]   Emmanuel Levinas, *Beyond the Verse: Talmudic Readings and Lectures,* trans. Gary D. Mole (London: Athlone Press, 1994) 17.
[36]   Ibid., 21.

that lies outside the contingency and flux of historical life. Everything human is caught up in process."[37] Nihilism has overtaken the biblical studies, but has anyone noticed?

In light of this loss of a historical foundation for belief and ethics, it is not surprising that biblical scholars have largely lost the conviction that they can relate their research to contemporary issues of faith and the attendant challenges of living in a postmodern world. Whether individual biblical scholars in their professional life are capable of experiencing this crisis is beside the point: it is this very crisis that constitutes *the* dominant theme of postmodernity. Biblical studies' unwitting surrender to nihilism constitutes just one more witness to its pervasiveness in society at large.

WILHELM DILTHEY'S ATTEMPT TO SAVE HISTORICALLY OBJECTIVE SENSE

The growing sense in the nineteenth century of the contingency of all historical knowledge became a problem, not only for the biblical studies but also for the humanities in general. In the face of the advances in the natural sciences, whose objectivity seemed to be above reproach, many scholars working in the humanities felt the need to develop new methodologies, whose scientific rigor would lead to similarly objective results. For example, in the face of the rapid emergence of "pure science" (*Reineswissenschaft*) in Germany, Wilhelm Dilthey (1833–1911) took up the challenge to develop a scientifically defensible hermeneutic theory that would establish the objectivity of the discipline of history and of the humanities and social sciences in general. Dilthey approached this undertaking by bringing together three modes of academic discourse, combining romanticism and neo-Kantianism with historicism.

Romanticism

As discussed in Chapter 2, Schleiermacher "deregionalized" the field of hermeneutics by developing a "universal" set of principles that could be applied to the interpretation of all types of texts, secular as well as sacred. Given the fact that Wilhelm Dilthey was Schleiermacher's devoted biographer (about whom he wrote a seven-hundred-page biography), it is not surprising that he was greatly influenced by Schleiermacher's hermeneutical theory and especially by his interest in psychological theory.[38] Schleiermacher's "psychological" interpretation, which involved

---

[37] Reynolds, *Broken Whole*, 19.
[38] Though Schleiermacher died the year after Dilthey's birth, Dilthey encountered Schleiermacher's disciples in Berlin and committed himself to writing *Leben Schleiermachers* (Berlin: E. Reimer, 1870). The second volume did not appear until 1891, twenty-one years later.

tracing the meaning of texts back to the intentions of their historical authors, required him to develop a hermeneutic procedure whereby he could move from a grammatical understanding of a text to its "inner" psychological meaning. Dilthey, following in Schleiermacher's footsteps, was also interested in great men of history who, he believed, transformed the intellectual, cultural, and social forces around them through their own personal genius.[39] Thus, for Dilthey, the study of history was the study of the great minds of history. He maintained that historical meaning is imposed upon us neither from outside history nor by providence or God, but by the great men of history.[40]

Neo-Kantianism

Dilthey was also influenced by Neo-Kantianism. Immanuel Kant had previously investigated the preunderstanding, or cognitive structure, that human beings bring to the act of understanding the world around them. Kant called this cognitive structure a "schema." On the basis of this insight, Dilthey concluded that he could not develop a *science* of history without first addressing the problem of the cognitive framework (preunderstanding) of the investigating historian. Indeed, one of the unforeseen implications of the historicist paradigm was the realization that historians – like the historical persons they study – are historically contingent beings. As such, they too possess a preunderstanding of things. For example, Dilthey observed that even the scholars of the Reformation approached biblical texts with a preunderstanding, namely that scripture possesses a *theological* unity of meaning.[41] Likewise, nineteenth-century historians also possessed a preunderstanding concerning such matters as historical causality, historical progress, and the linearity of time.

In the first instance, Dilthey addressed the problem of historical consciousness on the basis of a descriptive psychology, by analyzing the shared cognitive structures shared by all human beings.[42] In order to appreciate Dilthey's solution, we must grasp what he meant by "understanding." In contrast to the natural sciences,

---

[39] Wilhelm Dilthey, *Leben Schleiermachers*, vol. I (*Gesammelte Schriften* I), xxxiii.

[40] Wilhelm Dilthey originally published *Einleitung in die Geisteswissenschaften* in 1883; it was subsequently republished as *Gesammelte Schriften* I. Among Dilthey's recent followers are E. Hirsch and E. Betti, who argue that interpretations become more valid as they incorporate more knowledge about the author and the author's values, rather than reflect the interpreter's own interpretive horizons: E. Hirsch Jr., *Validity in Interpretation* (New Haven: Yale University Press, 1967); E. Betti, *Contemporary Hermeneutics: Hermeneutics as Method, Philosophy, and Critique* (London: Routledge & Kegan Paul, 1980), 51–94.

[41] Wilhelm Dilthey, *Weltanschauung und Analyse des Menschen seit Renaissance und Reformation* (*Gesammelte Schriften* II), 126, n. 3.

[42] Though Dilthey was not a neo-Kantian, many of his ideas were formed in conversation with neo-Kantians such as Wilhelm Windelband and Heinrich Rickert. Dilthey understood Kant's philosophy well. His thinking was influenced more by Kant's *Critique of Judgment* than by his *Critique of Pure Reason*.

which study physical and tangible objects, the humanities study the human *Geist,* which is to say, the human "spirit" or "mind." In his early writings, Dilthey primarily understood the term *Geist* (in *Geisteswissenschaften*) in the sense of the inner psychological human "spirit" or "mind." Thus, the German term for the "humanities and social sciences" is *Geisteswissenschaften,* a term that can be broken down into two words, *Geist* (human "spirit") and *Wissenschaften* (denoting "sciences")." In other words, the *Geisteswissenschaften* are the "sciences of the human spirit."

Dilthey reasoned that since the humanities' object of study is different – the human "spirit" – its goal must also be different. The real goal is "understanding," not scientific "explanation." Thus, Dilthey made the important distinction between "explanation" (*Erklärung*) and "understanding" (*Verstehung*) as two *contrasting* approaches to the acquisition of knowledge: as he explained, "we *explain* nature, but we *understand* mental life."[43] While the natural sciences are concerned with the explanation of *general* laws and ascribing *causal* effects in the world, the goal of the "sciences of the human spirit" (*Geisteswissenschaften*) is concerned with understanding. On the basis of this distinction, he argued that the task of the historical is not to explain the past but rather to arrive at a *shared understanding* of the past with the great men of history.

Dilthey developed his theory of shared understanding on the basis of the twin concepts of "sympathy" and "imaginative transposition." Through "sympathy" with a historical author, Dilthey believed, the modern interpreter can condition his own mind so as to achieve an intimate connection with the historical author himself.[44] Similarly, through a process he termed "imaginative transposition" (*Heineinverstehen*), he believed that the historian can enter into the inner world of an ancient author, to appreciate his thoughts and experiences from his own perspective. Dilthey argued that such "imaginative transposition" is indeed possible because the interpreter and ancient author *share the same cognitive structure,* a structure that is shared by all historical human beings:[45] "The first condition of possibility of a science of history is that I myself am a historical being, that the person studying history is the person making history."[46] The concept of "imaginative transposition" is based on the principle of analogy: on the basis of his supposition that the cognitive structure of human beings in the present is analogous to that of

---

[43] Wilhelm Dilthey, "Die geistige Welt: Einleitung in die Philosophie des Lebens," in *Gesammelte Schriften* V, 144; Dilthey, "Ideen über eine beschreibende und zergliedernde Psychologie," in *Die geistige Welt,* ed. Georg Misch (*Gesammelte Schriften* V), 144.

[44] Dilthey, *Die geistige Welt,* 278.

[45] Dilthey states that "Understanding (*Verstehen*) is what we call this process by which an inside is conferred on a complex of external sensory signs" ("The Rise of Hermeneutics," in *W. Dilthey: Selected Writings,* ed. and trans. H. P. Rickman [Cambridge: Cambridge University Press, 1976], IV, 236).

[46] Dilthey, *Der Aufbau der geschichtlichen Welt in den Geisteswissenschaften* (*Gesammelte Schriften* VII), 278.

human beings in the past, Dilthey argued that the historian can actually "relive" (*nacherleben*) the experiences and enter into the realm of the "private mental life" (*Seelenleben*) of the great figures of the past.[47] On this basis, he described the act of understanding the mind of a person of the past as "the re-discovery of the I [the interpreter] in the Thou [historical person]."[48]

At first, this concept of "imaginative transposition" seemed to provide Dilthey with a theoretical structure by which to explain how the historian can arrive at a mutually shared understanding with the great men of the past. But given the heuristic nature of actually applying "imaginative transposition," Dilthey confessed that the "result reached in interpretation can never have demonstrative certitude."[49] Nonetheless, he believed that it was possible for interpreters to overcome their own historical situatedness and achieve an unbiased understanding of the past. Thus, Dilthey's theory of a shared cognitive structure functioned as the foundation for his legitimation of historical studies.[50]

Over time, however, Dilthey became increasingly aware of the problematic nature of his theory of imaginative transposition. He later abandoned his psychological approach in 1900, after reading the first volume of Edmund Husserl's *Logical Investigations* (*Logische Untersuchungen*), a book that developed a *phenomenological* theory of human consciousness.[51] This work had a profound influence upon Dilthey's own thought, as it would on later generations of philosophers, including Heidegger, Gadamer, Ricoeur, and Levinas. Dilthey praised *Logical Investigations* as "epoch-making." In order to appreciate the contribution of Edmund Husserl's phenomenology to Dilthey's thought, we must pause here to summarize the basic outlines of his phenomenological method.

THE PHENOMENOLOGY OF EDMUND HUSSERL

The starting point of phenomenology is the insight that our experience of "reality" is the *product of an active meaning-adding process*. Reality is not something that is "out there," beyond our bodies, which is passively inscribed upon, or registered by, one's human consciousness as experience. That which we take to be "reality" is actually *constructed* by our own consciousness. Phenomenology is the study of *how* human consciousness constructs our everyday, nontheoretical, nonscientific, and nonpropositional experience into that which we take to be the real world.

---

[47] Theodore Plantinga, *Historical Understanding in the Thought of Wilhelm Dilthey* (Toronto: University of Toronto Press, 1980), 40.

[48] Dilthey, *Selected Writings*, 208.

[49] David West, *Introduction to Continental Philosophy* (Cambridge: Polity Press, 1996), 87.

[50] Dilthey believed that the coherence of human consciousness of the world, "mental facts" (*geistige Tatsachen*), could be employed as a valid point of reference because of the shared structure of human thought (*Einleitung in die Geisteswissenschaften, Gesammelte Schriften* I [Leipzig: G. B. Teubner, 1922], xvii; West, *Introduction to Continental Philosophy*, 83–84).

[51] Edmund Husserl, *Logische Untersuchungen*, 2 vols. (Halle: Max Niemeyer, 1900–2).

Edmund Husserl set out to study the transcendental conditions for the possibility of human consciousness through an analysis of the "intentionality" of consciousness. According to Edmund Husserl, human consciousness is not an entity that can be studied in isolation. Human consciousness is more like a *function* that coordinates our "experiences" (*Erfahrungen*) into a set of meaningful relations. Human consciousness thematizes the flow of "sense-data from the world" (*Erlebnisse*) according to a cognitive structure.

In his later writings, Husserl's own theory turned toward the historical, most notably with his adoption of the term "horizon." Husserl termed this cognitive structure a phenomenological "horizon." A "horizon" is a complicated network of precognitive mental structures that makes sensate data meaningful, within preestablished parameters. For example, it is your phenomenological horizon that allows your mind to correctly interpret what your ear hears at the beach *as* the sound of waves, and what your nose smells in the garden *as* the scent of a rose, and what your eyes see in the sky *as* the shape of a flying kite. To perceive anything in one's environment meaningfully *as* something always entails such an *interpretative* moment. It is also your phenomenological horizon that allows your mind to interpret the shape of a cloud in the sky, say, as the profile of a rabbit. But a person who has never seen a rabbit might construe the same cloud *as* the shape of something else. In order for sensory data to be unified into a meaning, whether it be a flying kite or the shape of a cloud, it must be locatable, by consciousness, somewhere within its structures. Human consciousness never experiences its surrounding world in an uninterpreted way. The *objects* of perception, such as waves, a rose, or a flying kite, are always experienced *through* one's horizon of meaning.

We must not think of human consciousness as a thing. Consciousness is not a brain in a skull, or a soul in a body, or even an ego wrapped in human flesh. In fact, from a phenomenological perspective, there is no thing called "consciousness" to study. Consciousness is really a coordinating *process*, which functions by forming connections between our experience of things in the world and our preexisting interpretive structure, termed a "horizon."

We are normally unaware of *how* our mind interprets our external experiences (raw sensory data) and transforms them into meaningful phenomena, which we experience as the "Real" world.[52] In fact, included within your own horizon is the preunderstanding that you have direct access to reality, without any horizon at all. But even your sense of being an independent "I" – independent of all other "I's" – is part of your own phenomenological horizon.

We are most aware of our own horizon of meaning when it breaks down and fails us, as sometimes happens when traveling in a foreign country. Sometimes one's experiences in a foreign culture do not "make sense" to us. What we

[52] For an explanation of the capitalization of "Real," see Chapter 8.

perceive in the world around us registers to us as *abnormal*. But because our sense of "normal" is always dictated by our horizon, that which we experience as "abnormal" offers the possibility of gaining some insight into the nature of our particular phenomenological horizon, perhaps even calling it into question or putting it at risk.

According to Husserl, human consciousness is "intentional," which is to say that it purposefully, or intentionally, takes in the experience of things in order to posit them as something meaningful (e.g., the experience of a smell *as* the scent of a rose). Husserl termed this meaning-giving, interpretative moment "noesis." Noesis is an act of the "apprehension" (*Auffassung*) of sensate data (whether it be a smell, a sound, or a visible mark) *as* something. The final result of "noesis" is "noema." The term "noema" designates one's *interpreted* experience of things. For instance, when one's consciousness construes a particular smell, sound, or visible mark, as the smell of baking bread, or as the sound of a train, or as the image of a Greek word on a page, a "noema" (interpretation of experience) has been produced. In every instance of "noema," there is a *surplus of meaning* resulting from consciousness's productive interpretation of sensory data. Thus, when your consciousness construes an object on your kitchen table *as* a cell phone (*as* a communication tool), then it has added meaning (whereas if Jean Calvin were to see the same object on a table, no "noema" would be formed).

Husserl's famous phenomenological slogan is that "all consciousness is consciousness *of* something." In other words, one's own consciousness is detectable only when it is in the process of "apprehending" the experience of something. Only when your mind is thematizing the flow of experience (*Erlebnisse*) of sensory data within your interpretive horizon is it possible for you to become self-aware of having any consciousness at all. This is to say that consciousness does not "show up" except when it is in the process of apprehending that which is *not* consciousness. We are aware of things in the world around us only because our consciousness is always energetically directed out of itself toward the world, and is always in the process of "apprehending" (making sense of) sense-data in terms of preexisting sets of relations (one's phenomenological horizon).[53]

Husserl likened consciousness to a "theater stage" on which actors appear and perform. If consciousness is like a stage, then we become aware of this "stage" (consciousness) whenever we are having the experience of a performance or play being performed *on* the stage. In other words, when entities in our environment appear on the stage of consciousness, it becomes possible for us to shift our gaze and behold the stage itself on which they appear.

[53] Edmund Husserl, *Die Krisis der europäischen Wissenschaften und die transzendentale Phänomenologie*, ed. Reinhold N. Smid (The Hague: Kluwer, 1992), 91. Husserl distinguishes the "I," experienced as "intentional consciousness," from the transcendental subjectivity that lies behind the "I" and generates it. He terms this transcendental subjectivity the "primal I" (*Ur-Ich*).

This brings us to Husserl's technique, which he variously termed "phenom-enological reduction," "eidic reduction," and *epochē* (ἐποχή). Husserl developed a technique that allows one to shift one's gaze (as it were) and behold the stage of consciousness itself. This technique involves a bracketing out of things in the world in order to leave only the "intentional structure" of noesis that interprets them.[54] This technique can be summarized in terms of the following threefold process: first, one lets one's consciousness apprehend a phenomenon; second, one brackets out from consideration the external content of the phenomenon (i.e., the entity); finally, having disregarded the external content, one then exam-ines the inner structure that formed its meaning (noesis) in the mind. The goal of this technique is to reveal the "horizon" that organized the sensory perception of an entity into a meaningful phenomenon and then to describe the structures of the horizon apart from the entity itself.[55] Thus, phenomenological reduction is not concerned with the nature of things in the world: its goal is to make explicit the horizon (cognitive structures) responsible for making such things meaning-ful to the observer.

Perhaps the most important point for our consideration of the theory of Wilhelm Dilthey is that phenomenological analysis obscures the Enlightenment's traditional distinction between the observing "subject" and the observed "object." When one demands that biblical interpretation be "objective," one is implicitly invoking this same Enlightenment epistemology, which assumes that "there are subjects and there are objects." Phenomenology demonstrates that this assump-tion is *false*. Because human consciousness is not a passive registration of reality beyond it (including biblical texts), the so-called subject is never independent of the phenomena being perceived. Your consciousness of a thing is always a unity comprising the relation between yourself, as an observer, and the perceived thing, arising from your own phenomenological horizon. Therefore, the notion of objec-tive biblical interpretation is a myth of the Enlightenment. It is not a theological principle, or a principle of the Reformation, or even a biblical principle. It is sim-ply a myth.

---

[54] Husserl, "Phenomenology," in *The Encyclopedia Britannica* [1929], 659: "He [the phenomenologist] must inhibit every ordinary objective 'position,' and partake in no judgment concerning the objec-tive world. The experience itself will remain what it was, an experience of this house, of this body, of this world in general, in its particular mode.... Our comprehensive *epokhē* (ἐποχή) puts, as we say, the world between brackets, excludes the world which is simply there! from the subject's field, presenting in its stead the so-and-so-experienced-perceived-remembered, judged-thought-valued-etc., world, as such, the 'bracketed' world. Not the world or any part of it appears, but the 'sense' of the world."

[55] Ibid., 660.

DILTHEY'S ADOPTION OF HUSSERL'S PHENOMENOLOGY

Husserl's concept of a horizon of consciousness provided Dilthey with a new theoretical basis – distinct from psychology – from which to theorize historical method.[56] After reading Husserl, he grasped the important distinction between empirical and phenomenological description.[57] Dilthey's subsequent turn toward phenomenology was a turn toward what he termed "lived experience" (*Erlebnis*). Under the influence of Husserl, he interpreted *Geist*, psychologically, no longer as the inner psychological human "spirit" or "mind" but rather in terms of the universal spirit (*Geist*) or humanity, or the universal structures of human consciousness, which are shared by all people. This reconceptualization of the concept of *Geist* functioned as the center of Dilthey's new "life-philosophy" (*Lebensphilosophie*). Here, the term "life" does not mean life forms in the world but rather one's life *experience* of the world. This life experience is always a product of the thematizing action of the horizon of consciousness: meaningful life experience "is inseparable from sensate data, but not reducible to it."[58] Building on this insight, Dilthey argued that our own human lives constitute a node of "little history" formed by our "lived experience" (*Erlebnis*). This little history supplies the structure whereby we thematize historical facts into a meaningful narrative whole. Dilthey reasoned that because human beings are themselves historical, they can know themselves only "in history, never through introspection. The human being is only given to us at all in terms of its realized possibilities."[59] By implication, the meaning of history is always revealed from within the temporal horizon of the historian. This phenomenological factor precludes the possibility of arriving at final objectivity about any past event, including such biblical events as the Exodus of the Jews from Egypt and the crucifixion of Jesus.

Dilthey departed from Husserl's phenomenology in one important way: he asserted that there is no universal or transcendental subject. Husserl, working in the Kantian tradition, was not concerned with particular, or individual, human existence. He set out to expose the "subjectivity of [human] consciousness *in general*."[60] In his *Logical Investigations*, Husserl's phenomenology was somewhat static, owing to its foundation in Kantian epistemology. This ahistorical focus was ill-suited to Dilthey's *historical* framework, which, of course, must model change over time. This issue eventually led to their parting of ways. Dilthey, a historian

---

[56] Georg Misch addresses Dilthey's use of Husserl's phenomenology in his introduction to Dilthey's *Die geistige Welt, Gesammelte Schriften* V (Paris: Aubier, 1947); cf. G. Misch, *Lebensphilosophie und Phänomenologie; eine auseinandersetzung der Diltheyschen richtung mit Heidegger und Husserl* (Stuttgart: Teubner, 1967 [1930]).

[57] Michael Ermath, *Wilhelm Dilthey: The Critique of Historical Reason* (Chicago: University of Chicago Press, 1978), 202.

[58] Ibid., 205.

[59] Dilthey, *Der Aufbau der geschichtlichen Welt*, 179.

[60] Husserl, "Phenomenology," 662 (emphasis added).

by training, could not exclude historical and contextual factors from his theory of "lived experience." In his view, all people possess a *historically contingent,* changeable, and revisable phenomenological horizon of meaning, which he termed a "life world" (*Lebenswelt*).

Dilthey believed that this inner human "spirit" (*Geist*) is made visible and tangible through the production of material objects such as texts and artifacts (e.g., statues, architecture, ceramics, glassware, jewelry, coins, ritual objects), especially in the realm of religion, art, and philosophy. Dilthey refers to these tangible expressions of the "spirit" as the "objective spirit." On the basis of this premise, he theorized hermeneutics as a "process whereby we discern something inward by means of signs outwardly given to the senses."[61] He thus redefined the term *Geisteswissenschaften* as "sciences based on inner mental and psychological experience *as they are expressed and objectified in public life.*" This new theoretical model would require the historian to strive to understand the human spirit by tracing its material objectifications ("the world of the [human] spirit") back "into the mental life from where they came."[62] By means of this "detour" (*Umweg*) through the world of material objects, Dilthey believed that the historian could progressively become "freed from" his own "particularity and transience" and gradually understand the world of the past through "sympathy" with the spirit that created them. By this means, he argued that historians can overcome their *own* historical relativity and achieve greater and greater objectivity, in the sense of understanding the past in the same terms as the people of the past understood themselves.

Having tried to address the problem of the foundation of historical knowledge in this way, Dilthey still remained uncertain about the precise nature of the connection between the tangible objects of the past and the inner human spirit (*Geist*) that formed them. Indeed, far from providing a way out of the hermeneutic circle, Dilthey's application of Husserlian phenomenology seemed to confirm just how inescapable the hermeneutic circle really is. Toward the end of his life, he came to recognize that neither Schleiermacher's psychologism nor Husserl's phenomenology could provide him with the means by which to construct hermeneutics as a procedure conducted on the basis of scientifically valid rules. Despite this setback, Dilthey remains an important figure, particularly because of his immense influence upon Martin Heidegger, who employed Dilthey's thought in his own reinterpretation of the phenomenological theory of his own teacher, Husserl (see Chapter 5).

---

[61] Dilthey, *Die geistige Welt*, 318.
[62] Ibid., 265; cf. Dilthey, *Der Aufbau der geschichtlichen Welt*, 150. W. Dilthey, *Einleitung in die Geisteswissenschaften* (*Gesammelte Schriften* I), vol. II, pt. 4; Dilthey, *Der Aufbau der geschichtlichen Welt*, 232; cf. Ermath, *Wilhelm Dilthey*, 310, 312; cf. Michael Ermath, "Objectivity and Relativity in Dilthey's Theory of Understanding," in *Dilthey and Phenomenology*, ed. Rudolf A. Makkreel and John Scanlon (Washington, DC: University Press of America, 1987), 73–93.

THE DEEPENING OF THE CRISIS OF HISTORICISM: ERNST TROELTSCH

Whereas Wilhelm Dilthey set out to address the crisis of historical objectivity, Ernst Troeltsch (1865–1923) has the distinction of having helped both to precipitate the crisis of historicism and then, subsequently, to have raised the alarm concerning its devastating effects. Troeltsch was many things: a German Protestant theologian, a founder of a sociological approach to religion, and a leading exponent of the use of historicism in biblical studies. One of the most noteworthy events in Troeltsch's life is recorded by his biographer, Walter Köhler. In 1896, Troeltsch—previously known for his strident defense of the use of historicism in the field of biblical studies—leapt to the podium in Eisenach and proclaimed to his senior colleagues, "Gentlemen, it's all tottering!"[63] In short, he declared that historicism was a house of cards that was now collapsing around their ears. As is clear from the title of his later essay, "The Crisis of Historicism and Its Problems" ("Der Historismus und seine Probleme," 1922), Troeltsch had come to believe that historicism was in serious crisis.[64] Troeltsch applied historical method consistently to Christianity to elucidate a true "essence" of Christianity, which, over time, is historically changing and relative. It was this insight that led to his later conviction that the *relativism* inherent in historicism "shakes all eternal truths."[65] According to Herman Paul, Troeltsch's fear was not so much that moral universals did not exist but rather that the specific Christian values of German society (*bildungsbürgerliche Kulture*) could no longer be justified on purely historical grounds as universal values.[66] If this were true, then the academic world would possess no historically justifiable universal values for critiquing the historical cultures and societies of the biblical past. Troeltsch's repeated attempts throughout his later life to address the challenge of historical relativism ultimately proved unconvincing.[67]

Troeltsch was by no means alone in perceiving this crisis of historical meaning. Throughout Germany, the initial optimism over the benefits of historicism before World War I gave way to a pervasive pessimism. During the politically

---

[63] Walther Köhler, *Ernst Troeltsch* (Tübingen: J. C. B. Mohr, 1941), 1; cf. Hans-Georg Drescher, *Ernst Troeltsch: His Life and Work* (Minneapolis: Fortress, 1993), 86; H. Stuart Hughes, *Consciousness and Society: The Reorientation of European Social Thought, 1890–1930* (New York: Knopf, 1958), 229–30.

[64] Ernst Troeltsch, "Die Krisis des Historismus," *Die neue Rundschau* 33/1 (1922): 572–90; cf. Ernst Troeltsch, *Der Historismus und seine Probleme* (*Gesammelte Schriften* 3) (Aalen: J. C. B. Mohr (Paul Siebeck), 1961 [1922]); Robert J. Rubanowice, *Crisis in Consciousness: The Thought of Ernst Troeltsch* (Tallahassee: University Presses of Florida, 1982).

[65] Troeltsch, "Die Krisis des Historismus," 573.

[66] Herman J. Paul, "A Collapse of Trust: Reconceptualizing the Crisis of Historicism," *Journal of the Philosophy of History* 2 (2008): 63–82.

[67] Cf. Troeltsch's distinction between partial relativism and total relativism, as explained by Joanne Miyang Cho, "The Crisis of Historicism and Troeltsch's Europeanism," *History of European Ideas* 21 (1995): 195–207.

and socially chaotic Weimar years, the historicist worldview attracted growing opposition, with many coming to believe that a state of emergency had overtaken the disciplines of theology and early Christian history in particular.[68] In fact, by the time that Troeltsch published his famous essay, the belief that a crisis had overtaken historicism had virtually become a cliché in the German academic world. Thus, far from being the first to sense the crisis, Troeltsch's *own* admission only served to demonstrate *how* wide the skepticism regarding historicism's continuing value had spread.[69] In fact, historicism had become a symbol of modern society's profound social malaise, with many coming to view it as a dehumanizing force that subverted the ethical values and truth of Christianity and Judaism. The Jewish philosopher Franz Rosenzweig called attention to historicism's epistemological hubris, vividly describing its tendency "to understand the Divine as the self-projection of the human" as "the monstrous birth of the Divine out of the human."[70] Rosenzweig's *The Star of Redemption* represents his own attempt to revivify the Hebrew Bible as the basis for a renewed Jewish identity.[71] Rosenzweig was not alone in his condemnation of historicism. He is representative of many Jews who were critical of historicism's tendency to reduce biblical history to its own categories, resulting in the reduction of the Jewish faith to a purely historical phenomenon.[72] Other Jewish scholars, such as Hermann Cohen, Isaac Breuer, and Walter Benjamin (pronounced "ben-ya-meen"), all attacked historicism's reductionistic tendencies. For example, Benjamin's famous essay "On the Concept of History" ("Über den Begriff der Geschichte"), published in 1939, attempted to modify the historical determinism that was passed onto Marxism through its reception of historicism.[73] Benjamin went so far as to argue

---

[68] On antihistoricist attitudes, see Hermann Heimpel, "Geschichte und Geschichtswissenschaft," *Vierteljahrshefte für Zeitgeschichte* 1 (1957): 1–17; for a survey of the concept of antihistoricism, see Kurt Nowak, "Die 'antihistorische Revolution,'" *Troeltsch-Studien* 4 (1987): 133–71.

[69] Jeffrey A. Barash, *Heidegger and the Problem of Historical Meaning,* rev. and expanded ed. (New York: Fordham University Press, 1988).

[70] Franz Rosenzweig, "Atheistische Theologie" [1937], in his *Philosophical and Theological Writings,* ed. Paul Franks and Michael Morgan (Indianapolis: Hackett, 2000), 10–24, esp. 24.

[71] According to Mara Benjamin, Rosenzweig's response to this crisis of modernity was paradoxical: while he challenged his readers to encounter the biblical text as revelation in order to invigorate Jewish intellectual and social life, his method of argument ultimately reinforced the foundations of German Jewish post-Enlightenment liberal thought. See Mara H. Benjamin, *Rosenzweig's Bible: Reinventing Scripture for Jewish Modernity* (Cambridge: Cambridge University Press, 2009).

[72] In his recent book, *Resisting History: Historicism and Its Discontents in German-Jewish Thought* (Princeton: Princeton University Press, 2003), David Myers has documented this Jewish backlash against historicism.

[73] Walter Benjamin, "On the Concept of History," in *Illuminations,* introd. and ed. Hannah Arendt, trans. Harry Zorn (Pimlico: Random House, 1999 [1955]), 245–55. According to the Marxist concept of Historical Materialism, "it is not the consciousness of men that determines their existence, but, on the contrary, their social existence that determines their consciousness"; see Karl Marx, preface to *A Contribution to the Critique of Political Economy,* http://www.marxists.org/archive/marx/works/1859/critique-pol-economy/preface.htm. Redemption consists of using our own "weak messianic power" to redeem the past.

that historical materialists, such as Marxists, must recover their capacity for true "experience" (*Erfahrung*) by recovering a *theological* gaze.[74] Through this means he hoped to recover the spiritual dimension of the Marxist struggle to bring about a communist utopia.

In Protestant circles, critics such as Eugen Rosenstock-Huessey and Karl Barth belonged to a whole generation of theologians who had grown highly skeptical of historicism's usefulness as a way of addressing the question of the historical meaning of the New Testament. Rosenstock-Huessey, himself a Christian convert from Judaism, went so far as to call upon Christians and Jews to join together in common cause to combat what he colorfully termed "the idols of relativism (in which not even Einstein believed)" and "historical objectivity."[75] All this is to say that more than a century ago, a great many Jewish and Christian scholars held the view that historicism was incapable of dealing with the significance of divine revelation.

At the center of the crisis of historicism was the problem of the cultural relativity of all religious beliefs. As Charles Bambach has argued, at its root this crisis was more *theological* in nature than it was a problem of historiological practice: it was precipitated not so much by the realization of the relativity of all historical knowledge as it was by the implications of this relativism for religious faith.[76] Edgar McKnight observes that "the critical distancing of the [biblical] text in the historical approach" had "transformed biblical writings into museum pieces without contemporary relevance."[77] How can one set of beliefs or ethical teachings be held up as superior over others, or even superior to philosophies of life that are actually hostile to our values and ethics, if they are culturally and socially contingent. Thus, in the eyes of many Jews and Protestants alike, historicism leads to

---

[74] Here Benjamin is contrasting true "experience" (*Erfahrung*) with experience as the simple "lived moment" (*Erlebnis*). Drawing upon the writings of Marcel Proust, he believed this could happen only in the locus of memory (Tomoko Masuzawa, "Tracing the Figure of Redemption: Walter Benjamin's Physiognomy of Modernity," *MLN* 100/3, German Issue [1985]: 514–36, esp. 519). Benjamin remarks, "Where there is experience (*Erfahrung*) in the strict sense of the word, certain contents of the individual past combine with materials of the collective past" (Benjamin, as cited in Richard Wolin, "Benjamin's Materialist Theory of Experience," *Theory and Society* 11 [1982]: 17–42, esp. 33). Experience opens an "allegorical" space. As Bainard Cowan observes, "In Benjamin's analysis, allegory is pre-eminently a kind of experience" (Bainard Cowan, "Walter Benjamin's Theory of Allegory," *New German Critique* 22 [1981]: 109–22, esp. 110).

[75] Eugen Rosenstock-Huessy, *Judaism Despite Christianity: The Letters on Christianity and Judaism* (Tuscaloosa: University of Alabama Press, 1969), 71; though Einstein proposed the theory of relativity, his statement "God does not play dice" demonstrates that he still maintained a kind of foundationalism.

[76] Charles R. Bambach, *Heidegger, Dilthey, and the Crisis of Historicism* (Ithaca, NY: Cornell University Press, 1995).

[77] Edgar McKnight, *Postmodern Uses of the Bible: The Emergence of Reader-Oriented Criticism* (Nashville: Abingdon Press, 1988), 14.

nihilism, that is, the view that truth, meaning, and morals are socially, culturally, and historically relative.[78]

This crisis of nihilism extended beyond the disciplinary boundaries of theology and biblical studies to the discipline of history itself. By historicizing the consciousness of the historian, historicism subverted the possibility of its own objectivity. As Thomas Reynolds observes, it is most ironic that in the act of recognizing "the historicism of human life," human rationality itself ran "aground while trying to advocate objectively valid truths."[79] In the end, historicism not only failed to provide a secure historical foundation for a Christian faith, as it had once hoped to do, but its *discovery of historical consciousness* subverted the epistemological structure of the Enlightenment, which had originally begotten historicism. Thus, through some hidden oedipal impulse, historicism committed the ultimate sin, patricide.

---

[78] Annette Wittkau, *Historismus: Zur Geschichte des Begriffs und des Problems* (Göttingen: Vandenhoeck & Ruprecht, 1992).

[79] Reynolds, *Broken Whole,* 38.

4

෬

The Twilight of Idols

Historicism is more than a set of research methodologies: it depends on, and is made possible by, a particular metaphysics or an unspoken set of beliefs. As Charles Bambach argues,

[Historicism] signifies a metaphysical reading of history which is founded on the history of metaphysics; in other words, it represents a privileging of metaphysical concepts of time, narrative, order, succession, continuity, and totality which derive from the single-point perspective of Cartesian and Kantian subjectivity and its corresponding insistence on the values of objectivity, methodological clarity, and scientific truth.[1]

The most important characteristic of the metaphysics of historicism is the presupposition that "there are subjects and there are objects." This subject-object binarism is the cornerstone of the metaphysics of historicism. Nineteenth-century historicism understood the historian as a sovereign subject whose task, like that of the "Wanderer" in David Caspar Friedrich's painting (see fig. 3.1), is to survey the historical past as an object from a great distance.

In his analysis of this metaphysics of subject-object binarism, Martin Heidegger interpreted the German term for "object," *Gegenstand,* literally as *Gegen-stand,* that is, that which the subject "stands over and apart from." In his lecture "Ontology: Hermeneutics of Facticity," Heidegger warns, "Steer clear of *the schema: there are subjects and objects, consciousness and being.*"[2] Because the theory of historicism presupposes a metaphysics of the rational subject (who stands over and apart from an object), the crisis of historicism is actually a crisis of the metaphysics of the rational subject.

Before I elaborate on this point, it is first worthy of mention that human rationality has not always functioned as the foundation for what counts as knowledge. Before the Enlightenment, the Platonic notion of the "Good" and, subsequently, the medieval philosophical concept of God served to stabilize the structure of Western knowledge by supplying it with a permanent, unchanging foundation. Each, in

---

[1]   Charles R. Bambach, *Heidegger, Dilthey, and the Crisis of Historicism* (Ithaca, NY: Cornell University Press, 1995), 11.
[2]   Martin Heidegger, "Ontology: Hermeneutics of Facticity," in *Contributions to Philosophy,* trans. Parvis Emad and Kenneth Maly (Bloomington: Indiana University Press, 1999), from *Ontologie: Hermeneutik der Faktizität, Gesamtausgabe 63* (Frankfurt am Main: Vittorio Klostermann, 1923), 81.

turn, functioned as the highest Truth, to which all other truths referred as their ultimate guarantor. But when the Enlightenment redefined knowledge as *what is knowable* by *the historical human subject* through the exercise of observation and reason, all this changed: human reason (not the Good or the concept of God) was instituted as the final guarantor or foundation of truth. René Descartes, the so-called Father of Modern Philosophy, has pride of place in this construction of a system of knowledge founded upon human reason. Richard Bernstein observes how Descartes' *Meditations* reflect his search "for some fixed point, some stable rock upon which we can secure our lives against the vicissitudes that constantly threaten us."[3] Through the application of reason, Descartes sought one *firm* place, an unchanging foundation, upon which the subject could stand and objectively observe the objects about him.[4] For Descartes, this unchanging, thinking "soul" (*anima*) functioned as a subject by intellectually manipulating and controlling its objects of analysis. Following in this Cartesian tradition, historicism established human reason of the historian as the sole arbiter for what counts as historical knowledge and, in so doing, reduced history to an object of analysis.

But this new status accorded to human reason created a problem: the metaphysics of the subject-object binarism, upon which historicism was based, made knowledge of *anything* – including history – dependent on the perspective of the *interpreting* subject. If all knowledge is interpretation, and every subject who interprets is historically situated, then *interpretation must always be limited by the perspective of the historically situated subject.*[5]

Having stated the problem, let us step back for one moment and observe that the emergence of the concept of the autonomous subject is, itself, a historical event. In other words, human "subjecthood" (over and against the world) is not a naturally occurring fact. It is a cultural idea, which has its own history of development, arising, as it did, out of the Enlightenment tradition. As Michel Foucault observes, the very "constitution of the self as an autonomous subject," above history and outside of history, is a *historical concept*, which is "rooted in the Enlightenment."[6] Certainly the concept of the *biblical* interpreter as a sovereign subject cannot be found in the history of Christian interpretation prior to the Enlightenment. Thus,

3 Richard Bernstein, *Beyond Objectivism and Relativism: Science, Hermeneutics and Praxis* (Philadelphia: University of Pennsylvania Press, 1985), 18.
4 René Descartes, *The Philosophical Works of Descartes*, trans. Elizabeth S. Haldane and G. T. Ross, 2 vols. (Cambridge: Cambridge University Press, 1969), vol. I, 149.
5 In the words of Friedrich Nietzsche, "A nihilist is a man who judges of the world as it is that it ought *not* to be, and of the world as it ought to be that it does not exist. According to this view, our existence (action, suffering, willing, feeling) has no meaning: the pathos of 'in vain' is the nihilists' pathos – at the same time, as pathos, an inconsistency on the part of the nihilists" (*The Will to Power*, trans. Walter Kaufmann and R. J. Hollingdale [New York: Vintage Books, 1967], § 585; cf. *Kritische Studienausgabe*, ed. Giorgio Colli and Mazzino Montinari [Berlin: Walter de Gruyter, 1975], 12:2, 6, 9).
6 Michel Foucault, "What Is Enlightenment?" trans. Catherine Porter, in *The Foucault Reader*, ed. Paul Rabinow (New York: Pantheon, 1984), 42 (emphasis added).

when we, as contemporary biblical interpreters, assert our own subjecthood, we are not affirming our natural selves but rather situating ourselves in a cultural construction formed by the epistemology of the Enlightenment. The second feature of the metaphysics of historicism is the Enlightenment concept of "overcoming" (*Aufhebung*) the past through intellectual progress. Jacques Derrida has observed how Western metaphysics of history is linked to the concepts of "teleology, eschatology, interiorizing accumulation of meaning, a certain type of traditionality, a certain concept of truth, etc."[7] No doubt Hegel's philosophy of the education of the human spirit (*Geist*) over time continues to inform our own implicit belief in the disciplinary progress of biblical studies. Many of its practitioners seem to share the belief that the discipline of biblical studies continually produces new forms of knowledge that supersede and replace past (defective) forms of knowledge. Thus, a contemporary survey of the syllabi of introductory courses in the New Testament across North America would reveal that the biblical interpretation of the Middle Ages, the Reformation, and the Enlightenment is generally not considered to belong to the discipline of New Testament studies. Those interested in pursuing graduate studies in, for example, the biblical exegesis of Erasmus, Luther, or Jonathan Edwards must apply to some other department, such as church history or theology. How can we account for the fact that the first seventeen hundred years of New Testament interpretation has no place within the contemporary discipline of New Testament studies? This question is rarely asked, no doubt, because the answer is deemed to be self-evident: through the application of human observation and reason, the discipline's theoretical basis, conceptual structures, and methodologies have become more sophisticated, with the result that the biblical interpretation of previous eras has been corrected, superseded, and replaced. It follows from this that only the most recently produced knowledge is worthy of being passed on and studied.

For example, the field of "Christian origins," when viewed according to this teleology of disciplinary progress, appears as a chronicle of the unending replacement of imperfect, historical accounts of the Jesus of Nazareth, the "Jesus movement," and Pauline Christianity, with increasingly more factual reconstructions of the same. There can be no doubt that many of the historical reconstructions of past scholarship were indeed flawed, and it seems commonsensical to view the present-day discipline of biblical studies as a movement away from the scholarship of the nineteenth century toward more historically objective reconstructions. But even if such new knowledge does correct past historical misunderstandings, by what value or ethical standard can we attribute progress to this perpetual circulation of knowledge? In short, is the alleged progress of biblical studies a myth?

7   Jacques Derrida, *Speech and Phenomena, and Other Essays on Husserl's Theory of Signs,* trans. David B. Allison (Evanston, IL: Northwestern University Press, 1973), 57.

Indeed, even as long as fifty years ago, Max Horkheimer and Theodor Adorno warned that the Enlightenment program, which had promised *liberation* to humanity, was itself a myth (cf. Chapter 9): far from liberating humanity, the unchecked use of rationality has actually functioned to mold human beings into "human resources" for the exploitation of the environment in the blind pursuit of profit and power.[8]

In the 1970s Jean-François Lyotard famously defined the term "postmodern" as an "incredulity" of the "meta-narrative" that has legitimated the Enlightenment paradigm of knowledge.[9] The Enlightenment has traditionally been viewed as the era when human rationality overthrew religious myth and blind superstition and liberated civilization from ignorance, installing humanity as master of its own destiny.[10] This metanarrative continues to dominate much of Western culture. But with the benefit of hindsight, it is now obvious that the knowledge produced by Enlightenment empiricism has functioned in tandem with strategies of power and oppression in a mutually generative manner. In fact, these very strategies of power and oppression have derived their coherence not from their transcendental foundation in some kind of universal truth but rather from the concrete strategies of power they have produced, aimed at normalizing and colonizing others. In truth, much of the greater part of the world's population groans under the negative effects of "progress" of Western knowledge. The discipline of biblical studies is also rooted in this same metanarrative of disciplinary progress, which has normalized the discipline's dominant ideological framework, historical positivism, and the knowledge produced by it. In so doing, this metanarrative has also succeeded in excluding or at least marginalizing other possible forms of knowledge about biblical texts.

According to Lyotard, Western society's metanarrative of knowledge has *lost its legitimacy*. As a result, we now live in what he terms a "postmodern era," which is to say, we now live in a time of a "crisis of narratives" with regard to the legitimation of knowledge. This is what Horkheimer and Adorno previously termed

---

[8] Max Horkheimer and Theodor W. Adorno, *Dialectic of Enlightenment: Philosophical Fragments,* ed. Gunzelin Schmid Noerr, trans. Edmund Jephcott (Stanford, CA: Stanford University Press, 2002 [1987]), 1.

[9] Jean-François Lyotard, *Postmodern Condition: A Report on Knowledge,* trans. Geoff Benninton and Brian Massumi, foreword by Fredric Jameson (Minneapolis: University of Minnesota Press, 1984 [1979]), xxiv, 7.

[10] Lyotard articulates two kinds of narratives of legitimation: the "emancipatory" grand narrative, which is more political in emphasis, and the "speculative," which is more philosophical. The emancipatory grand narrative legitimizes the status quo by asserting that humanity naturally rises up in dignity and freedom by acquiring knowledge. In other words, it describes the human subject as a hero of liberty, who, through science, opposes the "priests" and "tyrants" of the former age and ushers in human freedom. According to Lyotard, this grand narrative is most in evidence in the education system: "The State resorts to the narrative of freedom every time it assumes direct control over the training of 'people' … in order to point them down the path of progress" (ibid., 32).

our "disenchantment" with the world.[11] Many have grown incredulous of the Enlightenment's promise of progress and disenchanted with much of the knowledge that has been legitimized by it. Even some biblical interpreters have grown skeptical of the purported progress of purely historical approaches to the Bible and the history of early Christianity. Given the fact that historicism is itself a child of the Enlightenment paradigm, it is not surprising (at least in hindsight) that it also has failed to produce many of its promised benefits. Not only has it failed to provide a secure historical and reasoned foundation for Christian faith (as was originally hoped), but, by drawing attention to the rootedness of the biblical texts in their respective historical contexts, the "progress" of the discipline has inadvertently severed the connection between biblical texts and ourselves in the present.

The third feature of the metaphysics of historicism is its understanding of time as a quantified, linear series of "nows." Historicism quantifies the time of everyday human experience in terms of uniform units of days, weeks, months, and years and then arranges these units of time into a linear sequence and divides them into the past, present, and future. From this historical perspective, the "present" is conceptualized as the end point of the past, and the past is believed to exist as an objective datum, independent of human existence or perception. This concept of linear time also implies a linear continuity of cause and effect. As I discuss in the next chapter, Heidegger argued that this manner of conceiving time must be learned: our primordial experience of time is different from this publicly shared perception of quantitative clock time.[12] More recently, Gianni Vattimo has observed how this perception of linear, quantified time undergirds and reinforces *the logic of overcoming the past through an act of will*: "[I]n establishing a metaphysical vision of time as pure temporal succession it persistently undergirds, and *reinforces*, the modernistic logic of *overcoming*."[13]

The fourth feature of the metaphysics of historicism is its assumption that all historical movements, societies, and civilizations manifest a *narrative coherence* over time. In his famous essay on narrative historiography, "The Discourse of History," Roland Barthes challenged this assumption, pointing out that even when historians do try to absent themselves from their historical reconstructions so that "history seems to be telling itself all on its own," the evidence of their presence remains in the imposition of continuity and coherence, the softening of gaps, and the filling in of dislocations, all of which are linguistical operations.[14] Contrary to scholarly

---

[11]   Ibid., xxiii; Horkheimer and Adorno, *Dialectic of Enlightenment*, 1 (emphasis added).

[12]   Martin Heidegger, *Concept of Time,* trans. William McNeill (Oxford: Blackwell, 1989), 20.

[13]   Gianni Vattimo, *End of Modernity,* trans. Jon R. Snyder (Baltimore: Johns Hopkins University Press, 1991 [1985]), 25. Similarly, Brook Thomas demonstrates "to what extent post-structuralism, and especially deconstruction, is a historical response to the crisis in historicism from which western thought has not yet recovered" (*The New Historicism and Other Old-Fashioned Topics* [Princeton: Princeton University Press, 1991], 35).

[14]   Roland Barthes, "The Discourse of History" [1967], in *Comparative Criticism: A Year Book,* III, ed. E. S. Schaffer (Cambridge: Cambridge University Press, 1981), 7–20.

reconstructions of "biblical" history, there is good reason to suspect the factuality of the narratives of early Judaism and Christianity, which have been constructed by scholars. Such reconstruction always involves intuitive leaps, guesswork, and even imagination. Indeed, this *must* be the case because, despite the fact that the first book of the Bible, Genesis, begins with the creation of the world, and the last book of the Bible, Revelation, narrates its end, the intervening texts record not a unilinear narrative between these two poles but a series of micronarratives, or narrative fragments that *obscure any overarching thematic unity*. A close reading of the Bible exposes many historical discontinuities and illogical elements, all of which subvert scholarly attempts to construct a single coherent "grand narrative." In fact, the Bible undermines the reconstruction of "grand narratives" because it possesses no universal theme or primary idea that allows it to be organized into such a unified narrative structure. By implication, the continuity and coherence of any history of early Judaism and Christianity are themselves signs of scholarly interference.

Actual history (*Geschichte*), which is to say, "what actually happened" (biblical and otherwise), is not linear.[15] Real history exhibits an *infinite polycentricism*, with many events occurring within the same period of time. Any and every historical event can be regarded as the beginning, middle, or end of any number of possible linear historical narratives. Thus, the very concept of Christianity having a discrete, historical "origin" (or "origins") implies an evolutionary narrative. The concept of Christianity having an origin is derived from the literalizing of a biological (Darwinian) metaphor. In reality, early Christianity cannot be condensed into a unified narrative without reducing its inherent complexity. It possesses more dimensions than can ever be represented by any set of narratives imposed upon the historical data by scholars. There is an almost indefinite number of *possible* early Christian histories, each with their own organizing centers (origins). Thus historicism's presumption of narrative coherence is itself another myth.

Fifth and finally, the metaphysics of historicism is grounded in the further belief that "history" exists as an independent, objective fact, apart from the perception and constructive activity of the historian. It is this belief that makes it possible for traditional historians to address their subject matter in terms of the subject-object binarism. The traditional historian construes his own being as a rational, autonomous self, who is distinct from, and outside of, the historical field being investigated. He investigates this object – history – with an attitude of disinterested neutrality. For example, Leopold von Ranke advocated that historians should strive to eliminate the effects of their subjectivity by cultivating detachment.[16]

---

[15] Gabrielle M. Spiegel, "History, Historicism, and the Social Logic of the Text in the Middle Ages," *Speculum* 65 (1990): 59–86, esp. 77–78, cf. 62.

[16] Leopold von Ranke, *Das politische Gespräch und andere Schriftchen zur Wissenschaftslehre*, ed. Erich Rothacker (Halle: S. Niemeyer, 1925), 43, cf. 52.

He famously advocated that the historian must "extinguish himself."[17] According to Wilhelm Dilthey, Ranke's doctrine of "self-extinction" signifies not the disappearance of the psychological person (historian) but the opposite, the pantheistic expansion of the historian's *cogito* to the level of a global perspective, in order that the historian might perceive the whole of history from a "God's eye" view: Ranke writes, "I imagine the Deity ... as seeing the whole of historical humanity in its totality ... and finding it all equally valuable."[18] Through the cultivation of such "self-extinction," the traditional historian of early Christianity seeks to contemplate a preexisting, coherent narrative of the development of Christianity from an Archimedean point outside the historical world itself.

It is now obvious that this ethic of the "self-extinction" of the historian is nonsensical: by extinguishing the self of the historian, one also extinguishes the possibility of the writing of history. Friedrich Nietzsche famously declared that "there are no facts, only interpretations," made by historians.[19] Likewise, in 1919 Benedetto Croce stated that "the past does not live otherwise than in the present, resolved and transformed in the present" by the historian.[20] Whatever the reality of actual history (*Geschichte*) may have been, it is no longer objectively existent, patiently waiting to be discovered by historians. The ancient past is not ready-made: there is only *our* perspective on it, interpreting isolated facts and documents and then reconstructing history on the basis of this evidence.[21] As Gareth Stedman Jones states, history "is an entirely intellectual operation which takes place in the present and in the head."[22] Similarly, Raymond Aron remarks that the past has disappeared and "attains existence only in minds, and changes with them."[23] He refers to this instability of history as "the dissolution of the [historical] object."[24]

In his famous book *Metahistory* (1973), Hayden White has demonstrated the story-shaping character of all historiography, citing example after example of how the strategies of explanation and (what he refers to as) "emplotment" used by historians often differ when studying the *same* historical data, depending on their

17 Ibid., 5.
18 Ranke, as quoted by Hans-Georg Gadamer, *Truth and Method*, 2nd rev. ed., trans. Joel Weinsheimer and Donald G. Marshall (London: Continuum, 1994), 207.
19 Nietzsche, *The Portable Nietzsche*, trans. Walter Kaufmann (New York: Viking Penguin, 1982), 458.
20 Benedetto Croce, *Theory & History of Historiography*, trans. Douglas Ainslie (London: Harrap, 1921 [1919]), 91.
21 Nietzsche, *The Will to Power*, 301–3 (§§ 556–60).
22 Gareth Stedman Jones, "From Historical Sociology to Theoretic History," *British Journal of Sociology* 27 (1976): 295–305, esp. 296.
23 Raymond Aron, *Introduction to the Philosophy of History* (London: Weidenfeld and Nicolson, 1961), 289.
24 Ibid., 118.

respective ideological presuppositions.[25] White concludes by arguing that *ideological saturation* always figures prominently in seemingly neutral, historical reconstructions.[26] Commenting on this phenomenon within historical reconstructions of Israelite history, David Clines remarks that we must admit that

we are not all engaged in some objective quest for determinate meanings, and that our ideologies, our locations, and our interests and our personalities determine our scholarship – and separate us from one another … there is a lot we don't like, don't approve of, and will not stand for, in our colleagues, a lot that has yet to be brought into the light, taken measure of, and fought over.[27]

To a great extent, this metaphysics of historicism, as outlined in the preceding five points, continues to constitute the possibility for the creation of new historical knowledge about early Christianity in the twenty-first century. In truth, no unconstructed, uninterpreted historical Jesus or Paul, or Corinthian church, or Matthean congregation, or Jewish Christianity is available to us. In point of fact, the earliest manuscripts of the Greek New Testament are more historically real than the historical reconstructions that scholars create on the basis of such manuscripts.

How then have scholars come to confuse the "history" (historiology), which they have constructed, with the factuality of history (*Geschichte*) as it actually happened? According to Roland Barthes, the mistaking of our own constructions for what "actually happened" is attributable to the power of "the apparently all-powerful [semiotic] referent."[28] By representing history with "assemblages" of semiotic "signs," the historian creates what Barthes refers to as the "effect of the real" or "the reality effect."[29] Historical reconstructions can take on the patina of factuality by diminishing the degrees of difference between the linguistic representation of history (historiology) and actual history (*Geschichte*), thereby creating a "referential illusion." Following this line of logic, one could say that New Testament scholars have created the reality *effect* of diaspora Judaism, and the reality *effect* of the

25 Hayden White, *Metahistory: The Historical Imagination in Nineteenth-Century Europe* (Baltimore: Johns Hopkins University Press, 1973), ix, 7–9, 13, 30–31, 426–31. Elsewhere, White argues that the heritage of nineteenth-century realism actually disguises in a pseudoscientific, sublimated form the ideology of humanism of the self-present subject; cf. Hayden V. White, "The Question of Narrative in Contemporary Historical Theory" [1984], in his *The Content of the Form: Narrative Discourse and Historical Representation* (Baltimore: Johns Hopkins University Press, 1987), 26–57.

26 Hayden V. White, "Method and Ideology, in Intellectual History: The Case of Henry Adams," in *Modern European Intellectual History: Reappraisals and New Perspectives,* ed. Dominick LaCapra and Steven L. Kaplan (Ithaca, NY: Cornell University Press, 1982), 280–310, esp. 288.

27 David J. A. Clines, *Interested Parties: The Ideology of Writers and Readers of the Hebrew Bible,* JSOTSup 205 (Sheffield: Sheffield Academic Press, 1995), 92–93.

28 Barthes, "The Discourse of History," esp. 16–17.

29 Roland Barthes, "From History to Reality" [1984], in *The Rustle of Language* (New York: Blackwell, 1986), 127–56, esp. 141–48.

historical Jesus (in the many contradictory portraits of him), and the reality *effect* of the apostle Paul, by conflating their rhetorically and ideologically informed constructions with the actual.[30]

To be fair, most scholars would admit – if asked – that their findings are perspectival, and they also would grant that multiple perspectives must always be provided through the use of a variety of complementary methods. Yet, as William Dray notes, far fewer scholars are prepared "to give up the claim to tell us how the past really was" without "any pretensions to epistemological respectability."[31] Keith Jenkins argues that historiography is "the attempted imposition of a meaningful form onto a meaningless past."[32] For this reason, the biblical interpreter must be incredulous of all historical reconstructions, especially those that seem the most convincing.

THE TEXTS AND CONTEXTS

Biblical scholars frequently conceive of a biblical text as a product or residue of particular historical context. But if no unconstructed historical past is available to scholars, then neither are unconstructed historical contexts. As Dominick LaCapra remarks, historians' "reconstruction of a 'context' takes place on the basis of 'textualized' remainders of the past."[33] The historical contexts to which New Testament scholars appeal are always products of discursive construction in the present.[34] Historical contexts such as the church in Corinth, the Johannine community, and the church of the Pastoral epistles do not exist independently of the contemporary historians who construct them. In the case of the exegesis of the Pentateuch, the canonical Gospels, and the Pauline and Deutero-Pauline epistles, interpreters must choose between competing reconstructions of the purported historical contexts of these texts. For this reason, the "notion that any one 'context' provides a unified framework for the interpretation of a given text is always dubious,"[35] and the assertion that one specific context is determinative of a text's "sense" must always be argued.

---

[30] Robert E. Berkhofer Jr., *Beyond the Great Story: History as Text and Discourse* (Cambridge, MA: Harvard University Press, 1995), 60, 63, 71.

[31] William Dray, *On History and Philosophers of History* (Leiden: Brill, 1989 [1978]), 65, cf. 4.

[32] Keith Jenkins, *On "What Is History?" From Carr and Elton to Rorty and White* (London: Routledge, 1995), 137.

[33] Dominick LaCapra, "Rethinking Intellectual History and Reading Texts" [1980], in *Modern European Intellectual History: Reappraisals and New Perspectives,* ed. Dominick LaCapra and Steven L. Kaplan (Ithaca, NY: Cornell University Press, 1994), 57–78, esp. 57.

[34] In a seminal essay, "The Model of the Text: Meaningful Action Considered as a Text" [1971], Ricoeur set forth the essential constituents of all actions and demonstrated how meaningful actions can be viewed as "texts" (reprinted in his *From Text to Action: Essays in Hermeneutics II,* trans. Kathleen Blamey and John B. Thompson [Evanston, IL: Northwestern University Press, 1986], 146–67).

[35] Dominick LaCapra, "AHR Forum: Intellectual History and Its Ways," *American Historical Review* 97 (1992): 425–39, esp. 430.

Not only are the possible historical contexts for a given text multiple, but the act of choosing one over another is often motivated by ideological motives. On this point, Jacques Derrida argues that the choosing of one historical context over another is never a "neutral, innocent, transparent, disinterested" act, nor is it a "purely theoretical gesture."[36] Similarly, Hans Kellner observes how historical reconstructions always exhibit an "unfailing ability to make sense out of things and to present them in a form that seems natural," even when shaped by different and even antithetical ideological commitments.[37] This ideological side of appeals to context necessitates that one always ask *which* politics and *which* ideology are implied in a given choice of historical context.[38] When the constructive role of ideology is ignored, contexts can take on the patina of verisimilitude.

And not only are contexts constructed and multiple; the very concept of a material context is not as self-evident as it may at first seem. The obviousness of the distinction between the text (as product of context) and the material context (as cause of a text), and the supposed unidirectional causal relationship between context and text, have been problematized over the past few decades. Dominick LaCapra has argued that texts are not simply determined by, or mimetic of, their respective historical contexts. While it is true that ancient texts *do* rework their historical contexts within their own symbolic registers, it is equally true that texts also possess their own illocutionary power to shape the communities that read and write them and to inform the authors who later redact them. In other words, texts play a role in the formation of their own material contexts in which successive versions of the same text are produced, revised, and expanded.[39] For example, many early Christian writings, such as the Gospel of Mark, the Fourth Gospel, the Q Sayings Gospel, and the Gospel of Thomas, all evolved and expanded over time through a series of recensions (i.e., revisions), allowing time for these texts to shape the communities for whom they had authority (e.g., Ur-Markus > Deutero-Markus). Ancient texts possess an illocutionary power to shape the communities and authors and thereby produce material contexts, according to their own symbolic universes.[40] This means, as Jean Howard observes, that "instead of a hierarchical relationship" in which texts are "parasitic" reflectors of historical facts, we should

---

[36] Jacques Derrida, *Limited Inc*, trans. Samuel Weber (Evanston, IL: Northwestern University Press, 1990), 111–60, esp. 131–32.

[37] Hans Kellner, *Language and Historical Representation: Getting the Story Crooked* (Madison: University of Wisconsin Press, 1989), 24.

[38] Richard Kearney (ed.), *Dialogues with Contemporary Continental Thinkers: The Phenomenological Heritage; Paul Ricoeur, Emmanuel Levinas, Herbert Marcuse, Stanislas Breton, Jacques Derrida* (Manchester: Manchester University Press, 1984), 115–16.

[39] Dominick LaCapra, "Intellectual History and Critical Theory," in *Soundings in Critical Theory* (Ithaca, NY: Cornell University Press, 1989), 182–209, esp. 205; Dominick LaCapra, "History, Language, and Reading: Waiting for Crillon," *American Historical Review* 100 (1995): 799–828.

[40] LaCapra, "Intellectual History and Critical Theory," 182–209, esp. 205; LaCapra, "History, Language, and Reading: Waiting for Crillon."

imagine a complex textualized universe in which texts participate "in historical processes and in the political management of reality."[41]

Jacques Derrida is well known for the deconstruction of the context-text binarism. His famous dictum that "there is no outside the text" (il n'y a pas de hors-texte) has frequently been misunderstood, either as a denial of extralingual reference to material contexts (i.e., as inscribing a boundary between world and text) or, conversely, as a total erasure of any boundary by transforming the world into a text.[42] However, Derrida's point is more subtle than this: he is neither textualizing context nor simply inverting the context-text hierarchy. While it is true that a material "outside" of biblical texts did exist, this outside material world itself was semiotically encoded. According to the symbolic anthropologist Clifford Geertz, contexts can also be theorized as texts because they too consist of interworked systems of signs and assemblies of texts.[43] Therefore, the point of departure for understanding all ancient contexts is also semiology. By demonstrating how textuality "embraces and does not exclude the world, reality, history," Derrida has deconstructed their rigid opposition and thereby subverted the implied subordination of texts to their contexts.[44] As far as finite human beings are concerned, *there is nothing outside the textuality of all of life.* Indeed, one of the governing tenets of New Historicism is that both texts and contexts should be unified under the concept of "textuality."[45] John Montrose, another exponent of New Historicism, states that historians should be concerned with "the historicality of texts and the textuality of history."[46] In effect, Derrida's deconstruction of the context-text binarism transforms the relationship between biblical texts and their contexts from that of "copy" (text) versus "original" (context) to one of homology between *two semiotically encoded domains.*[47] By implication, the conventional appeal by biblical scholars to the "real" historical contexts *behind* semiotically coded texts ought to be replaced with interpretive approaches that respect the semiotic homology that characterizes the interwoven text-context world as one unified "regime of signs."

---

[41] Jean Howard, "The New Historicism in Literary Study," *English Literary Renaissance* 16 (1986): 13–43, esp. 25 (emphasis added).

[42] Jacques Derrida, *Of Grammatology,* trans. Gayatri Spivak (Baltimore: Johns Hopkins University Press, 1974 [1967]), 158; cf. Jacques Derrida, "Outwork" [1972], in *Dissemination,* trans. Barbara Johnson (Chicago: University of Chicago Press, 1981), 1–60, esp. 36; cf. Jacques Derrida, "Living On: Border Lines" [1979], in *Deconstruction and Criticism (Question What You Thought Before),* ed. Harold Bloom (New York: Continuum, 1980), 75–106, esp. 84.

[43] Clifford Geertz, *The Interpretation of Cultures* (New York: Basic Books, 1973), 14, 27.

[44] Derrida, "Living On: Border Lines," 137; cf. Kearney, *Dialogues with Contemporary Continental Thinkers,* 123–26.

[45] John E. Toews, "Intellectual History after the Linguistic Turn: The Autonomy of Meaning and the Irreducibility of Experience," *American Historical Review* 92 (1987): 886.

[46] Louis Montrose, "Renaissance Studies and the Subject of History," *English Literary Renaissance* 16 (1986): 5–12, esp. 8.

[47] Jonathan Culler, "Literary History, Allegory, and Semiology," *New Literary History* 7 (1976): 259–70.

THE CRISIS OF HISTORICISM AS AN OPPORTUNITY

According to Martin Heidegger, Nietzsche's writings represent the crisis of Western metaphysics in its clearest form. In *Human All too Human* (1878), Nietzsche foretold the advent of an eschatological "overman" (*Übermensch*), who would replace all former values, especially the Hegelian value of "overcoming" (*Aufhebung*), with values of his own choosing, through an exercise of his "will-to-power" (*der Wille zur Macht*).[48] But by emphasizing the priority of human will, Heidegger argues that Nietzsche inadvertently *continued* the primary tendency of subject-object metaphysics, which is the logic of overcoming the past through human will.[49] In Heidegger's view, Nietzsche's attempt to solve the problem of nihilism through his concept of the "will-to-power" failed because his solution unwittingly employed the very system of thought that it set out to combat, for, if the logic of the Enlightenment epistemology, which created the crisis of nihilism, is one of overcoming the past knowledge through an act of human will, then the attempt to willfully overcome nihilism through another act of will actually furthers and extends nihilism.[50] For this reason, Heidegger called Nietzsche, who was the first to recognize the emergence of this metaphysical crisis, the "last metaphysician of the West": "In the thought of the will to power, metaphysical thinking itself completes itself in advance. Nietzsche, the thinker of the thought of will to power, is the *last metaphysician* of the West. This age, whose consummation unfolds in his thought, the modern age, is a final age."[51]

In Heidegger's view, historicism has now exhausted itself as a viable approach to history. It survives only as a vestige of a nineteenth-century, metaphysical view of human being as subject. It now exemplifies such obsolete concepts of the independence of the subject, the linearity of historical cause and effect, the unidirectional narrative of progress through overcoming the past, and especially the methodological access to truth.

---

[48] In an unpublished note from 1873, Nietzsche writes: "Why you are there, that you should ask yourself: and if you have no ready answer, then set for yourself goals, high and noble goals, and perish in pursuit of them! I know of no better life purpose than to perish in attempting the great and the impossible." Phillip R. Fandozzi, *Nihilism and Technology: A Heideggerian Investigation* (Lanham, MD: University Press of America, 1982), 9; Ernst Behler, *Confrontations: Derrida/Heidegger/Nietzsche*, trans. Steven Taubeneck (Stanford, CA: Stanford University Press, 1991), 17, 23.

[49] Bambach, *Heidegger, Dilthey, and the Crisis of Historicism*, 1.

[50] Heidegger, "Overcoming Metaphysics," in *The End of Philosophy*, trans. Joan Stambaugh (New York: Harper & Row, 1973), 95.

[51] Heidegger, *Nietzsche*, vol. III: *The Will to Power as Knowledge and Metaphysics*, ed. David Farrell Krell, trans. Joan Stambaugh (New York: Harper & Row, 1987), 7–8; Heidegger, *Nietzsche*, vol. I: *The Will to Power as Art*, ed. David Farrell Krell (New York: Harper & Row, 1979), 479–80. By "consummation" Heidegger means the "unimpeded development of all the essential powers of being, powers that have been reserved for a long time, to what they demand as a whole." It is the "conditional and complete installation for the first time and in advance, of what is unexpected and never to be expected" (Heidegger, *Nietzsche*, vol. III, 7).

Thus, in Heidegger's view, the modern era is the "final age" of the metaphysics of historicism that brings us to a point of "historical decision" in the present "as to whether this final age is the conclusion of Western history or the counterpart to another beginning."[52] For Heidegger, the very name of "Nietzsche" symbolized the collapse of this Western culture into nihilism and the corresponding call for a decision from us: "The age whose consummation unfolds in his [Nietzsche's] thought, the modern age, is the final age, which means an age in which the historical decision arises as to whether this final age is the conclusion of Western history or the counterpart to another beginning."[53] Thus, to follow the path of Nietzsche is "to catch sight of this historical decision" to reply to nihilism.[54]

Heidegger outlined three typical responses to the problem of nihilism.[55] One could accept the fact of historical relativism at face value, as Oswald Spengler did, and reject outright the possibility of suprahistorical values and eternal truths; alternatively, one could take the opposite position, as did such Platonists as Eduard Spranger, and attempt to deduce intuitively from history eternal truths and values; or one could endeavor to construct a compromise solution between these two contrary positions by searching for a minimum of universal values as "they are embodied in the historical context only in a relative form."[56] In Heidegger's view, all three of these solutions fail to explicate the manner in which the history is formed as knowledge and made present (*gegenwärtig*) to the historian. All three approaches fail to appreciate the hermeneutic conditions – namely, human "facticity" – that make historical inquiry possible.[57]

Whereas many construed the crisis of historicism as a crisis of nihilism, Heidegger interpreted the crisis differently, by pursuing the crisis of historical consciousness to its very core: he argued that because historicism is a form of metaphysical thinking, the crisis of historicism is a metaphysical crisis of the metaphysics of historicism and, therefore, a crisis of the metaphysics of the knowing subject. As such, this crisis not only signals the death of subjecthood and the death of traditional history; it also holds within itself the promise of a new beginning, which is imminent within the end.

---

[52] Heidegger, *Nietzsche*, vol. III, 8.
[53] Ibid. Heidegger uses the term "consummation" in the sense of "unimpeded development of all the essential powers of being, powers that have been reserved for a long time, to what they demand as a whole." It is the "conditional and complete installation for the first time and in advance, of what is unexpected and never to be expected" (*Nietzsche*, vol. III, 7).
[54] Heidegger, *Nietzsche*, vol. III, 8.
[55] Martin Heidegger, *The Phenomenology of Religious Life,* trans. Matthias Fritsch and Jennifer Anna Gosetti-Ferencei (Bloomington: Indiana University Press, 2004), 27–30; cf. Martin Heidegger, "Introduction to the Phenomenology of Religion," in Theodore Kisiel, *The Genesis of Heidegger's Being and Time* (Berkeley: University of California Press, 1993), 151–91.
[56] Heidegger, *Phenomenology of Religious Life*, 30.
[57] The term "facticity" (*Faktizität*) is derived from the Latin *factum*. Interpreting the term *factum* as "constructed knowledge," Heidegger employs this term with the inference that the "world" is not "out there" to be analyzed but is always interwoven into the very structure of human existence.

Heidegger believes that we can experience this promise of new beginning only by first calmly and contemplatively experiencing the *essence* of the nihilism, which we have brought upon ourselves. He argued that "we must attempt to first turn in toward [nihilism's] essence," because "turning into its essence is the first step through which we may leave nihilism behind us."[58] By meditating on the end of the Western metaphysics of the subject (*cogito*), and the dissolution of the grammar of "subjects" versus "objects," he believed we can find a way of "turning" toward such a new beginning.[59]

THE TWILIGHT OF IDOLS

Because historicism is founded upon the nineteenth-century metaphysics of the subject, the crisis of historicism is actually a crisis of our own subjecthood. Heidegger's understanding of the "end" of history as a new "beginning" and of the necessity for us to make a "historical decision" inaugurates the postmodern attitude toward history.[60] In fact, according to Gianni Vattimo, *the actual meaning of our present age is this death of this subject-object metaphysics*, which functioned as the foundation of nineteenth-century historiography.[61]

The metaphysics of subjecthood is fully dead. But we still mourn its loss and cling to its cold exterior for some small comfort. As Nietzsche foresaw so many years ago, *our* destiny has become that of living in the "twilight of idols," the greatest of which is the metaphysics of our own subjecthood.[62] Despite the fact that historicism is founded upon an obsolete view of the human being as a "subject," its ghost lingers on in biblical studies. But how could we not mourn the passing of our sovereign subjecthood. According to Vattimo, we should feel the same respect toward this "idol" as one would feel for ancient "monuments, tombs, traces of past life, or even family memories."[63] Vattimo's image of a decaying tomb is an ambivalent symbol of both the preservation and loss of cultural memory. Historicism, being itself a product of the metaphysics of subjecthood, is but another monument in ruins.

But I would argue that it is a "splendid ruin" nonetheless.[64] For this reason, historicism continues to have an honored place within a post-historical hermeneutic

---

[58] Martin Heidegger, "On the Question of Being," trans. William McNeill, in *Martin Heidegger: Pathmarks*, ed. William McNeill (Cambridge: Cambridge University Press, 1998), 319.
[59] Martin Heidegger, *The History of the Concept of Time*, trans. Theodore Kisiel (Bloomington: Indiana University Press, 1985), 4.
[60] Bambach, *Heidegger, Dilthey, and the Crisis of Historicism*, 2.
[61] Vattimo, *End of Modernity*, 145–63.
[62] Nietzsche, *Portable Nietzsche*, 463–563.
[63] Vattimo, *End of Modernity*, 177.
[64] I am here borrowing the phrase "splendid ruin" from a passage in Robertson Davies's novel *Rebel Angels*, in which he likens the Hellenistic Greek of the New Testament to a "splendid ruin ... splendid in decay" (*Rebel Angels* [Harmondsworth: Penguin, 1983], 46).

paradigm within the following framework. First, historical inquiry continues to serve a vital function in its ability to call attention to *historical difference*, and to contribute to a strategy of resistance to all totalizing discourses – theological and otherwise. Indeed, the genius of historicism has always been its ability to disclose the disconcerting uniqueness of historically situated biblical texts and, thereby, to *defamiliarize* them to their readers. This disclosure of historical difference challenges us to go beyond the narrow limits of our own culturally and historically bound horizons of meaning to contemplate the "other." The privileging of historical difference can also serve a vital role in discourses of resistance. In contrast, a lack of awareness of historical difference often accompanies the use of the Bible in strategies of oppression and violence, and to justify intolerance and prejudice.

Second, the implied downward causation found in historical positivism, which construes authors as efficient causal agents, is false. As we discuss in Chapter 12, it is because sense-events arise from the restructuring of the virtual surface of textual networks that authors function only as quasi causes, or triggers of sense-events. Therefore, the traditional appeal to authors should, as part of a strategy of limiting and controlling the meaning of biblical texts, be replaced with a multidimensional view of textuality, which considers the role of the author within a more complex set of variables.

But despite the fact that an "author" is a zone of indiscernibility – always remaining both distinct and obscure at the same time – and even though contexts manifest their own forms of textuality, both authors and contexts nonetheless embody an extralingual reference to the *material* world that should not be excluded from the hermeneutic act. Indeed, as already noted, "denotation" is the component of language that *connects* the domains of signification and manifestation to real material contexts. This being said, the naiveté of conceiving of a biblical text as a mere product, or residue, of a particular historical context, and the practice of appealing to such contexts as a way of objectifying textual meaning, should be replaced with approaches that respect the reciprocity between texts and contexts.

Third, as the vigorous exertions of Nietzsche's "overman" remind us, biblical studies cannot overcome nihilism through an act of human will, such as by the invention of new methodologies.[65] In fact, nihilism cannot be overcome by *any* act of will because it is a symptom of something deeper, namely a crisis of the metaphysics of the sovereign subject. Any attempt to overcome nihilism by an act

---

[65] In his 1923 lecture "The Hermeneutics of Facticity," Heidegger remarks that the task of hermeneutics is not the developing of a set technique but "of informing; of making each Da-sein, in its being, accessible to this Da-sein itself; of going back to the self-alienation with which Da-sein is oppressed. Far from being a technique, this practice of interpretation will be necessarily different for different people. In hermeneutics the possibility is of Da-sein's becoming and being for itself understandingly" (*Gesamtausgabe*, 63:20). Its object is to overcome its own "fallenness" and "self-alienation" and to rediscover its freedom to choose authenticity over inauthenticity.

of the rational subject can extend nihilism further.[66] On the other hand, the honest experience of the nihilism, which we have brought upon ourselves, can open up the possibility of a new beginning, in which we reappraise how knowledge is legitimated within the discipline of biblical studies and the purposes for which we seek this knowledge.

Fourth, any form of thought that claims to reconstruct the biblical past objectively, as an isolated historical artifact, is founded on an obsolete metaphysics of the knowing subject. The continued use of historicism in its purely antiquarian mode of expression, dedicated solely to uncovering the minutiae of the past, and disconnected from life, represents a form of thought that *alienates* biblical interpreters from themselves, as well as their real material contexts. All such forms of historicism have lost their critical and emancipatory edge and therefore have no place in a renewed practice of hermeneutic inquiry.

Fifth and finally, with the transformation of New Testament studies into a purely methodologically guided form of inquiry, the notion of scholarly accountability has shifted from that of an ethical accountability to others to a methodological accountability to disciplinary rigor. I would argue that our exploration of the historical "founding sense-event" of biblical texts should not overshadow the possible implications of such research for the present. Biblical interpreters are ethically accountable to those outside their guild by virtue of the fact that their embodied lives are indissolubly linked with a series of other human relations, which – taken together – make them contextually situated interpreters. As such, the act of interpreting biblical texts has the potential to create intensive connections with others, both locally and globally. The very self of the interpreter is always connected to multiple, dynamic dimensions of life in widely different registers – religious, social, ethical, economic, and material. These multiple dimensions of human existence complicate the making of interpretive choices, which are implicit within the practice of all biblical hermeneutics. While this is not to argue that biblical studies should restrict its work to the elucidation of ethically motivated readings, neither should hermeneutics overlook the fact that biblical scholars carry out their research within a broader ecology of life. Any interpretative strategy that focuses on the repeatability of methods of interpretation at the cost of losing sight of our accountability to others can only banish all spiritual impulses within our work.

---

[66] Martin Heidegger, *Nietzsche*, vol. IV: *Nihilism*, ed. David Farrell Krell, trans. Frank A. Capuzzi (San Francisco: Harper Collins, 1991), 241; Martin Heidegger, *Nietzsche*, vol. II: *The Eternal Recurrence of the Same*, ed. David Farrell Krell (New York: Harper & Row, 1984), 386.

PART II

⌀

ON THE WAY TO POST-HISTORICAL

HERMENEUTICS

5

The Interpreter as the Location of Meaning: Martin Heidegger

> We are ourselves the entities to be analyzed. The being of any such entity is in each case mine.[1]

The First World War was a military conflict involving seventy million military personnel that embroiled the whole of Europe, Russia, North America, and the Ottoman Empire. By its end, more than fifteen million people had been killed, the German, Austro-Hungarian, Ottoman, and Russian empires had disappeared, and the map of Europe had been redrawn. In the years that followed, starvation and disease wiped out tens of millions more. This was the context for the establishment of a new liberal democracy in Germany in 1919 known as the Weimar Republic. The so-called Weimar years, which stretched from 1919 to the beginning of Hitler's Third Reich in 1933, were filled with political and economic instability, social dislocation, and violence. Not surprisingly, these were also years of growing disillusionment, cynicism, and a sense of nihilism, as exemplified by such movements as Dadaism, which embraced the chaos and irrationality of the times.

Against this background of slaughter, chaos, and human suffering, the skepticism that had arisen regarding historicism took on even greater proportions and resulted in a profound disillusionment concerning the continuing relevance of historicism and liberal Protestantism alike.[2] As previously noted, even Ernst Troeltsch, well known for his strident defense of historicism, came to recognize its shortcomings. When viewed against the carnage, misery, and upheaval of the Weimar years, historicism's scientistic objectives seemed irrelevant and even bourgeois. Many Christian scholars felt this generational crisis acutely, with a corresponding desire to tear down the old, which helps to explain why Karl Barth's ground-breaking *Commentary on Romans,* Ernst Troeltsch's classic essay "The Problem with Historicism," and Martin Heidegger's epic *Being and Time* were all

---

[1] Heidegger, BTMR 67 (§ 9). The traditional translation of *Sein und Zeit* (1927) is that of John Macquarrie and Edward Robinson, who translated it into English in 1962 (Harper & Row) with the title *Being and Time* (hereafter abbreviated BTMR). We are now indeed fortunate to have a new, updated and corrected translation available to us, by Joan Stambaugh, which was published in 1966 (State University of New York Press) (hereafter abbreviated BTS).

[2] Jeffrey A. Barash, *Heidegger and the Problem of Historical Meaning,* rev. and expanded ed. (New York: Fordham University Press, 1988).

published at this critical time, within a few short years of each other, in 1919, 1922, and 1927, respectively.

As previously discussed, Martin Heidegger addressed the crisis of historicism by arguing that it was not, in fact, an *epistemological* problem but rather an *existential* phenomenon of human existence. As such, it creates a new opportunity: because the enigma of history concerns what it means to *be* historical, then the contemporary crisis of historicism actually opens up an opportunity for us to explore our own human historicality. Heidegger's tome *Being and Time* is such an exploration of human historicality. It represents an ever-deepening analysis of the structures of human life in time, which constitute the very hermeneutic conditions for all interpretation.

HEIDEGGER'S EARLY YEARS

Martin Heidegger (1889–1976) was raised in the Roman Catholic tradition and received an education in Catholic theology and medieval philosophy.[3] When he later commenced his studies for the priesthood at Albert-Ludwig University in Freiburg, he read both Edmund Husserl's *Logical Investigations* (*Logische Untersuchungen*) and writings of Wilhelm Dilthey. His fresh acquaintance with Husserl and Dilthey marked the beginning of the profound influence of these writings upon his thought. Following the completion of his dissertation, he was appointed as an unsalaried lecturer (*Privatdozent*) at Freiburg University. Though he was later drafted into the war, health problems led to his return to the university, where he met Edmund Husserl in person. But even before meeting him, Heidegger had become involved in editing Husserl's papers for publication with Edith Stein. In fact, Stein had followed Husserl to Freiburg from the University of Göttingen and had been appointed his assistant along with Heidegger.[4] It was also in Freiburg

---

[3]   Thomas Scheehan, "Reading a Life: Heidegger and Hard Times," in *The Cambridge Companion to Heidegger*, ed. Charles Guignon (Cambridge: Cambridge University Press, 1993), 70–96.

[4]   Edith Stein (1891–1942) was born in 1891 into an observant Jewish home in Breslau, Silesia, in what is now Poland. In 1916, she completed her doctorate of philosophy with Edmund Husserl in the area of phenomenology. Her dissertation was entitled "On The Problem of Empathy" (*Zum Problem der Einfühlung*). Following her appointment as a faculty member at the University of Freiburg, she served, along with Heidegger (appointed the previous year), as a teaching assistant to Husserl. In 1919 she completed her postdoctoral thesis (*Habilitationsschrift*), entitled "Psychic Causality" (*Psychische Kausalität*). However, her thesis was rejected solely because she was a woman, blocking her appointment as a university professor. While on holiday, she read the autobiography of the medieval mystic Saint Teresa of Avila. This autobiography precipitated Stein's conversion to Christianity. She was baptized as a Roman Catholic on 1 January 1922. In the years following her conversion, she abandoned her phenomenological orientation, which she had learned from Husserl. She was subsequently received as a nun into the Discalced Carmelite Order at Cologne in 1933, the same year that Heidegger resigned his rectorship at the University of Freiburg. In 1939 she moved to Echt, in the Netherlands, to avoid the Nazis, who were then arresting all Jewish converts. But in retaliation for a Catholic bishops' public letter, condemning Nazi anti-Semitism, the Nazis began to arrest converts to Christianity, who had previously been spared. Thus, in 1942 Stein was arrested and sent to the Auschwitz concentration camp, where she was murdered in the gas chamber. In 1998 Pope John Paul II canonized her by her Carmelite monastic name, Saint Teresa Benedicta of the Cross.

that Heidegger met his future wife, Elfride Petri, a Lutheran. Perhaps it was under Elfride's influence that Heidegger began to read Protestant theologians such as Martin Luther and Friedrich Schleiermacher and take an interest in Protestant interpretations of Pauline theology. The story of Paul's Damascus road conversion in particular came to exercise a significant influence over Heidegger's imagination. In the years 1917–19, Heidegger experienced a crisis of faith, following which he turned his back on Catholic theology and abandoned traditional Western metaphysics and epistemology.[5] When Heidegger was subsequently appointed professor in philosophy at the University of Marburg, he met Hans-Georg Gadamer and Rudolf Bultmann (whose writings we discuss in Chapters 6 and 8, respectively). Upon Husserl's retirement in 1928, Heidegger returned to Freiburg and became Husserl's successor.[6]

THE PUBLICATION OF *BEING AND TIME*

In 1927 Heidegger published *Sein und Zeit* (*Being and Time*), which is indisputably one of the most important philosophical works of the twentieth century. This work is an ever-deepening analysis of the structures of human life that constitute the very hermeneutic conditions of all interpretation. It can be read as an exploration of the situatedness of the interpreter – *as nonsubject* – in a particular place and time, within an ever-expanding world of relations.

Following the introduction (§§ 1–8), *Being and Time* is divided into two parts, Division One (§§ 9–44) and Division Two (§§ 45–83). At the outset it is important to bear in mind that Division One constitutes what Heidegger refers to as a preliminary "interpretation of the human being in its everydayness," that is, in terms of our everyday practice of coping with the world around us. Because our understanding of our environment (including biblical texts) always involves interpretation, it is necessary to begin any analysis of hermeneutics with a consideration of the everyday phenomenological horizon of interpreters themselves.

Heidegger's fundamental question in *Being and Time* is the "question concerning the meaning of being" ("Die Frage nach dem Sinn von Sein").[7] Because the

---

5   Martin Heidegger, *Zur Bestimmung der Philosophie, Gesamtausgabe* 56/57 (Frankfurt am Main: Vittorio Klostermann, 1987), 215. In a letter dated 9 January 1919, he writes that "epistemological insights, extending to the theory of historical knowledge, have made the system of Catholicism problematic and unacceptable to me – but not Christianity and metaphysics (although these in a new sense)." Cf. Hugo Ott, *Martin Heidegger: Unterwegs zu seiner Biographie* (Frankfurt: Campus, 1988) 106. In a letter to the eminent Lutheran theologian Rudolf Otto in 1919, Husserl wrote of "radical changes" in Heidegger's "basic religious convictions" (Thomas Scheehan, "Heidegger's 'Introduction to the Phenomenology of Religion,' 1920–21," in *A Companion to Heidegger's "Being and Time,"* ed. Joseph Kockelmans [Washington, DC: University Press of America, 1986], 43).

6   We return to the subject of Heidegger's university career and his association with Nazism in Chapter 11.

7   It is now normative practice to not capitalize "being" (see Joan Stambaugh, BTS, introduction).

whole of *Being and Time* represents an extended attempt to answer this question, any attempt to formulate a concise definition of being at this point would be premature. Nonetheless, a few preliminary remarks will help orient the reader to the overall argument of this work. What then does Heidegger mean by being? First, Heidegger states that "being is not a *genus*." In other words, being is not a category or taxonomical unit by which we can classify things in the world. For example, the term "Canis" is the genus (a taxonomical category) for dogs, wolves, foxes, coyotes, and jackals. In contrast, being is not a taxonomical category for any grouping of entities. Being actually transcends all such categories and taxonomical units.

Second, being is not an entity or thing in the world. It cannot be observed or measured. It cannot be classified or defined by means of progressively more general, or higher, properties and categories (e.g., species → genus →family → order → class). In other words, being is unclassifiable. Nonetheless, being is always implied in the process or faculty of thinking about all things, forming assertions, and posing questions.

Suffice it to say, Heidegger observes that only human beings inquire into the meaning of being. In contrast to animals, the human being (or "Da-sein" in Heidegger's terminology) is endowed with a self-reflective consciousness that allows it not only to relate itself to its environment but also to inquire into the significance of existence. Because the human being is the only place where the meaning of being can be disclosed, Heidegger reasons that to answer the question, What is the meaning of being? we must begin with an examination of the human being, who asks this question.[8] In philosophical terms, ontology (which is the study of being) must begin with a phenomenological examination of the human being: *"Only as phenomenology is ontology possible."*[9]

BEING AND TIME: DIVISION ONE

Heidegger's phenomenological analysis of human beings is termed an "existential" (*existenzial*) examination. An existential analysis is concerned with ontological structures of human beings, which cannot be directly observed. For example,

---

[8]   See Jean Grondin, *Le tournant dans la pensée de Martin Heidegger* (Paris: Presses universitaire de France, 1987); Theodore Kisiel, "Das Kriegsnotsemester 1919: Heideggers Durchbruch zur hermeneutischen Phänomenologie," *Philosophisches Jahrbuch* 99 (1992): 105–23; Martin Heidegger, "The Turning," in *The Question Concerning Technology*, trans. William Lovitt (New York: Harper & Row, 1977); Peter Eli Gordon, *Rosenzweig and Heidegger: Between Judaism and German Philosophy* (Berkeley: University of California Press, 2003), 425. Contemporary scholarship now dates Heidegger's so-called turning to the years following 1917, though traditionally it has been dated to the 1930s following his abandonment of the concept of Da-sein, but denied by Heidegger, in a letter published by William J. Richardson in *Heidegger: Through Phenomenology to Thought*, 4th ed. (New York: Fordham University Press, 2003).

[9]   BTMR 60 § 71. For an explanation of phenomenology and a summary of Husserl's phenomenological method, see Chapter 3.

human beings possess the capacity to care, understand, and be free. These capacities are not directly observable. In phenomenological terms, these are "structures" that precede all particular *acts* of caring, all *moments* of understanding, and all individual *expressions* of freedom. The importance of studying such existential structures lies in their ability to reveal the modes in which human beings experience the world, live in the world, and make important choices.

In contrast to such an "existential" examination, an "existentiell" (*existenziell*) analysis is concerned with the *observable* facts of human material existence. Heidegger argues that one cannot perform an "existential" (ontological) analysis of human beings without also paying due attention to their actual "existentiell" ways of existing and acting. In fact, Heidegger famously stated that the essence of the human being *"lies in its existence."*[10]

Da-sein: The Being of the Interpreter

Even though Heidegger was a student of Edmund Husserl, the father of phenomenology (and he even dedicated *Being and Time* to him), Heidegger developed his phenomenology in a different direction. Perhaps the best way to clarify this issue is to explain Heidegger's neologism for the human being, namely "Da-sein."[11] In everyday German, the word "Da-sein" means "life," "existence," or, more literally, "to be" (*sein*) in a particular "there" (*Da*) or "here." In other words, the "being" (*sein*) of every Da-sein – you or I – is embedded in both a particular "place" and "time." The importance of the hyphen in "Da-sein" should not be overlooked: because "Da" signifies a historical place and "sein" signifies "being" in an actual historical time, the hyphen signifies that each human being, as Da-sein, constitutes the unique intersection of a specific place and a time. In its most profound depths, Da-sein is always inextricably connected to the inexhaustible complexity of the particular, unique, nonsubstitutable, lived experience in its own time, and its own body. Every Da-sein is a hyperdifferentiated singularity. In many ways, Heidegger's Da-sein is the antithesis of Husserl's idealized, human consciousness. Unlike Husserl, Heidegger was interested in *particularized* human existence. The term Da-sein allowed him to refer to an individual, particular human life, which is to say in *your* life, and in *my* life: "The being which is an issue for this entity in its very being, is in each case mine" (BTMR 150).

Da-sein is neither characterized by a stable, unchanging essence nor determined by any such essence. Whereas an entity (a thing) is the sum of its fixed properties, Da-sein does not have fixed properties. Its particular characteristics at any given

---

[10] BTS, 40, § 9.

[11] Though Macquarrie and Robinson (BTMR) rarely hyphenate 'Da-sein,' Joan Stambaugh states in her introduction that Heidegger himself came to prefer the hyphenated version because it was less prone to psychological connotations. Heidegger believed that human beings are "uncanny," which is to say we do not really know what a human being is, because we *are* it (BTS, xiv).

moment are only possible ways, among many, for it to exist in the world. Its characteristics "are in each case possible ways for it to be, and no more than that."[12] In other words, Da-sein is an open possibility: it is a "becoming" more than a "being." It is a "be(com)ing." For this reason, authentic Da-sein is never being self-identical from one moment to the next. It is always becoming what it presently is not.

Da-sein always understands itself in terms of its existence, in terms of its possibility to be itself or not be itself. Da-sein has either chosen these possibilities itself, stumbled upon them, or already grown up in them. Existence is decided only by each Da-sein itself in the manner of seizing upon or neglecting such possibilities. We come to terms with the question of existence always only through existence itself. We shall call this kind of understanding of itself existentiell understanding.... For this the theoretical perspicuity of the ontological structure of existence is not necessary. The question of structure aims at the analysis of what constitutes existence. We shall call the coherence of these structures existentiality. Its analysis does not have the character of an existentiell understanding but rather an existential one. (BTMR 52)

Heidegger's use of the term Da-sein, in place of a term such as "Man" or "human being," also allows him to avoid the traditional subject-object binarism of Western metaphysics (cf. Chapter 4). We previously discussed David Caspar Friedrich's painting *Wanderer above a Sea of Mists*, which depicts the ideal of the modern sovereign subject contemplating the world from afar. Da-sein is not such a Cartesian subject: it is not a thinking soul implanted into a human body. In fact, Heidegger uncovers a dimension of human existence that is more primordial than both Aristotle's "Man" (as an "animal augmented with rationality" [ζῷον λόγον ἔχον], BTMR 74 § 10) and Descartes' "ego sum." Da-sein is more than an Aristotelian "rational animal" or a Cartesian "cogito." In fact, the term "Da-sein" implies a rejection of any attempt to compartmentalize human subjectivity as a thinking subject who stands over against the world. By implication, the term "Da-sein" implies a rejection of the self-understanding that many biblical scholars bring to their own acts of biblical interpretation.

Thrownness and Facticity

According to Heidegger, every human being – as Da-sein – is "thrown" into its own world (*Welt*). By "thrown," he means that Da-sein always finds itself *already* in a certain social, cultural, linguistic, historical, and religious environment, which is *not of its own choosing*. Heidegger terms this condition Da-sein's "thrownness" (*Geworfenheit*).

However, the world into which Da-sein is "thrown" is not "out there," exterior to its own being, waiting to be observed and analyzed. Da-sein is not thrown into its

---

[12] BTMR 68, § 9.

world the way a goldfish is dropped into a goldfish bowl. The world, within which Da-sein lives, is its environment. The world is not a container or receptacle for Da-sein to act. It is *interwoven* into the very structure of Da-sein's own existence.

You and I are characterized by such thrownness. Our thrownness extends back to our births (and even beyond through our awareness of and rootedness in the past). For this reason, we can never get outside of our particular world, or stand apart from it, in order to interpret it from a detached point of view beyond it or outside of it.[13] As "thrown" Da-seins, we always understand the things in our world – including biblical texts – in terms of the totality of our own involvements with our environment.

Da-sein is capable of catching "sight" (*Sicht*, §§ 31, 36, 69b) of its own thrownness. Heidegger terms this catching sight of itself "transparency" (*Durchsicht*). Transparency is not a self-absorbed introspection upon one's own interiority or inner soul. Transparency is always in relation to Da-sein's environment as "being-in" the world: "Understanding of existence, as such, is always an understanding of the world" (BTMR 186). Thus, by achieving such self-transparency, Da-sein actually sees itself not as a separate entity but as being relationally in its world:

The sight which is related primarily and on the whole to existence we call "transparency" [*Durchsichligkeit*]. We choose this term to designate "knowledge of the Self" in a sense which is well understood, so as to indicate here it is not a matter of perceptually tracking down and inspecting a point called the "Self," but rather one of seizing upon the full disclosedness of Being-in-the-world *throughout all* the constitutive items which are essential to it, and doing so with understanding. In existing, entities sight "themselves" [*sichtet "sich"*] only in so far as they have become transparent to themselves with equal primordiality in those items which are constitutive for their existence: their Being-alongside the world and their Being-with Others. (BTMR 186)

Perhaps the most important implication of Da-sein's thrownness is its "factical" nature. By "factical" (*faktisch*), Heidegger does not mean "factual" (*tatsächlich*). The term "facticity" (*Faktizität*) is derived from the Latin term *factum* ("constructed knowledge"). Owing to Da-sein's "factical" nature, the world is not "out there," ready to be analyzed by Da-sein. It is always, already, interwoven into the very structure of one's human existence (BTMR 56). By implication, factical experience is much more varied than just cognitive experience. It includes a wide range of existential concerns bound up with the "strife and struggle" (*Sturm und Drang*) of living. But Heidegger cautions that Da-sein often *fails* to catch sight of its own facticity. Heidegger describes this event as "opaqueness" (*Undurchsichtigkeit*) (BTMR 186–87).

---

[13] From Plato onward, philosophy has argued that essence precedes existence, though Jean-Paul Sartre was famous for reversing the order.

Everydayness

As noted, Division One begins with an examination of Da-sein's "everydayness" (*Alltäglichkeit*), which is to say, its *everyday,* uncritical mode of coping with things in daily life. In this "everyday" mode of living, Da-sein is generally opaque to itself because Da-sein is accustomed to *turning away* evasively from the truth of its own being. All people (including biblical scholars, ministers, and priests) spend much of their life in this self-evasive mode of living. As a result, Heidegger argues that we have an ingrained tendency to view ourselves in terms of what we are *not,* that is, as independent, sovereign subjects, detached from our context. In this everyday, self-evasive mode, we rarely question the significance of our own existence and, for this reason, we often live inauthentically.

Authenticity and Inauthenticity: The Proper and the Improper (§ 9)

As Da-sein, we find ourselves thrown into a particular context (our "there"), which we cannot step out of – much less escape from. Since every Da-sein is thrown into a particular family, culture, language, and society, its own being is *contingent.* Nevertheless, authentic Da-sein is not determined by these various contexts because its true being is characterized by having possibilities: as Da-sein, you are an open possibility of becoming that which you presently are not. As Da-sein, your life is not determined by your thrownness because your future is always more important than your past. You may "take up" your particular existence either "authentically" (*eigentlich*) or "inauthentically" (*uneigentlich*).

The term "authentic" can be explained as follows. The German term *eigentlich* is derived from the commonplace German adjective *eigen,* meaning "proper." The opposing adjective to *eigen* is the German term *fremd,* meaning "alien," "another's," or "strange." Thus, the meaning of *eigen* is comparable to the use of the English term "own" in the expressions "having one's *own* mind" and "being one's *own* person." In other words, living "authentically" (*eigentlich*) means being true to one's *own* self. It means living out the possibilities that arise out of your *own* "proper" being. This is the possibility that Da-sein *is:*

Da-sein is my own, to be always in this or that way.... Da-sein *is* always its possibility. It does not "have" that possibility only as a mere attribute of something objectively present. And because Da-sein is always essentially its possibility, it *can* "choose" itself in its being, it can win itself, it can lose itself, or it can never and only "apparently" win itself. The two kinds of being of authenticity and inauthenticity … are based on the fact that Da-sein is in general determined by always being mine. (BTS 40)

According to Heidegger, if Da-sein fails to choose to take up one of its *own* possibilities, it will "fall" into a possibility that is not of its own choosing. By failing to choose from among its *own* possibilities, and by allowing its existence to be determined by its environment, Da-sein always "falls" into the untruth of "inauthenticity." By "falling" into a possibility that it did not choose, Da-sein actually conceals its true being from itself. Heidegger calls this failure to realize one's ownmost authentic possibilities "inauthentic" existence.

Ready-to-Hand and Present-at-Hand (§§ 21–22)

In Heidegger's examination of the *manner* in which Da-sein interacts with things and people in its everyday mode, he introduced an important distinction between viewing things as "ready-to-hand" (*Zuhandenheit*) and as "present-at-hand" (*Vorhandenheit*). In Heidegger's terminology, the phrase "ready-to-hand" describes our *prereflective* familiarity with our environment and our intuitive practical knowledge. To say that the world is "ready-to-hand" means that it is tacitly meaningful and useful to us, prior to any rational or scientific analysis.

Heidegger argues that Da-sein's primordial (foundational) relationship to entities in its world is in a "ready-to-hand" (*Zuhandenseit*) mode. To view an entity as ready-to-hand is to view it in terms of its ways of usefulness. In other words, to view your environment as ready-to-hand is to see it in terms of your own daily ways of coping and interacting with your world and getting things done. In contrast, to view an entity as "being present-at-hand" (*Vorhandenseit*) is to see it as disengaged from its usefulness, as an isolated thing, possessing physical properties. For example, consider the distinction between viewing a ballpoint pen as ready-to-hand during the process of writing a letter with it and, when its ink runs out, viewing the same pen as present-at-hand, that is, as an object possessing physical properties. In daily life, we are so accustomed to seeing things as ready-to-hand that it actually requires an adjustment of our attitude to see them as mere objects, that is, as present-at-hand: "When we have to do with anything, the mere seeing of things which are closest to us bears in itself the structure of interpretation, and in so primordial a manner that just to grasp something *free*, as it were, *of the 'as,'* requires a certain readjustment" (BTMR 190). For example, we are so accustomed to seeing a hammer *as* a tool for nailing that an effort is required to see it as merely a physical object endowed with properties.

In his Freiburg lectures, Heidegger describes the experience of looking at a table in his house.[14] He did not simply see *a* table, but a particular table in a particular room of his house. In the first instance, he did not see the table as a present-at-hand object, possessing geometric and physical properties (e.g., dimensions, type of wood, types of joining, decorations, finish). Rather, he saw it as ready-to-hand, for writing letters upon, or for the sharing of food with family and friends. He could also look back into the past and recall past events celebrated around this table and look forward to future events around this same table. In each case,

---

[14] Martin Heidegger, *Ontologie: Hermeneutik der Faktizität* [1923], *Gesamtausgabe* 63 (Frankfurt am Main: Vittorio Klostermann, 1975), 88–92.

the table's precise physical dimensions and composition are not as important as whether the table is the appropriate size for his purposes (e.g., for dining, for writing), and whether it is in an appropriate relation to other things in the room (e.g., its proximity to a source of light, to a radiator for heat). In every case, his primordial perception of the table is not as an object with physical characteristics but as a *relational* entity, which is imbued with "sense" (*Sinn*). This is to say that when we see a table as ready-to-hand, we see it as belonging to the totality of our personal involvements with things and people within our lives. This totality of his involvements constituted a web of possible significances for the table.

Because we normally view the things in our world as ready-to-hand, they are primarily familiar to our consciousness in a nonpropositional way. For example, in contrast to a purely academic study of the Bible, many people read the Bible as ready-to-hand, that is, as part of the totality of their existential world of involvements, in ever-widening circles of relations.

Heidegger's distinction between ready-to-hand and present-at-hand is also important for his deepening analysis of Da-sein. Inauthentic Da-sein perceives itself as present-at-hand, that is, as a disengaged, self-sufficient, and independent subject. However, this self-perception is false. *We can never be present-at-hand to ourselves.* We can never stand outside of ourselves and observe ourselves objectively. Authentic Da-sein always understands itself as being ready-to-hand, that is, as belonging to a larger system of relations. As we shall see, Da-sein is full of concern for these relations, as part of its own care for itself. Because Da-sein is not a subject, and can never authentically become a subject, the Bible can never authentically be a present-at-hand *object* of scientific inquiry, for one cannot have an object without a subject (a basic premise of post-historical hermeneutics).

Being-in-the-World and Being-with Others (§§ 25–27)

Da-sein is not merely spatially "in the world," as a goldfish is *in* a bowl of water, or as an engagement ring is *in* a velvet box. The "world" is woven into the very existence-structure of Da-sein, in its "everydayness," and, consequently, the being of Da-sein is inextricably connected with innumerable kinds of relations beyond it. Heidegger refers to this mode of living as "being-in-the-world" (*In-der-Welt-Sein*). By virtue of its "being-in-the-world," the "world" (*Welt*) is never objectively present to Da-sein. Rather, the "world" constitutes the sum of Da-sein's environmental relations. It is the place where Da-sein has its concernful relations of "being-with" (*Mitsein*) others (BTMR §§ 25–27). "Being-with" others, in personal relationships and various kinds of communities, is a primordial (ontological) feature of Da-sein's own existence-structure. By implication, one's quest for authenticity does not involve isolating oneself in an effort to catch a glimpse of one's own interiority. Rather, part of the truth of Da-sein's being is that it cares for other people and that its own being is bound up with the being of others. In other words, Da-sein is *existentially* in-the-world *with others*. This observation has one important implication for biblical hermeneutics: because an interpreter's own horizons of "sense," and the interpreter's future projections of possible ways of living, are always bound up with one's being-in-the-world and being-with others, these *relations* must form the basis of the interpreter's own self-knowledge.

Fallenness and the Anyone-Self (§§ 25–27)

Heidegger terms the character of the inauthentic life the "anyone-self" (*das Man*). By "anyone," Heidegger does not mean other people.[15] The "anyone-self" refers to Da-sein itself to the extent that it conceives of itself in terms of how other people think of it and, as a consequence, becomes closed off to its ownmost possibilities for existence. Da-sein has a tendency to overlook its own possibilities for becoming. Indeed, according to Heidegger, for the most part, Da-sein is unaware of its ownmost possibilities for *existence*. As a result, Da-sein becomes just an "anyone-self" and "constantly lags behind its possibilities."

Heidegger terms such lagging behind one's possibilities Da-sein's "fallenness" (*Verfallen*).[16] "Fallenness" means *falling away from one's own possibilities for living*. Da-sein is *primordially* fallen. It can break free from its fallen mode of existence only by "finding itself again in its possibilities."[17] But Heidegger, who had previously studied Augustine's *Confessions*, comes to the conclusion that the achievement of a fully authentic existence is impossible: Da-sein's everyday existence will always be characterized by some degree of fallenness. Authenticity will always be a matter of degree.

Da-sein's Three Modes of "Being-in-the-World" (§§ 29ff.)

At this point in Division One, Heidegger undertakes a more fundamental analysis of the structures of Da-sein's being-in-the-world. By digging beneath Da-sein's everydayness, Heidegger disclosed three more foundational existential modes of existence, namely the structures (capacities) of "attunement" (*Befindlichkeit*), "understanding" (*Verstehen*), and "talk" (*Rede*, § 15). Taken together, these structures of existence comprise three interrelated "existentials" (*Existenzialen*) that characterize Da-sein's existence.[18]

---

[15] Das Man, BT §§ 25–27, 35–38, 51, 52, 59, 68 c, 71, 73, 81 (hereafter *Being and Time*, either English edition, abbreviated as BT).

[16] Verfallen, BT §§ 25–27, 35–38, 51, 52, 59, 68c, 71, 73, 81.

[17] BTMR 183 § 31.

[18] "Existentials" are different from "categories." Categories concern the properties of entities in general (e.g., hardness, heaviness), whereas existentials are structures that are proper to Da-sein alone. In contrast to these three authentic modes, Heidegger describes three corresponding inauthentic modes: namely, ambiguity (*Zweideutigkeit*), curiosity (*Neuigier*), idle talk/prattle (*Gerede*) (35–77). In contrast to "attunement," "ambiguity" arises when Da-sein becomes so engaged in "going along with the world" that it can no longer distinguish between the assertions given by the world and the truths revealed in its own understanding.

ATTUNEMENT (BEFINDLICHKEIT). Heidegger's strange term *Befindlichkeit* is notoriously difficult to translate. Macquarrie and Robinson misleadingly translated it as "state-of-mind." More recently, Joan Stambaugh suggests "attunement." More idiomatically, this term could be translated as "how one finds oneself." In other words, "attunement" is a form of prereflective awareness that guides Da-sein's day-to-day concernful dealings with the things in its world. More specifically, attunement is the ontological structure that allows Da-sein to be aware of its "moods," "thrownness," and its general outward-oriented character of "being-in-the-world."

The English term "moods" does not convey the breadth of meaning of the German term *Stimmung*. The term *Stimmung* connotes the manner in which one is concernfully disposed toward the world: "*Mood has always already disclosed being-in-the-world as a whole and first makes possible directing oneself toward something*" (BTS 129). Da-sein is always predisposed toward its world in one "mood" or another.[19] Moods are general attitudes that predispose us to view the world in a particular way such as threatening, or nurturing, or funny. For example, consider such negative moods as boredom and suspicion, and positive moods such as cheerfulness and hopefulness. When we are in a depressed mood, a particular person might appear to us as annoying and irritating, while the same person might seem comical when we are in an ironic or silly mood.

Interestingly, the German term *Stimmung* can also be used to describe the "tuning" of a musical instrument such as a violin. Likewise, Da-sein's moods *attune* it to its world in a particular way or bring it *into tune* with its own environment (Da). The main point is that biblical interpreters, as Da-seins, are always attuned to their world in a particular way and, like a violin, can even *re*tune themselves to their world.[20]

UNDERSTANDING. The second of the three existential structures is "understanding" (*Verstehen*),[21] which, according to Heidegger, is the most fundamental activity of Da-sein. Heidegger's term "understanding" does not name a specific process of cognition such as reasoning, interpreting, hypothesizing, or deducing. In fact, understanding precedes all such forms of knowing and interpretation. It actually constitutes the very possibility of Da-sein knowing or interpreting anything.

---

19 "[W]hen we master a mood, we do so by way of a counter-mood; we are never free of moods" (BTMR 175 § 29).

20 Though your moods cannot reveal this enigma to you, they do have the potential to disclose to you the manner in which you turn away from your own "thrownness": "The way in which the mood discloses is not one in which we look at thrownness, but one in which we turn towards or turn away [*An- und Abkehr*]. For the most part the mood does not turn towards the burdensome character of Da-sein which is manifest in it, and least of all does it do so in the mood of elation when this burden has been alleviated. It is always by way of attunement that this turning-away is what it is" (BTMR 174).

21 Cf. BT §§ 31, 32, 44, 58, 68.

The role of understanding is to disclose to Da-sein its own existence-structure, which is characterized by its authentic or inauthentic possibilities for becoming. First and foremost, Da-sein *understands* itself as being endowed with possibilities. Its very being is dynamic and future oriented: this is why Heidegger refers to understanding as the "to-be-able-to-be" (*Sein-können*) of Da-sein's existence.[22] Da-sein "*is* existentially that which, in its potentiality-for-Being, is *not yet*" (BTMR 185–86). Authentic Da-sein primordially experiences itself as having possibilities of becoming what it presently is not. This experience is *immanent* within Da-sein and ready to be expressed.[23] For this reason, Da-sein is always more than it is factually (*tatsächlich*) but is never more than it is virtually or factically (*faktisch*) (BTMR 185). Put simply, Da-sein's potentiality is prior to its actuality. Da-sein's "existence" implies that within Da-sein is the very possibility for it to express, in its existence, its true inner self.[24] In a very real sense, Da-sein is its ownmost possibility: its ownmost possibility is to become in actuality what it already is immanently.

The two existential modes, understanding and attunement, are equiprimordial.[25] In other words, "attunement" is *always* accompanied by understanding. Nevertheless, in Heidegger's view, understanding is existentially more significant to Da-sein than attunement because, while attunement reveals various aspects of Da-sein's actuality, it is understanding that discloses Da-sein's being a nest of possibilities for authentic existence. Authentic Da-sein is "attuned" to its own being and understands that it "has already got itself into definite possibilities. It either lets these possibilities pass by, or seizes them and makes mistakes" (BTMR 183).

Da-sein has the capacity to *understand* itself as being endowed with possibilities because of another existential structure, called "projection" (*Entwurf*).[26] By virtue of the fact that Da-sein is its ownmost possibilities, it is not determined by its thrownness: it possesses the capacity to project itself into its future. This projection is not thematic. In other words, it has no specific content, in the sense of a specific plan, project, or goal.[27] But through projection, Da-sein is able to hand

---

[22] Macquarrie and Robinson translate this term as "potentiality-for-Being."
[23] Thus, Da-sein is constantly more than it is factually (*tatsächlich*) but never more than it is factically (*faktisch*) (BTMR 185 § 31).
[24] BT § 4.
[25] "Equi-" here has the sense of "equally," therefore "equally primordial with." Primordial means close to the essential nature of *Being*.
[26] Cf. BT § 31. As projecting, Da-sein "throws before itself the possibility as possibility, and lets it *be* as such" (BTMR 185).
[27] Projecting is an ontological structure. "It has nothing to do with comporting oneself toward a plan that has been thought out, and in accordance with which Da-sein arranges its Being. On the contrary, any Da-sein has, as Da-sein, already projected itself; and as long as it is, it is projection. As long as it is, Da-sein always has understood itself and always will understand itself in terms of possibilities. Furthermore, the character of understanding as projection is such that the understanding does not grasp thematically that upon which it projects – that is to say, possibilities.... As projecting, understanding is the kind of Being of Da-sein in which it *is* its possibilities as possibilities" (BTMR 185).

over to itself its own possibility, which it itself immanently is in its own being: "[A]s projecting, understanding is the kind of being of Da-sein in which it *is* its possibilities as possibilities" (BTMR 185).

Despite the fact that you are thrown into a world that is not of your own choosing (which conditions and limits your possibilities for authentic existence), and even though you always experience the world through moods, you are still able to see new possibilities for living in the world. You are capable of seeing these possibilities only because you always see your environment as being significant to your being. By implication, your thrownness into the world is not significant for what it starkly and factually is but rather for what possibilities it presents to you for the future. In other words, through projection, your life is endowed with possibilities.

INTERPRETATION. Your mode of understanding *functions* as a way of knowing through "interpretation" (*Auslegung*). The term "interpretation" really means living out, in real life, the possibilities projected by the understanding:

This development of understanding we call "interpretation" [*Auslegung*].... In interpretation, understanding does not become something different. It becomes itself. Such interpretation is grounded existentially in understanding; the latter does not arise from the former. Nor is interpretation the acquiring of information about what is understood; it is rather the working-out of possibilities projected in understanding. (BTMR 188–89)

At this point, it must be observed that Heidegger's term "interpretation" (*Auslegung*) has a much broader meaning than the term "exegesis." The German term *Auslegung* means interpretation in a very broad sense. It is not a specific, or thematic, cognitive activity such as interpreting the meaning of a text. In contrast, the German term *Interpretation*, translated by the English term "Interpretation" (note the capital "I"), refers to the more practical and systematic forms of interpretation that we associate with biblical exegesis. In *Being and Time,* Heidegger is attempting "to determine the essence of interpretation [*Auslegung*]," not "Interpretation."[28] In simple terms, Heidegger is attempting to determine the *general* process by which we interpret anything. His starting point is the interpretation we employ in everyday life, when we are not even aware of interpreting. Throughout each day, we are constantly *interpreting* the world around us, which makes our experience of the world meaningful and real to us. Interpretation also allows us to accomplish everyday tasks and cope with life's challenges. In other words, each of us has a *hermeneutic* relation to our world.

Because Da-sein primordially understands the entities in its world as "ready-to-hand," it always interprets things *as* something with respect to their

---

[28]   Martin Heidegger, *Unterwegs zur Sprache* (Pfullingen: Neske, 1959), 98.

usefulness to itself: "We never perceive equipment that is ready-to-hand without already understanding and interpreting it" (BTMR 190). This brings us to what Heidegger calls the "as-structure" of interpretation. Interpretation views entities *as* (useful for) something, with respect to some kind of referential totality that is sketched out in advance by Da-sein. These possibilities for usefulness are not inherent in things themselves but are part of Da-sein's own existence-structure. However, as previously discussed, Da-sein's existence-structure is not isolated from the world: Da-sein is *in* the world and *with* others. Therefore, Da-sein does not throw a "signification over some naked thing which is present-at-hand. We do not stick a value on it; but when something within-the-world is encountered as such, the thing in question already has an involvement which is disclosed in our understanding of the world, and this involvement is one which gets laid out by the interpretation" (BTMR 190–91). Interpretation is always based on, and preceded by, Da-sein's many ways of relating to the world into which it has been thrown. As a result, in the very act of interpreting any thing, Da-sein illuminates its own existential-structure, which, as we have seen, is one of being-in-the-world. In any act of interpretation, that which is illuminated is not the present-at-hand thing itself or Da-sein as an isolated present-at-hand interpreting subject but is its existence-structure of Da-sein, as it exists in its "here" (Sein) and "now" (Da).

This concept can be illustrated with a quotation from Saint Augustine: "Unless you believe, you will not understand" (*Nisi credideritis, non intelligitis*),[29] which means that understanding is possible only when there is *pre*-understanding. This dictum can also be compared to Anselm's motto "faith seeking understanding" (*fides quaerens intellectum*). All this is to say that there is a long-standing awareness within the Christian tradition that every act of interpretation is grounded in, and is preceded by, forms of (faith-inspired) preunderstandings.

Heidegger terms this preunderstanding a "fore-structure." A "fore-structure" is an interpretive framework that we employ when we interpret events in daily life as meaningful. By implication, our experience of the world as meaningful is rooted in an ontological structure within Da-sein, which "exists" before the act of interpretation, which is why Heidegger terms it a *fore*-structure. He subdivides this fore-structure into three interrelated aspects: "fore-having" (*Vorhabe*), "fore-sight" (*Vorsicht*), and "fore-conception" (*Vorgriff*):

1. Fore-having means that you cannot interpret the meaning of an object, such as a hammer, unless you first have in your mind a preunderstanding of the "totality" of the hammer's "involvements which is already understood"

---

[29] Augustine, *De Libero Arbitrio* (On Free Choice of the Will), book I, chapter 2, section 4 (quoting from Isa 7:9).

(BTMR 191). In other words, fore-having is a *prior understanding* of a thing's totality of involvements: a hammer is connected to the totality of construction tools and equipment, such as saws, screwdrivers, measuring tapes, nails, and screws. This totality of equipment allows Da-sein to view a hammer from the perspective of this broader referential context of equipment. This taken-for-granted framework provides a structure for thought that predetermines the range of ways in which Da-sein can interpret and use any particular object such as a hammer.

2. Fore-sight is a prior point of view that directs one's attention, in advance of interpreting any one thing, to a specific issue or problem. For example, prior to a hammer being meaningful to me as ready-at-hand, I have the need to repair or build something, or I am able to anticipate such a need in my future (BTMR 191). In other words, fore-sight situates the meaning of an entity in terms of a specific form of usefulness.

3. Fore-conception concerns our ability to make an object's "as-structure" explicit (BTMR 191). One must be able to *make a connection* between one's fore-sight (as taxonomical framework) and one's fore-having (as a specific form of usefulness). For example, *prior to* interpreting a hammer, you have the conception of a hammer *as* a tool (within the totality of involvements of building tools) *and* you have the conception of your need of building a shed in your backyard. Put simply, fore-conception allows you to make a connection between the tool and the project.

All interpretation is guided by this tripartite fore-structure.[30] When Da-sein sketches out how it will make use of something, this is its meaning or "sense" (*Sinn*, §§ 32, 65). For example, the meaning of my hammer is to connect boards together with nails to build my shed. The significance of my furnace is to give off heat in my house and keep my family warm during the cold winter months. Thus, things in our own environment are *significant* to us because they fit somewhere within the "as-structure" of the whole of our fore-structure. Heidegger refers to this meaningfulness as the "hermeneutic *as*." By implication, the significance of things is formed by the very being of Da-sein itself:

Meaning is an *existentiale* of Da-sein, not a property attaching to entities, lying "behind" them, or floating somewhere as an "intermediate domain." Da-sein only "has" meaning, so far as the disclosedness of Being-in-the-world can be "filled in" by

---

[30] "Whenever something is interpreted as something, the interpretation will be founded essentially upon fore-having, fore-sight, and fore-conception. An interpretation is never a presuppositionless apprehending of something presented to us. If, when one is engaged in a particular concrete kind of interpretation, in the sense of exact textual Interpretation, one likes to appeal [*beruft*] to what 'stands there,' then one finds that what 'stands there' in the first instance is nothing other than the obvious undiscussed assumption [*Vormeinung*] of the person who does the interpreting ... that is to say, as that which has been presented in our fore-having, our fore-sight, and our fore-conception" (BTMR 191–92).

the entities discoverable in that disclosedness. *Hence only Da-sein can be meaningful* [sinnvoll] *or meaningless* [sinnlos]. That is to say, its own Being and the entities disclosed with its Being can be appropriated in understanding, or can remain relegated to non-understanding. (BTMR 193 § 32)

Understanding how something is significant requires that one understand the Da-sein for whom it is significant: "Da-sein is that entity which, as Being-in-the-world, is an issue for itself" (BTMR 182 § 31). With each new act of interpretation – including the interpretation of biblical texts – *Da-sein's fore-structure* is illuminated. To say that such-and-such a biblical text is significant to me is to say that it is significant within my fore-structure. Therefore, the sense of a biblical text is not a static concept concealed in the text. Sense is always a function of the organizing fore-structure of the interpreter. Da-sein is the place or site where this meaning-event happens. If we are to understand the present sense-event of biblical texts, it is necessary to understand the person of the interpreter, where this present sense-event unfolds. Thus, Heidegger concludes that in a hermeneutic inquiry *Da-sein is the being to be investigated.*

At this point, it is important to clarify that a fore-structure is not a set of consciously held beliefs, ideas, or ideological commitments. A fore-structure is a way of looking at the world that does not require legitimation or explanation. For example, the preunderstanding that God oversees all things and loves the world might be part of one's fore-structure. Similarly, most westerners assume that individuals take precedence over family and society and that society should be egalitarian, whereas many people who have been raised in East Asian cultural settings, based on Confucian values, assume the opposite. These are both *preunderstandings* of the world. Similarly, the concepts of "God," "history," "author," "normal," and "gender" often belong to one's fore-structure, and, as such, the fore-structure behind these concepts forms the basis of what we take to be Real.[31]

We should bear in mind that the examples Heidegger employs to elucidate Da-sein's fore-structure (e.g., the meaning of a hammer, a furnace, and a table) are intended to demonstrate only the *general conditions* of all interpretation. Needless to say, Heidegger is not particularly interested in the meaning of hammers per se. It is important to bear in mind that these examples in Division One serve to demonstrate how understanding belongs to Da-sein's everydayness. But Heidegger considers Division One to be a *preliminary* sketch, in which Da-sein is analyzed in its mundane "everydayness."[32] In such everydayness, the truth of our existence remains hidden because we habitually avoid authentic being. We routinely turn away from catching sight of our own being and instead prefer to view ourselves

---

[31] In contrast, one's conscious assent to the Westminster Confession, or Catechism of the Catholic Church, or to the Apostles' Creed would *not* be part of one's phenomenological fore-structure. But one's precritical faith would be part of one's horizon.

[32] *Alltäglichkeit*, BT §§ 9, 26, 27, 35–38, 51, 52, 59, 71.

in terms of what we are not, namely, independent subjects, who are independent from the world. In this uncritical, evading mode of living, we do not question the significance of our own existence. We return to this subject in our exploration of Division Two of *Being and Time*, where the question of significance is related to the realm of history, one's own people, heritage, and tradition. But first we must complete our discussion of Heidegger's preliminary interpretation of Da-sein, in its everyday mode in Division One.

The Hermeneutic Circle and the Disclosure of Truth

In our previous discussions of Schleiermacher and historicism (Chapters 2 and 3), we explained the concept of a hermeneutic circle, that is, the necessity of moving back and forth between the whole and the parts in the interpretive process. In the precritical exegesis of the Reformation, this hermeneutic circle involved the linguistic task of interpreting the individual parts of the Bible with reference to the whole canon of Scripture and, beyond this, to the whole of classical literature and then, in turn, understanding the whole of the canon in terms of its constituent parts. In the case of nineteenth-century historicism, the hermeneutic circle involved the historical interpretation of the discrete parts of history – individual persons, events, societies – in terms of an overarching historical narrative of progress and, then, reinterpreting this narrative totality in terms of these discrete parts. Heidegger revolutionized the hermeneutic circle by asserting that it is actually an ontological circle, not an epistemological one. In other words, the hermeneutic circle concerns the very being of Da-sein and its relation to its own world. As previously discussed, Da-sein's world is not "out there," beyond Da-sein, waiting to be analyzed; it is always interwoven into the very structure of Da-sein's own human existence. As being-in-the-world and being-with others, Da-sein is already inextricably caught up in innumerable kinds of relations with its environment (BT §§ 25–27).

Interpretation is an expression of these relations in terms of the fore-structure that makes them meaningful. As such, the general task of all interpretation is to describe *how* the world becomes significant to us. In his lecture "The Hermeneutics of Facticity," Heidegger states that the task of hermeneutics is not to develop a technique of interpretation but to make each Da-sein accessible to itself, that is, to allow Da-sein to come to itself "understandingly."[33] By implication, the goal of such interpretation is not the attainment of objective knowledge of things in the world but the overcoming of Da-sein's alienation. This implies that interpretation will necessarily have different characteristics for different interpreters.

But how is the process of interpretation circular? As you will recall, Husserl's phenomenological reduction has three steps: apprehending a phenomenon in

---

[33] Heidegger, *Ontologie*, 20.

consciousness, bracketing out from consideration the external objective content of the phenomenon, and reflecting on the inner transcendental process whereby its meaning (*noesis*) was formed. Similarly, Heidegger's hermeneutic circle begins when Da-sein interprets an entity in the world. But in order to appreciate *how* this entity has become significant to Da-sein, Da-sein must turn inward and circle back to disclose its own fore-structure that made this present sense-event possible. Da-sein, having moved out of itself in apprehending an entity, returns back into itself, repeatedly, in a circular motion, then circles back to the entity being interpreted with successive iterations. Each circle cycle provides greater insight into Da-sein's own fore-structure, thereby allowing Da-sein to interpret the significance of the entity in successively different ways as Da-sein progressively brings deeper and deeper levels of its fore-structure into focus.[34]

Heidegger is not searching for a way to escape this circle. There is no need to do so because, as Heidegger observes, this is not a "vicious" circle. The very limitations of the circular structure of interpretation also provide the positive conditions for understanding the significance of things. Indeed, without this circle, nothing would be meaningful to Da-sein. Thus, our "thrownness" is not an obstacle to be overcome in pursuit of final objectivity. Our own historical finitude is a positive starting point of all biblical interpretation. The objective is not to discover a way to break out of the circularity of interpretation but rather to enter into the circle resolutely:

But if we see this circle as a vicious one and look out for ways of avoiding it, even if we just "sense" it as an inevitable imperfection, then the fact of understanding has been misunderstood from the ground up. The assimilation of understanding and interpretation to a definite ideal of knowledge is not the issue here.... If the basic conditions which make interpretation possible are to be fulfilled, this must rather be done by not failing to recognize beforehand the essential conditions under which it can be performed: What is decisive is not to get out of the circle but to come into it in the right way. This circle of understanding is ... the expression of the existential fore-structure of Da-sein itself. It is not to be reduced to the level of a vicious circle, or even of a circle which is merely tolerated. In the circle is hidden a positive possibility of the most primordial kind of knowing. To be sure, we genuinely take hold of this possibility only when, in our interpretation, we have understood that our first, last, and constant task is never to allow our fore-having, fore-sight, and fore-conception [i.e., our horizon of interpretation] to be presented to us by the fancies and popular conceptions, but rather to make the scientific theme secure by working out these fore-structures in terms of the things themselves. (BTMR 194–95)

---

[34] Heidegger concludes that, because the logic of interpretation is circular, then "the business of historiological interpretation is excluded a priori from the domain of rigorous knowledge. We must give up the quest for a universal epistemology of hermeneutics. In so far as the Fact of this circle in understanding is not eliminated, historiology must then be resigned to less rigorous possibilities of knowing" (BTMR 194–95 § 32).

In the case of biblical interpretation, the validation of one particular interpretation over another does not lie in the verification of a hypothesis or proposition but rather in the ability of the interpretation to aid the interpreter in the living out of authentic possibilities of existence. In freedom, Da-sein chooses how it will open up the present sense-event of a biblical text. A "good" interpretation is one that causes the interpreter to exclaim "this is the truth which I've been looking for!" The ultimate goal of such an interpretation is to *enact* the truth that one discovers in one's own life. Your preunderstanding of yourself and your world guides what you focus on in a biblical text, whom you identify with in biblical narratives, and how you feel when you read a particular story (e.g., anxious, guilty, joyful, vindicated, angry). For example, the story of Jesus' compassion on the woman caught in an act of adultery (John 8:1–11), or the story of Jesus' harsh treatment of a Canaanite woman (Matt 15:21–28), or Jesus' explanation to the rich young man about how to enter into heaven (Mark 10:17–25) will all evoke different reactions in readers, depending upon factors such as gender, social status, and economic status. This fact illustrates how textual interpretation really requires an interpretation of one's own being. It requires that we open up ourselves to discover the fore-structure that made a text significant *to us* in a particular way.

Clearly, this hermeneutic circle is not an epistemological or methodological circle. It does not lead to the scientific advancement of disciplinary knowledge. It does not even subordinate a present sense-event to a preexisting independent, objective founding sense-event. Indeed, it cannot, because there is no subject and no object, which together constitute the metaphysical foundation for the concept of objective truth.[35] Whether objective truth exists independently of human understanding is beside the point. The point is that no such truth is accessible to Da-sein. Neither Da-sein nor that which is interpreted can ever be present-at-hand. Therefore, the point of interpretation is not to progress toward greater objectivity but rather to catch a glimpse of the revelation of truth in one's own be(com)ing.

The Clearing and the Happening of Truth (§ 44)

According to Heidegger, Da-sein's own existence-structure opens a space, or horizon, within which truth is revealed to Da-sein. But what does Heidegger mean by

---

[35] Heidegger states that the traditional philological and historical concerns of biblical studies are secondary: "[Philological Interpretation] belongs within the range of scientific knowledge. Such knowledge demands the rigour of a demonstration to provide grounds for it.... But if interpretation must in any case already operate in that which is understood, and if it must draw its nurture from this, how is it to bring any scientific results to maturity without moving in a circle, especially if, moreover, the understanding which is presupposed still operates within our common information about man and the world?" (194.2) Heidegger concludes that since the logic of interpretation is circular, then "the business of historiological interpretation is excluded a priori from the domain of rigorous knowledge. We must give up the quest for a universal epistemology of hermeneutics. In so far as the Fact of this circle in understanding is not eliminated, historiology must then be resigned to less rigorous possibilities of knowing" (BTMR 194).

"truth" (*Wahrheit*). What does it mean to speak of the truth of the New Testament? Traditional philosophical theories locate truth in propositions or judgments, that is, a proposition is true when it either corresponds to the facts or ideas as they really are (a correspondence theory of truth), or is consistent with and contained within an extensive system of knowledge (a coherence theory of truth),[36] or is practical or useful in terms of human wellness (a pragmatic theory of truth). These three theories of truth share one feature in common: they all locate truth in assertions or propositions.

Heidegger does not set out to contest any of these theories of truth. However, he does argue that these are derivative, or secondary, definitions of truth because each of them, in its own way, locates truth in the making of assertions. In contrast, Heidegger does not lay out criteria for determining whether an assertion is true or false. Rather, he explores the essence of truth. Put simply, he is not asking what is true but what is truth.

Heidegger argues that these theories of truth all depend on the primary meaning of truth, which is the phenomenon of *uncovering* something hidden. Heidegger's famous definition of truth is based on the Greek term for "truth," which is ἀλήθεια (*alithia*). Heidegger treats the initial *alpha* of this word as an "*alpha* privative." In other words, *alithia* is a negation of *lithia* (ληθεία), which would mean "hiddenness" or "concealment."[37] According to Heidegger, the essence of truth consists in uncovering something that was previously hidden or concealed. In effect, truth is the revelation of something in its "unhiddenness" (*Erschlossenheit*). Conversely, falsehood is a covering up, or distorting of truth as it really is.

It is important to stress that this concept of truth is prelinguistic. In other words, such truth is not identical to an assertion, a proposition, or a statement. Truth is a *disclosure* of the way things really are, which may or may not be subsequently formulated into the words of an assertion. For example, you might walk into your living room and see that the picture on the wall is askew. You recognize this truth, even though you probably will not linguistically formulate the proposition "the picture is askew." Hans-Georg Gadamer gives a more interesting example of beholding a work of art, or hearing a piece of music, and having the experience of being addressed by it directly, such that the experience becomes truth to you. You are seized by the truth of a work of art or music. Gadamer terms this an "authentic experience" of art.[38] In such an experience, you recognize the truth claim that proceeds from it, even though you may lack the linguistic ability to express adequately this truth in language.

[36] Heidegger remarks that "science in a general way may be defined as the totality established through an interconnection of true propositions" (BTMR 32 § 4).
[37] Though λήθεια is not actually attested in the Greek language, but cf. λήθη and forms of λανθάνω.
[38] Hans-Georg Gadamer, "The Universality of the Hermeneutic Problem" [1966], in *The Hermeneutic Tradition from Ast to Ricoeur*, ed. Gayle L. Ormiston and Alan D. Schrift (Albany: State University of New York Press, 1990), 147–58.

According to Heidegger, Da-sein is the place, or location, where such truth is uncovered and revealed. After all, only Da-sein asks the question, What is truth? Heidegger observes that "there is truth only in so far as Da-sein is and as long as Da-sein is" (BTMR 227). At the beginning of *Being and Time*, Heidegger states that Da-sein gets its own character from the act of inquiring into the truth of being:

The very asking of this question [of the meaning of being] is an entity's mode of *being*; and as such it gets its essential character from what is inquired about – namely, being. This entity which each of us is himself and which includes inquiring as one of the possibilities of its being, we shall denote by the term "Da-sein."[39]

To explain this concept, Heidegger employs the metaphor of a "clearing" (*Lichtung*).[40] A "clearing" is a piece of land within a forest in which trees have been cut down so as to create an *open space*. Whereas animals and birds can easily remain hidden and undetectable in a forest, they can easily be sighted when they walk or fly through such a forest clearing. According to Heidegger, Da-sein is such a clearing. In other words, Da-sein is a place – a "there" (Da) – in the world where truth can be sighted. But this is possible only because Da-sein is attuned to being, or *in tune* with being, in a unique way.

At this point, it must be stressed that Heidegger is *not* arguing that Da-sein determines what is truth. Da-sein is not a solipsistic ego, which introspectively searches its own interiority in an attempt to catch sight of its own hidden workings. Heidegger is not advocating a "subjective" or individualized concept of truth over an "objective" concept of truth. Remember that the terms "objective" and "subjective" are meaningless in a phenomenological analysis. The object-subject dualism is a myth of the Enlightenment (cf. Chapters 3 and 4). Therefore, asking what is truth apart from Da-sein is pointless because without Da-sein the question would never be asked. Besides, why would any person want to know a truth that is disconnected from human existence?

In any case, Heidegger is arguing that the only truth that Da-sein can catch sight of is the truth that becomes visible in the clearing, which Da-sein is. Da-sein is the place of the uncovering of truth. It is neither the foundation of truth nor the efficient cause of truth. Its role is not to actively and willfully construct truth but rather to wait for the truth of being to manifest itself within Da-sein. This advent of truth always belongs to truth's own destiny. But without Da-sein, there is no clearing for truth to be manifested. Da-sein is the time and place where an incessant repetition of various trial ways of truth can uncover itself.

According to Heidegger, truth normally remains concealed because Da-sein misinterprets itself as a subject and its environment as an object, owing to its own

---

[39] BTMR 27, § 2.
[40] "Clearing": our background experiences that allow things to show up in consciousness (BTMR 171, § 28, and n. 2; 215, § 36).

"fallenness" (BT §§ 35–38). When Da-sein thinks of itself as a subject, abstracted from its context, Da-sein becomes a nonrelational entity, which is to say, inauthentic. The truth of a biblical text can show up only in the clearing of Da-sein to the degree that Da-sein lives authentically. Because the attainment of authenticity is always partial, the sighting of truth will also always be partial. But even in the ideal case, when Da-sein's being is perfectly transparent to itself, the truth of a biblical passage would still be colored by Da-sein's mood, thrownness, fore-structure, and temporality. Therefore, there can be no noncontextual biblical truth: all we can have are poor sightings of truth and better sightings of contextual truth.

Assertions and Language (§§ 33–34)

The third existential mode of Da-sein is "discourse" (*Rede*). It is closely related to, and equiprimordial with, "attunement" and "understanding" (*Verstehen*). Heidegger discusses discourse in terms of Da-sein's being-in-the-word. The world already makes sense to Da-sein. But it is discourse, as an ontological structure, that endows Da-sein with the capacity to express what is significant to it, which is what Heidegger means by his statement: "To significations, words accrue."[41] Most of our day-to-day interpretations of the world take place without being formulated into assertions. When you see a hammer, it is immediately significant to you *as* a hammer. (You would think somebody quite odd who said, every time he sees a hammer, "This is a hammer.") Likewise, you may interpret the water falling from the sky as rain without ever making the assertion, "It is raining."

Heidegger calls the preverbal recognition of the meaning of things the "hermeneutic *as*." You see the hammer *as* a tool for hammering nails, and rain *as* a risk requiring one to take precautions (open your umbrella) or as an opportunity (your vegetable garden will get watered). But now imagine working all day with a hammer that is extremely heavy. As the day passes, your arm becomes tired and sore from hammering; you then interpret the hammer *as* having the property of heaviness, and you lay it down. The hammer, which you previously viewed as being ready-to-hand, you now view in its isolated "thingness" *as* present-at-hand, possessing the quality of heaviness. Heidegger terms this the "predicative (or apophantic) *as*."[42] In contrast to the "hermeneutic *as*," this "predicative *as*" points out one particular property of a thing. In asserting that "the hammer *is* too heavy," you are viewing it as a thing, possessing the property of heaviness, independent of your involvement with it as a tool.

---

[41] BTMR 161; "The doctrine of signification is rooted in the ontology of Da-sein" (BTMR 209). "Discourse is existentially equiprimordial with attunement and understanding.… Discourse is the articulation of intelligibility. Therefore it *underlies both interpretation and assertion. That which can be articulated is interpretation, and thus even more primordially in discourse, is what we have called 'significance'*" (BTMR 203–4).

[42] Or "apophatic *as*."

Heidegger's point is that one can derive propositional (assertive) truth from existential truth.[43] However, this shift from a "hermeneutic *as*" to a "predicative *as*" involves a modification of the practice of interpretation: what is interpreted is not the hammer as a ready-to-hand tool but the hammer as a present-at-hand object. In other words, the making of an assertion requires that Da-sein view itself as a detached subject, who makes an assertion about an object (a hammer), rather than as an entity located within a broader field of its existential relations. This is to say that assertions involve a stepping back from Da-sein's lived referential totality of involvements (BTMR 204–5). Whereas Da-sein would primordially relate to biblical texts as ready-to-hand, in the making of assertions about biblical texts these texts become detached objects of analysis.

According to Heidegger, all assertions are formed by "calculative" thinking. Calculative thinking "lets all beings count only in the form of what can be set at our disposal and consumed."[44] Calculative thinking is the form of thought that is endemic within our technological world: it is responsible for our "compulsion to *master everything* on the basis of the consequential correctness of its procedure."[45] Heidegger is not condemning the use of assertions. Indeed, the humanities and social sciences – including biblical studies and theology – all depend upon the formulation of such assertions. Assertions are necessary because they can be passed on to others as information and knowledge. Nonetheless, Heidegger considers assertions to represent a secondary, or derivative, form of interpretation. The formulation of assertions is a subset of the universal human practice of interpreting the world as ready-at-hand.

The necessity of formulating assertions should not overshadow the problems that they pose for us. First among these is the fact that all assertions are detached from their existential moorings. When one accepts an assertion in daily life, as one might in hearing a sermon, or class lecture, or watching the news on the television, one thereby detours the phenomenological structure that formed the assertion in the first place. My young son might assert that my hammer is heavy. I can accept this assertion as true. But when I might pick up the same hammer, I discover that I do not find it heavy at all. A friend who phones me from a nearby neighborhood might tell me that it is raining; but if I were to look out the window, I might see that it had not yet begun to rain in my neighborhood. Heidegger argues that when Da-sein lives in its inauthentic mode of everydayness, it accepts such assertions without testing them out and without having any direct experience of the entity itself. Similarly, when assertions are made about biblical texts, the existentially

---

43   "Communication" in which one makes assertions – giving information, for instance – is a special case of that communication which is grasped in principle existentially. In this more general kind of communication, the articulation of Being with one another understandably is constituted (BTMR 205).

44   Heidegger, "Postscript to 'What Is Metaphysics?'" in *Martin Heidegger: Pathmarks*, ed. and trans. William McNeill (Cambridge: Cambridge University Press, 1998), 231–38, esp. 235.

45   Ibid., 235 (emphasis added).

significant hermeneutical "as" is no longer available to the person who receives the assertion, unless she examines the text herself.

Care and Anguish (§§ 39–40)

As you will recall, in the process of exploring Da-sein's everydayness, Heidegger discovered three deeper ontological structures – namely attunement, understanding, and discourse. In this next section, he argues that beyond these three structures lies an even more foundational ontological structure, which he terms "care" (*Sorge*).[46] Authentic Da-sein does not interpret the world as an end in itself: Da-sein interprets the world because it cares, which takes such diverse forms as caring, anxiety, worry, and, especially, angst.

In Heidegger's terminology, "care" has a double sense. First, it means "caring," or being full of concern, about something. In daily life, care involves both concern about things (*Besorgen*) and solicitude toward others (*Fürsorge*). "Care" also means "taking care," or "being careful." When Da-sein anticipates or encounters challenging or threatening situations, it immediately takes care.[47] Of course, the importance of care is succinctly summed up in the Lord's Prayer, with the concernful request that God might supply the bread that we require for tomorrow (Matt 6:11). Thus, care is the fundamental structure that underlies and unites all aspects of your existence, especially with regard to your deep-seated concern for your future. Your possibilities for your future always arise out of you taking care. Through care, Da-sein can catch sight of its own being in two ways. First, care brings Da-sein to perceive its own, individual responsibility to serve as a horizon or clearing for the disclosure of the truth. As noted earlier, only Da-sein is able to open a space within itself in which truth is revealed.

Second, the gravity of this responsibility to serve as a "clearing" for Truth is qualified by a second realization, which is that Da-sein's being – as such a clearing – is radically finite and imperfect. The disclosure of truth in Da-sein is always finite and partial because Da-sein habitually lives inauthentically. Da-sein is a radically imperfect clearing for Truth. The apparent solidity of Da-sein's perspective, and of what it takes to be the meaning of life, is all formed by Da-sein's own radically imperfect horizon.

Thus, Da-sein recognizes – perhaps for the first time – that, ultimately, it is the clearing of nothing (*Nichts*). This experience of its own nothingness gives rise to an experience of profound "angst," which explains why, for Heidegger, angst is *the* fundamental mood: angst makes Da-sein aware that it is a "no where" (*nirgends*) and a "nonplace." It is the "placeholder" (*Platzhalter*) of nonbeing, of nothingness (*das Nichts*). To experience oneself as a "no where" (*nirgends*) and as a "nonplace"

---

[46] BT §§ 39–45, 57, 63–65.
[47] On the term "factical," see previous section on "Da-sein: The Being of the Interpreter."

is to feel "strange" or "uncanny" (*unheimlich*). It feels "strange" to recognize that one is not a permanent foundation for any truth: phenomenologically, each of us is actually an "abyss" (*Abgrund*, ἄβυσσος) and a "groundless place" (*das Grundloss*). Heidegger describes this experience of our own groundlessness as being cast out of one's own home. Da-sein is homeless being.[48]

Da-sein's experience of its own abysmal nothingness fills it with "terror."[49] While most people retreat from this frightful experience to the security of delusions of the inauthentic life, a few will dare to allow themselves to experience this abyss fully.[50] They are willing to open themselves up to this experience because they recognize that this experience can become a source of revelation (BTMR 224). Angst has a role in *rescuing* Da-sein from self-concealment and from becoming lost in the "anyone self." Through angst, Da-sein can recognize its own freedom to choose its own possibilities for authentic living. In other words, angst has the positive function: Da-sein now realizes that it must make some important choices in its life.

BEING AND TIME: DIVISION TWO

Heidegger's interpretation of Da-sein in Division One of *Being and Time* does not constitute his final definitive analysis of Da-sein's structures of being. After all, not even *Heidegger* could escape the hermeneutical circle in his own phenomeno-logical interpretation of Da-sein. His own preliminary analysis in Division One led him to the realization that his elucidation of "care," as a fundamental onto-logical structure, did not bring his analysis of the structural unity of Da-sein to a completion. Therefore, he continued his analysis of Da-sein in Division Two, in an attempt to deepen his preliminary analysis. He accomplished this by ground-ing Da-sein's care structure in a yet more fundamental structure, "temporality," working his way toward this goal via an analysis of angst, death, guilt, conscience, freedom, and resoluteness.

Angst and Being-toward-Death (§§ 46–53)

Heidegger resumes his analysis in Division Two with an examination of Da-sein's existence in time. He begins this process by identifying Da-sein's outer temporal limits, which is to say, its birth and death. As previously noted, Da-sein exists authentically by projecting itself toward its future possibilities. It is Da-sein's abil-ity to project itself into its future that causes it to anticipate its greatest future

---

[48] "Un-homeliness": cf. Charles R. Bambach, *Heidegger, Dilthey, and the Crisis of Historicism* (Ithaca, NY: Cornell University Press, 1995), 262.
[49] Heidegger, *Pathmarks*, 99, 102, 108.
[50] Bambach, *Heidegger, Dilthey, and the Crisis of Historicism*, 128.

limitation, namely its own death. Heidegger refers to this circumstance of antic-ipating death as "being-toward-death" (*Sein zum Tode*). In contrast to animals, which seem to lack the capacity to foresee their own nonexistence, Da-sein is able to anticipate its own death. Such "being-toward-death" begins the moment that Da-sein grasps the fact that all its words, deeds, and accomplishments are subject to the same outcome, that of nonexistence in the material world.

However, the term "death" in the phrase "being-toward-death" does not specify a future event that brings Da-sein's existence to an end, nor does being-toward-death denote the mere philosophical acknowledgment of the fact that everyone will sooner or later die. Rather, the anticipation of death functions by disclosing to Da-sein the "here" (*Da*) and "now" (*Sein*) of its material existence. In other words, death is not so much a future event that terminates its existence as it is a future inevitability *that brings Da-sein's present life into focus*. For this reason, Heidegger argues that the anticipation of death should become a source of authentic exis-tence, for only when Da-sein realizes that death is its ownmost, nonrelational, certain, yet indefinite possibility can it adopt an authentic attitude toward its own present life. Such an authentic attitude is the proof that Da-sein truly understands its own existence.

The ever-present knowledge that life is finite and that Da-sein could die at any moment permeates Da-sein's present with angst. This angst is neither a cowardly fear in the face of death, arising out of a weakness of the spirit, nor a hopeless despair in the face of death. Rather, angst is a basic mood that reveals that Da-sein is a "thrown being *towards* its own end" (BTMR 435). By bringing the reality of Da-sein's present existence into focus through the anticipation of death, angst also brings all of Da-sein's present decisions into focus, for Da-sein's sense of angst arising from being-toward-death compels it to explore, here and now, the actual possibilities that lie at the heart of one's own life.

Da-sein's Guilt and the Call of Conscience (§§ 54–62)

As noted previously, Da-sein habitually flees in the face of its own thrownness and falls into inauthentic existence. This is also true of being-toward-death: "Proximally and for the most part Da-sein covers up its ownmost being-toward-death, *fleeing in the face* of it."[51] By virtue of its inordinate desire for "comfortableness, shirking, and taking things lightly" (BTMR 435), Da-sein habitually conceals the uncertainty that lay at the very core of its own existence. Nonetheless, despite its predilection for self-concealment, its life also displays the countermovement of honest probing and struggle against its own everyday indifference. This countermovement allows Da-sein to become aware of its own inherent "negativity" (*Nichtigkeit*).

---

[51] BTMR 295 § 50; cf. Martin Heidegger, *Phänomenologische Interpretationen zu Aristoteles*, 2nd ed., *Gesamtausgabe* 61 (Frankfurt am Main: Vittorio Klostermann, 1994), 108–9.

Heidegger calls the ontological structure by which Da-sein becomes aware of its own negativity "conscience" (*Gewissen*).[52] Da-sein's conscience silently "summons" Da-sein from its lostness in the "anyone self" by making it aware of what Heidegger terms its "guilt" (*Schuld*). Heidegger does not employ the term guilt in a theological sense to specify the state of having committed a sin or transgression against a divine law. In Heidegger's phenomenological framework, guilt is the recognition of Da-sein's ontological fallenness. Consequently, it is never fully in control of its own being, and it constantly lags behind its own possibilities. This lack of control and lagging behind one's potential are two aspects of Da-sein's negativity. As such, the disclosure of Da-sein's guilt is really the disclosure of the negativity and abysmal strangeness that lies at the very core of Da-sein's own being.[53]

Once faced with its guilt, Da-sein's conscience directs it to make a choice in the present from among those choices available to it. But more primordial than Da-sein's freedom to choose are Da-sein's "attunement" (*Befindlichkeit*) to its world, its "moods" (*Stimmung* and *Bestimmung*), especially angst, and the "call" (*Anruf*) of its conscience. Da-sein's freedom is always qualified by the givenness of Da-sein's being. It must also be stressed that the conscience does not direct Da-sein to make any particular choice. Indeed, it is incapable of doing so because the "call" of conscience says "nothing" (*Nichts*). The call of conscience is actually an empty silence. Da-sein's conscience silently calls Da-sein and summons it from its lostness in the "anyone self" to "take care" (BTMR 318). If Da-sein is living authentically, it will accept this silent summons, first, by "taking care" and, second, by affirming its own "nothingness," which is a sign of its authentic anticipation of death (BT § 62). It is this affirmation of its own nothingness that constitutes Da-sein's authentic attitude toward itself. In contrast, inauthentic Da-sein evades its own inherent negativity and turns away from the inevitability of its own death.

Resoluteness before Death

The angst suffered in the anticipation of death can lead to authentic existence because, in response to this angst, Da-sein's conscience directs it to make a choice. Da-sein – whether living authentically or inauthentically – is destined to make a choice: "Once one has grasped the finitude of one's existence, it … brings Da-sein into the simplicity of its individual destiny" (BTMR 435 § 74). Authentic Da-sein adopts "*an impassioned freedom towards death – a freedom which has been released from the illusions of the 'they,' and which is factical, certain of itself, and anxious*" (BTMR 311 § 53). As being-toward-death, Da-sein reviews its life from its

---

52 Cf. the traditional notion of "conscience." While every Da-sein has a "Conscience," it may not have a "conscience."
53 Cf. Giorgio Agamben, *Language and Death: The Place of Negativity*, trans. Karen E. Pinkus with Michael Hardt (Minneapolis: University of Minnesota Press, 1991), 1.

anticipated death to its birth and, in a moment of "clarity of vision" (*Augenblick*), resolutely *chooses* its ownmost "destiny."[54]

Making such a choice is not a one-time event. It requires "resoluteness" (*Entschlossenheit*, § 60). Heidegger's account of Da-sein's "resoluteness" is shaped, in part, by his interpretation of the accounts of the conversion of the apostle Paul in the book of Acts (Acts 9, 22, 26), as well as by Plato's famous allegory of the cave (*Republic* VII, 514–17). Paul, having experienced a moment of "clarity of vision" on the road to Damascus, came to see his life from a radically altered perspective. With this new clarity of vision, Paul, "who formerly persecuted" the church and "tried to destroy it," then proclaimed the faith he once tried to destroy (Gal 1:23). Similarly, the allegory of Plato's cave tells the story of ordinary men who were held prisoners in a cave. On the wall of the cave, they observed the shadows of the things in the real world outside the cave, cast there by the bright sun. Eventually, a few of these men left the cave and went out into the world and saw for the first time the things of the world as they really were. They then realized that all they had previously seen were mere shadows of the real. With this new clarity of vision, they returned to the cave to persuade their fellow prisoners to leave behind the shadows of the real to experience the real world as it is in itself. In Heidegger's view, Da-sein, like Saint Paul and the men of Plato's cave, can experience a similar moment of clarity of vision, brought on by the action of angst and the call of conscience. Together, they assist in revealing to Da-sein that it has contented itself too long with mere shadows of the real. Like Paul and the men in Plato's cave, authenticity hinges on Da-sein leaving behind falsehoods, half truths, and the shadows of the real. In Heidegger's estimation, it is Da-sein's "individual destiny" (*Schicksal*) to make this choice.[55]

Authentic Da-sein will *resolutely* choose a future from among the many possible futures available to it. Such possible futures are always related to, but not determined by, Da-sein's past, including its religious heritage and the history of its people (*das Volk*). Da-sein is also thrown into the heritage of its religious tradition as a horizon of its future possibility. By implication, Da-sein's "individual destiny" (*Schicksal*) is grounded in a "destiny" (*Geschick*) that it shares with others: "But if fateful Da-sein, as being-in-the-world, exists essentially in being-with-others, its historicizing (of its religious heritage) is a co-historicizing and is determinative for it as a *destiny of a people*" (BTMR 384). This "shared destiny" of a people (*Geschick*) is not merely an aggregate or summation of the destinies (*Schicksal*) of its individual members. Individual destinies become part of a shared destiny by means of their interaction in a shared world of meaning. Heidegger insists that only in

---

[54] Martin Heidegger, "Letter on Humanism," in *Martin Heidegger: Pathmarks,* ed. William McNeill (Cambridge: Cambridge University Press, 1998), 239–76.

[55] BTMR 435–36. Here, the term "destiny" has nothing to do with predestination. Da-sein's future is not limited to one specific outcome or to a predetermined series of events.

the labor of common life and work, and in the exchange of ideas and struggle of debate, can this corporate destiny of a "generation" be fashioned (BTMR 384–85).

Temporality (§§ 65–71)

Having examined the outer limits of Da-sein's extension in time – its anticipated death and its "thrownness" at birth – and the related structures of conscience, call, guilt, freedom, and resoluteness, Heidegger argues that Da-sein's care structure is grounded in a still deeper and more fundamental structure, namely, "temporality" (*Zeitlichkeit*). Da-sein's "care-structure" cannot serve as the ultimate unity of all of its modes of being because the very structure of care is actually constituted by its temporality.[56]

The term "temporality" does not designate our publicly shared perception of quantitative clock time. We have been socialized to perceive time as an unending sequence of quantified units of time, of minutes, hours, days, and weeks, for dealing with those things that affect our present well-being (e.g., my meals, my home, my health, my protection, my place in the world).[57] From a historical and scientific perspective, time is a linear succession of identical "nows," a kind of "neutral time," by which all events can be measured objectively.[58] Heidegger refers to this perception of time as "mundane" time or "world-time."[59] From the perspective of mundane time, your past and future are merely past and future times for getting things accomplished.[60]

This manner of conceiving time must be learned. It is a cultural construct. Children are not born with this sense of quantitative time. At birth, a child experiences time as a *unity* in which its future-oriented mode of expectation and its past-oriented mode of retrieval become fused within a present moment of resoluteness. By implication, each Da-sein has its *own* authentic time: authentic time is always *my* time: "In so far as time is in each case mine, there are many times."[61] This unity of existential time – which Da-sein is – is not an objective datum available to the historian.

Heidegger attempted to dismantle our acculturated understanding of mundane time by rooting time in Da-sein's own primordial structures. He argued that the connection of Da-sein's past to the present is not the fundamental relation because the present of authentic Da-sein is not just a deterministic working-out of the past. Ultimately, what is important to Da-sein is not the relation of the past to the

---

56   BTMR 19; Heidegger, *Concept of Time,* trans. William McNeill (Oxford: Blackwell, 1989 [1924]), 20.
57   Bambach, *Heidegger, Dilthey, and the Crisis of Historicism,* 236–37.
58   Ibid.
59   BTMR 429–34, § 73; cf. 499, n. xiii.
60   Heidegger, *Concept of Time,* 20E.
61   Ibid., 21.

present but the relation of the future to the past because it is the future that opens up a way to break free from the historical causality of the past.[62]

The Three Ek-stases (§§ 65–69)

The future, past, and present constitute three structural moments, or what Heidegger refers to as the three "ek-stases" of Da-sein's temporal existence. The Greek term *ek-stasis* (ἔκ-στασις) literally means "standing out."[63] Heidegger employs it to specify the manner in which Da-sein's existence stands out *in time*.[64] Da-sein's fundamental *ek-stasis* is in the future (*Zukunft*): Da-sein's existence "stands out" in the future whenever it projects its potentiality-for-being (*Seinkönnen*). Da-sein also "stands out" in its own past, but its past is not a linear series of "nows" that have ceased to be; Da-sein continually *retrieves* its past in its own present being.[65] Da-sein equally "stands out" in its present because the present is where the future and past *ek-stases* meet: the future-oriented mode of projection and past-oriented mode of retrieval are both "made present" (*gegenwärtig*) within the present moment: this is what Heidegger means by "temporality" (*Zeitlichkeit*). Heidegger's point is not that Da-sein's being is shaped by temporality. Rather, he is arguing that *Da-sein's being is its temporality*. This insight transforms our concept of time from that of a linear series of "nows" beyond our own individual essences into the process that each of us individually embodies. In his Kassel lectures, Heidegger states:

Da-sein is nothing other than the being of time [*Zeit-Sein*]. Time is nothing that one meets with in the world outside but is what I myself am.… Time determines the totality of Da-sein. Not only in a temporally particular moment is Da-sein there, but it is itself only as a being stretched along between its possibilities and its past.[66]

---

[62] Cf. Proust, Joyce, Aldo Rossi's *"Theatre of Memory" in Venice*.

[63] Ecstasy, that is, out of time: because the ground of Da-sein is free for its own possibilities, it is essentially futural. Thus, it is not only a (thrown) child of its time, but also a child beyond its time (cf. "fate").

[64] In fact, for Heidegger, *Ek-sistence* means "standing out into the truth of being" (249). Ek-sistence, according to Heidegger, is the only proper way for a human "to be." This is what he means by "essence is ek-sistence," a statement made in direct response to Sartre's lecture on humanism (247). This lecture had lumped Heidegger with "the other humanists" (Fell 156). Heidegger responded by stating that Sartre, while having reversed Plato's "essence precedes existence," had nevertheless been taking the *traditional metaphysical* meaning of "essence." "Sartre's 'subject' is a modification of the Cartesian *cogito* that rejects the *cogito's* substantiality or nontemporal instantaneous self-inherence but retains its character as an irreducible or absolute *fundamentum inconcussum*" (159). In Sartre's view, then, subject and object are at opposite ends of the spectrum and defined by one another (159). In Heidegger's thought, by contrast, nothing is separate: neither thought nor world, neither subject nor environment (162). Indeed, the only thing that separates Da-sein as "interpreter" as opposed to an "interpretee" is its status as being-aware of its own Being (162). Hence, concludes Heidegger, if we hold to the traditional metaphysical and Western definition of "essence," then we have not given humanism its "proper dignity" (Heidegger 251).

[65] "An entity of the character of Da-sein is its 'there' in such a way that, whether explicitly or not, it finds itself [*sich befindet*] in its thrownness" (BTMR 174).

[66] Heidegger, "KV," 22.

Heidegger's Lectures on Galatians and 1 Thessalonians

Before the publication of *Being and Time*, Heidegger taught a course entitled "Introduction to the Phenomenology of Religion" (1920–21).[67] The purpose of these lectures was not to interpret Galatians and 1 Thessalonians theologically or historically but to interpret Paul's letters phenomenologically. In other words, Heidegger was not interested in the overt conceptual content of Paul's ideas (*Vorstellungsgehalt*) about the Christ's Parousia (παρουσία), or "second coming." Instead, he set out to elucidate the early Christian experience of time itself. He set out to discover what is "primal" or "original" about early Christianity (*Urchristentum*), as experienced in the factical lives of the first Christians, particularly in the churches of Galatia and Thessalonica.[68] Heidegger believed that these letters reveal aspects of the primal experience of the earliest Christian experience of time.

In his letter to the Thessalonians, the climax of Paul's message is found in 1 Thessalonians 4–5, where he clarifies the fate of those Christians who died before the Parousia of Christ (1 Thess 4:13–18). In these chapters Paul sets out to answer the Thessalonians' question, "When will the Lord return?" (1 Thess 5:1–12). If we are to understand Paul's response to this question, we must appreciate his understanding of time. Kairotic time is not measurable in terms of days, weeks, and months. It cannot be observed as something present at hand. The distinction between historical time and kairotic time is the distinction between when and how.[69] Heidegger argues that Paul understood human life to be implicated in two heterogeneous kinds of time, termed respectively *kairos* (καιρός) and *khronos* (χρόνος).

For the purposes of this discussion, let us call *kairos* "kairotic time" and call *khronos* "historical time." Historical time refers to our everyday, publicly shared perception of quantitative (clock) time. But, as noted earlier, at the time of one's birth one experiences time more as kairotic time, which is to say, as a unified flow of life that opens up to future possibilities. Kairotic time always possesses the ungraspable quality of the "now" of the present moment.[70] Kairotic time and mundane time are coextensive. In other words, kairotic time is not the future of historical time, nor is it separable from historical time.[71] In one of the writings of

---

[67] "Phänomenologie des religiösen Lebens" (Wintersemester 1920/21), *Gesamtausgabe* 60, part 2, ed. Matthias Jung and Thomas Regehly (Frankfurt am Main: Vittorio Klostermann, 1995).

[68] These lectures also dealt with Paul's letter to the Galatians, but his treatment of this letter is much briefer and, for our purposes, less interesting.

[69] Klaus Held, "Phenomenology of 'Authentic Time' in Husserl and Heidegger," *International Journal of Philosophical Studies* 15/3 (Sept. 2007): 327–47.

[70] Elsewhere, in Ephesians and Colossians we find the expression ἐξαγοραζόμενοι τὸν καιρόν, that is, "buying up kairotic time." This phrase conveys a special dimension of kairotic time (Eph 5:16; τὸν καιρὸν ἐξαγοραζόμενοι, Col 4:5).

[71] The "experience (of 'kairotic time') doesn't pass before me as a thing that I set there as an object; rather, I myself 'appropriate' (*er-eigne*) it to me, and it properly happens or 'properizes' (*es er-eignet*) according to its essence" (Heidegger, *Gesamtausgabe* 56/57, 75).

the Hippocratic Corpus (a collection of ancient medical writings associated with Hippocrates), the following maxim is found: "*Chronos* [historical time] is that in which there is *kairos* [kairotic time], and *kairos* is that in which there is a little *chronos*."[72] In other words, they are folded into one another. When one seizes one's own kairotic time, one is not seizing a time that is different from historical, every-day time: kairotic time is a moment of historical time, which one has taken hold of and brought to fullness.

Thus, when the Thessalonian Christians ask Paul when Christ will return (1 Thess 5:1), they are asking a question about historical time. But Paul thinks that this is the wrong question. The right question is about kairotic time, namely "*How* should we wait?"[73] This explains why Paul does not answer the Thessalonians' question at all. Instead, he redirects their question by observing, "You know very well that the day of the Lord is coming like a thief in the night" (1 Thess 5:2). With this statement, he redirects their interest away from historical to kairotic time, that is, on *how* they should live in expectation of the Parousia.

Heidegger argues that understanding the Parousia from a phenomenological perspective requires that we abandon our mundane Western conceptions of historical time, and especially the cultural trappings of Jewish and early Christian apocalypticism, and instead contemplate the "how" of living in the present. Rather than answering the Thessalonians' question about the historical "when" of Christ's return, Paul probes the very core of the Christian experience of time as *time struggled*. For Paul this meant "keeping awake" in the present (γρηγορῶμεν, 1 Thess 5:6). According to Heidegger, Paul experienced time as a "struggle" (*der Kampf*), characterized by wakefulness, in which every moment demands an existential decision because one's very being is at stake.[74] Thus, kairotic time is always a time of struggle, crisis, and decision. It is always characterized by a wakefulness in the present moment.[75]

Theoretical detachment is impossible within kairotic time because the authenticity of one's own life is always at risk. This explains why, in 1 Thess 5:3–6, Paul compares two ways of living based respectively on historical and kairotic time. On the one hand, there are those who live in a way that ignores the kairotic dimension of time and are lulled into a false sense of security. According to Paul, such people will one day be caught by surprise: "Ruin will fall on them with suddenness of pains overtaking a woman in labor and there will be no escape" (1 Thess 5:3). On

---

[72] Cf. Giorgio Agamben, *The Time That Remains: A Commentary on the Letter to the Romans* (Stanford, CA: Stanford University Press, 2005), 68.

[73] Sheehan, "Heidegger's 'Introduction to the Phenomenology of Religion,'" 1920–21," 57–58.

[74] Cf. Paul's admonition to the Thessalonians to "keep awake" (γρηγορῶμεν). The verb γρηγορέω is derived from the perfect of ἐγείρω, ἐγρήγορα; "So then let us not sleep, as others do, but let us keep awake and be sober" (1 Thess 5:6).

[75] Heidegger described this experiential time as "the enacted-historical situation" (*die vollzugsge-schichtliche Situation*) (*Gesamtausgabe* 9:93).

the other hand, there are those who live by the slogan, "Let us be watchful and self-controlled" (γρηρῶμεν καὶ νήφωμεν). Such people will not be caught by surprise (1 Thess 5:6b).

Wakefulness is not about counting down the days until Christ's coming. It is not about "killing time," as one would wait for a train or a bus to arrive at a station. The distinction between the experiences of time as "killing time" and "time struggled" captures the difference between living in historical time and living in kairotic time. Living in kairotic time is the experience of living in a state of constant wakefulness and readiness, which draws together one's time-consciousness into one unifying moment of engaged decision making.

Actualization involves a peculiar "kairotic" moment of illumination that comes from full alertness to my situation. The when of the Parousia (being "before God") is now determined by the how of my self-comportment ... and this in turn by the actualization of my factic life-experience in and through every moment. How the Parousia stands in my life refers back to the full temporal actualization of my life, and not to a passing when.[76]

In Heidegger's view, this kairotic time-consciousness is a central dimension of early, primordial Christian experience. The authentic Christian does not live *in* time but rather *lives* time: "Understanding is ... from the outset established a *Da-sein's being wakeful* for itself."[77] Living wakefully means that every moment calls for a decision that may lead to greater authenticity or inauthenticity. In this light, Paul's exhortation to "be watchful and self-controlled" (1 Thess 5:6) conveys the need to be alert to the present moments as an opportune time to take up one's existence authentically, while recognizing that our "attunement" to our world, our angst, and the "call" (*Anruf*) of conscience always precedes and qualifies such choices. As such, the early Christian eschatological consciousness provided Heidegger with a model of the factical-historical life, which was more fundamental to Da-sein's being than the quantifiable past, present, and future time. In so doing, Heidegger changed historical inquiry from a mode of explaining the past to an exploration of the urgency of living time in the present.[78]

History, Historicality, and Historiology (§§ 72–77)

In Heidegger's view, our commonplace understanding of history is a bundle of incompatible concepts. Is history a story about something that is past, cut off from the present, and therefore more or less irretrievable, or is history inextricably bound up with the present, in a people's sense of their background, origin, or descent? Or is history a kind of endowment that is handed down to the present in the form of

---

[76] Theodore Kisiel, *The Genesis of Heidegger's "Being and Time"* (Berkeley: University of California Press, 1993), 186.
[77] Heidegger, *Gesamtausgabe* 63:15.
[78] Bambach, *Heidegger, Dilthey, and the Crisis of Historicism*, 220.

tradition? Heidegger argues that all three of these understandings of history arise out of Da-sein's inauthentic historicality (*Geschichtlichkeit*). In Heidegger's view, the problem of history is essentially rooted in the problem of the historicality of Da-sein. As previously explained in Chapters 3 and 4, history does not exist *independently* of the historians who write history. In a very real sense, history for us is always historiology, that is, a product of the thematizing of the isolated facts of history. Such thematizing is termed "historiology." According to Heidegger, historiology (*Historie*) is rooted in Da-sein's own "historicality" (*Geschichtlichkeit*).[79]

The term "historicality" can be explained as follows. Since time *is* process that Da-sein embodies, in the form of the three *ek-stases* and being-toward-death, history finds its unity in the temporality of Da-sein's present existence. If one imagines Da-sein's existence is a kind of story, or a "little history," that begins at the time of one's birth and ends at the moment of death, then it is the temporal existence-structure of Da-sein that provides the foundation for the possibility of thinking historically. In other words, it is only because Da-sein's existence is itself a little story that past events, construed as continuous narrative, can be significant to Da-sein. Thus, the historicality of the interpreter or historian is itself the source of all views of history: "If Da-sein's being is in principle historical, then every factical science is always manifestly in the grip of this historicizing" (BTMR § 76). By implication, the foundation of history is not historical persons, artifacts, or historical facts but rather the existence-structure of Da-sein. We can grasp actual history (*Geschichte*) only through historiology because historical inquiry always implicates Da-sein in its own primordial relation to time.

There is a necessary relation between the "happening" (*Geschehen*) of Da-sein and the "happening" of history. These two happenings interconnect in the following way: since Da-sein's futural orientation (*ek-stasis*) is primary, authentic Da-sein's historical understanding will also be fundamentally future oriented and the historical past will always be felt as something that impinges on, and shapes, the Da-sein's future: "History as *Geschichte* signifies a happening that we ourselves are, where we are there present.... We are history, that is, our own past. Our future lives out of its past. We are carried by the past."[80]

Charles Bambach observes that Heidegger's radical idea of the historicality of time transformed "the meaning of history from a question of logical method and scientific research to an ontological exploration of the roots of human beings in the world."[81] This interconnection between history and our own historicality is an

---

[79] The German term "historiology" (*Historie*, §§ 76, 77), that is, the science of writing history.

[80] Heidegger's 1925 lecture, "Wilhelm Dilthey's Research and the Struggle for a Historical Worldview," in *Supplements: From the Earliest Essays to Being and Time and Beyond*, ed. John van Buren (Albany: State University of New York Press, 2002). 147ff.; "Wilhelm Diltheys Forschungsarbeit und der Kampf um eine historische Weltanschauung," quoted in Bambach, *Dilthey, Heidegger, and the Crisis of Historicism*, 242.

[81] Bambach, *Heidegger, Dilthey, and the Crisis of Historicism*, 131.

essential feature of human existence. By implication, it is the projective structure of the interpreter of historical facts that makes history significant: "The 'selection' of what is to become a possible object for historiology *has already been met with* in the factical existentiell *choice* of Da-sein's historicality, in which historiology first of all arises, and in which alone it *is*" (BTMR 447). In other words, the interpreter is the source of historical significance.[82] After all, it is Da-sein who asks, What difference does today introduce with respect to yesterday?

Post-historical hermeneutics recognizes that interpreters cannot understand historical inquiry without a hermeneutical reflection on the factical nature of their own historicality. Da-sein's caring (*Sorge*) about the past is part of Da-sein's temporal structure. By implication, any historical inquiry that is dedicated solely to uncovering the antiquarian minutiae of the past actually represents a form of thought that alienates Da-sein from its own authentic historicality (BTMR 448).

Heidegger's Reflections on Nietzsche's The Use and Abuse of History

In §§ 75–76 of *Being and Time*, Heidegger discusses the second of Friedrich Nietzsche's *Untimely Meditations*, entitled *The Use and Abuse of History* (1874).[83] In this tract, Nietzsche described three modes of historiography: namely, a monumental, an antiquarian, and a critical mode. According to Nietzsche, when history is viewed from a monumental perspective, we appreciate that "the great which once existed was at least *possible* once and may well again be possible sometime."[84] He declares that such monumental history is needed by "the active and powerful person ... who requires models, teachers and comforters, and cannot find them among his associates and contemporaries." Such a person wants to "create greatness" (§ 2). From monumental historiography, the powerful man derives "great *driving impulses*" (§ 2.5). But Nietzsche cautions that the monumental view of history has some disadvantages, for "if the monumental consideration of the past rules over the other forms of analyzing it, I mean, over the antiquarian and the critical methods, then the past itself suffers *harm*."

History, when viewed from an antiquarian perspective, belongs to the historian, who "with loyalty and love looks back upon his origins ... [trying] to preserve the conditions in which he grew up,"[85] that which is "the customary and traditionally

---

[82] Heidegger, *Gesamtausgabe* 61:76; cf. Theodore R. Schatzki, "Living Out of the Past: Dilthey and Heidegger on Life and History," *Inquiry* 46/3 (2003): 301–23.

[83] Friedrich Nietzsche, *On the Advantage and Disadvantage of History for Life,* trans. Peter Preuss (Indianapolis: Hackett, 1980 [1874]); cf. Foucault's appropriation and modification of this in "Nietzsche, Genealogy and History," in *Language, Counter-memory, Practice,* ed. Donald F. Bouchard, trans. Donald F. Bouchard and Sherry Simon (Ithaca, NY: Cornell University Press, 1977), 139–64.

[84] Nietzsche, *On the Advantage and Disadvantage of History for Life,* § 2.

[85] Ibid., § 3.1.

valued."[86] But Nietzsche argues that the antiquarian historian looks at *too few* things, and what he does see he

> looks at too closely and in isolation. [He] cannot measure it and therefore takes everything as equally important. Thus for the antiquarian sense each single thing is too important.… Here there is always the imminent danger that at some point everything old and past … is taken as equally worthy of reverence but that everything which does not hold this respect for ancient things, like the new and coming into being, is rejected and treated as hostile.[87]

Antiquarian history tends to bury "further living … when the historical sense no longer conserves life, but mummifies it.… Antiquarian history knows only how to *preserve* life, not how to generate it. Therefore, it always undervalues what is coming into being."[88]

In contrast, what Nietzsche terms critical historiography (§ 3.5) belongs to the *living* person, who suffers from the oppressive weight of history and who feels that "history … sits in judgment and passes judgment [on him]." Such a person "wants to cast off" this burdensome "load at any price."[89] Nietzsche recognizes that neither monumental, antiquarian, nor critical mode is above suspicion. Each can be used or abused. For example, he mocks the "moldy" work of the antiquarian historian whose writings serve only to paralyze human action and instincts (§ 3) and, in so doing, have "mummified" modern man (§§ 1–4, 10):

> A person must have the power and from time to time use it to break a past and to dissolve it, in order to be able to live. He manages to do this by dragging the past before the court of justice, investigating it meticulously, and finally condemning it.… Here it is not righteousness which sits in the judgment seat or, even less, mercy which announces judgment, but life alone, that dark, driving, insatiable self-desiring force.… When we condemn that confusion [of the past] and consider ourselves released from it, then we have not overcome the fact that we are derived from it. (§ 3.5)

Nietzsche argues that there are two ways in which one can break away from the stultification of academic history. The first way is to embrace the "unhistorical" by learning to forget the past (§ 10) like a placid herd of cattle.[90] The second option, which of course Nietzsche recommends, is to become "super-historical." To become "super-historical" means to turn aside from the transitory to that which is eternal, especially art and true religion (in contrast to the denatured historicized Christianity of nineteenth-century Germany) and, with a creative spirit and religious vision, create a "harmonious whole" (§ 6). In Nietzsche's view, this is the only way to bestow an eternal character upon the history (§ 10). His final advice to

---

86 Ibid., § 2.7.
87 Ibid., § 3.2–3.
88 Ibid., § 3.2–3, 4.
89 Ibid., § 2.7.
90 Ibid., preface 1.

historians, which could also be directed at biblical interpreters today, is to make a "loving study" of the ancient documents, with the creative vision and artistic spirit required to create out of them a "harmonious whole" (§ 6).

According to Heidegger, when Nietzsche described the monumental, antiquarian, and the critical modes of historiography, he may have "understood more than he has made known to us" (BTMR 396), for these three modes of historiography correspond to the three temporal *ek-stases* (as outlined earlier). Da-sein's existential journey cannot begin with Nietzsche's antiquarian mode, in which one sifts through dusty historical records to preserve the past because the primary moment of Da-sein's existence is the future (BTMR 446): "Da-sein exists authentically as futural" when, by coming "back resolutely to itself, it is, by repetition, open for the 'monumental' possibilities of human existence" (BTMR 448). Authentic Da-sein always explores the past in terms of its future: "*[H]istoriological* disclosure temporizes itself *in terms of the future.* The 'selection' of what is to become a possible object for historiology *has already been met with* in the factical existentiell *choice* of Da-sein's historicality, in which historiology first of all arises, and in which alone it *is*" (BTMR 447).

According to Heidegger, Nietzsche's monumental mode corresponds to future *ek-stasis* because it is full of anticipation. As resolutely futural, Da-sein is "open for the 'monumental' possibilities of human existence" (BTMR 396). From this futural perspective, history (historiology) has the potential to disclose what Heidegger refers to as "the quiet force for the possible."[91] History can present possibilities because it is multilayered (*vielschichtig*) and fateful (*geschicklich*) in the sense that it provides the foundation for all of Da-sein's decisions for authentic or inauthentic choices (BTMR 448). This is because the past constitutes "the existentiell possibility in which individual destiny, corporate destiny, and world history have been factically determined" (BTMR 447). Having caught sight of its own future possibility, Da-sein then surveys the possibilities for existence which it has inherited from the past and inserts its own future into them. It is this understanding of history *as a future-directed quest* that lets the course of events be "brought to fruition" in one's own actions.

Only an entity which, in its being, is essentially futural ... and can let itself be thrown back upon its factical "there," ... that is to say, only an entity which, as futural, is equiprimordially *having-been*, can, by handing down to itself the possibility it has inherited, take over its own thrownness and be in the moment of vision for "its time." (BTMR 437)

To this it must be added that Nietzsche's monumental mode of history remains incomplete without the antiquarian mode, which is a kind of remembering that throws Da-sein back onto the past. As Heidegger observes, "For the most part, it

---

[91] BTMR 447; cf. Heidegger, *The Concept of Time,* 20E.

is only through the work of traditional history, passed down to us, that historiology penetrates what has-been-there itself" (BTMR 447). In Heidegger's view, this mode of remembering and preserving of the past corresponds to Da-sein's past *ek-stasis*. Only by "reverently preserving" the past can Da-sein find a way of "seizing upon" a possibility for its future (BTMR 443, 448). Heidegger argues that this antiquarian mode requires a humble and respectful attitude of *pietas* toward one's religious heritage and a "loyalty" to history in the sense of "revering ... the repeatable possibilities of existence":

> The Resoluteness in which Da-sein comes back to itself discloses its current factical possibilities of authentic existing, and discloses them in terms of the *heritage* which that resoluteness, as thrown, *takes over....* If everything "good" is a heritage, and the character of "goodness" lies in making authentic existence possible, then the handing down of a heritage constitutes itself in Resoluteness. (BTMR 425)

But it cannot be emphasized enough that authentic historiography *does not begin* with the antiquarian mode of "acquisition, sifting, and securing" the biblical documents and archaeological remains of the ancient Mediterranean world. Da-sein's future-oriented being provides "the existential foundation for historiology as a science, even for its most trivial and 'mechanical' procedures" (BTMR 446). In other words, *repetition of the past is always repetition forward*. Da-sein reviews the heroes of the past, *only after it has run ahead to its own future* and gazed with angst upon its own coming death. By reverently preserving the religious heritage and tradition passed on to us, Da-sein is brought face to face with its own "individualized" possibilities for existence, which are its own "unshakeable joy."[92]

Da-sein's destiny is to make a choice from among its possibilities. Da-sein, having returned to its past, its history, heritage (*das Erbe*), and tradition (*Überlieferung*), is presented with possibilities for living. Da-sein surveys the heroes of its heritage, those women and men who have lived lives characterized by faith, courage, integrity, and service, and discovers in these lives new possibilities for living in the present. For example, the narrative of Sarah and Abraham holds up the possibility of leaving the safe and familiar behind and going to unknown places with God as their only security. The life of Jeremiah embodies the possibility of proclaiming God's Word in dangerous circumstances. The story of Anna and Simeon exemplifies the possibility of living in hope, year after year, with patience and faithfulness. The life of the apostle Paul epitomizes the possibility of breaking down old barriers of faith that divide people. The life of Thecla raises up the possibility of serving

---

[92] Martin Heidegger, "Letter on Humanism," in McNeill, *Martin Heidegger: Pathmarks*, 239–76. But Heidegger adds that "proximally and for the most part the Self is lost in the 'they.' It understands itself in terms of those possibilities for existence which 'circulate' in the 'average' public way of interpreting Da-sein today" (BTMR 435); cf. Gianni Vattimo, *The End of Modernity* (Baltimore: Johns Hopkins University Press, 1991 [1985]), 86.

God faithfully in the midst of persecution. To respect such heroes does not mean to literally repeat their historical lives in one's own life but rather to repeat the *possibilities for living* that their lives have demonstrated. As Heidegger observes,

The resoluteness which comes back to itself and hands itself down, then becomes the *repetition* of a possibility for existence that has come down to us. Repeating *is handing down explicitly* – that is to say, going back into the possibilities of existence that have come down to us. The authentic repetition of a possibility of existence that has been – the possibility that Da-sein may choose its hero – is grounded existentially in anticipatory resoluteness, for it is in resoluteness that one first chooses the choice which makes one free for the struggle of loyally following in the footsteps of that which can be repeated. (BTMR 485)

Thus, whereas historicism viewed history as unique and unrepeatable, in principle, Heidegger argued that history sheds light on possibilities for life that can be repeated and counteractualized in the future. This would require us to meditatively recollect these historical lives with a view to the possibilities inherent in them. This form of recollection transforms historical inquiry from an antiquarian reconstruction of the facts of the past for its own sake to a respect for the past as a disclosure of a future possibility on the basis of "the factical existent possibility that *has been*" (BTMR 441–47).[93] The seizing of one of these possibilities for existence is made possible only in a moment of clarity of vision.

Consequently, "the struggle of loyally following in the footsteps" of a past hero does not involve the literal reproduction of a particular historical life, say of Jesus, Mary Magdalene, or Paul, in one's own life. The essential importance of the great women and men of the past lies not in the bare facts of their historical lives but in the possibilities inherent in their lives that can be taken hold of again. This means that the question that you must ask is, What difference does your future introduce with respect to possibilities for existence offered up by the heroes of the past, *as passed on to us by our shared history, tradition, and religious heritage?*

The Repetition, Dismantling, and Destruction

Da-sein does not abandon itself to the past in some form of historical literalism. A "repetition" (*Wiederholen*) of the past would not take the form of a mimetic reenactment, or reproduction, of the historical lives of Jesus, Paul, or the early Christian saints.[94] Heideggerian hermeneutics does not aim at uncritically restoring one to

---

[93] Similarly, in the field of history, David Harlan argues that presentist history raises up texts "from the graveyard of dead contexts ... helping them take up new lives among the living." Harlan urges historians to take a stance in writing history as a form of "moral reflection"; David Harlan, *The Degradation of American History* (Chicago: University of Chicago Press, 1997), xxxii–xxxiii (emphasis added).

[94] John D. Caputo, *Radical Hermeneutics: Repetition, Deconstruction, and the Hermeneutical Project* (Bloomington: Indiana University Press, 1987), 60–61.

an uncritical or idealized understanding of the past, nor would it attempt to over-come the imperfect historical reconstructions of scholars by distilling some sort of generic moral truth or maxim.

The theme of historiology is neither that which has happened just once for all nor some thing universal that flows above it, but the possibility that has been factically existent. This possibility does not get repeated as such – that is to say understood in an authentically historiological way – if it becomes perverted into the colorlessness of a supratemporal model. (BTMR 447)

Heidegger argues that repetition requires that we cultivate "recollective think-ing" (BTMR 443–44), through which the possibilities for existence, offered up by the past, can be redirected. In his later writings, Heidegger also called for taking "a creative view of tradition," reinterpreting what came before in the light of a monu-mentalized vision of what we can be.[95] But Heidegger argues that such repetition of the possibilities offered up by the past may require some form of "dismantling" (*Abbau*) and even "destruction" (*Destrucktion*).[96] He remains suspicious of tradi-tion and is prepared to carry out a destruction of aspects of it in light of the pull of the future.

We must not lose sight of this *necessary* tension in Heidegger's view of tradition as that which is both necessary and indispensable, but also something that can be dangerous, requiring that aspects of it be bracketed out or dismantled. Nietzsche had previously argued that the critical historian "must have the power ... to break with the past and to dissolve it, in order to be able to live ... by dragging the past before the court of justice, investigating it meticulously, and finally condemning it."[97] In a similar manner, Heidegger argues that recollective thinking may require that the traces of the past be "twisted" so that they can function in new ways.[98] Having caught sight of various past possibilities for existence, Da-sein must make a reciprocal rejoinder to these possibilities with the counterpossibilities.

But when one has, by repetition, handed down to oneself a possibility that has been, the Da-sein that has-been-there is not disclosed in order to be actualized over again. The repeating of that which is possible does not bring again something that is "past," nor does it bind the "Present" back to that which has already been "outstripped." Arising, as it does, from a resolute projection of oneself, repetition does not let itself be persuaded of something by what is "past," just in order that this, as something which as formerly

---

[95] Heidegger, *Introduction to Metaphysics*, 155.

[96] *Destruktion* is a key term in Heidegger's early writings. It was first used by Heidegger in a course he taught in the summer semester of 1920. His use of this term is rooted in Luther (Bambach, *Heidegger, Dilthey, and the Crisis of Historicism*, 197). The term *Destruktion* summarizes his idea of phenomenology with respect to the uncertainty of one's own existence. In the years following his "turning" (*Kehr*), he attempted *Destruktion* of *Geisteswissenschaften* (Bambach, *Heidegger, Dilthey, and the Crisis of Historicism*, 201–3; Caputo, *Radical Hermeneutics*, 60–61).

[97] Nietzsche, *On the Advantage and Disadvantage of History*, § 3.5.

[98] Vattimo, *End of Modernity*, 172, 179.

actual, may recur. Rather the repetition makes a *reciprocal rejoinder* to the possibility of that existence which has-been-there.... But when such a rejoinder is made to this possibility in a resolution, it is made in a *moment of vision; and as such,* it is at the same time a *disavowal* of that which in the "today," is working itself out as the "past." Repetition does not abandon itself to that which is past, nor does it aim at progress.[99]

CONCLUSION

For the past two centuries, the "subject" versus "object" binary opposition has constituted the epistemological foundation for the legitimation of the biblical interpretation, with its emphasis on "explaining" (*erklären*) biblical texts as historical objects of knowledge. The ensuing crisis of historicism was, first and foremost, a crisis of the metaphysics of the knowing subject. But the quest for the objective meaning of early Christian history has ended by establishing biblical studies in a nihilism from which it has yet to escape.[100] This rationalist model did not achieve its noblest goals because it failed to appreciate the manner in which its objects of inquiry – early Christian history and texts – are formed as knowledge and made present (*gegenwärtig*) by the interpreter (Da-sein). Consequently, this objectifying mode of inquiry has led to a dislocation between the person, as academic interpreter of the Bible, who creates new historical knowledge about the Bible, and the same person, who desires to live an authentic human existence as time struggled.[101] Ironically, though many contemporary biblical interpreters are dissatisfied with the discipline's inability to address existential issues, they nonetheless remain attached to the metaphysics of subjecthood that lies at the core of this crisis. One of the legacies of Heidegger's phenomenological analysis is the recognition that the life of the biblical interpreter cannot be separated from human existence. In a letter to his student Karl Löwith, Heidegger wrote, "I work concretely and factically out of my 'I am.' ... I do not separate ... the life of scientific, theoretical, conceptual research and my own life."[102] The implication of this crisis of subjecthood is that we can grasp the present sense of the Bible only by appropriating it from within our historicality. As such, our own historical consciousness, including our angst, beliefs, hopes, values, and commitments, is not an obstacle to be overcome but rather the very source of hermeneutical significance.

---

[99] BTMR 437–38, § 74.
[100] "Historicism characterizes modernity" because in establishing a metaphysical vision of time as pure temporal succession, it persistently undergirds, and reinforces, the modernistic logic of overcoming." Gianni Vattimo, "*Verwindung:* Nihilism and the Postmodern in Philosophy," *Substance* 16/2, issue 53 (1987): 7–17, esp. 25.
[101] See Heidegger's *Beiträge zur Philosophy* (*Gesamtausgabe* 65 [Frankfurt am Main: Vittorio Klostermann, 1989], 494), where he compares *Geschichte* and *Historie* with respect to a point of decision.
[102] Dietrich Papenfuss and Otto Pöggeler, *Zur Philosophischen Aktualität Heideggers: Symposium der Alexander von Humboldt-Stiftung, vom 24–28. April 1989, in Bonn-Bad Godesberg* (Frankfurt am Main: Vittorio Klostermann, 1990–92), 29.

Heidegger addressed this crisis by arguing that it is not an epistemological problem but rather a crisis of Western consciousness. As such, this crisis creates an opportunity: for if "the enigma of history lies in what it means to *be* historical," then the crisis of historical positivism actually opens up an opportunity for us to abandon the inauthentic models of what it means to be human and to explore our own human historicality more deeply.[103] By implication, the real challenge before us is to cast off the outer cloak of the autonomous, rational subject. Biblical interpretation does not require neutrality.[104]

According to Heidegger, the basic meaning of "crisis" (κρίσις) is a "breaking away" from something, leading to a point of decision. Thus, the "crisis" of historicism leads us to a point of decision about "the use and abuse of history." Because the quest for an objective, early Christian history cannot be reconciled with the facticity of one's own being, Heidegger argues that the three modes of historiography – monumental, antiquarian, and critical – should be *unified* into one authentic historiology, which would make the "past vital again – and bring it into a future."[105] In the words of Gianni Vattimo, we can conceive of the past "as a message that we have to knowingly interpret and transform ... accepting history," not as a cause but "as open to the future."[106]

Thus, Heidegger's analysis of Da-sein provides a way for the biblical interpreter to think outside the "subject versus object" epistemological structure. A certain

---

[103] Heidegger, *The Concept of Time*, 20E. "The essence of *Historie* is grounded in the subject-object relation; it is objective because it is subjective and insofar as it is the one, it must be the other. Consequently, any 'opposition' between 'subjective' and 'objective' *Historie* has no meaning. All *Historie* ends in anthropological-psychological biographism" (Heidegger, *Beiträge zur Philosophy*, 494).

[104] "We still have scholars today who busy themselves with philosophy and who consider freedom-from-every-standpoint not to be a standpoint, as though such freedom did not depend upon those very standpoints. These curious attempts to flee from one's own shadow we may leave to themselves, since discussion of them yields no tangible results. Yet we must heed one thing: this standpoint of freedom-from-standpoints is of the opinion that it has overcome the one-sidedness and bias of prior philosophy, which always was, and is, defined by its standpoints. However, the standpoint of point-lessness represents no overcoming. In truth it is the extreme consequence, affirmation, and final stage of that opinion concerning philosophy which locates all philosophy extrinsically in standpoints that are ultimately right in front of us, standpoints whose one-sidedness we can try to bring into equilibrium. We do not alleviate the ostensible damage and danger which we fear in the fact that philosophy is located in a particular place – such location being the essential and indispensable legacy of every philosophy – by denying and repudiating the fact; we alleviate the danger only by thinking through and grasping the indigenous character of philosophy in terms of its original essence and its necessity, that is to say, by posing anew the question concerning the essence of truth and the essence of human Da-sein, and by elaborating a radically new response to that question." M. Heidegger, *Nietzsche*, vol. II: *The Eternal Recurrence of the Same*, ed. David Farrell Krell (New York: Harper & Row, 1984), 118.

[105] Heidegger, *Die Frage nach der Wahrheit*, Gesamtausgabe 21 (Frankfurt am Main: Vittorio Klostermann, 1976), 14.

[106] Gianni Vattimo, *A Farewell to Truth*, trans. William McCuaig (New York: Columbia University Press, 2011 [2009]), xxxiii.

freedom comes from knowing that authentic hermeneutic understanding is never objective or scientific. It is always valid and invalid at the same time. Though it is an ungrounded discourse, persons of Christian faith must still pay heed to it: having been divested of their subjecthood, they are nonetheless confronted with the necessity of coming to a decision about the significance of the Bible *for their own lives in the present*. An authentic understanding of the Bible should be occupied not solely with the assembling of antiquarian facts into a coherent, grand (historical or theological) narrative but rather with discerning the possibilities for life that have been passed on to us by the past. Such a renewed form of interpretation will always require that we take seriously our own existential challenges and the challenges of the contemporary world. Those who dare to adopt such a hermeneutic mode will discover that it has the potential to usher one into the kairotic dimension of time.

6

Faith and History: Bultmann's Debate with Barth

In every moment slumbers the possibility of being the eschatological moment.
You must reawaken it.[1]
Always in your present lies the meaning of history.[2]

Like many of their contemporaries, Rudolf Bultmann and Karl Barth experienced the crisis of historicism profoundly. In response, Bultmann and Barth, along with Paul Tillich and Emil Brunner, broke with the optimism of nineteenth-century German Protestantism and developed what is now known as a theology of crisis, or "crisis theology." For his part, Bultmann (1884–1976) developed his theology of crisis in the direction of existentialism, owing to the profound influence upon his thought of Heidegger's early writings, especially *Being and Time*. Bultmann and Heidegger met each other at the University of Marburg, where Bultmann was appointed lecturer in New Testament in 1921. Heidegger's appointment there in the following year afforded them the opportunity to become close colleagues. Interestingly, these were the very years when Heidegger was writing *Sein und Zeit* (*Being and Time*).[3]

The first edition of *Sein und Zeit* (*Being and Time*) was published in 1927. However, it was not until 1962 that it was translated into English, more than thirty years later. This considerable delay in the production of an English translation may explain not only why Heidegger's existential phenomenology was slow to be taken up by the English-speaking world but also why Bultmann, a leading exponent of Heidegger's early existentialism in the field of New Testament studies, has often been misunderstood and, more recently, ignored by English-speaking scholarship.[4] Curiously, the fact that both Bultmann and Heidegger died in the same year (1976) underscores the fact that they belonged to the same generation of German scholarship.[5]

---

[1] R. Bultmann, *History and Eschatology: The Presence of Eternity; The Gifford Lectures, 1955* (New York: Harper & Brothers, 1957), 155.
[2] R. Bultmann, "Christian Faith and History," in his *History and Eschatology*, 138–55, esp. 155.
[3] Hans-Georg Gadamer and Paul Tillich were also appointed at Marburg.
[4] Though Bultmann's thought was popularized in Great Britain by Bishop John A. T. Robinson in his book *Honest to God* (London: SCM Press, 1963).
[5] See Rudolf Bultmann, "Autobiographical Reflections," in *Existence and Faith*, trans. Schubert M. Ogden (New York: Harper & Row, 1966), 283–88.

DEMYTHOLOGIZING THE NEW TESTAMENT

In his now well-known book *New Testament and Mythology* (1941), Rudolf Bultmann argued that the theology of the New Testament is expressed in the *mythological* language of the first-century Mediterranean world. In his essay "New Testament and Mythology," he writes:

The cosmology of the New Testament is essentially mythical in character. The world is viewed as a three-storied structure, with the earth in the centre, the heaven above, and the underworld beneath. Heaven is the abode of God and of celestial beings – the angels. The underworld is hell, the place of torment. Even the earth is more than the scene of natural, everyday events.... It is the scene of the supernatural activity of God and his angels on the one hand, and of Satan and his daemons on the other. These supernatural forces intervene in the course of nature and in all that men think and do. Miracles are by no means rare. Man [*sic*] is not in control of his own life. Evil spirits may take possession of him. Satan may inspire him with evil thoughts.... This aeon is held in bondage by Satan, sin, and death (for "powers" is precisely what they are), and hastens towards its end. The end will come very soon, and will take the form of a cosmic catastrophe. It will be inaugurated by the "woes" of the last time. Then the Judge will come from heaven, and dead will rise, and last judgment will take place, and men will enter into eternal salvation or damnation.

This then is the mythical view which the New Testament presupposes when it presents the event of redemption which is the subject of its preaching.... All this is the language of mythology, and the origin of the various themes can be easily traced in the contemporary mythology of Jewish Apocalyptic and the redemption myths of Gnosticism. To this extent the kerygma [Christian proclamation] is incredible to modern man [*sic*], for he is convinced that the mythical view of the world is obsolete.[6]

Bultmann reasoned that the Jewish apocalyptic and gnostic worldview of early Christian proclamation is "incredible" – which is to say, unbelievable – to modern people and that this *mythical* language cannot, and should not, be modernized or "repristinated." In fact, it is impossible to repristinate a past world picture by sheer resolve, especially a *mythical* world picture, because our contemporary worldview is irrevocably formed by reason and science. To demand blind acceptance of the

---

[6] Rudolf Bultmann, "New Testament and Mythology," in *Kerygma and Myth*, ed. Hans Werner Bartsch, trans. Reginald H. Fuller (London: SPCK, 1953), 1–44, esp. 1–2. The Jewish apocalypticism of Paul's day was characterized by the expectation of the imminent end of the world and God's vindication and salvation of his covenantal people. The heavenly world was thought to include angelic beings and a preexistent savior. It was separated from the realm of human existence by a series of intermediate worlds that were occupied by good and evil spirits. God himself was cosmologically removed from this world but made use of intermediaries such as the Son of Man, the heavenly *logos*, and angels to intervene in human affairs (cf. Klaus Koch, *The Rediscovery of Apocalyptic: A Polemical Work on a Neglected Area of Biblical Studies and Its Damaging Effects on Theology and Philosophy*, Studies in Biblical Theology 2/22 [London: SCM Press, 1972], 18–35).

mythological elements in the New Testament would be to reduce Christian faith to an act of will, or fideism.[7]

However, Bultmann argued that Christian faith possesses a true essence that can be distinguished from the mythological worldview in which it is suspended: this essence concerns the saving work of God in Christ for humanity. The true significance of Christ's life and death concerns our existence in the present. The real purpose of the Bible's mythical language was to lead its original readers to a true understanding of themselves before the presence of almighty God.[8] Ernst Fuchs, a follower of Bultmann, summarized Bultmann's viewpoint as follows: either "faith has significance for the self in the world *now*, or it has no significance at all ... [the] locus [of the truth of the gospel] is precisely in the question about the self, as it finds itself estranged from itself, burdened with guilt.... The question of the self, in short, is the existential condition, or concern, upon which [biblical] interpretation depends."[9]

In our own time, in the twenty-first century, the mythological thought-forms of the Bible pose the real danger of *obscuring* the true essence of the gospel. This is why Bultmann famously argued that the New Testament must be "demythologized."[10] In his book *The Problem of Demythologizing the New Testament Message*, Bultmann explained how this program should be carried out: to demythologize the New Testament is to replace its Jewish apocalyptic and Hellenistic "mythical world picture" with contemporary, existential categories, especially as expounded by Heidegger in his *Being and Time*.[11] For example, Bultmann employed Heidegger's concept of "fallenness," in which Da-sein forgets its own possibilities, and his concept of "angst" to clarify the biblical concepts of sin and guilt, respectively. He borrowed Heidegger's concept of "being-toward-death" in his theology of dying to the world and to oneself, and he used Heidegger's concept of "authentic" existence to explicate the life of true Christian faith.[12] By so replacing the New Testament's mythical elements with existential categories, Bultmann attempted to emancipate

---

[7] Bultmann, *New Testament and Mythology and Other Basic Writings*, ed. Schubert M. Ogden (Philadelphia: Fortress, 1984), 3.

[8] Bultmann, "New Testament and Mythology," 4–11.

[9] Ernst Fuchs, as quoted by Paul J. Achtemeier, *An Introduction to the New Hermeneutic* (Philadelphia: Westminster Press, 1969), 127 (emphasis added).

[10] Bultmann, "New Testament and Mythology," 16.

[11] However, Bultmann criticized Heidegger's philosophical views on three points: whether achieving authentic existence goes beyond attaining a correct understanding of human nature, whether and how authenticity can be obtained, and the possibility and place of divine action. G. D. Chryssides, "Bultmann's Criticisms of Heidegger," *Sophia* 24/2 (1985): 28–35.

[12] Bultmann also adopted many other Heideggerian concepts such as "every-dayness," "fallenness," and "temporality." Cf. M. Lill, who compares Heidegger's *Sein und Zeit* and Bultmann's *Das Evangelium des Johannes,* with respect to the relation between philosophy and theology, in *Zeitlichkeit und Offenbarung: Ein Vergleich von Martin Heideggers "Sein und Zeit" mit Rudolf Bultmanns "Das Evangelium des Johannes,"* European University Studies (Frankfurt: P. Lang, 1987).

modern people from the primitivism and superstition of the ancient first-century worldview and disclose to them the true essence of the gospel of Christ. Bultmann employed the term *kerygma* to refer to this demythologized essence of the Christian gospel, stripped of its first-century "mythical world picture."[13] It is this demythologized *kerygma* that invites human beings to enter into a new dimension of historical life in the present with God, one that is set free from guilt and anxiety, and open to others in love.[14] From this it should be clear that Bultmann's project of demythologizing the canonical Gospels was not an academic exercise but rather a task related to the proclamation of the church, whose goal was to clarify the true gospel of Christ. True Christian faith can arise only in response to the proclamation of this *kerygma*.

THE "JESUS OF HISTORY" AND THE "CHRIST OF FAITH"

In his books *The History of the Synoptic Tradition* (1921) and *Jesus and the Word* (1926), Bultmann rightly argued that the Jesus of history, as portrayed in the canonical Gospels, has *already* been recast in the mythical thought forms of the Jewish apocalyptic and Hellenistic world. Though Bultmann had no doubts that the historical Jesus actually existed, he maintained that nothing can be objectively known about the life and personality of the historical Jesus. He famously declared: "I do indeed think that we can now know almost nothing concerning the life and personality of Jesus, since the early Christian sources show no interest in either, are moreover fragmentary and often legendary; and other sources about Jesus do not exist."[15] Moreover, in Bultmann's view, the concept of an objective account of the historical Jesus is unattainable because historical phenomena "do not exist at all without a historical subject who understands them."[16] The facts of the life of Jesus become historical phenomena only when they become significant to us in some way: "They become historical phenomena only when they speak, and this they do only for a subject who understands them."[17] Therefore, Bultmann argued that the knowledge of the historical Jesus, as acquired through the historical-critical exegesis of the New Testament, is objective *only* in the sense that this knowledge "comes within a certain way of asking questions" out of our existential "being-in-the-world."[18]

---

[13] τὸ κήρυγμα (cf. Rom 16:25, 1 Cor 1:21, 2:4, 15:14; cf. 2 Tim 4:17, Tit 1:3).

[14] Gary Dorrien, *The Word as True Myth: Interpreting Modern Theology* (Louisville, KY: Westminster John Knox Press, 1997), 112; Martin J. De Nys, "Myth and Interpretation: Bultmann Revisited," *International Journal of the Philosophy of Religion* 11/1 (1980): 27–41.

[15] Rudolf Bultmann, *Jesus and the Word* (New York: Scribner's, 1958 [1921]), 8 (emphasis added).

[16] Bultmann, "The Problem of Hermeneutics [1950]," 137–57, esp. 151–52, in Roger A. Johnson (ed.), *Rudolph Bultmann: Interpreting Faith for the Modern Era* (London: Collins, 1987). We have previously discussed this point in Chapters 3–4.

[17] Bultmann, "The Problem of Hermeneutics," 151–52.

[18] Ibid., 152.

This is not to suggest that Bultmann rejected historical inquiry. He did not. In fact, Bultmann is arguably the most famous New Testament historical critic of the twentieth century. He even argued that theology must begin with historical-critical exegesis and that it must remain bound to it.[19] Nonetheless, in his view, true Christian faith and the quest for God can never be supported by demonstrable facts, much less by faith in the facts of history: true Christian faith can never depend on history because justification is "by faith alone" (*sola fide*).[20] God's pardon for guilty sinners is granted to, and received, only through faith, to the exclusion of all human efforts, including efforts to reconstruct an objective account of the historical Jesus.[21]

Because justification is by faith alone, any attempt to support faith through a reconstruction of the historical Jesus is actually rooted in unbelief. In his view, any bare fact concerning the historical Jesus, which might be employed as a support for faith, must be put aside. In Bultmann's estimation, the "basic human attitude" behind all such scholarly efforts to prop up faith with history is that of "highhandedness."[22] Standing against the highhandedness of all such historical reconstructions is God's *kerygma*, "which claims that we can in no way free ourselves from our factual 'fallenness' in the world but are freed from it only by an act of God ... (namely) the salvation occurrence that is realized in Christ."[23] This explains why Bultmann welcomed all attempts to discredit what he referred to as "the fanciful portraits of Life-of-Jesus" because such portraits mean "nothing other than 'Christ after the flesh,'" which is "no concern of ours."[24] In his view, the true task of the biblical scholar is not that of proving the hand of God in history but rather the opposite: to prove that the act of God in Christ cannot be proved through historical reconstruction.

In many ways, Bultmann was following in a particular tradition of scholarship that had established a definitive *disjunction* between the "Jesus of history" and the "Christ of faith."[25] The "Jesus of history" is bound to the past, and the details

---

[19] Wilhelm Anz, "Die existentiale Theologie Rudolf Bultmanns," *Wort und Dienst* 23 (1995): 9–22. Andreas Großmann discusses the dialogue between Heidegger and Bultmann on the relationship between philosophy and theology in "Zwischen Phänomenologie und Theologie: Heidegger's 'Marburger Religionsgespräch' mit Rudolf Bultmann," *Zeitschrift für Theologie und Kirche* 95/1 (1998): 37–62.

[20] Bultmann, "New Testament and Mythology," 41–44.

[21] In making this declaration, Bultmann's specific target was the liberal "Jesus of history," as reconstructed by German liberal Protestants such as Schleiermacher, who viewed Jesus as one who proclaimed universal truths, such as the brotherhood of humanity, the infinite value of the soul, the higher righteousness of love, and the importance of establishing God's kingdom on earth through love and goodwill.

[22] Bultmann, "New Testament and Mythology," 28.

[23] Ibid., 26.

[24] Rudolf Bultmann, *Faith and Understanding*, ed. Robert W. Funk, trans. Louise Pettibone Smith (Philadelphia: Fortress, 1969), 132.

[25] Gotthold Lessing (1729–81) was the first to draw a distinction between the "Jesus of history" and the "Christ of faith," a distinction that was subsequently expanded upon by Martin Kähler (1892) in *The So-Called Historical Jesus and the Historic Biblical Christ*, trans. C. E. Braaten (Philadelphia: Fortress, 1964 [1896]).

of his life remain largely uncertain, unverifiable, and irrelevant to Christian faith. Bultmann even went so far as to declare: "How things looked in the heart of Jesus I do not know and do not wish to know."[26] Even though the theological meaning of the cross originated from a historical event – the crucifixion of Jesus – Paul never proclaims a historical crucifixion. He always proclaims Christ as *crucified and risen,* as one inseparable theological idea; in other words, the Cross and Resurrection encompass one *single* cosmic event, not two historical events that can be objectified by biblical scholars.

In Bultmann's view, the Jesus of history is irrelevant to faith; what is essential is that we know the Christ of faith. By implication, the Christian *kerygma,* which is the *essence* of Christian faith, contains no authenticated historical facts. The *kerygma* is the preaching of the Christ of faith, of Christ crucified and resurrected, *not* the preaching of the Jesus of history. God's revelation to humanity is an announcement of the *truth of human existence,* not a recitation of the antiquarian facts of Jesus' historical life in Galilee and Judea.[27] Bultmann colorfully describes the quest for the facts of history as "a kind of pathology of the necrophiliac theological archivist."[28] In contrast, the *kerygma* challenges us to put our faith where Jesus put his faith, namely in God's future, and not in the veracity of our own historical reconstructions.

THE PROBLEM OF HERMENEUTICS

In his famous essay "The Problem of Hermeneutics" (1950), Bultmann tried to hold Christian existentialism and historical skepticism together in a creative tension by mediating between the Heideggerian existentialism of *Being and Time* (1927) and Wilhelm Dilthey's earlier attempt to develop a scientifically rigorous method for human sciences (*Geisteswissenschaften*) for historical research.[29]

The fact that Bultmann wrote an essay entitled "The Problem of Hermeneutics" in 1950 clearly demonstrates that philosophical hermeneutics continued to have an honored place within the discipline of New Testament studies in the mid-twentieth century. In other words, by as late as the 1950s, biblical scholars continued to reflect on the present sense-event of biblical texts. In this essay, Bultmann begins by noting how both Schleiermacher and Dilthey stressed the importance of going

---

[26] Bultmann, *Faith and Understanding,* 132.
[27] Bultmann, "The Problem of Hermeneutics," 155–57.
[28] Ibid., 146–50.
[29] Ibid., 137–57; cf. Hans Hübner's discussion of a letter from Bultmann to Hübner (dated June 5, 1972) in which Bultmann states that his contact with Heidegger began when he read Heidegger's not yet published book on Jesus. Heidegger advised him to add the term *Wirkungszusammenhang* (coherence of effect), which was so central to Dilthey's philosophy, to the first page of the introduction ("Bultmanns 'existentiale Interpretation' – Untersuchungen zu ihrer Herkunft," *Zeitschrift für Theologie und Kirche* 100/3 [2003]: 280–324).

beyond a purely grammatical interpretation of texts to uncover the inner "psychical life" of their authors.[30] As we discussed in Chapter 2, for Schleiermacher, the actual goal of the grammatical side of interpretation was to *move past* the "outer form" of a text – past its words, sentences, and paragraphs – to grasp its true "inner origin," namely the intention of its author.[31] Indeed, Schleiermacher believed that texts exist "like miracles, only to direct our attention towards the [individual human] spirit that playfully generates them."[32] In reply, Rudolf Bultmann argued that it is not necessary to go beyond the writings of Paul to reconstruct the psychology of Paul, or the mind of Paul. In an essay simply entitled "Paul," Bultmann states:

If we are concerned to inquire about the actual content of Paul's theology, then it would be wrong to go back to his "personality" in order on that basis to understand his theology. For in the first place, a picture of his personality and character can only be obtained by reconstructing it on the basis of having first understood his theological and non-theological statements; and so one deceives oneself if one imagines that one can understand what Paul says by understanding his personality. In the second place, however, what one customarily refers to as the "character" of a man [*sic*] is not something outside of his work to which one can refer to in order to explain it; ... conversely, his work is something that is detached from his "character." Rather a man [*sic*] first acquires his "character" in his work, and his work is a presentation of his "character." Thus it is certainly correct to say that the prominent features in a picture of Paul are his concern with his subject and his passion, which together combine to make for a radicalism of thought and judgment. However, in saying this, one is not speaking about presuppositions from which his work has grown, but rather is characterizing that work itself.[33]

In this passage Bultmann argues along similar lines as Roland Barthes later did: "Paul" is really an *effect* of the text itself. Our sense of Paul's *presence*, lying in wait behind his writings, is actually an effect of the texts themselves. But there is no need to try to go beyond this textualized presence.

Bultmann observes that scholars do not routinely apply Schleiermacher's psychological method to *all* ancient documents, citing as examples the writings of the Egyptians, Babylonians, Assyrians, and Romans. This prompts him to ask why then did Schleiermacher treat biblical documents differently, especially since he claimed to be developing a general or universal hermeneutic that applies to all literature.[34] According to Bultmann, the reason can be found in Schleiermacher's own *pre-understanding* of the subject matter.[35] Schleiermacher's universal hermeneutical

---

[30] Bultmann, "The Problem of Hermeneutics," 138–41.

[31] F. Schleiermacher, *Werke Schleiermachers*, ed. Hermann Mulert (Berlin: Prophläen Verlag, 1924), III/3, 355, 358, 364.

[32] As quoted by Wilhelm Dilthey, in *Das Leben Schleiermachers*, 2 vols. in 4 (Berlin: Walter de Gruyter, 1970), appendix, 117.

[33] Bultmann, "Paul" [1930], in his *Existence and Faith*, 111–46, esp. 121.

[34] Bultmann, "The Problem of Hermeneutics," 142–44.

[35] Ibid., 153–55.

theory is not really universal at all: it is actually "guided by a certain way of asking questions or to a certain objective.... It is always guided by a pre-understanding of the subject matter about which it questions the text."[36] Real biblical interpretation is never presuppositionless: the interpreter is never a subject and always an "I," who approaches the text with preundertandings. Bultmann is not arguing that we should rid ourselves of our preunderstandings, for without "preunderstanding and the questions guided by it, the texts are dumb." But he does argue that biblical interpretation requires that we raise our preunderstandings to the level of consciousness and test them, thereby putting them at risk.

The preunderstandings of authentic interpretation are always directed toward the future. Bultmann describes this future directionality as follows: one "is always on the way; each present hour is questioned and challenged by its future ... [one] can either gain ... genuine life or miss it."[37] Biblical interpreters who understand themselves as historically situated, future-oriented beings recognize that their "genuine self can only be offered" to them "as a gift by the future."[38] Whenever we undertake to interpret a biblical text, we do so on the eve of our future, which calls us to authenticity.

This is not our customary disposition toward the future. Most often, we want to have power over the future. Bultmann argues that "very historicity" awakens in us "the illusion of having power" over the future. But the authentic person is the one who receives freedom as a gift from God.[39] The authentic person is not allowed to look to the past for guarantees about the future. Biblical interpretation, informed by such freedom, is not limited to the recovery of the past sense of biblical texts, because the interpreter is charged with the responsibility of interpreting the past on the eve of God's future, which is at the same time "the responsibility *over against* the heritage of the past in the face of the future."[40] This means that authentic biblical interpretation will always require an existentiell decision to appropriate the present sense-event of biblical texts afresh in our present historical situation: "Genuine understanding is a matter of hearing the question raised in the work or claim encountered in it, and the 'completion' of one's own individuality consists in the richer and deeper disclosure of one's own possibilities...."[41] Bultmann elaborates this thought in his essay "Is Exegesis without Presuppositions Possible?" (1957):

Because the text speaks to existence it is never understood in a definitive way. The existentiell decision out of which the interpretation emerges cannot be passed on, but

---

[36] Ibid., 141.
[37] Bultmann, *History and Eschatology*, 140.
[38] Ibid., 150.
[39] Ibid.
[40] Ibid., 143.
[41] Ibid., 149.

must always be realized anew. This does not mean, of course, that there cannot be continuity in the exegesis of Scripture.... [E]very exegesis that offers itself as a guide is at the same time a question that must always be answered anew and independently. *Since the exegete exists historically and must hear the word of Scripture as spoken in his special historical situation, he will always understand the old word anew.* Always anew it will tell him who he, man [*sic*], is and who God is, and he will always have to express this word in a new conceptuality. Thus it is true also of Scripture that it only is what it is with its history and its future.[42]

RECOVERING FROM HISTORICISM

As previously discussed in Chapters 3 and 4, the historicist worldview increasingly came under suspicion from the late nineteenth through the early twentieth century owing to its tendency to reduce biblical texts to its own categories of analysis and worldview. This had the effect of reducing the Christian gospel to a purely historical phenomenon arising from mundane, material causes. Historicism's view of the human being, as being determined by historical conditions, would imply that we are at the mercy of history. Bultmann describes the problem as follows: "Historicism is perfectly right in seeing that the present situation grows out of the past; but it misunderstands the determination by the past as purely causal determination and fails to see it as leading into a situation of questions, of problems."[43]

In Bultmann's view, historicism failed because it did not recognize the present situation as a time of decision: historicism "does not understand the present situation as the *situation of decision* – a decision which is at one and the same time a decision over against our future, and a decision over against our past *concerning the way in which it is to determine our future.*"[44] In the words of Gianni Vattimo, the past does not determine the present because it "summons us and offers itself up to interpretation."[45] We have a role in how the past becomes significant to us. Bultmann agrees with Heidegger that the crisis brought on by historicism is not a dead end for it actually opens up a way of escape from its own historical relativity. The relativity of every historical situation does have positive meaning in the sense that it presents us with a moment of decision. But, at the same time, it also fills this moment with risk.[46]

---

[42] Rudolf Bultmann, "Is Exegesis without Presuppositions Possible?" [1957], in his *Existence and Faith: Shorter Writings of Rudolf Bultmann*, 289–96, esp. 296 (emphasis added).

[43] Bultmann, *History and Eschatology*, 141–42 (emphasis added).

[44] Ibid. (emphasis added).

[45] Gianni Vattimo, *A Farewell to Truth*, trans. William McCuaig (New York: Columbia University Press, 2011 [2009]), xxxv.

[46] Bultmann states, "Historicism has also the merit itself of showing the way in which it is to be overcome" (*History and Eschatology*, 143).

The concrete possibilities for human action are, of course, limited by the situation arising from the past.... But the future is open in so far as it brings the gain or the loss of our genuine life and thereby *gives to our present its character as a moment of decision.* Historicism in its traditional form overlooks the *dangerous character of the present,* its character of risk. The *relativity of each present moment,* rightly seen by historicism, is therefore not relativity in the sense in which any particular point within a causal series is a relative one, but has the positive sense that the present is the moment of decision, and *by the decision taken the yield of the past is gathered in and the meaning of the future is chosen.* This is the character of every historical situation; in it the problems of the past and future are enclosed and are waiting, as it were, *to be unveiled by human decisions.*[47]

Even though our present is rooted in, and limited by, the past, it is not *determined* by the past, and indeed cannot be so determined, because the present sense-event of the past is always ambiguous. The past does not have only one sense; "it is ambiguous. In consequence of its misunderstanding of the present, historicism also misunderstands the future as determined by the past through causality instead of being open."[48] The ambiguous meaning of the past forces each individual to make decisions in the present regarding his or her future, and any decision that one makes regarding the future "is at the same time a decision over against our past *concerning the way in which it is to determine our future.*"[49] In short, "by the decision taken [in the present], the yield of the past is gathered in and the meaning of the future is chosen."[50] Thus, this gift of freedom in the present is always existential:

The meaning in history lies always in the present, and when the present is conceived as the eschatological present by Christian faith [then] the meaning of history is realized.... Always in your present lies the meaning of history, and you cannot see it as a spectator, but only in your responsible decisions [now]. In every moment slumbers the possibility of being the eschatological moment. You must awaken it."[51]

Bultmann also warns that the way of escape from historicism is dangerous because with the recognition of the present moment as a situation of decision comes the further realization that we are not passive bystanders in the act of interpretation. The biblical interpreter has a responsibility to make a decision about how he or she will open up the meaning of a biblical text in the eschatological present, in light of God's pull toward the future:[52] "[E]very moment is the *now* of

---

47   Ibid., 141–42 (emphasis added).
48   Ibid.
49   Ibid., 143.
50   Ibid., 141.
51   Ibid., 155.
52   For example, David Clines asks what ethical responsibility interpreters carry if they help potentially oppressive texts to stay alive ("The Postmodern Adventure in Bible Studies," in *Auguries: The Jubilee Volume of the Sheffield Department of Biblical Studies,* ed. David J. A. Clines and Stephen D. Moore, JSOTSup 269 [Sheffield: Sheffield Academic Press, 1998], 286).

responsibility, of decision.... In this responsibility, as responsibility over the past as over against the future, the unity of history is grounded."[53] For, "by the decision taken [in the present], the yield of the past is gathered in and the meaning of the future is chosen."[54] Here we are confronted with the realization that the true meaning of biblical exegesis lies not in the objectivity of its results but rather in the manner in which we decide to open up the meaning of a text. To the extent that we fail to grasp this existential truth, we risk becoming alienated from our very selves. By implication, the very act of interpretation leaves its mark on the interpreter. Insofar as biblical scholars understand their task to be that of simply applying historical methods of interpretation to biblical texts, they overlook the dangerous character of risk to themselves, which always attends the hermeneutic act.[55]

THE CRISIS THEOLOGY OF BARTH AND BULTMANN

Both Karl Barth (1886–1968) and Bultmann are associated with crisis theology. The Greek noun *krisis* (κρίσις) is derived from the verb *krinin* (κρίνειν), meaning "to judge." For Barth, this crisis announced God's judgment, which required a response in the form of a human decision. Barth famously applied his crisis theology in his commentary *Epistle to the Romans* (*Der Römerbrief*), which was first published in 1919 at the outset of the Weimar Republic and then thoroughly revised three years later (1922).[56] With this publication of *Epistle to the Romans*, Barth became a recognized exponent for displacing the centrality of the historicist paradigm within liberal German Protestantism.

The starting point for Barth's crisis theology was "the judgment of God" (τὸ κρίμα τοῦ θεοῦ), as announced by Paul in Romans 2:1–6. In Barth's view, this divine judgment is *beyond the reach of historical inquiry*. He argued that this judgment is also "*krisis* of [human] knowledge" (9:30–10:3). In fact, Barth argued that the Christian gospel actually *contradicts* historically grounded knowledge. Like Bultmann, Barth emphasized that human beings are justified "by faith alone" (*sola fide*) and that any attempt to support faith by applying historical analysis to the New Testament is rooted in unbelief. True Christian faith does not depend upon having objective facts concerning the historical Jesus. Indeed, it could not so depend, for if it did, then faith would be meaningless. True faith is not a faith in the historical reliability of the canonical gospels, or even in the veracity of scholarly reconstructions of the historical Jesus. According to Barth, true faith requires a surrender of our human freedom to the will of God. True faith does not rest on a

---

53 Bultmann, *History and Eschatology*, 143–44.
54 Ibid., 141.
55 Ibid.
56 On Barth's *Epistle to the Romans*, see Charles R. Bambach, *Heidegger, Dilthey, and the Crisis of Historicism* (Ithaca, NY: Cornell University Press, 1995), 187–92.

demonstrable historical foundation. In fact, "genuine faith *is a void,* an obeisance before that which we can never be, or do, or possess."[57]

This insight provided the backdrop for Barth's later famous proclamation of the arrival of a *crisis of time,* and the collapse of faith in historical knowledge. He termed this crisis of time the "zero hour" (*Stunde Null*). In this "zero hour" one experiences "abandonment and doubt and uncertainty."[58] This is the experience of standing at the threshold between the past and future ages. Barth argued that the past age – dominated by historicism – must be left behind, while the future has yet to come. The present – our present – is empty space between the obsolete past and an uncertain future. It is precisely in this present "zero hour" that God calls us to make a decision for or against God's self-revelation. True Christian faith is demonstrated by responding to God's own self-revelation in the present moment. The only appropriate human response is faith and obedience.

BARTH AND THE WORD OF GOD

Barth's critique of historicism should not be viewed as a retreat to biblical fundamentalism. Barth, who is arguably *the* preeminent Protestant theologian of the twentieth century, actually rejected the identification of scripture as the Word of God. In his view, the *words* of scripture are not identical with God's Word, nor are they infallible. The sixty-six books of the Bible were written by human beings and, as such, are marked by human imperfections. They reflect the historical and cultural contexts in which they were written.

But Barth believed that God's revelation of God's own self is independent of all human history and culture.[59] Barth did not contest Bultmann's point that Paul's letters contain mythical elements borrowed from Jewish apocalyptic and Hellenistic culture. Nonetheless, in Barth's view, the mythological character of the scriptures is irrelevant because the whole of scripture "is placed under the KRISIS of the Spirit of Christ":

The problem is whether the whole must not be understood in relation to the true-subject matter which is – The Spirit of Christ.... The commentator is thus presented with a clear 'Either – Or.' The question is whether or not he is to place himself in a relation to this author of utter loyalty.... Even so, the extent to which the commentator will be able to disclose the Spirit of Christ in his reading of Paul will not be elsewhere the same. But he will know that the responsibility rests on his shoulders; and he will not let himself be

---

[57] Karl Barth, *The Epistle to the Romans,* trans. Edwyn C. Hoskyns (London: Oxford University Press, 1933), 88 (emphasis added).

[58] Barth, *Church Dogmatics: IV. The Doctrine of Reconciliation,* 2nd ed. (London: T. & T. Clark International, 1956), 431.

[59] V. Harvey, *The Historian and the Believer: A Confrontation between the Modern Historian's Principles of Judgment and the Christian's Will-to-Believe* (New York: Macmillan, 1966), 133.

bewildered by those other spirits, which so often render inaudible the dominant tones of the Spirit of Christ.[60]

In his commentary *Epistle to the Romans,* Barth rejected the historicist requirement that Romans be interpreted in terms of the particular historical contexts of Paul (when composing the letter) and that of the church in Rome. Barth erased the boundary between Paul (as historically conditioned author) and the contemporary interpreter. In Barth's view, biblical exegesis does not necessitate the reconstruction of Paul's historical context or the mind of Paul. Rather it requires that we, as interpreters, stand in the very presence of Paul and understand that "our problems are the problems of Paul."[61] Whereas Bultmann's starting point was ontological, that is, our human capacity *to experience* God's revelation, Barth's starting point was theological: namely, God's sovereign act of self-revelation apart from the limitations of human understanding. This starting point is evident at the outset of his *Church Dogmatics,* where Barth begins with a question: "What is the Word of God and who am I in relation to God's Word?" Thus, rather than developing a hermeneutic theory of textual interpretation, Barth began with God's divine self-disclosure to humanity. He wanted to demonstrate the priority of the Word of God above all things, and how the sacred scriptures, when proclaimed, become for us the Word of God.

In Bultmann's view, Barth had overreacted to the errors of historicism. There is no uninterpreted *kerygma,* not even in Barth's own theological writings. For a biblical text to have significance for human beings, it must always be grounded in a human existential horizon of meaning, which functions as the condition of possibility for any interpretation: to say that a biblical text has significance in the present is to say that it has significance for particular historical human beings, living within a particular tradition, heritage, and culture, with a shared horizon of meaning.

But Bultmann and Barth *did* agree on one central point, that the appropriation of God's Word by human beings is always an act of God. It is never the result of human striving. I have argued that the metaphysics of the striving "subject" *is* nihilism proper. In their separate ways, Bultmann and Barth both help us to recognize that the significance of Christ's cross and resurrection cannot be objectively grasped through any act of human will, including the willful exercise of historical analysis in biblical studies.

BULTMANN'S LEGACY

Bultmann's writings provide one critical perspective on the complex phenomenon that I have termed the crisis of historicism. As we have seen, he attempted to

---

[60] Barth, *Epistle to the Romans,* 17.
[61] Ibid., 451.

demythologize the gospel, which is suspended in a first-century mythical world-view of the ancient Mediterranean world, into the *kerygma*, using the language of Heideggerian existentialism. He also cautions us against putting our faith in any of the portraits of the historical Jesus produced annually by New Testament scholars. With the benefit of hindsight, it is clear that aspects of Bultmann's interpretive framework are outdated owing to his dependence on the early writings of Heidegger, especially *Being and Time*, as a framework for his thought. In contrast to Bultmann, Ernst Fuchs and Gerhard Ebeling in Germany, and James Robinson and Robert Funk in the United States, focused on Heidegger's later writings. They developed what is now known as the "new hermeneutic." In the years following the publication of *Being and Time*, even Heidegger abandoned the term Da-sein, on account of what he perceived to be the residual subjectivity in the concept of Da-sein.

Nonetheless, Bultmann remains one of the few biblical scholars to have attempted to address the problem of nihilism inherent in the historicist paradigm. His legacy reminds us, first, that the past is uncertain and its significance is always ambiguous and, second, that God calls us in the midst of the eschatological present. Therefore, interpreters always possess a degree of freedom, tempered by the responsibility to decide how they will open up the sense-event of biblical texts in the present moment. This freedom and responsibility fills the practice of biblical interpretation with risk. Interpretation always involves existential decisions.

Perhaps Bultmann's greatest legacy is not his attempt to employ Heidegger's phenomenology to demythologize the New Testament or his effort to purify a Christian *kerygma* but rather his reminder that biblical interpretation is vested with the responsibility of awakening in the present historical moment an "eschatological moment." He was able to recognize, in a way that we perhaps have failed to recognize, that even in the midst of the ambiguity of the present moment, we remain addressed by the *kerygma* of God, a *kerygma* that can never be made over into an object of historical inquiry.

7

❧

The Linguistic Turn: Language as a Symbolizing System

Perhaps the immobility of things that surround us is forced upon them by our conviction that they are themselves and not anything else, by the immobility of our conception of them.[1]

The Mojave Desert is a vast expanse of wilderness located in southern California. Its natural geographic formations include sand dunes, salt flats, mountains, volcanic formations, and lava beds. For thousands of years this natural landscape remained virtually devoid of human symbolization until it was surveyed in 1906 by the Union Pacific Railroad for the development of a new railroad line and the construction of a new railway station.

With the incursion of human beings to this wilderness came the practice of human signifying: this new town required a name. The task of selecting a name was left to a warehouse worker named John Kelso and two other railroad workers, who decided to choose a name for the town by drawing their surnames out of a hat. Each man wrote his own surname on a scrap of paper and deposited it into a hat, and, as luck would have it, the first paper drawn out had the signifier "John Kelso" written on it. And so it was that, through the arbitrary process of drawing of names out of a hat, this sunbaked patch of wilderness, which for thousands of years had eluded human signifying practices, had the proper name "Kelso" thrust upon it by these strangers from elsewhere. Once again, nature had fallen under the power of the signifying practice of human beings, who attach their own words to the things they imagine and observe, such as a nonexistent town and an unmarked patch of desert (fig. 7.1).

A RECORD OF THE UNUSUAL

Human beings have not always proved able to distinguish what they imagine and what they observe in the world around them. In 1640 a man named Aldrovandi wrote a nonfiction book about dragons. Under the heading "On the serpent in general," his table of contents lists the following sections:

---

[1] Marcel Proust, *Remembrance of Things Past*, vol. 1: *Swann's Way: Within a Budding Grove*, trans. C. K. Scott Moncrieff and Terence Kilmartin (New York: Random House, 1981), 6.

7.1. Mojave National Preserve

1. equivocation (i.e., various meanings of the word serpent); 2. synonyms and ety-
mologies; 3. differences; 4. form and description; 5. anatomy; 6. nature and habits; 7.
temperament; 8. coitus and generation; 9. voice; 10. movements; 11. places; 12. diet; 13.
physiognomy; 14. antipathy; 15. sympathy; 16. modes of capture; 17. death and wounds
caused by the serpent; 18. modes and signs of poisoning; 19. remedies; 20. epithets;
21. denominations; 22. prodigies and presages; 23. monsters; 24. mythology; 25. gods
to which it is dedicated; 26. fables; 27. allegories and mysteries; 28. hieroglyphics; 29.
emblems and symbols; 30. proverbs; 31. coinage; 32. miracles; 33. riddles; 34.devices;
35. heraldic signs; 36. historical facts; 37. dreams; 38. simulacra and statues; 39. use in
human diet; 40. use in medicine; 41. miscellaneous uses.[2]

How was it possible for Aldrovandi, as late as the year 1640, to write a nonfiction
book about dragons? He could do so because he was able to consult other books
on the same subject. The simple fact that other books were published about dragons provided a sufficient basis for Aldrovandi to write yet another book on the
same subject.[3] Prior to the Enlightenment, no clear distinction was made between
"signs" in books and "signs" in nature. But with the transition from the Renaissance

---

[2]   As quoted by Michel Foucault, *The Order of Things: An Archaeology of the Human Sciences* (New
      York: Vintage Books, 1970 [1966]), 39.
[3]   Richard A. Muller and John Thompson, "The Significance of Precritical Exegesis," in *Biblical
      Interpretation in the Era of the Reformation*, ed. Richard A. Muller and John Thompson (Grand
      Rapids, MI: Wm. B. Eerdmans, 1996), 335–42, esp. 339.

to the Enlightenment, came a new principle of knowledge: one must distinguish what is written in books from what can actually be observed in the material world. For the past three hundred years, this principle has functioned as a fundamental tenet for the advancement of Western knowledge, including biblical studies.

The problem of discriminating between linguistic "signs" in books and observable "signs" of things in the world was taken up by Miguel de Cervantes in his two-part classic novel *Don Quixote* (1605, 1615). Its main character, Don Quixote, interpreted the things he encountered in his world on the basis of the tales found in the medieval chivalric romances, which he loved to read. Michel Foucault has argued that Don Quixote was suspended between the two eras, the Renaissance and the Enlightenment. In the era of the Renaissance, people viewed the world as a kind of "text," full of "signs," which could be deciphered. Things in the world all possessed signs that pointed to other things in the world. Knowledge consisted of discovering the resemblances between these "signs." Through such resemblances, things were believed to be signs that pointed to other things, whether in nature or books. These resemblances, or "similitudes," were of four different types.

First, "convenience" (*conventia*) denotes a kind of resemblance that results from things being close to one another – for example, the body and the soul. The soul, being close to the body, receives the affects of the body's actions and assimilates itself to the body; the body, on the other hand, was thought to be altered and corrupted by the passions of the soul.[4] In the Renaissance, the world was also viewed as a tangled grid of adjacencies, with things adjusting themselves to one another or communicating with one another (e.g., plants and animals, earth and sea, humanity and everything, God and matter).

Second, "emulation" (*aemulatio*) is really "convenience" that has been freed from the law of place: we can think of emulation as a kind of "mirroring" of things or a "twinship" between things. For example, the human intellect was viewed as an imperfect *mirror* or reflection of God's wisdom; human eyes were thought to be a mirror of the illumination of the sun and moon. The human mouth was a reflection of Venus, the goddess of love, because it gives passage to kisses and words of love. In such ways, things were believed to emulate one another from afar.[5]

Third, "analogy" also makes resemblances possible across space. However, it does not deal with visible resemblances but rather with more subtle relations. People looked for analogies between plants and the earth, between animals and the world, between diamonds and the rocks in which they were buried. Thus, the wing of a bird and the fin of a fish were thought to be analogies of a human arm. Similarly, by "analogy," a plant is a human being with its head down, and its "mouth" (roots) buried in the dirt. The world was thought to be saturated with

---

[4]   Foucault, *The Order of Things*, 18.
[5]   Ibid., 19.

analogies between things. Humanity was the center upon which all these relations were focused.[6] In fact, through analogy, all things in the world could be drawn together and related to humanity. However, the fact that there was no single privileged point of view, or no single correct analogy, allowed for the endless piling up of analogies and no definitive statement.

Fourth, "sympathy" deals with the attraction between things. "Sympathy" excites the world into movement. For example, by sympathy, the root of a plant grows toward water; by sympathy, the head of a sunflower turns to face the sun. Sympathy results in assimilating, mingling, and causing differences to disappear. Fire, because it is warm and light, is attracted to the sky, but it disappears in the air as smoke, vapor, and clouds: in other words, by mingling with the air, it "assimilates" to air, and the difference between fire and air disappears.[7] Sympathy was contrasted antipathy, which maintains the isolation of things and prevents their assimilation. For example, fire (as hot and dry) has an antipathy for water (as cold and damp). Thus, in the Renaissance, all things in the world had resemblances to other things through these four "similitudes." These similitudes allowed nature, like books, to be read as a vast text. "Knowledge" was understood to be based on the discovery of these "similitudes" (correlations) in nature, which was then recorded in books.[8]

From the perspective of the Renaissance understanding of knowledge, as a reading of the similitudes in the world, part 1 of *Don Quixote* can be read as Don Quixote's quest to discover the connections or resemblances between the signs in his books and the signs in his world. Michel Foucault observes that "every episode, every decision, every exploit" of Don Quixote "will be yet another sign" that he "is a true likeness" of the chivalric knights he read about in his books.

Don Quixote's failure to distinguish between what he observed in the world and what he read in his books resulted in his perceiving them as a unity of meaning. This was Don Quixote's downfall because by the time of the Enlightenment these similitudes had broken down.[9] Since the dawn of the Enlightenment, the Renaissance's belief in the profound kinship between signs in the world and signs in texts has been *dissolved*. Words are no longer believed to be essentially connected to things in the world. Instead of resemblances between the signs in books and signs in nature, we, as people whose thinking has been formed by Enlightenment, are more inclined to see the *differences* between them.[10] As Aldrovandi's book of dragons reminds us, words even possess the power to dissimulate the real.[11] For this reason, the study of literature, including biblical literature, always leads us

---

[6]   Ibid., 21.
[7]   Ibid., 23.
[8]   Ibid., 31–32.
[9]   Ibid., 46–48.
[10]   Ibid., 42ff.
[11]   Ibid., 47.

back to what Foucault terms "the untamed, imperious being of words." It has lost its status of being a prose of the world.[12]

When Don Quixote finally discovered that the linguistic signs in his books did not resemble the things and people he met on his travels, he experienced the *negative* image of the Renaissance world. Writing had ceased to be a prose of the world. Thus, in part two of the novel *Don Quixote*, with the similitude between the "order of words" and the "order of things" having broken down, what is most obvious to Don Quixote now are the *differences* between his medieval books and his own reality. Cervantes' novel can be read as a tale of lost innocence. In the post-Enlightenment era, in which we live, literature – including biblical literature – has broken off its kinship with things and has long ceased to be a "prose of the world."[13]

As previously noted in Chapter 1, Ferdinand de Saussure argued that words do not designate things in the world. They actually designate our culturally shared concept of things (signifieds). Even though Louis Hjelmslev revised and corrected Saussure's bilateral theory (words ↔ concepts) by incorporating the component of *denotation* (see Chapter 1), which is language's domain of reference, it remains true nonetheless that linguistic signs do not, and cannot, simply "point to" things in the world because language's other two components, signification and manifestation, condition denotation. Taken together, the three components condition one another with the result that the questioning of denotation always leads to a questioning of signification and manifestation in a circular fashion.

In point of fact, language employs words generically. Language employs linguistic signs, such as the sign "cat," categorically, to group together *dissimilar* real things (e.g., real cats) that share some common characteristics. For example, even though every cat is unique and dissimilar to one degree or another from all other cats, all these different cats are grouped together under the same linguistic sign, "cat." In its "significatory" dimension, language groups things together into categories on the basis of an *attribution of similarity. But every such attribution of similarity involves a comparison by which dissimilar things are grouped into categories of sameness*: for example, a tiger, lion, jaguar, and leopard are all dissimilar, but are all grouped together on the basis of similarity under the genus of *Panthera*. While this may seem like common sense, one might ask why whales, bats, and cats are all grouped under the genus of mammals, according to the same logic. In truth, there is no model cat, ideal cat, or original cat, after which all other cats have been modeled; there are only an infinite number of different – past, present, and future – dissimilar cats. What is true of cats is equally true of all real things. In the real world, *difference precedes similarity, and existence precedes sameness*.[14]

---

[12] Ibid., 300.
[13] Ibid., 48.
[14] Gilles Deleuze, *Difference and Repetition*, trans. Paul Patton (New York: Columbia University Press, 1994 [1968]), 28–30.

Language covers up all natural difference by attributing sameness through its culturally determined taxonomic categories and frameworks.

But what if we were to dispense with such taxonomic frameworks and gave every individual thing its own specific name. For example, imagine a language that lacked the word "cat" but had a distinct word for every single cat that has existed and does exist. In his short story "Funes, His Memory," the Argentine writer Jorge Borges imagines such an "impossible" language "in which each individual thing – every bird, every branch – would have its own name."[15] Of course, such a language, consisting of billions and billions of lexemes, would immediately break down and human communication would cease. Languages cannot function in this way, with the limited exception of proper names.

THE SAPIR-WHORF HYPOTHESIS

The primary point is that human concepts, including our modes of conceptualization, are fundamentally shaped by the words we use. This principle of *linguistic relativity* is officially known as the "Sapir-Whorf hypothesis" (or "Whorfianism"), named after two American anthropologists, Edward Sapir and his student Benjamin Lee Whorf, the primary proponents of this theory. According to this principle, the structures of individual languages influence the ways in which we linguistically conceptualize our world (either in speech or writing). For example, by virtue of the fact that the English language lacks certain terms, certain concepts go unthought by English speakers. To cite a few examples, the word *mokita*, which means "the truth no one speaks" in the Kivila language of Papua New Guinea, refers to the implied agreement among people to avoid speaking of specific shared, shameful secrets.[16] The term *mbuki-mvuki* (pronounced "m boo key – m voo key") is a word in the African Bantu language meaning "to cast off one's clothes spontaneously in order to dance unhindered."[17] The Japanese term *mono-no-aware*, which literally means the "pathos of things," designates a pervasive sadness arising from the awareness of the transience of things (*mujo*).[18] The Greek word *kefi* (κέφι) describes the inclination that Greeks have to dance and sing at a moment's notice, for which no exact English equivalent exists. Because the English language lacks any direct equivalent to these terms, these particular directions of thought are not readily available to speakers of the English language. These four simple examples are only intended to illustrate the importance of the structuring role of language on human

---

[15] Jorge Luis Borges, *Collected Fictions*, trans. Andrew Hurley (New York: Penguin, 1998), 136.

[16] Gunter Senft, "Ain't Misbehavin? Trobriand Pragmatics and the Field Researcher's Opportunity to Put His (or Her) Foot in It," *Oceanic Linguistics* 34/1 (1995): 211–26.

[17] Howard Reingold, *They Have a Word for It: A Light-Hearted Lexicon of Untranslatable Words and Phrases* (Louisville, KY: Sarabande Books, 2000), 28–29.

[18] Ivan I. Morris, *The World of the Shining Prince: Court Life in Ancient Japan* (New York: Kodansha International, 1994), 197.

thought. Because all human languages are themselves historical, changeable, and culturally situated (including the biblical Hebrew and Hellenistic Greek), it follows that both the concepts found in biblical texts and the methodological terminology of biblical studies possess their own *material history*.

LANGUAGE AS A TAXONOMY

Words are really categories or taxonomies that group dissimilar things together according to categories of sameness. Such categorizations are cultural constructions. It takes a linguistic community to bring into being such linguistic taxonomic frameworks. For example, through language, human identity is constructed on the basis of a framework that brings together such concepts as gender, race or color, ethnicity, class, nationality, and religion. Such concepts (signifieds) ignore the natural differences between people in favor of attributing sameness to them (e.g., blacks, Koreans, consumers, Asians, lesbians, Jews, Americans), on the basis of a shared set of "labels." By such means, unique individuals are labeled and grouped, despite the infinite variety of individual differences that such labels conceal (cf. Chapter 12). Jorge Luis Borges humorously mocked this "nominalizing" function of language by supposing to cite an "excerpt" from a "certain Chinese encyclopedia." In this encyclopedia, animals are divided into the following categories:

(a) belonging to the emperor
(b) embalmed
(c) tame
(d) suckling pigs
(e) sirens
(f) fabulous
(g) stray dogs
(h) included in the present classification
(i) frenzied
(j) innumerable
(k) drawn with a very fine camelhair brush
(l) et cetera
(m) having just broken the water pitcher
(n) that from a long way off look like flies[19]

Under the guise of quoting this fictitious Chinese encyclopedia, Borges calls attention to the linguistically determined categories that shape human thinking, such as the classification of "animals." What is an "animal" and what is not an "animal"? Commenting on this passage, Michel Foucault observes that this entertaining depiction of a foreign (Chinese) signifying system reminds us that we too,

---

[19]   As quoted by Foucault, *Order of Things*, xv.

as English speakers (or speakers of other languages), are unable to simply express reality as it is in itself. Our thoughts are always shaped by the taxonomy of the language we speak: "In the wonderment of this taxonomy, the thing we apprehend in one great leap, the thing that, by means of the fable [of Borges], is demonstrated as the exotic charm of another system of thought, is the limitation of our own [language], the stark impossibility of thinking that."[20]

As the Sapir-Whorf hypothesis explains, language determines the semiotic categories and terminology that structures and directs our cognitive processes, including the cognitive processes of both the earliest Christians and contemporary biblical interpreters. What is more, even our *experience* of reality, past and present, is actually mediated by language. We interpret the world around us through the conceptual categories of the language we speak. Thus, Louis Montrose, an exponent of the New Historicism, argues that language is "the medium in which the Real is constructed and apprehended."[21] Language functions as a kind of code that structures the way we interpret the meaning of the world around us. Language constructs our "Real" on the basis of reality. In the interpretive process, the natural complexity of life, not to mention the "complexity" of God, is reduced to language's categories of sameness.

This turn toward language in contemporary theory can be found as far back as the writings of later Heidegger, not to mention nineteenth-century thinkers such as Wilhelm von Humboldt. In his "Letter on 'Humanism'" (1949), Heidegger famously referred to language as the "house of being": "Language is the house of being. In its home, human beings dwell. Those who think and those who create with words are the guardians of this home."[22] Heidegger's phrase "house of being" connotes the manner in which language grants and bestows the possibility of "thinking" (*Denken*) upon humankind. Language, as a form of "being," graciously gives "being" to human thought. According to Heidegger, "being" is "holy" and is God's dwelling place, and language as the "house of being" provides an ontological framework within which God manifests God-self.[23] Thus, to study the being of language in its full materiality and historicality is not to deny God's revelatory activity. Just as the *emptiness* of Christ's tomb revealed divine presence, likewise, the emptiness of language shelters the trace of God that survives in the

---

[20] Ibid.
[21] Louis Montrose, "Renaissance Studies and the Subject of History," *English Literary Renaissance* 16 (1986): 5–12, esp. 6.
[22] Martin Heidegger, "Letter on 'Humanism,'" in *Martin Heidegger: Pathmarks*, ed. William McNeill (Cambridge: Cambridge University Press, 1998), 239–76, esp. 239.
[23] According to Heidegger, "The High One … inhabits the Serene of the holy"; M. Heidegger, "Remembrance of the Poet," trans. Douglas Scott, in *Existence and Being*, ed. Werner Brock (Chicago: Henry Regnery, 1949), 283, cf. 133. Cf. Joseph Kockelmans who comments, "Holding Himself back in the vastness of the holy (i.e., Being as what is whole), God waits there and sends holiness out before Him as his trace"; J. Kockelmans, *On the Truth of Being: Reflections on Heidegger's Later Philosophy* (Bloomington: Indiana University Press, 1984), 141.

remembrance of God as manifested in times past. However, the emptiness of language that shelters the trace of God who has come also *conceals* the God who will come. Biblical interpretation, whose medium is language, occurs at this interface between the remembrance of the God, who has come, and the anticipation of the God, who is to come. In the latter case, biblical language actually conceals that which is undetermined about God's future self-disclosure.

Positively speaking, the Sapir-Whorf hypothesis implies that one's language creates the very conditions of possibility for us to meaningfully experience anything including religious meaning. For example, Andor Gomme observes that it is "religious language" itself that "makes religious experience possible: it is a precondition of whatever understanding the religious person can have of the world and of whatever he can do in it."[24] In the case of biblical hermeneutics, passing *beyond* biblical language is possible only by passing *through* biblical language.

But, negatively speaking, the Sapir-Whorf hypothesis implies *we are not fully "in charge" of our thoughts and experiences.* As John Toews explains, the "creation of meaning" becomes "impersonal, operating 'behind the backs' of language users, whose linguistic actions can merely exemplify the rules and procedures of languages they inhabit, but do not control."[25] This issue, which is now termed the "semiotic challenge," was recognized more than a century ago by Friedrich Nietzsche, who described language as

a mobile army of metaphors, metonyms, and anthropomorphisms – in short, a sum of human relations, which have been enhanced, transposed, and embellished poetically and rhetorically, and which after long use seem firm, canonical, and obligatory to a people: truths are illusions about which one has forgotten that this is what they are.[26]

Similarly, Raymond Williams describes language as a "form of codification," that is, a kind of structure that determines what is thinkable, and therefore expressible.[27] Because the normative activity of language is representation, it is the linguistic categories of language that establish, at the outset, the means by which we represent in words the world of our experience, religious beliefs, values, and imagination.

This recognition of a language as a form of codification that guides and limits human thought is illustrated by another story of Jorge Luis Borges. In "Of Exactitude in Science," the cartographers of an imaginary kingdom "draw up a map so detailed that it ends up covering exactly the territory."[28] In other words, the scale

---

[24] Andor Gomme, "The New Religious English: A Form of Unbelief of the Day," in *Ritual Murder: Essays on Liturgical Reform,* ed. Brian Morris (Manchester: Carcanet Press, 1980), 75.

[25] John E. Toews, "Intellectual History after the Linguistic Turn: The Autonomy of Meaning and the Irreducibility of Experience," *American Historical Review* 92 (1987): 879–907, esp. 882.

[26] Nietzsche, "On Truth and Lie in an Extra-Moral Sense," in *The Portable Nietzsche,* ed. and trans. Walter Kaufmann (New York: Viking Penguin, 1954), 46–47.

[27] Raymond Williams, *Marxism and Literature* (Oxford: Oxford University Press, 1977), 167.

[28] Jorge Luis Borges, *Collected Fictions,* trans. Andrew Hurley (New York: Penguin, 1998), 325.

of the map is 1:1. Understandably, "succeeding generations came to judge a map of such magnitude cumbersome, and … abandoned it to the rigors of sun and rain."[29] This story of Borges was later reinterpreted by the French theorist Jean Baudrillard (1929–2007), who employed it to illustrate the concept of simulation. According to his retelling of the story, the citizens of the kingdom became so accustomed to the map that when it finally disintegrated owing to effects of weather and wear, the real territory under the map became exposed, but seemed alien to them. The citizens of the kingdom soon became *nostalgic for map*.[30] According to Baudrillard, we too have grown to prefer the simulation of maps to reality as it actually is. Whether or not you agree with Baudrillard, my primary point is that it is necessary to distinguish between biblical and theological language (as a map) and the reality presupposed by it.

As explained in Chapter 1, all signifieds function relationally within a linguistic system on the basis of their difference from other signifieds within the paradigmatic structure of language as a whole. Signifieds are defined negatively, according to their difference from other similar and opposite signifieds within the paradigmatic structure.[31] I have termed this "negative value." By adding this "paradigmatic" (synchronic) dimension to the traditional study of the words (syntagmatic groupings), Ferdinand de Saussure drew attention to a previously ignored dimension of language and, in so doing, paved the way for the study of the *structurality of language*.[32]

Whereas the post-Enlightenment era understood language as a medium whereby one can transparently communicate one's own thoughts and ideas, Saussure's exploration of the structurality of language demoted language from being an expression of pure human thought into a *structure*, which provides an impersonal, limiting framework for the formulation and expression of human thought.[33]

THE RISE OF STRUCTURALISM

In France during the 1950s an intellectual movement was born known as "structuralism." The origins of structuralism can variously be traced back to the influence

---

[29] Jorge Luis Borges, "Of Exactitude in Science," in *A Universal History of Infamy*, trans. Norman Thomas di Giovanni (New York: Dutton, 1972), 141.

[30] Jean Baudrillard, *Simulacra and Simulation,* trans. Sheila Faria Glaser (Ann Arbor: University of Michigan Press, 1994 [1981]), 1–42.

[31] Saussure, *Course in General Linguistics*, 115.

[32] Foucault, *Order of Things*, 281, 290.

[33] Nancy F. Partner, "Making Up Lost Time: Writing on the Writing of History," *Speculum* 61/1 (1986): 90–117; Christopher Blake argues that the fact that the past cannot be observed by direct sense perception has one significant consequence, namely that we must abandon a correspondence theory of language because a correspondence theory depends on the fact that correspondences can be verified by direct observation. Christopher Blake, "Can History Be Objective?" [1955], in *The Theories of History,* ed. Patrick L. Gardner (Glencoe, IL: Free Press, 1959), 340.

of the Copenhagen Linguistic Circle and to the writings of the ethnologist Claude Lévi-Strauss. In the 1930s the Copenhagen Linguistic Circle, founded by Louis Hjelmslev and Viggo Brøndal, rediscovered Boethius's theory of signification and the semiotic theory of Saussure. The writings of both Hjelmslev and Brøndal, on the one hand, and Lévi-Strauss, who applied Saussure's semiotic theory to the fields of anthropology and ethnology, on the other, led to the advent of French structuralism.[34] Lévi-Strauss famously argued that the symbolic structures within human societies, such as kinship systems, can be analyzed in the same way that Saussure analyzed language. In the wake of Lévi-Strauss's discovery of the structurality of human social practices and myths, others came to recognize the wider applicability of Saussure's semiotic theory for the analysis of repeating structures in such diverse fields as literary criticism (Roland Barthes), mythology (A. J. Greimas), psychotherapy (Jacques Lacan), developmental psychology (Jean Piaget), neo-Marxism (Louis Althusser), and biblical studies (Daniel Patte, Edmund Leach, D. Alan Aycock).[35] All applications of structuralism were based on the premise that many dimensions of human society can be interpreted as systems of signs comparable to language. Within a structuralist framework of analysis, meaning is grounded not in self-present knowing subjects but in structures such as culture and language. By implication, human beings do not themselves intentionally create their culture and language. Rather, they are *formed by* such structures.

The primary features of structuralism can be summarized as follows: first, language is understood as a structure that organizes human thought and creates the possibility for knowledge. From a structuralist perspective, the source of meaning is not the individual but the linguistic and cultural structure that governs a social collective. Whereas a romanticist, such as Schleiermacher, might have made the anthropocentric claim that "I (as author) speak language," a structuralist would counter "language speaks us." Second, this structure is viewed as an object that can be scientifically investigated. Third, like Saussure's subordination of *parole* to *langue*, the structuralists subordinated actual instances of any structure to the structure that produced them. Fourth, within the structure, there are no absolute terms but only differential relations of interdependence between terms. Finally, the structure is deemed to be autonomous and closed off to being changed by human actions.

A common analogy for the structuralist perspective is the game of chess. While these rules (structure) of chess are intelligible to an outsider to the game, such as chess players, they are not *fully* known to any of the individual chess pieces. For example, a bishop only "knows" what moves it is allowed to make at any point in

---

34 Saussure's lectures on linguistics were published posthumously in 1916 by his students as *Course in General Linguistics*.
35 For example, Daniel Patte and Aline Patte, *Structural Exegesis: From Theory to Practice* (Philadelphia: Fortress, 1978); Edmund Leach and D. Alan Aycock, *Structuralist Interpretations of Biblical Myth* (Cambridge: Cambridge University Press, 1983).

the game; it knows it can only move diagonally and that it cannot jump over other pieces; it knows it can capture other pieces by occupying the square on which they sit. All *this* a bishop knows, but it knows nothing else. For example, it does not know what a knight or rook can do, or even why it is engaged in the conflict constituted by the whole game. In fact, no chess piece knows the total rules or purpose of the game (i.e., its structure).

By analogy, a human cultural structure (e.g., American society, Korean society, first-century Mediterranean society) can be said to function like a chess game, or structure, that creates the rules for meaning and human symbolization of a given culture and society. Each individual in a given society (like a bishop or pawn in a game of chess) knows only what he, or she, individually is allowed to do within that structure, but no individual understands the structure as a whole. Each person's options for action are always constrained by, and limited to, those provided by the structure. Similarly, to be "in a tradition," such as the Reformed tradition, or the Confucian tradition, or the Brahman tradition, is also to be "in" a structure. It means having a certain way of using language and thinking about the world, and of inhabiting the world. In the case of both one's society and one's tradition, the structure we inhabit both creates *and* limits the possibilities available to us for knowing God and for conceptualizing the meaning of biblical texts and Christian faith.

Though many of the insights of structuralism live on in contemporary intellectual movements, structuralism itself had a relatively short life-span. It came to an end when its critics turned the structuralist strategy upon structuralism itself, effectively holding it captive to its own theory. They reasoned that if the humanities and social sciences are imprisoned within their own modes of discourse, and if their classificatory systems (including such abstractions as "society" and "culture") are all products of the signifying system, as structuralism maintained, then the *structuralism itself must be imprisoned within its own signifying system.* Structuralism was unable to answer this indictment. Its own metalanguage turned out to be yet another signifying system.

In the eyes of many theorists, including Jacques Lacan, Luce Irigaray, Julia Kristeva, Judith Butler, and the three great poststructuralists, Gilles Deleuze, Michel Foucault, and Jacques Derrida, the death of structuralism signified the end of the possibility of describing reality with any metalanguage or totalizing theory. Language is something humans receive rather than make. Perhaps the greatest continuing legacy of structuralism for us is its invitation to reflect on how our language creates a symbolic space within which we can talk and write about G-d.

THE LINGUISTIC TURN

Structuralism lives on, particularly in the form of the "linguistic turn," which is to say, in the turning of Western philosophy toward a linguistic philosophy. This "turn" arose out of the recognition that language is not a transparent medium of human thought.[36] Language is not a value-neutral, culture-free, scientific instrument for the representation of reality. It is a *taxonomic and symbolic* system that shapes what we take to be reality. To use Jacques Lacan's terminology, language constitutes our "Real."[37] Lacan famously distinguished between the "Real" and "reality." The "Real," namely that which we take to be the world, existing independently of our perceptions of it, is actually an *effect* produced by the symbolic order of language within our own unconscious: "The Real is not synonymous with external reality, but rather with *what is real for the subject*."[38]

Whereas Baudrillard's term *simulacra* presupposes that one can move beyond simulations to an experience of reality, Lacan argued that there are *only simulacra*. What we take to be reality is *always* a cultural construction. All we can ever experience is the "Real." Even our human perception that we have direct access to nature – unmediated by the symbolic order – is itself *an effect produced by the symbolic order*. In other words, the perception of nature as an absence of symbolization is *itself* a symbolization, which is based on the nature-culture binarism of language. "Nature" has "negative value" as part of a larger differential set of paradigmatic relations. Thus, when I began this chapter by describing the Mojave wilderness as a *natural* landscape devoid of human symbolization, I construed its meaning in terms of what it is not. My observation was structured on the nature-culture binarism. This is an example of the "Sapir-Whorf hypothesis." To look at the Mojave Desert and see it as a sign of the absence of human beings is another example of the construction of the "Real."

---

[36] The phrase "linguistic turn" actually brings together a number of diverse philosophical movements, beyond those associated with structuralism, including the philosophies of later Wittgenstein, Johann Georg Hamann, Wilhelm von Humboldt, and Richard Rorty (cf. his *The Linguistic Turn: Recent Essays in Philosophical Method* [Chicago: University of Chicago Press, 1967], though Rorty later dissociated himself from linguistic philosophy). For a summary of the far-reaching effects of this linguistic turn, see Elizabeth A. Clark, *History, Theory, Text: Historians and the Linguistic Turn* (Cambridge, MA: Harvard University Press, 2004), 42–62. The power of certain rhetorical tropes in historical discourse was explored by Hayden White in *Metahistory: The Historical Imagination in Nineteenth-Century Europe* (Baltimore: Johns Hopkins University Press, 1973); J. L. Austin, *How to Do Things with Words,* 2nd ed. (Cambridge, MA: Harvard University Press, 1975); G. Lakoff, *Women, Fire, and Dangerous Things* (Chicago: University of Chicago Press, 1987); Toews, "Intellectual History after the Linguistic Turn: The Autonomy of Meaning and the Irreducibility of Experience," 879–907; J. Vernon, "Who's Afraid of the 'Linguistic Turn'? The Politics of Social History and Its Discontents," *Social History* 19 (1994): 81–97.

[37] According to Lacan, even the human unconscious is structured according to the rules of language (*langue*). This semiotic structure exists in the unconscious prior to the differentiation of the "subject" from the undifferentiated self. Thus, the subject is essentially generated through this symbolic order of the unconscious. It "is caught in [the symbolic structure] from the first in his being. The illusion that he has formed [the symbolic order] by his consciousness results from the fact that it was by way of a *béance* (desire) specific to his imaginary relation to his counterpart, that he was able to enter into this order as a subject"; Jacques Lacan and A. Wilden, *Speech and Language in Psychoanalysis* (Baltimore: Johns Hopkins University Press, 1968), 107.

[38] Ibid., 161 (emphasis added).

In the following chapters, we discuss the impact of the "linguistic turn" on the hermeneutic tradition in the writings of Hans-Georg Gadamer, Paul Ricoeur, Emmanuel Levinas, and Gilles Deleuze and Félix Guattari. In various ways, their hermeneutic theories explore how the limitations imposed upon us by language simultaneously constitute the *positive conditions* for all hermeneutic practice.

CONCLUSION

By virtue of the nature of language's component of signification, and its intrinsic connection to the components of denotation and manifestation, biblical texts should not be read as mere reports or commentaries on the ancient worlds behind the text. The languages of biblical texts – Hebrew and Greek – provided the taxonomic registers and symbolic regimes by which their ancient authors understood and conceptualized their worlds, their religious communities, and their religious beliefs. This phenomenon, which is explained by the Sapir-Whorf hypothesis, is what precipitated the so-called linguistic turn of twentieth-century Western philosophy: language has since been demoted from the status accorded to it in the Enlightenment, namely, that of medium of the pure expression of human ideas and knowledge, to the status of being a *form of codification and symbolization*, which actually *shapes* human ideas and knowledge.[39]

The profound implications of the Sapir-Whorf hypothesis cannot be evaded by those whose task it is to interpret biblical texts. With our new insight into the phenomenon of linguistic relativity comes the negative realization that *our* "Real," as well as the "Real" of the ancient authors of biblical texts, is *always, already, semiotically encoded*. This insight awakens us to the realization that the beliefs, ideas, and faith commitments that are most familiar to us, all consist of *regimes of signs*. Our recognition of the effect of linguistic relativity empties the interpretive space of biblical studies of such traditional concepts as the grand narrative of disciplinary progress and the concept of noncontextual truth.[40] In Part III of this book, I argue that it is because the discursive conditions of traditional biblical studies have no primordial unity, or fixity, that its procedures can be reappropriated to achieve new ends.[41]

As a result of the linguistic turn, the world of biblical interpretation now takes on a very different appearance, at least to those of us who are citizens of twentieth-century thought. On the one hand, we find ourselves positioned outside the

---

[39] Foucault, *Order of Things*, 295–96.
[40] According to Foucault, even the concept of contextually free "truth" is itself a discursive construction, which does not correspond to any constant reality that exists as a historical fact. Truth is "a system of ordered procedures for the production, regulation, distribution and operation of statements." Michel Foucault, *Power/Knowledge: Selected Interviews & Other Writings, 1972–1977*, ed. Colin Gordon (New York: Pantheon, 1972), 133.
[41] Homi K. Bhabha, *The Location of Culture* (London: Routledge, 1994), 36.

"scientistic" mindset of the previous generation of scholars, who generally shared an Enlightenment conception of language and subjecthood. On the other hand, our new appreciation of the implications of linguistic relativity does not automatically reposition us in some kind of higher, methodological realm that is above or outside of the discursive field of traditional biblical studies.

In Chapter 12, I return to this point and discuss a kind of Deleuzian "higher empiricism," which may have the potential not only to expose the conditions of possibility of traditional, scientistically oriented forms of biblical interpretation but also to help biblical interpreters reimagine how the praxis of hermeneutics can be redirected in new ways. But, for the present, suffice it to say that this modified interpretive space, which accrues from an appreciation of linguistic relativity, changes our role as interpreters from that of creators of knowledge to that "speaking" of things and that of "associating" things together.[42] Such "speaking" and "associating" can perform a vital hermeneutic role because these are the very means by which biblical interpreters both discover and enact the potentialities inherent in biblical texts. In other words, the realization that our thought has been shaped by the very language we employ to create thought *has the positive effect of transforming us into active agents, who are empowered to associate.* Thus, the post-historical interpreter, who has been decentered from being a sovereign subject by the relativity of language, is simultaneously *enabled by the relativity of language* to participate in the "present sense-event."

---

[42] Kristeva, "Psychoanalysis and the Polis," in *Transforming the Hermeneutic Context,* ed. Gayle L. Ormiston and Alan D. Schrift (Albany: State University of New York Press, 1990), 92.

PART III

POST-HISTORICAL HERMENEUTICS

8

Interpretation as Dialogue: Hans-Georg Gadamer

Hans-Georg Gadamer (1900–2002), perhaps more than any other scholar, has raised the subject of hermeneutics to the level of public discourse in the twentieth century. Gadamer's hermeneutic theory is rooted in the phenomenological tradition of Husserl and Heidegger. Gadamer's interest in phenomenology began in 1922 when he read Husserl's *Logical Investigations*, the same work that had previously inspired both Wilhelm Dilthey and Martin Heidegger, as well as Ricoeur and Levinas. But Gadamer's long relationship with Heidegger was reflected in the greater influence of Heidegger's philosophical thought over Gadamer's hermeneutical theory, in comparison to that of Husserl.[1] Gadamer was particularly struck by the way Heidegger was reading pre-Socratic philosophical texts. He read them not as having purely historical value. Instead, he read the pre-Socratic philosophers with the expectation that their thought was relevant to our own contemporary questions.[2] Gadamer was changed by this new approach, and he too became convinced that the ancient texts of the great Western tradition could continue to have contemporary relevance for us today. This conviction culminated in the publication of his monumental *Wahrheit und Methode* in 1960, with the first English translation, *Truth and Method*, appearing fifteen years later in 1975.[3] This book is now regarded as one of the most important philosophic texts of the twentieth century.

GADAMER AND THE LINGUISTIC TURN

As discussed in Chapter 7, the so-called linguistic turn concerns the growing appreciation by philosophers of the essential connection between language and thought. Of course, the publication of Heidegger's *Being and Time* in 1927 preceded this turn

---

[1] At the end of Heidegger's career, it was Gadamer who edited his *Festschrift* on the occasion of his sixtieth birthday, and presented it to him on 12 January 1949. During World War II, Gadamer, being an anti-Nazi, did not receive an academic appointment until near the end of the conflict. He finished his career at Heidelberg University, where he remained until his death in 2002 at the age of 102.

[2] The term pre-Socratic designates Greek philosophers, including Thales (624–546 B.C.E.), Anaximander (610–546 B.C.E.), and Anaximenes (585–525 B.C.E.), who were active before Socrates.

[3] A second revised German edition was published in 1965 (Tübingen: J. C. B. Mohr), which was employed for the first English translation in 1975 (New York: Continuum). In the preface of the second German edition Gadamer responds to his early critics.

of philosophy toward language. In contrast, Gadamer's mature works, which were written much later, do take account of the structuring role of language on human thought. Part 3 of *Truth and Method* presents Gadamer's general discussion about language, providing a general argument for the close relationship between linguistic expression, understanding, and interpretation:

The fact is that the problems of linguistic expression are already problems of understanding. All understanding is interpretation, and all interpretation takes place in the medium of a language which would allow the object to come into words and yet is at the same time the interpreter's own language.[4]

Gadamer insists that there exists an "essential connection between understanding and language."[5] He remarks that "in the mirror of language, everything that exists is reflected."[6] He explains the fundamental connection between understanding, interpretation, and language through two basic premises: first, he argues that *all understanding is interpretation*. In other words, all understanding involves the *addition of meaning* because understanding is necessarily a dialogical process that fuses the horizon of the interpreter and the text.[7] Gadamer's second premise is that *all interpretation is linguistic*. Because all human thinking is tied to language, language functions as a kind of lens through which we symbolize our world in terms of degrees of similarity and difference. All human thought is preconditioned by language – by its categories, its hierarchies, its inherent binary oppositions, and so forth. Language functions as a kind of unspoken authorizing structure that is continually "affirmed, embraced, cultivated" in the day-to-day activity of interpreting the world around us.[8] The language of Western biblical interpretation and the language of the biblical texts themselves are both likewise imbued with the preconceptions of language and with language's particular ways of representing the religious world of the ancient Near East.

THE UNIVERSALITY OF THE HERMENEUTIC PROBLEM

As discussed in Chapter 3, an invidious comparison arose in the late nineteenth century between the objective knowledge produced by the natural sciences and the kind of knowledge created by the humanities. Scholars working in humanities

---

4 Gadamer, *Truth and Method*, 350.
5 Ibid.
6 Gadamer, "Rhetorik, Hermeneutik und Ideologiekritik," in *Kleine Schriften* I (Tübingen: J. C. B. Mohr, 1967), 118; cf. Gadamer, *Truth and Method*, 388.
7 On this point Gadamer remarks, "If a person transfers an expression from one thing to the other, he has in mind something that is common to both of them, but this need not be in any sense generic universality. He is following, rather, his widening experience, which sees similarities, whether of the appearance of an object, or of its significance for us. It is the genius of linguistic consciousness to be able to give expression to these similarities" (*Truth and Method*, 388–89).
8 Ibid., 280.

and social sciences, such as biblical studies, felt mounting pressure to answer this challenge by recourse to methodologically guided inquiry, which was deemed to be more objective. Gadamer addressed this challenge posed by the physical sciences differently: he argued that the humanities and the natural sciences are *both* a subspecies of a universal practice of hermeneutics. In his famous article "The Universality of the Hermeneutic Problem" (1966), he claimed that, far from being a problem restricted to the humanities, hermeneutics is a universal activity in which all human beings engage.[9] In everyday communication, people arrive at mutual understanding through a *hermeneutic* process. As Schleiermacher had previously observed, we are most aware of this hermeneutic process when misunderstanding arises. Only when intersubjectivity *breaks down*, and there is a failure to communicate, do we examine our prior interpretive process in order to ascertain the cause of the failure. Because hermeneutics is a universal problem, the primary challenge faced by biblical studies is not that of developing better methods of interpretation but rather that of applying hermeneutic theory to its own failures of understanding.

THE HORIZON OF UNDERSTANDING: A BORROWED VIEW

In the face of the sciences' emphasis on the acquisition of objective, universally valid knowledge, Gadamer developed an alternate model that emphasized the importance of appreciating one's own phenomenological *fore*-understanding (or preunderstanding), which both precedes interpretation and makes interpretation possible: "The first of all hermeneutic requirements remains one's own fore-understanding."[10] As such, one's own fore-understanding determines what meaning can be realized in the act of interpretation.

As previously discussed, human beings always interpret entities within their environment in terms of a phenomenological "horizon." Heidegger's analysis explored human beings (Da-sein) in their historical situatedness, recognizing that no horizon of meaning is held in common by all people. Gadamer also employed the term horizon itself to explain the role of one's preunderstanding in all interpretation. In Gadamer's words, a "horizon" is a "range of vision that includes everything that can be seen *from a particular vantage* point."[11] A "horizon" is a nontheoretical *preunderstanding* or fore-structure that makes all beliefs, ideas, and concepts possible.

The term "horizon" is derived from the Greek term *oros* (ὅρος), meaning a "limit" or "boundary." Thus, a phenomenological "horizon" imposes a limit or

⁹ Hans-Georg Gadamer, *Philosophical Hermeneutics*, trans. David E. Linge (Berkeley: University of California Press, 1976), 3–17.
¹⁰ Gadamer, *Truth and Method*, 262.
¹¹ Ibid., 269 (emphasis added).

boundary beyond which one cannot see, perceive, or understand. This concept of a horizon, as that which *limits* one's perspective, calls to mind the Chinese expression "to see the sky from the bottom of a well." In other words, a horizon actually *narrows* one's point of view, impeding one's perception from alternative points of view.

One of the implications that this limitation put on understanding by one's horizon is that we do not all experience the world the same way. For example, whereas I might experience the smell of freshly brewed coffee as inviting and comforting, a person from East Asia might experience the same smell as off-putting or repulsive. Similarly, a young boy living in the middle of the Sahara desert may not experience the sound of waves breaking on a beach or the scent of a perfume that smells like roses as the sound or smell of any particular thing at all, and he might interpret the sight of a flying kite as a large bird of prey.

A phenomenological horizon is a cognitive structure that supplies the conditions for us to meaningfully interpret the world around us. This cognitive structure can be thought of as a kind of "borrowed" view. It is borrowed in the sense that no individual possesses his or her own private, individualized horizon. A horizon always belongs to a collective of people, who share a common culture and worldview. Individuals only "borrow" this horizon. Because one's experience of the world is always shaped by this horizon, and this horizon is historically revisable from era to era, and age to age, it is equally true that *forms of human experience have their own history*.

For example, we have already discussed Rudolf Bultmann's analysis of the horizon of the first Pauline Christians, which included an apocalyptic view of time. Their expectation of the imminent end of the world and God's judgment through the agency (*parousia*) of the Son of Man and various angelic beings was a mythological view of the world that was borrowed from apocalyptic Judaism.[12] This mythological worldview functioned more as a horizon of shared meaning for early Christians than it did a conscious set of beliefs.

By way of a more contemporary example of a phenomenological horizon, consider the model of the Ptolemaic, earth-centered universe, which functioned as the interpretive horizon of meaning for Europeans before the Renaissance (fig. 8.1). For Christians, the earth-centered universe functioned more as a shared phenomenological horizon than as a theological belief. It seemed obvious to Europeans that if the earth was the center of the universe, then humanity (particularly European humanity) constituted the center of God's redemptive plan.

In the sixteenth century, Nicolaus Copernicus (1473–1543) developed a new model of the universe, in which the sun – not the earth – was located at the center

---

[12] Klaus Koch, *The Rediscovery of Apocalyptic: A Polemical Work on a Neglected Area of Biblical Studies and Its Damaging Effects on Theology and Philosophy*, Studies in Biblical Theology 2/22 (London: SCM Press, 1972), 18–35.

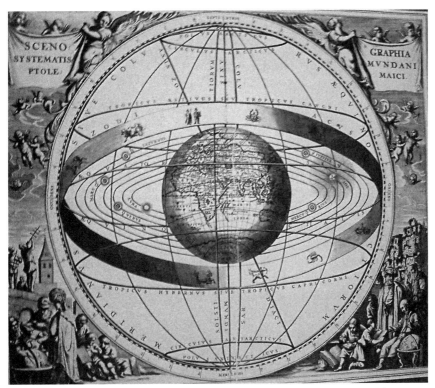

8.1. Andreas Cellarius's geocentric universe, *Harmonia macrocosmica Atlas* (Amsterdam 1661), Huntington Library, San Marino, California

of all things (fig. 8.2). Copernicus's heliocentric cosmology not only displaced the earth from the center of the universe but also dislodged humanity from the center of the cosmos. In the centuries that followed, the geocentric (Ptolemaic) horizon of the Western world has shifted to a heliocentric horizon, with the result that most people today presume the Copernican worldview, but not as a firmly held belief, but rather as a commonsense horizon or unconscious borrowed view.

In hindsight, this shift from a geocentric to heliocentric horizon may seem like a mere epistemological correction. But few individuals ever put this theory to the test to verify that it is true. In any case, most of our interpretive horizons are not so easily disproved. For example, Western societies tend to share a phenomenological horizon that assumes the priority of the rights of individuals over the rights of family and society. In contrast, many Confucian-based societies share the opposite horizon. Likewise, horizons of meaning concerning the *linearity* of time, the *progress* of Western civilization, the freedom of the human condition, and the capacity of language to *transparently* communicate one's own ideas have all contributed to

8.2. Andreas Cellarius's heliocentric universe, *Harmonia macrocosmica Atlas* (Amsterdam 1661), Huntington Library, San Marino, California

the formation of a pretheoretical, interpretive structure (horizon) that makes the world meaningful to most Westerners.

THE HISTORICALLY EFFECTED CONSCIOUSNESS

One dimension of our horizon of meaning is our consciousness of the historical past. According to Gadamer, our "horizon of the past" (*Vergangenheitshorizont*) influences us "in everything we want, hope for, or fear in the future."[13] He calls this historically influenced consciousness our "historically effected consciousness." By *historically effected*, he means that human consciousness is always shaped by history, culture, tradition, and language, in such a way that every act of interpretation is always "effected" by these factors. Our sense of belonging to a history, culture,

---

[13] Hans-Georg Gadamer, "The Universality of the Hermeneutic Problem" [1966], in *The Hermeneutic Tradition from Ast to Ricoeur,* ed. Gayle L. Ormiston and Alan D. Schrift (Albany: State University of New York Press, 1990), 147–58, esp. 151.

tradition, and language always *effects* our horizon of meaning, how we think, what questions we ask, how we relate to the past, and what we hope for in the future.

Our interpretation of the past (including the biblical past) is also made possible by our historically effected consciousness because we are always already part of the history that we set out to interpret. According to Gadamer, "the naiveté of so-called historicism" consisted in the fact that, "in trusting its own methodological approaches," it disregarded the historically effected consciousness of the historian.[14] Because the path to knowledge always begins by deciding what questions to ask, what methods to use, our historically effected consciousness plays a significant role in understanding all historical phenomena:[15]

If we are trying to understand a historical phenomenon from the historical distance that is characterized by our hermeneutical situation, we are always already affected by history. It determines in advance both what seems to us worth inquiring about and what will appear as an object of investigation, and we more or less forget half of what is really there – in fact, we miss the whole truth of the phenomenon – when we take its immediate appearance as the whole truth…. In relying on its critical method, historical objectivism conceals the fact that historical consciousness is itself situated in the web of historical effects.[16]

In Gadamer's view, this discovery of our own historically effected consciousness is "very likely the most important revolution among those we have undergone since the beginning of the modern epoch," whose "spiritual magnitude probably surpasses what we recognize in the application of natural science."[17] Its discovery has three implications for the practice of biblical interpretation.[18] First, the concept of the historically effected consciousness undercuts a subject-centered conception of rationality and objectivity. Second (and this is a Heideggerian theme), our recognition of the historically effected consciousness requires that we must attempt to "recognize beforehand the essential conditions under which it [our interpretations] can be performed." In other words, biblical interpretation necessarily requires that one bring one's own horizon of meaning *to the level of consciousness* in order to acquire a heightened degree of self-reflective awareness of our own particular "historical orientation" in finding history meaningful.

However indissoluble the ground of historical life from which it emerges, historical consciousness can still understand historically its own capacity to take up a historical orientation…. Historical consciousness no longer simply applies its own criteria

---

[14] Gadamer, *Truth and Method*, 266–67.
[15] Ibid., 299–300.
[16] Ibid., 300.
[17] Hans-Georg Gadamer, "The Problem of Historical Consciousness," in *Interpretive Social Science: A Reader*, ed. Paul Rabinow and William A. Sullivan (Berkeley: University of California Press, 1979), 109.
[18] Gadamer, *Truth and Method*, 263.

of understanding to the tradition in which it is situated, nor does it naively assimilate tradition and carry it on. Rather it adopts a reflective posture toward both itself and the tradition in which it is situated. It understands itself in terms of its own history. *Historical consciousness is a mode of self-knowledge.*[19]

Third, biblical interpreters must also attempt to gain a heightened degree of self-reflection on their *limits* in elucidating their own horizons of meaning. To one degree or another, our historically effected consciousness always remains inaccessible to our own self-scrutiny, as Gadamer observes, because it is "more being than consciousness."[20] We can never fully perceive the radical contingency of our own perceptual world. In fact, only with difficulty can we experience what Heidegger calls our own "strangeness" (*Unheimliche*). Each of us, in the core of our very beings, *constitutes a limit to our own self-knowledge.* Our own realization that this limit can never be fully overcome should guard us from any compulsion to totalize our own perception of things, of biblical texts, and of God, as if these perceptions were reality itself.

THE ROLE OF TRADITION

According to Gadamer, one's historically effected consciousness is also formed by the religious and intellectual tradition in which one finds oneself. By "tradition" Gadamer means the ongoing "effective history" (*Wirkungsgeschichte*) of the past upon the present. In making this observation, Gadamer was very aware that modern people tend to view tradition with suspicion, and place a much higher value on the role of human reason (as emphasized by the Enlightenment) to sweep away the burden of tradition. But, in Gadamer's view, the Enlightenment actually deformed the very concept of tradition: he argues that tradition is not an object passed down to us that we either accept or reject. Rather, it is a "happening" that has *already* taken hold of us and shaped us, whether or not we are aware of it.[21] In fact, tradition is so very close to us that it is *always* silently working at the back of our minds, beyond our control: "We are always preoccupied, hopefully and fearfully, with what is *closest to us.*"[22]

Gadamer never refers to "*the* tradition." Tradition has no fixed boundaries. It is not contained in a discrete set of texts that one can point to on a library shelf, nor is it a set of fixed theological doctrines and creedal confessions that can be listed on a sheet of paper. Indeed, in Gadamer's view, tradition even includes the Enlightenment ideal of rationality and objectivity, which we have all internalized, to one degree or another, as part of our horizon of meaning. In other words, the

---

[19] Ibid., 228.
[20] Gadamer, *Kleine Schriften*, 1:127, 158; cf. Gadamer, *Truth and Method*, xxxiv.
[21] Gadamer, "Universality of the Hermeneutic Problem," 150.
[22] Gadamer, *Truth and Method*, 271–73.

Enlightenment, and our understanding of the role of reason, are also part of tradition. Thus, Gadamer conceives of tradition fluidly as a historical happening arising from our ongoing dialogue with the past. In this light, human "understanding
itself should not be thought of so much as an action of one's subjectivity but as
entering into the happening of tradition (*Überlieferungsgeschehen*), by which the
past and the present are constantly fused."[23] This dialogue was under way long
before we were born and is never expressed with finality in our own lives because
it continues to change through our own engagement with it. Thus, far from being
a static body of texts, doctrines, and creeds, which have been passed on from
generation to generation, tradition is more like a dynamic *force* in which the old
and new are always recombining in the present into something new, which is of
living value.

The "happening" of tradition in the present has implications for biblical interpretation: because the interpreter of scripture can never step outside his or her
tradition, the truth of a biblical passage can be uncovered *only* from within one's
tradition. We can never approach the biblical texts as isolated objects of inquiry,
apart from tradition, or as somehow conceived as prior to our tradition. Our
horizons of meaning, our historically effected consciousnesses, and the questions
we ask about biblical texts are always guided by one's *own* tradition. In fact, the
Bible belongs to the whole of our tradition, and is in no way separable from the
course of history, which carries tradition. Consequently, as Gadamer observes,
"the actual meaning of a (biblical) text, as it speaks to the interpreter, is not
dependent on the (historical) occasion represented by the author and his original
public. At least it is not exhausted by it; *for the meaning is also determined by the
historical situation of the interpreter and thus by the whole of the objective course
of history*."[24]

Every book of Christian scripture belongs to a living tradition. As such, it is
more appropriate to speak of the Bible *as* tradition, rather than of the Bible *and*
tradition. Our individual acts of interpreting scripture always reflect the historical process that hands on tradition from one generation to the next. This fact
changes the role of the biblical interpreter from that of creating new, objective
knowledge about the Bible to that of forming new associations and relations from
within one's own living tradition. A particular biblical text becomes significant
to us when we discern that it answers questions that are being asked from within
our own tradition. Because our acts of interpretation always constitute engaging
tradition in dialogue (whether we realize it or not), our practice of interpretation
will improve if we bring the effective history of our tradition *fully to the level of
consciousness*.

---

23 Jürgen Habermas, "A Review of Gadamer's *Truth and Method*" [1967/1971], in Ormiston and Schrift,
   The Hermeneutic Tradition from Ast to Ricoeur, 235–36.
24 Gadamer, *Truth and Method*, 263–64 (emphasis added).

PREJUDICE

According to Gadamer, every tradition has its own particular prejudice. Consequently, owing to the effective history of tradition, every interpreter likewise has his or her own prejudice as well.[25] To appreciate Gadamer's point we must appreciate what he means by the term "prejudice." During the age of the Enlightenment, the term "prejudice" (*praejudicium*) was synonymous with false judgments, which cannot be legitimated by reason. The rationality was assigned the role of emancipating humanity from normalizing tendencies of religious prejudice (as false judgments), replacing falsehood and superstition with true, rational, verifiable knowledge. Enlightenment philosophers, such as Immanuel Kant, Baruch Spinoza, Thomas Hobbes, David Hume, and Jean-Jacques Rousseau, all argued that the religious prejudice in favor of tradition should be cast aside in order to understand the world rationally and objectively, as it actually is.[26] This high value that the Enlightenment accorded to rationality continues to influence greatly our own historically effected consciousness in the present, including the discipline of biblical studies.

Gadamer is well known for his attempt to rehabilitate the concept of prejudice, arguing that prejudice is a necessary component of all human understanding. In his view, prejudice constitutes the "conditions whereby we experience something – whereby what we encounter says something to us."[27] Far from arguing that we must leave our prejudices behind, Gadamer claimed that our prejudices are *indispensable,* for, without them, we cannot interpret anything.[28] Indeed, the very prejudices that preclude one's objective knowledge of the Bible also supply the *indispensable* conditions for knowing anything at all about the Bible, for it is through prejudice that the interpreter "anticipates" the meaning of a text: "[O]ur expectation and our readiness to hear the new [is] also necessarily determined by the old that has already taken possession of us."[29] Therefore, Gadamer argues that the goal of hermeneutics is not to eliminate prejudices but rather to bring them fully to the level of consciousness.

In response to Gadamer's emphasis on the positive function of prejudice in biblical interpretation, one might ask (as Jürgen Habermas did) how one can distinguish between correct and incorrect prejudices. But, in Gadamer's view, this very question is a product of the Enlightenment's historically effected consciousness. In fact, he even asserts that the Enlightenment's attack on prejudice is itself *part of the*

---

[25] Ibid., 266.
[26] Ibid., 304.
[27] Gadamer, "Universality of the Hermeneutic Problem," 151.
[28] Gadamer, *Truth and Method*, 397.
[29] Gadamer, "Universality of the Hermeneutic Problem," 152. Similarly, Gadamer remarks that the interpreter "appropriates the tradition from the horizon of expectations that is already formed by this tradition." Jürgen Habermas's "A Review of Gadamer's *Truth and Method*," 213–44, esp. 222.

prejudice of the Enlightenment. From this vantage point, even the Enlightenment failed to free itself from prejudice.

INTERPRETATION AS DIALOGUE

We have previously discussed how Saussure developed a theory of language (*langue*) as a synchronic semiotic structure shared by a linguistic community. A synchronic analysis privileges the importance of the structure of language (*langue*) over any particular instantiation of the structure in actual spoken or written communication (*parole*). Similarly, in his early writings, Ludwig Wittgenstein tried to study particular instances of speech acts (utterances) by treating them formally as ideal sentences, independent of the material contexts in which they were spoken. In Gadamer's view, the privileging of propositional language is the wrong starting point for understanding language because real language performs many functions beyond that of communicating ideas and propositions. For example, people also employ language to persuade, assert, defend, joke, thank, apologize, suggest, promise, request, and command. On this basis, Gadamer argued that the model that is best suited to understanding the use of real language is not propositional logic (as Wittgenstein maintained) but rather the give-and-take of actual human *dialogue.* In Gadamer's view, human communication does not have autonomous meaning apart from the specific social and material contexts in which it is socially employed between people. Therefore, if one is to understand human communication, it is necessary to take into consideration the wider social and material context that gives rise to it, which always involves other people and, therefore, always involves *dialogue.*

If Heidegger claimed that the fundamental task of being human is that of *understanding* through interpretation, Gadamer stressed that interpretation always takes the form of dialogue. In everyday life, we normally employ statements dialogically. As Gadamer remarks, "language is most itself" not in propositions but in the question-and-answer process of dialogue. Indeed, even propositions encountered outside of a dialogue (such as in a course textbook) can be understood as belonging to a preceding scholarly, question-and-answer dialogue concerning the subject. In fact, "there is no possible statement that cannot be understood as the answer to a question, and can only be understood":[30]

Every proposition has presuppositions that it does not express. Only those who think with these presuppositions can really assess the truth of a proposition. I maintain, then, that the ultimate logical form of the presuppositions that motivate every proposition is the *question.*[31]

[30] Jean Grondin, *Introduction to Philosophical Hermeneutics* (New Haven: Yale University Press, 1994), 119.
[31] Gadamer, *Truth and Method,* 299, cf. 331–33.

In the case of the historicocritical methods of biblical studies, each method might appear to be a scientific procedure that yields objective *monological*, factual propositions about biblical texts. But every proposition can also be conceived of as a *reply* to a question, arising out of an extended dialogue. For example, in the case of statements concerning textual criticism, the implicit question is, What was the original text of each of the documents of the New Testament? Redaction criticism presumes the implicit question, What theological point of view shaped the redactor's portrayal of Jesus in each of the canonical Gospels? Source criticism asks the question, What is the nature of the literary dependency between the three synoptic Gospels? Form criticism asks the question, In what literary form was early Christian material orally circulated, and what was its "situation in life" (*Sitz im Leben*)? All this is to say that even the propositions that one encounters in an introductory textbook about the New Testament have originated from a question-and-answer dialogue over generations between the historically effected consciousnesses of scholars. All academic propositions (including theological propositions) and *all* methodologies of biblical interpretation arise out of particular ways of asking questions about biblical texts. For this reason, the conclusions of biblical scholars should always be considered in the context of the prior dialogues and questions that shaped them. By implication, the practice of hermeneutics does not require that we step out of the ordinary practice of dialoguing with others: biblical interpretation is itself a form of human dialogue.[32]

INTERPRETATION AS DIALOGUE: WHO AM I, AND WHO ARE YOU?

Gadamer devoted much of his career to the study of the writings of Plato. These writings consist of extended dialogues between Plato's teacher, Socrates, and various characters, who attempt to answer Socrates' many probing questions. In view of Gadamer's interest in the dialogues of Plato, it is not surprising that Gadamer also founded his own theory of interpretation on the concept of dialogue.[33]

One of the challenges of reading Plato's dialogues is that he never speaks with his own voice: his dialogues consist of questions and answers between Socrates and his interlocutors. Though one might suppose that Plato inserted his own ideas into the mouth of his teacher, Socrates, this may not be the case. Gadamer maintained that neither Socrates nor his interlocutors communicate Plato's own understanding of truth. Rather, truth is worked out in the dialogical process itself: "It is not judgments but questions that have primacy in logic, as the Platonic dialogues and the dialectical origins of Greek logic show as well."[34]

---

32 The later Wittgenstein took account of everyday language. He famously referred to language as a "game" because each linguistic act follows certain rules and strategies.
33 Gadamer, *Truth and Method*, 359–61, 38, 464–65.
34 Gadamer, *Gesammelte Werke* (Tübingen: J. C. B. Mohr [Paul Siebeck, 1986]), 2:52.

Gadamer describes two kinds of dialogue. The first type is based on the scientific model. Within a scientific framework, one's dialogical partner is treated as an object to be explained. By way of example, consider how a psychiatrist interacts with a patient: the psychiatrist believes that he can come close to transcending his own historical nature and understand the patient's disorder without prejudice. This is an example of a one-sided dialogue. The hermeneutic corollary to such a one-sided dialogue entails taking a biblical text as an object to be explained by a detached interpreter (as sovereign subject). To approach a biblical text in this manner is really a *monologue* because the interpreter is never personally addressed by the biblical text.[35] According to Gadamer, a *true* dialogue begins only when we find ourselves personally addressed. Indeed, in his view, "this is the primary hermeneutic condition."[36] This model of dialogue is based on an attitude of *fundamental openness* to a guest whom we invite into our house:

[W]e welcome just that guest who promises something new to our curiosity. But how do we know the guest whom we admit is one who has something *new* to say to us? Is not our expectation and our readiness to hear the new also necessarily determined by the old that has already taken possession of us?[37]

We approach our guests not as objects to be explained but as special visitors who have something new to tell us. We approach our guests with anticipation. To think of a biblical text as such a special guest, and biblical interpretation as a kind of dialogue, implies that both the interpreter and the text have their own roles to play in the dialogue. This dialogic process begins with the recognition that a *prior relationship* exists between the interpreter and the scriptures, which is mediated by the effective history of tradition.[38] To engage in such a dialogue requires that the interpreter must curb his tendency to assimilate the text to his own expectations of meaning.

It is this very preexisting relationship between the text and interpreter that precludes the objectification of a biblical text as a mere object to be explained. According to Gadamer, the text, as one's dialogical partner, has the status of "thou" (*Du*), with whom one can engage in an intimate conversation.[39] We know that a *true* dialogue has taken place when we find ourselves questioned by the text. We must always, in principle, remain open to the possibility that the text may have something significant to say to us.

But how is it possible to be so questioned by a text that is, after all, an inanimate object? To be so questioned is to experience one's own subjecthood, personal identity, values, and one's personal choices challenged. One is so questioned when one

---

[35] Gadamer, *Truth and Method*, 259, 360.
[36] Ibid., 266.
[37] Ibid., 153.
[38] Ibid., 361.
[39] That is, the German familiar *Du* as opposed to the formal *Sie*.

feels perplexed about life after reading a text. One is questioned when one finds one's own horizon of meaning put at risk.[40] I must hasten to add that this process of feeling perplexed, questioned, and challenged does not at all imply that one should always adopt the values and implied horizon of meaning of the world of the text. But it does mean that the person of the interpreter must remain open to being questioned in order to achieve a heightened degree of self-reflective awareness, especially with respect to one's own chronic inauthenticity and well-rehearsed habits of self-evasiveness.

From this explication of true dialogue, it should be clear that the role of the biblical interpreter extends well beyond that of listening to, and obeying, what the text may say. After all, this process is a dialogue. In the ensuing conversation, the rights of the interpreter, as well as the text, must be respected.[41] As a matter of principle, the interpreter always retains the right *to speak and be heard*; the interpreter also has the right to question the text, to seek clarification, to argue, and even finally to remain unconvinced and disagree. In the end, one knows that a true dialogue has taken place not when the interpreter has passively acceded to the literal meaning of a biblical text but rather when she or he has asked the fundamental hermeneutic question: "Who am I and who are you?"[42]

Similarly, in the case of our engagement with our own religious and academic tradition (of which biblical texts are always a part), we do not simply submit to tradition. Gadamer argues that our relationship with one's tradition should also take the form of dialogue. At times, this dialogue might be a quiet conversation and, at other times, a forceful debate. In both cases, and in forms less extreme, we find ourselves in conversation with tradition. Because this is a dialogue, not a monologue, tradition has *an aspect of nonobligation* and is, in principle, open to revision over time through our engagement with it. Nonetheless, through dialogue with tradition, we may also experience our subjecthood questioned and find ourselves challenged to go beyond the limits of our own limited horizon of meaning. When this happens, our own lives contribute to the unfolding of tradition in the present.

THE VIEWED SUBJECT

The concept of having one's subjecthood called into question is illustrated by Michel Foucault's reflections on the painting *Las Meninas* (The Maids of Honor), by the renowned Spanish artist Diego Velázquez (fig. 8.3).[43] This painting represents the artist himself, Velázquez, on the left, working on a large canvas, the back of which

---

[40] Gadamer, *Truth and Method*, 373–74.
[41] Cf. ibid., 150.
[42] Hans-Georg Gadamer, *Gadamer on Celan: "Who Am I and Who Are You?" and Other Essays*, trans. Richard Heinemann and Bruce Krajewski (Albany: State University of New York Press, 1997).
[43] *Las Meninas*, originally named *The Family* (1656), in Museo del Prado.

8.3 Diego Velázquez, *The Maids of Honor* (*Las Meninas,* 1656),
Museo del Prado, Madrid (Scala / Art Resource, NY)

is visible to the observer. In the center of the painting is pictured Margarida Maria, the *infanta*,[44] accompanied by her attendants. She is the daughter of King Philip IV of Spain. The focal point of Velázquez's painting seems to be Margarida Maria.

As an observer of this painting, you may think of yourself as the "Wanderer" in David Caspar Friedrich's *Wanderer above a Sea of Mists* (see fig. 3.1). You presume yourself to be a sovereign subject, observing this painting from a position *outside*

---

[44] "Infanta" is a title given to a daughter of the king of Spain or of Portugal.

the painting's self-referential world. But to find the subject matter of the painting, which Velázquez (as painted in the picture) is currently working on, you must look into the mirror that is hung on the wall in the background of the painting. In this mirror, you can catch a glimpse of the dim reflection of the faces of the king and queen of Spain, Philip IV and his wife Mariana. It is *they* who are in the process of being painted by Velázquez. They seem to be the true subject matter of Velázquez's own painting. But aside from this reflected image, the king and queen are not visible to our view, as observers.[45]

Foucault observes that these absent subjects – Philip and Mariana – and the observers (you and I) are located in the same position. They are looking at us through the mirror, and we are looking back at them through the same mirror. As such, one might say that we, as the observers, and they, as the observed, take part in a ceaseless exchange, with reversing roles. We are reminded of Einstein's insight that "the relativity of the frames of reference is included in the object studied," which, according to Roland Barthes, results in "the relativization of the relations of writer, reader and observer (critic)."[46] One might even wonder, Who is observing whom? With this new awareness, we feel perplexed. Who is the subject, and who is the object? After all, note that even the painter, Velázquez (in the painting), is also looking at us, not Philip and Mariana. In fact, he seems to be painting *us*.

We, the presumed subjects, now in shock, find ourselves the observed spectators. As Foucault remarks, the "spectator is already the spectacle."[47] Are we, as the observers of this painting, standing in the place of the king and queen? Is the reflection we see in the mirror our *own* reflection? Who then is actually being painted? It now seems that, with our exchange of gazes with Philip and Mariana, and even with Velázquez himself, we ourselves have become part of the painting. It now appears that this painting is not about an event in the past at all. It is not about the infanta, or even about the king and queen of Spain. It is about the *interaction in the present moment* between the painting and ourselves. We have become part of the picture and, as such, find ourselves *stripped of our subjecthood*. In the midst of our ensuing anxiety, we ask the hermeneutic question, Who am I, and who are you? We find ourselves questioned by the painting.

Similarly, in the very act of interpreting any biblical text, there always exists the possibility that our own subjecthood will also be challenged and that we will thereby be awakened to *our own participation* in the act of bringing the present significance of the text into life. Granted that the dynamics of the present sense-event involve much more than willing, intending interpreters (see Chapter 12), it remains true that without human interpreters there can be no text-reception complex and therefore no present sense-event.

[45] Michel Foucault, *The Order of Things* (New York: Pantheon, 1970), 3–16.
[46] Roland Barthes, *Image Music Text,* trans. Stephen Heath (New York: Hill and Wang, 1977), 156.
[47] Foucault, *The Order of Things*, 312.

THE FUSION OF HORIZONS

In the encounter between the interpreter and a biblical text, both dialogical partners have their own phenomenological horizons of meaning. When you question
a biblical text, you cannot leave your own horizon behind. In fact, every question you ask of the text presupposes your own horizon.[48] Therefore, whenever you
deliberately set out to understand the meaning of a biblical text, it is always your
"own thoughts" that "have gone into re-awakening the text's meaning."[49]

Biblical texts have their *own* horizons of meaning as well. As previously noted
in our discussion of Rudolf Bultmann, biblical texts are inscribed with ancient
beliefs concerning the system of patriarchy, the efficacy of sacrifice, and the reality
of humans becoming polluted and requiring purification, as well as the acceptance
of curses, apocalyptic timetables, gnostic dualisms, and many other trappings of
the mythological worldview of the Hellenistic era, all of which are grounded in
widespread ancient pretheoretical, precognitive horizons. These ancient horizons of meaning are diffused throughout biblical texts. They constitute the virtual
"unsaid" of every text. As such, the founding sense-event of a biblical text does
not reside solely in its semantic content, in its words, phrases, and sentences: its
"sense" is also structured by these phenomenological horizons, within which the
texts have been suspended.

Therefore, whenever we translate, read, or interpret a biblical text, we always
encounter as implied its phenomenological horizons, which are often, of course,
strikingly different from our own contemporary horizons of meaning. When
this happens, text presents "itself in all its otherness" as it "assert(s) its own fore-
meanings."[50] This helps to explain why you might experience a biblical text as
strange, bizarre, or even offensive. In Gadamer's view, the experience of some texts
as familiar and others as strange is an important part of biblical hermeneutics.
Gadamer explains that "the place of strangeness and familiarity that a text has
for us is that intermediate place between being an historically intended separate
object and being part of tradition. The true home of hermeneutics is this intermediate area."[51] At this point, it must be emphasized that a text's "strangeness" is not a
property of the text itself. A text seems strange to us when it does not fit comfort-
ably within our own horizon of meaning. A biblical text can only be meaningful
to us if it can somehow be located within our own phenomenological horizon.
By implication, the experience of a text's strangeness actually exposes important

---

[48] Gadamer, *Truth and Method*, 271–73. He remarks: "Indeed, it could very well be that only *insignificant* things in historical consciousness permit us to approximate this idea of totally extinguishing
individuality, while the great productive achievements of scholarship always preserve something of
the splendid magic of immediately mirroring the present in the past and the past in the present"
(Gadamer, "The Universality of the Hermeneutic Problem," 149–50).

[49] Gadamer, *Truth and Method*, 388.

[50] Ibid., 269.

[51] Ibid., 263.

details of one's own horizon of meaning. Thus we should always value this experience because through it can arise a heightened degree of self-awareness and self-transparency.

To take an example from everyday life, whenever we are confronted by strangeness and difference, such as we might when traveling in a foreign country, what we are most aware of is not pure difference itself but *how things differ from our sense of what is "normal."* In other words, we always experience difference in terms of *degrees of difference* from our own expectations (e.g., this person is different from people with whom I normally interact in terms of *x*, this food is different from the food I normally eat in terms of *y*, this way of interacting is different from the way the people I know interact in terms of *z*). Reflecting on our actual experiences of difference can help us elucidate our *own* interpretive horizons. Indeed, as noted earlier, one of the possible outcomes of interpretation is that the interpreter will find that his or her own horizons are not only elucidated but even questioned, tested, or put at risk.

This brings up Gadamer's concept of a "fusion of horizons" (*Horizont-verschmelzung*). First, it must be observed that this so-called *fusion* of horizons does not imply a unification, blending, or amalgamation of one's phenomenological horizon with the horizon of the text. Nor by "fusion of horizons" does Gadamer mean a fusion of conscious beliefs, ideas, or concepts. That which is brought into contact are not beliefs, ideas, and concepts, but those pretheoretical, precognitive *pre*understandings which make our beliefs, ideas, or concepts possible.

The outcome of this so-called fusion is primarily "to understand *the context of what is said* [or written]" from the perspective of a horizon that is not one's own.[52] In simple terms, the *fusion* of horizons creates the possibility for the interpreter to see her phenomenological horizon and the phenomenological horizon of the text *at one and the same time.* This simultaneous awareness of two horizons at once is the *experience of the contingent nature* of both one's own perceptual world *and* that of the biblical text. The fusion of horizons is the experience of becoming conscious simultaneously of the idiosyncratic nature of one's own perspective and the idiosyncratic nature of the perspective of the text, with the result that both horizons are surpassed and exceeded.[53] By "surpassing," I do not imply that one's own horizon of meaning becomes neutralized, or that one comes to achieve some form of final objectivity. Far from it. However, this fusion of horizons does *create a modified temporal space from which one can see beyond the former limits of one's own historically effected consciousnesses.*[54]

---

[52] Ibid., 262 (emphasis added).

[53] Ibid., 273.

[54] "In this the interpreter's own horizon is decisive, yet not as a personal standpoint that he maintains or enforces, but more as an opinion and a possibility that one brings into play and puts at risk, and that helps one truly to make one's own what the text says. I have described this above as a 'fusion of horizons'" (ibid., 388).

The pioneering American psychologist and philosopher William James (1842–1910) gives an example of such a fusion of horizons, drawn from his trip to the Appalachian Mountains. One day he saw an opening in the forest that had been clear-cut and replaced with a muddy garden, a log cabin, and some pigpens. James was appalled because "the forest had been destroyed; and what had 'improved' it out of existence was hideous, a sort of ulcer, without a single element of artificial grace to make up for the loss of Nature's beauty." But just then a farmer came out of the cabin and told him "we ain't happy here unless we're getting one of those coves under cultivation."[55] At that moment, James realized his horizon of meaning was different from that of the Appalachian farmers. He confesses,

> I had been losing the whole inward significance of the situation. Because to me the clearings spoke of naught but denudation, I thought that to those, whose sturdy arms and obedient axes had made them they could tell no other story. But when *they* looked on the hideous stumps, what they thought of was personal victory.... In short, the clearing which to me was a mere ugly picture on the retina, was to them a symbol redolent with moral memories and sang a very paean of duty, struggle and success.[56]

Thus this experience of difference made it possible for William James to become simultaneously aware of his own horizon of meaning *and* the horizon of meaning of the Appalachian farmers. His resulting heightened awareness created a dynamic space of interaction between these two phenomenological horizons within James's own consciousness. This new "hermeneutical" consciousness endowed him with "the real power ... to see what is questionable" on the basis of the whole of human experience.[57]

The event of the fusion of the present horizon of the biblical interpreter and the past horizon of a biblical text is not a one-time event.[58] Gadamer argues that the human imagination has a hermeneutical function in repeating this process, again and again, thereby exposing to oneself new and productive questions. This is possible because the imagination does not ask, What did this text mean in its original historical setting? but rather, Where does this text take us? This latter question turns the fusion of horizons into an ongoing, open-ended process, which can move in different directions as one rereads the same texts over time. Thus, in Gadamer's view, "it is imagination [*Phantasie*] that is the *decisive* function of the scholar."[59]

---

55 William James, "On a Certain Blindness in Human Beings," in his *Talks to Teachers on Psychology*, ed. Frederick Burckhardt and Fredson Bowers (Cambridge, MA: Harvard University Press, 1983), 134 (quoted by Richard Rorty, *Contingency, Irony, and Solidarity* [Cambridge: Cambridge University Press, 1989], 38). A cove is a small valley between two ridges that is closed off at one end.

56 James, "On a Certain Blindness in Human Beings," in Rorty, *Contingency, Irony, and Solidarity*, 38.

57 Gadamer, "Universality of the Hermeneutic Problem," 153.

58 "As soon as the historian acts at all, he produces new relationships that combine into a further story from a new perspective"; Habermas, "A Review of Gadamer's *Truth and Method*," 229.

59 "Universality of the Hermeneutic Problem," 154 (emphasis added).

In response to Gadamer's affirmation of the role of the imagination in interpretation, you might be tempted to demand that we restrict the practice of hermeneutics to the elucidation of the "literal," or historical, or (authorially) intended meaning of biblical texts, and abandon the imagination altogether. But, in Gadamer's framework, the conviction that real meaning of a text is its literal, or historical, or authorially intended meaning is itself another aspect of our Western, post-Enlightenment, historically effected consciousness, which has been formed most notably by the blending of the traditions of historicism and romanticism.[60] Given the fact that the traditions of historicism and romanticism are both relative new comers in comparison with the whole of the Christian interpretive tradition (stretching back almost two thousand years), it should be observed that, during the first seventeen hundred years of Christianity, biblical interpreters have never confined themselves exclusively to the literal, historical, or intended meanings of texts. For example, the Alexandrian school of interpretation made extensive use of allegory. Its leading expositor, Origen of Alexandria (185–254), argued that since everything in scripture consists of mysteries, all scripture should be interpreted *spiritually*. In book 4 of his treatise *On Principles*, Origen lays out a systematic discussion of the allegorical and typological interpretation of scripture, which requires the *suppression* of the literal meaning of biblical texts. According to Origen, the Holy Spirit actually conceals a deeper meaning under the veil of the literal meaning (*On Principles* 4.2.7). Origen's doctrine of the spiritual progression through three levels of meaning was ultimately believed to lead to divine wisdom. In the medieval period, Origen's theory of the three levels of meaning was reworked as a doctrine of the fourfold senses of scripture in the writings of Johannes Cassianus (360–430/35). This latter doctrine distinguished a literal meaning (what "happened"), an allegorical meaning (what one should believe), a moral or "tropological" meaning (how one should act morally), and an "anagogical" meaning (what one should hope for). Thus, the contention that the meaning of scripture should be confined to its literal or historical dimensions is actually contrary to the greater part of the Christian interpretive tradition.

Thus, Gadamer is on firm ground when he rejects romanticism's and historicism's assertion that a text possesses a "unitary meaning," and emphasizes the role of the interpreter's imagination in the discovery of the *multiple* present sense-events.[61] Gadamer actually defends the authority of texts over and *against* the intentions of their historical authors: in response to the romanticist notion of reliving, or reexperiencing, an author's intended meaning, Gadamer argues that interpretation is "not a mysterious communing of souls, but a sharing of common

---

[60] Gadamer, *Truth and Method*, 336–37.
[61] Dominick LaCapra, "Rethinking Intellectual History and Reading Texts," *History and Theory* 19 (1980): 245–61; reprinted in Dominick LaCapra and Steven L. Kaplan (eds.), *Modern European Intellectual History: Reappraisals and New Perspectives* (Ithaca, NY: Cornell University Press, 1982), 23–56.

meaning" through dialogue *with the text* (not the author).[62] On the basis of his conceptualization of tradition, Gadamer argues that a biblical text, once written, actually becomes distanced from the contingencies of its original historical author and historical context and is joined into the totality of the course of history that followed the text's composition.

Of course, from a practical perspective, biblical "authors" are long deceased and unavailable to us directly. As such, one cannot engage in a dialogue with a biblical historical author. That which *is* available to us are physical copies of copies of copies of the *texts* they once composed, as they have been salvaged, collected, edited and reshaped, copied, suppressed, and promoted over the course of centuries by the interpretive tradition. Only these later copies of biblical texts, as handed down by tradition, possess the capacity to enter into a dialogue with present-day interpreters. For example, we can dialogue with the book of Isaiah (but not with Isaiah the prophet), within the ongoing tradition of interpretation; and we can dialogue with the Letter to the Romans (not with the apostle Paul), within this same tradition. In each and every case, the resulting *present sense-event* does not ultimately depend upon the contingencies of the original historical author or the intended historical addressees or readers for the text, as a past authorial "said" disappeared two millennia ago. What has been passed on by our tradition is textual "saying," an ever-changing present sense-event.[63] By implication, this present sense-event for us will *always go beyond* the literal and historical meaning, according to our own changing contexts, challenges, and commitments.[64]

Gadamer privileges this textual "saying" (as part of tradition) as our dialogical partner, over the original, historical authorial textual "said." This privileging of the "saying" over the "said" changes the nature of hermeneutics from that of merely reconstructing the founding sense-event to one of discovering a text's new meanings through open-ended dialogue. By implication, hermeneutic understanding requires that one understand a text *differently* from how its original, historical authors and intended recipients understood it. Because interpretation always requires a *fresh* appropriation of the founding sense-event as a present sense-event, arising out of an open-ended dialogue, within the effective history of tradition, the present sense-event will always *go beyond* the founding sense-event.[65] Therefore, authentic biblical interpretation always entails an addition of value to the effective

---

[62] Gadamer, *Truth and Method*, 260.
[63] Ricoeur comments that, at the moment a text is written, *le dire* (the original authorial saying) disappears, and only *le dit* (the textual-said) survives; cf. Ricoeur, *Hermeneutics and the Human Sciences: Essays on Language, Action and Interpretation,* trans. and ed. John B. Thompson (Cambridge: Cambridge University Press, 1981), 92.
[64] Gadamer, *Truth and Method*, 354.
[65] Ibid., 46–50.

history of a text within a tradition. For this reason, the meanings of biblical texts in the present are inexhaustible.⁶⁶

When one seeks the present sense-event of a biblical text, what kind of knowledge is one seeking? Aristotle once distinguished between three kinds of knowledge: practical knowledge or wisdom, scientific knowledge, and technical knowledge.⁶⁷ The term "practical wisdom" or *phronisis* (φρονήσις) refers to the kind of knowledge required for dealing with the challenges of daily living in the real world. Such practical wisdom is never gained in a purely theoretical manner for it is a kind of wisdom that accrues from one's personal reflection on past experiences.

Gadamer borrowed Aristotle's concept of practical wisdom, arguing that interpretation should always lead to some kind of practical wisdom in the art of living.⁶⁸ By implication, the goal of biblical hermeneutics is not the mere attainment of *any* type of knowledge about the Bible because there is no "guarantee in any way" of "the productivity of … [the] application" of just any kind of knowledge. Indeed, "there is (even) such a thing as methodological sterility …, that is, the application of a method to something not really worth knowing."⁶⁹ Thus, in Gadamer's view, the primary goal of hermeneutics is not the factual elucidation of the founding sense-event of a text but the discernment of practical wisdom for living in the present. I have termed such wisdom the "present sense-event" of a text (cf. Chapter 1). Unlike the founding sense-event, the present sense-event always concerns the person of the interpreter, the care of the self, and one's thoughtful engagement with others and the world. By implication, *the quest for such practical wisdom is always an extension of the knowledge of oneself because knowledge of the self contributes to self-transformation.* Thus, the hermeneutic process is circular: the search for practical wisdom leads to self-transformation, and self-transformation leads to further practical wisdom. And so it follows that, *in the act of interpreting a*

---

⁶⁶ Agreeing with Gadamer, Habermas states, "A series of events acquires the unity of a story only from the point of view that cannot be taken from those events themselves. The actors are caught up in their histories; even for them – if they tell their own stories – the point of view from which the events can take coherence of a story arises only subsequently…. As long as new points of view arise, the same events can enter into other stories and acquire new significations." Cf. Gadamer, *Truth and Method*, 356; Habermas, "A Review of Gadamer's *Truth and Method*," 227.

⁶⁷ Gadamer, *Truth and Method*, 278–93. In the opening section of the anonymous Jewish philosophical treatise *4 Maccabees*, the author sets out his primary thesis, that "practical wisdom" (φρονήσις) is the "highest virtue" of all the four Platonic cardinal virtues: "The subject that I am about to discuss is most philosophical, that is, whether devout reason is sovereign over the emotions. So it is right for me to advise you to pay earnest attention to philosophy. For the subject is essential to everyone who is seeking knowledge, and in addition it includes the praise of the highest virtue – I mean, of course, *practical wisdom*" (*4 Macc* 1:1–2).

⁶⁸ Gadamer adopted from Heidegger Aristotle's notion of *phronesis* as "practical wisdom" (*Truth and Method*, 278–93); cf. Aristotle, *Nicomachean Ethics*, IV, 3–10.

⁶⁹ Gadamer, "Universality of the Hermeneutic Problem," 153.

biblical text, the very person of the interpreter is always at stake.[70] Such a privileging of practical wisdom over propositional or scientific knowledge would require
that one replace the traditional, positivistic model of biblical interpretation as sovereign subject (who treats biblical texts as objects to be explained) with a properly
hermeneutic model, which recognizes what is at stake for the interpreter is nothing less than self-transformation.

ASSESSING GADAMER'S USE OF HEIDEGGER'S PHENOMENOLOGY

Gadamer's hermeneutic theory clearly builds upon the foundations of Heidegger's
existential phenomenology: his critique of the Enlightenment ideal of objectivity,
his concept of the historically effected consciousness, the importance of the effective history of tradition, the productivity of prejudice, and the fusion of horizons
are all extensions, in one way or another, of Heidegger's phenomenological theory.
Like Heidegger, Gadamer also argues that understanding is not a *re*productive but
a *productive* process that always involves the horizon of the interpreter.[71] Granting
his profound indebtedness to Heidegger, Gadamer nonetheless remained attached
to what some scholars have termed a "metaphysics of recollection" (*Erinnern*),
in the sense that he remained committed to the notion that truth is passed on
in tradition. As previously discussed, Heidegger argued that tradition hands on
possibilities for existence, which can be incarnated in one's own life. According to
Heidegger, authentic Da-sein exists by projecting itself toward its own future possibilities, exploring its past in terms of its *ek-static* future. But, in Heidegger's view,
that which is carried forward by tradition is not a growing accumulation of truth
but rather existential possibilities of ways to live authentically in the future. In fact,
as we have previously discussed, Heidegger argues that the "repetition" of these
possibilities of living may actually require some element of their "dismantling"
(*Abbau*) or even "destruction" (*Destrucktion*) of the knowledge handed down by
the tradition.[72] Thus, in Heidegger's understanding of tradition, there is a *necessary* tension between its positive and negative dimensions, resulting in his overall
ambivalent attitude toward it: tradition is both necessary and dispensable, at the
same time. Owing to his suspicion of tradition, Heidegger is even prepared to
carry out a destruction of aspects of tradition.

---

[70] Michel Foucault, *The Hermeneutics of the Subject: Lectures at the Collège de France, 1981–1982,*
trans. Graham Bruchell, ed. F. Gross (New York: Palgrave Macmillan, 2005), xxiv.

[71] Gadamer, *Truth and Method,* 263–64.

[72] *Destruktion* is a key term in Heidegger's early writings. It was first used by Heidegger in a course
he taught in the summer semester of 1920. His use of this term is rooted in Luther (Charles R.
Bambach, *Heidegger, Dilthey and the Crisis of Historicism* [Ithaca, NY: Cornell University Press,
1995]). The term *Destruktion* summarizes his idea of phenomenology with respect to the uncertainty of one's own existence. In the years following his "turning" (*Kehr*), he attempted *Destruktion*
of *Geisteswissenschaften* (Bambach, *Heidegger,* 201–3; John D. Caputo, *Radical Hermeneutics:
Repetition, Deconstruction, and the Hermeneutic Project* (Bloomington: Indiana University Press,
1987), 60–61.

In contrast to Heidegger, Gadamer supposes that tradition hands on more than just possibilities for living: it actually hands on *truth*. Indeed, he believes there is a kind of progress of truth over the centuries, a concept that is reminiscent of the philosophy of Hegel. Whereas Plato defined the Truth beyond human affairs and in opposition to the flux of history, Hegel plunged Truth into the flux of history and then tried to reconcile them through the dialectical process of a synthesis of thesis and antithesis. Gadamer modified this Hegelian view, arguing that truth must always be reappropriated afresh, dialogically, by each successive generation. Nonetheless, he believes that the present generation does not begin from scratch. Even with his insistence on the indefinite plurality of expressions of Truth, and the need for the continuous reappropriations of Truth, Gadamer still follows in the tradition of Hegel's dialectics, leading some scholars to accuse him of domesticating the radicality of Heidegger's hermeneutical project.[73]

Whereas Heidegger emphasized that Da-sein always looks forward to the future *before* looking back to its past, Gadamer's ideal interpreter looks backward first before looking forward. By viewing the Western tradition as a "thou" handed on by the past, Gadamer has, in effect, redirected Heidegger's radical hermeneutics in a Hegelian direction and thereby supplanted Heidegger's "destruction" of Western metaphysics with his own metaphysics of a recollection of truth. Whether you view this aspect of Gadamer's hermeneutics as a necessary correction of Heidegger's radicalism or as a regrettable domestication of Heidegger's genius, it is important to appreciate what is distinctive about Gadamer's own hermeneutical theory.

CONCLUSION

In the exploration of the present sense-event of biblical texts, we cannot simply leap into past literal or historical meanings. Interpretation necessitates an open-ended and respective dialogue between the interpreter and a biblical text, as it is passed down to us by the effective history of tradition. In this process, an authentic dialogue will always move beyond the founding sense-event to a fresh experience of the text from within our own present possibilities. In this dialogue, one never interprets the Bible as a solitary interpreter: we always stand within a living tradition, whose effective history is woven into our own historically effected consciousness. This consciousness, in turn, guides the questions we ask of biblical texts. By implication, the present sense-event is not a fixed object awaiting recovery but rather something that changes over time according to how biblical texts are read within different traditions, by different interpreting communities, in different historical contexts, over the centuries. In the ensuing dialogue, the Bible, the interpretive tradition, and our own horizons of meaning constantly recombine into new wisdom for living in the present.

---

[73] Caputo, *Radical Hermeneutics*, 96, 111, 113.

9

☙

Interpretation and Critique: Jürgen Habermas

In this chapter, I discuss the role of reason in biblical interpretation, especially as a tool to critique the ideological use of the Bible to control and oppress others. According to the Lacanian philosopher Slavoj Žižek, the first example of the use of reason to oppose such a use ideology is found in the book of Job.[1] After Job's possessions were destroyed, his children killed, and his body became covered by a dreadful skin disease, three theologians came to visit him: Eliphaz, Bildad, and Zophar. They tried to convince him that *he* was the cause of his own suffering: in their view, Job must have sinned and provoked God's punishment. Indeed, *this* was the *hidden* meaning of Job's suffering. The three theologians then proceeded to rebuke Job for his unwillingness to confess his sins. In reply, Job insisted that his suffering had no deep meaning (Job 27). He then proceeded to critique their theological strategy of blaming the victim as an *ideological* strategy whose intended purpose was to legitimize theologically Job's suffering. To everyone's surprise, God intervened in this debate and took Job's side: the Lord praised Job for his truthful speech and declared that the theology of the theologians had distorted God's own truth.

I discuss not only the hermeneutic role of reason in critiquing ideology but also the problems that accompany the use of human rationality in general. As we shall see, the founders of the Frankfurt school, Max Horkheimer and Theodor Adorno, were critical of the ways in which rationality – as espoused by the Enlightenment paradigm – has been ideologically redirected in our own age to advance oppression, in the service of technology and the production of goods. Habermas, for his part, argued in favor of the continuing importance of human reason in pursuit of a more humane and just world.

The style, language, and concepts of the writings of Jürgen Habermas are very different from the phenomenological writings of Heidegger, Bultmann, and Gadamer because Habermas represents a different intellectual tradition, namely that of the so-called Frankfurt school, sometimes known as "critical theory." The term "Frankfurt school" is an informal term designating a group of neo-Marxist scholars who were affiliated with, or influenced by, the Institute for Social Research (Institut für Sozialforschung) at the University of Frankfurt am Main. In the wake

---

[1] Slavoj Žižek, "The Act of Its Vicissitudes," *The Symptom: Online Journal for Lacan* 6 (May 2005).

of the failure of working-class revolutions in Western Europe following the First World War, and the simultaneous rise of fascist governments in Europe, the University of Frankfurt brought together a number of dissident Marxists in an effort to reinterpret Marxist theory in the face of new, emerging social realities. The founding members of the Frankfurt school were Max Horkheimer, Theodor Adorno, Herbert Marcuse, and Walter Benjamin. In different ways, each argued that Enlightenment rationality, as reappropriated by science and technology, had become a vehicle of oppression and human suffering in the modern world. The publications of the Frankfurt school can be divided into three phases. The so-called first wave of the Frankfurt school was founded by Horkheimer (1895–1973) and Adorno (1903–69). Their coauthored book *Dialectic of Enlightenment* (*Dialektik der Aufklärung*, 1944) and Adorno's *Minima Moralia* (1951) have the status of founding texts of critical theory.[2] Jürgen Habermas is associated with the third wave of the Frankfurt school.

Habermas is important to the field of biblical hermeneutics for a number of reasons. First, he engaged in a famous debate with Gadamer concerning the nature of hermeneutic praxis. This debate now has the status of the classical hermeneutic debate of modern times. It focused on the universal, hermeneutic claims made by Gadamer in his book *Truth and Method*. Second, many contemporary modes of biblical interpretation, such as feminist criticism, postcolonial criticism, and liberation theology, have their roots in critical theory, which explains why these newer methods of interpretation tend to evaluate practices of interpretation *ethically*, that is, with respect to their impact upon others. For example, the feminist scholar Elisabeth Schüssler Fiorenza has called for an "ethics of valuation," arguing that biblical interpreters must consider the ethical consequences and political functions of biblical interpretation.[3] All this is to say that an understanding of Habermas's work provides a basic framework for comprehending and critiquing such newer interpretive approaches. Third, a knowledge of Habermas's theory also provides a nonphenomenological theoretical structure by which to critique the phenomenological tradition *outside* the tradition itself.

KARL MARX AND IDEOLOGY

To understand and situate the critical theory of Habermas, one must have some basic familiarity with Marxist theory, the work of Horkheimer and Adorno, and the meaning of the term "ideology." Liberal Protestantism has tended to view

---

[2]   Max Horkheimer and Theodor W. Adorno, *Dialectic of Enlightenment: Philosophical Fragments,*
    ed. Gunzelin Schmid Noerr, trans. Edmund Jephcott (Stanford, CA: Stanford University Press,
    2002 [1987]); Theodor W. Adorno, *Minima Moralia: Reflections from Damaged Life,* trans. E. F. N.
    Jephcott (New York: Verso, 1974).
[3]   Elisabeth Schüssler Fiorenza, *Rhetoric and Ethic: The Politics of Biblical Studies* (Minneapolis:
    Fortress, 1999).

Western intellectual history from a Hegelian perspective of the education of the human "Spirit" (*Geist*) over time, manifesting a progress of the history of ideas toward a greater manifestation of the Truth. As noted in Chapter 8, this theme is even found in Gadamer's own hermeneutic thought.

In contrast, Karl Marx (1818–83) rejected Hegel's narrative of the progress of the history of ideas, arguing that no such decontextualized or disembodied truth exists. *All human truths arise from existing material, politicoeconomic conditions.* Truth is always political. As such, *all* truths have a strategic aim. Moreover, many purported "truths" are actually ideologies produced by the dominant class to serve their own interests. As Marx bluntly asserted, "What else does the history of ideas prove, than that intellectual production changes its character in proportion as material production is changed? The ruling ideas of each age have ever been the ideas of its ruling class."[4] Marx's assertion that the "ruling" or commonplace ideas of a society are those of the ruling class formed the basis of his argument that such "ruling" truths are employed by the ruling class to further their own strategic purposes. By implication, the truths of any society transmit hidden meanings beneath their surface, literal meanings. Marx termed this hidden meaning "ideology." Marx argued that much of what we take to be self-evidently true about the natural order of society is actually an ideological construction, employed by those in power to rationalize the economic status quo, thereby justifying inequity and legitimizing their own economic self-interest.[5] Thus, in Marx's "base/superstructure" model, the term "base" refers to a society's means of economic production. The term "superstructure" refers to a society's ideology. According to Marx, the "base" (means of production) determines the "superstructure" (ideology). In other words, the particular nature of a given society's means of economic production will determine the content of the ideology used by the ruling class to stabilize and maximize economic production for its own benefit.

In Marx's view, ideology functions by confusing the "proletariat" (workers) by creating within them a false consciousness, which makes them compliant workers within an unjust system in which the surplus capital of production is accumulated by the "bourgeoisie."[6] By "proletariat," Marx means "the class of modern wage laborers who, having no means of production of their own, are reduced to selling their labor in order to live." The term "bourgeoisie" specifies "the class of modern capitalists, owners of the means of social production and employers of wage labor." The Italian Marxist political theorist Antonio Gramsci (1891–1937) argued that ideology is used to give the proletariat a false conception of its own interests,

---

4 Karl Marx, "Manifesto of the Communist Party," in *Marx and Engels: Basic Writings on Politics and Philosophy,* ed. with a new introduction by Lewis S. Feuer (New York: Doubleday, 1959), 1–41, esp. 26.

5 Cf. David McLellan, *The Thought of Karl Marx: An Introduction* (New York: Harper, 1971); John Plamenatz, *Karl Marx's Philosophy of Man* (Oxford: Oxford University Press, 1975).

6 Marx, "Manifesto of the Communist Party," 7, n. 1.

with the result that the self-interest of the ruling class is perceived to coincide with the interests of society as a whole: "The mode of production in material life determines the general character of the social, political and spiritual processes of life. It is not the consciousness of men that determines their being, but, on the contrary, their social being that determines their consciousness."[7] An "ideology" is a system of illusory beliefs and distorted thought that *conceals social contradiction and gives rise to false consciousness.*

Max Horkheimer and Theodor Adorno describe this false consciousness as the "mysterious willingness of the technologically educated masses to fall under the spell of any despotism, in its self-destructive affinity to nationalistic paranoia."[8] Theodore Adorno, recognizing the real danger posed by the "total organization" of truth, famously warned in *Minima Moralia: Reflections on a Damaged Life* (1951) that "the whole is untrue" (*das Ganze ist das Unwahre*).[9] By falling under the spell of any totalizing regime of truth, the ideology of their masters, workers actually become alienated from the harsh reality of their own material lives. Such alienation produces such psychiatric by-products as neurosis and psychosis. Given the changing content of the "base/superstructure" relationship, the forms of neuroses and psychoses in society will vary from society to society, according to forms of self-alienation produced by a given ideology. Each regime of power will produce its own spectrum of psychiatric illnesses.

Thus, human communication has the capability to transmit concealed messages that create a false and alienated consciousness among those who are governed, upon whose labor the economic system depends. This explains why Marx, in analyzing the Christian religion of his day, concluded that while it may appear to be concerned with God and the hope of salvation after death, its real function is to imbue the poor with a false consciousness that makes "the misery of life more endurable" and provides a way by which they might one day escape "from the reality of inhumane working conditions." This is the context of Marx's famous depiction of religion as "the opium of the masses."[10]

The purpose of Marx's ideological critique is not merely to understand how ideology functions but rather to emancipate those who are most affected by it.[11] Thus, in contrast to phenomenological theories of interpretation, which are aimed at understanding, the goal of Marxist-oriented suspicion of meaning is always to bring about social transformation and emancipation, to the end that the ones

---

[7] Karl Marx, "A Contribution to the Critique of Political Economy," in *Marx-Engels Reader*, ed. Robert C. Tucker (New York: Norton, 1978), 4; see also "The German Ideology," in Tucker, *Marx-Engels Reader*, 154–55.

[8] Horkheimer and Adorno, *Dialectic of Enlightenment*, xvi.

[9] Adorno, *Minima Moralia*, 50.

[10] Marx, "*Contribution to the Critique of Hegel's Philosophy of Right*," in *Early Writings*, trans. and ed. T. B. Bottomore (New York: McGraw-Hill, 1964), 44.

[11] Marx, "Theses on Feuerbach," in *Marx-Engels Reader*, 145.

who produce capital and goods also create the social relationships within which such capital goods are produced.[12] According to Habermas, Marxism represents the ultimate intellectual ordering of metropolitics, which returns "the appearance of politics *to the truth* of the productive forces and relations of production, and promising."[13] Paul Ricoeur hailed Marx as one of the "masters of suspicion" because, by means of his exercise of *suspicion*, he cleared "the horizon for a more authentic word, for a new reign of Truth."[14]

HORKHEIMER AND ADORNO AND THE MYTH OF THE ENLIGHTENMENT

Homer's great epic *The Odyssey* tells the story of Odysseus's contest with the colossal one-eyed Cyclops, Polyphemus. Having landed on the island of the Cyclops, Odysseus and twelve of his best men entered a large cave, the home of Polyphemus. When Polyphemus discovered these intruders he blocked the cave's entrance with a large boulder, thereby preventing their escape; he then proceeded to devour Odysseus's men, two by two, each night, for his evening meal. Odysseus, greatly outmatched by the brute force of Polyphemus, applied reason to outwit him: he served Polyphemus strong wine to make him drunk. When Polyphemus asked his name, Odysseus replied that his name was "Outis" (Οὖτις), which literally means "Nobody" in Greek.[15] Polyphemus, mistaking the word "Outis" for a proper name, promised that he would eat "Nobody" last. When he passesd out from drunkenness, Odysseus and his men drove a wooden stake through his only eye, thereby blinding him (fig. 9.1). When the wounded Polyphemus cried out to his fellow Cyclops for assistance, saying that "Nobody" had attacked him, they misunderstood him and surmised that he had gone mad. The next day, Odysseus and his remaining crew tied themselves to the undersides of Polyphemus's sheep and thereby escaped when the sheep were let out of the cave to graze the next morning.

In *Dialectic of Enlightenment*, Max Horkheimer and Theodor Adorno liken the plight of humanity to that of Odysseus, who, when faced with danger, applied rationality and discipline in order to survive.[16] If Polyphemus represents the violent power of nature, then Odysseus represents his antitype, Western civilization,

---

[12] Jacques Rancière, *Aesthetics and Its Discontents*, trans. Steven Corcoran (Malden, MA: Polity Press, 2009 [2004]), 37. The reference to "suspicion" here echoes Ricoeur's own characterization of the "school of suspicion" (or the doubters of tradition) in the fields of history (Marx), philosophy (Nietzsche), and the unconscious (Freud); cf. Paul Ricoeur, *Freud and Philosophy: An Essay on Interpretation*, trans. Denis Savage (New Haven: Yale University Press, 1970), 32–35.

[13] Rancière, *Aesthetics*, 33.

[14] Ricoeur, *Freud and Philosophy*, 33 (emphasis added).

[15] The name Οὖτις is a combination of οὐ (no) and τις (someone), meaning "nobody" (*Od.* 9.366, 408).

[16] Horkheimer and Adorno, *Dialectic of Enlightenment*, 44.

9.1. Odysseus blinding the Cyclops, Archaeological Museum, Eleusis (Scala / Art Resource, NY)

which tames nature through reason. But Odysseus's survival came at a cost: he was forced to become "Nobody" (Οὖτις) to survive. Similarly, Horkheimer and Adorno argue that modern people have had to renounce their own personal identities and become "nobodies" in order to survive in a world of technology and industrial production. Moreover, this world, having been reduced by human rationality to an object of control and exploitation, has now been emptied of any ultimate purpose or value.

This analysis of the story of Odysseus reflects Horkheimer and Adorno's own loss of faith in key aspects of Marxism, especially Marx's belief in the positive benefits of Enlightenment rationality and the possibility of emancipatory progress.[17] The exercise of reason has made it possible for science to endlessly reinvent itself and proliferate new technological wonders. By employing a principle of noncontradiction, Enlightenment rationality has reduced the ambiguities of the world to dialectical logic: either humanity must dominate the world or it will dominate humanity. This stark choice is based solely on fear and calculation.[18]

In reply to this cold logic, Horkheimer and Adorno argue that the Enlightenment program, which originally promised to liberate human beings by dispelling "myths" with knowledge, *is itself a myth*: "Myth is already enlightenment and enlightenment reverts to mythology."[19] With the advantage of hindsight, we can now see that this use of reason has not liberated humanity. Horkheimer and Adorno argue that science actually has no interest in human liberation and that its myth of liberation is just an ideology. The truth is that the only objective of Enlightenment rationality is to maximize production by inventing more efficient technologies for controlling the minds of the workforce through ideology. After all, the workers are the resources needed for the production of goods. In reply, the primary theme of Horkheimer and Adorno's *Dialectic of Enlightenment* is that continued use of rationality, according to the dictates of the Enlightenment paradigm, in the form of science and technology, now poses a threat to individual freedom and personal well-being.

Horkheimer and Adorno argued that science and technology have employed the myth of emancipatory progress as an ideology to control and exploit individuals as human resources for economic production.[20] Capitalism, the ultimate distillation of the logic of the Enlightenment, has nullified finite human beings, in its effort to control everything and everybody, turning them into calculable, substitutable resources for economic production. For this reason, employees today are literally called "human *resources*." Thus, the promise of emancipatory human progress actually masks technologies of human control and exploitation.[21] In other words, the rationality inherent in the world of science and technology conceals a hidden logic that is dehumanizing and repressive:[22] The advancement of economic productivity actually "allows the technical apparatus and the social groups which administrate

[17] Cf. Max Horkheimer, *The Eclipse of Reason* (New York: Seabury Press, 1974), 3–57.
[18] Horkheimer and Adorno, *Dialectic of Enlightenment*, 29.
[19] Ibid., xviii, cf. 1.
[20] Ibid., 27.
[21] Horkheimer, *Eclipse of Reason,* 30, 44, 56.
[22] Horkheimer and Adorno, *Dialectic of Enlightenment*, xiii.

[to have] a disproportionate superiority to the rest of the population."[23] Individuals are organized into productive bio-social-political-technical assemblages for purposes that have nothing to do with their own well-being. Far from leading humanity to its own freedom and well-being, corporate capitalism expends all its energy on self-preservation through competition and environmental exploitation. In light of growing poverty in the world today, the dehumanizing conditions that attend the mass production in the globalized world, and the resultant environmental devastation, it is obvious that the Enlightenment's so-called progress of reason has not been accompanied by a corresponding progress of humanity. Enlightenment rationality, as distilled in capitalism, as an economic structure, is actually a *closed* system of thought that *attacks* all values and beliefs that stand in the way of its own program of domination and control. In his critique of this emphasis on this instrumental use of rationality, Horkheimer states that "if reason itself is instrumentalized, it takes on a kind of materiality and blindness, becomes a fetish, a magic entity that is accepted rather than intellectually experienced."[24]

As part of their critique of the Enlightenment rationality, Horkheimer and Adorno reinterpreted another story about Odysseus: the story of his encounter with the Sirens. "Sirens" are dangerous mythical creatures, which possess the head of a woman and the body of a bird. The seductive songs of the Sirens had lured countless mariners to their deaths on the rocky coastline circling the island they inhabited.

Knowing this danger, Odysseus prepared to sail past the island, ordering that all of his crew plug their ears with bee's wax and divert their minds with the hard labor of rowing. Significantly, Odysseus desired to hear the fabled songs of the Sirens, and so he ordered his men to lash his body to the ship's mast. Thus, as his men slowly rowed the ship past the singing Sirens, Odysseus was able to listen to their songs safely, strapped to the mast (fig. 9.2). Even though his heart was filled with a deep longing to escape and swim to the Sirens, the ropes held fast. Meanwhile, his crew, absorbed in its disciplined labor, rowed the ship to safety (*Od*.12.39).

Horkheimer and Adorno interpreted this episode in the life of Odysseus in terms of Hegel's "master-slave" dialectic: when faced with a threatening situation (the Sirens' song), the key to the workers' survival lay in their *obedience to their master and in their commitment to disciplined labor*. The oarsmen, as "pliable proletariat," plugged their ears as ordered, both "literally and culturally," to the truth. It was this act that conscripted them *as slaves* to their master, Odysseus. But both the crew and Odysseus were caught in the double play of enslavement: each is a slave to the other. *Both were made captive to their socially determined roles.*

In their interpretation of this story, Horkheimer and Adorno invoke Aristotle's distinction between "bare life" (ζωή) and "full human existence" (βίος). Odysseus,

---

[23] Ibid., xiv.
[24] Horkheimer, *Eclipse of Reason*, 23–24.

9.2. Odysseus and the Sirens, Antikensammlung, Staatliche Museen, Berlin
(bpk, Berlin / Staatliche Museen / Art Resource, NY)

in allowing himself to hear the Sirens' song, partook of "full human existence,"
whereas his oarsmen, who commit themselves to obedience and labor, are per-
mitted only to know the "bare life" of survival. Odysseus's "full human existence"

comes at the expense of *their* sacrifice. He, in contrast, made no such sacrifice because he did "not believe in any objective necessity" to resist the experience of beauty.[25] Instead, he allowed himself, as master, the pleasure of contemplating the beauty of the song of the Sirens.[26]

But, by becoming their master, Odysseus also became captive to his own socially determined role.[27] Thus, within the system of domination, both the slaves (crew) and master (Odysseus) became captives to their socially determined roles, by virtue of their reciprocal obligations, as dictated by the rationality of survival. Similarly, Adorno and Horkheimer argue that Enlightenment rationality, once believed to be the final arbiter between reality and illusion, and the guarantor of human liberty, has actually implemented its own form of master-slave relationship upon us.[28] Our continued blind attachment to this form of rationality can never emancipate us but only perpetuate our servitude.[29] Biblical interpreters must find a way of escaping from such forms of rationality that enslave them to the "bare life," when they really yearn for the "full human existence."

LOUIS ALTHUSSER: THE STRUCTURE OF IDEOLOGY

It is ironic that even though many biblical scholars now investigate the role of ideology in the first-century Roman and Hellenistic world, comparatively few are willing to investigate the role of ideology within the contemporary discipline of biblical studies. This reluctance is all the more surprising given the lengthy history of theorizing on ideology over the course of the twentieth century. For example, Louis Pierre Althusser (1918–90) employed French structuralism to elaborate a new Marxist theory of ideology. At first glance, the combination of Marxist theory with structuralism may seem to be contradictory. After all, a Marxist analysis is historical and materialistic (diachronic), whereas a structuralist analysis is ahistorical and nonmaterialistic (synchronic). Althusser addresses

---

[25] Horkheimer and Adorno, *Dialectic of Enlightenment*, 36.
[26] Ibid., 34.
[27] Ibid., 46.
[28] Horkheimer, *Eclipse of Reason*, 3–57.
[29] Ibid., 42–55. Similarly, Adorno, in his critique of Hegel's dialectical narrative of progress, argued that "the whole is the false" (*Minima Moralia*, 33; as quoted in Martin Jay, *Adorno* [Cambridge, MA: Harvard University Press, 1984], 43). In this *Minima Moralia,* Adorno translates his philosophical-aesthetic theory of negative dialectics into a rhetorical theory of irony. In part 2 (pp. 137–208) Adorno assembles his categories, summarizes what has been achieved in the past, and sketches out where dialectics should go in the future. Through the use of what he termed "negative dialectics," Adorno attempted to develop a nondominating form of thought, which would appreciate its own limitations and accept the premise that reality can never be fully subsumed under the totalizing concepts of the knowing subject. Adorno's *Negative Dialectics* constitutes an attack on the notion of the autonomous individual as the locus of criticism.

this issue by making a distinction between diachronic "ideologies" and synchronic "Ideology."[30]

In essence, Althusser asks, why do people obey the unjust laws of oppressive governments, when it is not in their self-interest to do so? In answer to this question, he describes the two primary mechanisms whereby people are coerced to live according to the oppressive laws of the state. The first mechanism he terms the "Repressive State Apparatuses," whereby the state enforces behavior *directly* through repressive measures such as the police and incarceration. Althusser terms the second mechanism "Ideological State Apparatuses," which are institutions that influence behavior *indirectly* (e.g., the justice system, the media, banks, the military, churches, advertising agencies) by producing "ideologies" that are *internalized* by individuals.[31] Such institutions make the dominant ideology of a society (in our case, capitalism, patriarchy, and heterosexism) appear to be neutral and natural, whereas ideologies that differ from this norm are made to appear radical and unnatural.

Althusser sets out to explain the mechanism whereby people internalize these ideologies by distinguishing between "ideologies" and "Ideology."[32] The former term specifies actual systems of distorted thought that are local and culturally specific, such as specific instantiations of capitalism and patriarchy. The latter term, Ideology, is structural, with no specific content. Like Heidegger's ontological structures of "understanding," "care," and "temporality," "Ideology" is an ontological structure that can be *filled out* by many different local and culturally specific ideologies. This explains why Althusser states that "Ideology has no history."[33] The content of Ideology, as a universal human, ontological structure, will vary according to specific social, political, and historical contexts.

On the basis of this distinction between ideologies and Ideology, Althusser sketches out two possible explanations to explain *how* people internalize the ideologies they encounter in their environment. The first explanation (which is incorrect according to Althusser) is what he terms the "conspiracy theory": namely, the powerful of society have deceived everyone else into accepting a false conception of reality. Althusser's own alternative explanation is that human beings are *predisposed* to generate false representations (ideologies) of themselves, by virtue of the ontological structure of "Ideology." The process of becoming a "subject-in-Ideology" has three forms. First, each of us is born into subjecthood: we are

---

[30] Louis Althusser, "Ideology and Ideological State Apparatuses," in *Lenin and Philosophy and Other Essays*, trans. Ben Brewster (New York: Monthly Review Press, 1971), 127–86; reprinted in *Critical Theory since 1965*, ed. Hazard Adams and Leroy Searle (Tallahassee: University Presses of Florida, 1986), 239–51. This is an excerpt from a longer piece discussing the relation between the state and subjects in Louis Althusser, *Lenin and Philosophy*, trans. Ben Brewster (London: Monthly Review Press, 1971).

[31] Althusser, "Ideology and Ideological State Apparatuses," in *Critical Theory since 1965*, 239.

[32] Ibid., 241a.

[33] Ibid., 240.

"always-already" subjected to the power of others. Second, we "always-already" inhabit culturally specific ideologies that appear to us as natural and self-evidently true, such as heterosexism. Third, the structure of Ideology actually "interpellates" individuals into subjecthood.

The term "interpellation" is related to the term "appellation," meaning a naming or calling. "Interpellation" is a kind of naming, or a calling, or a hailing, of a person into subjecthood. When ideology calls to us, we reply, Are you speaking to me? We always reply because each of us possesses our own internal structure of Ideology.[34] For example, television commercials and television evangelists always employ an implicit or explicit "you" in their messages. This is interpellation. This "you" makes the viewer feel *personally* addressed and called, despite the fact that tens of thousands of people may be watching the advertisement or television show at the same time. This same effect was achieved by the well-known Uncle Sam poster, "I want YOU for the U.S. Army" (fig. 9.3). This recruiting poster predisposes one to be interpellated into the ideology of American soldiery. According to Althusser, this capacity of ours to feel individually addressed by ideology is an inherent part of the structure of being human.

This structure (Ideology) not only requires a subject (lowercase), that is, an individual person (you or I). It also requires a believing Subject (uppercase), which is to say, the structural possibility of subjecthood. This concept can be compared to Michel Foucault's theory of texts creating "Subject positions" for authors (subjects) to fill. In simple terms, when called by an ideology, each of us, as a particular subject, has structural potential to become a Subject that is interpellated into an ideology.

Why are we so susceptible to interpellation? Althusser believes that when individuals are unable to endure the reality of their lives, they naturally create distorting ideologies that convince them that life is not as bad as it seems to be. An ideology can even become a source of hope. The problem with this coping strategy is that it results in individuals becoming even further alienated from the reality of their own lives. It results in a *double* alienation, in which people become alienated *from themselves and their feelings and intuitions*, as well as from their physical environments. Forms of mental illness, such as neuroses and psychosis, often result from such alienated ways of living in the world. Indeed, mental illness is one of the "material" faces of Ideology.[35]

HABERMAS'S CRITIQUE OF GADAMER'S HERMENEUTIC PHILOSOPHY

Like Althusser, Jürgen Habermas also reflected deeply on the reality of ideology in contemporary life. He began his academic career as a graduate student of Horkheimer

---

34 Ibid., 245b.
35 Ibid., 242b.

9.3. James Montgomery Flagg, I want you for the U.S. Army nearest
recruiting station (1916–17) (Art Resource, NY)

at the University of Frankfurt. But he eventually rejected Max Horkheimer's direction as a doctoral supervisor and left Frankfurt, later completing his thesis under the direction of Wolfgang Abendroth. Habermas remained unconvinced by Adorno and Horkheimer's critique of rationality. In his view, their own critique of rationality had itself become another totalizing form of rationality: "If they do not want to renounce the effect of a final unmasking and still want to *continue with critique*, they will have to leave at least one rational criterion intact for their explanation of the corruption of *all* rational criteria."[36] Habermas attempted to reinstate the role of human reason for human betterment. The necessity of doing so is one of the key issues that arises in his debate with Gadamer. Thus, even though Habermas is considered to be a member of the Frankfurt school, he strongly disagreed with the institute's founders regarding the role of reason in achieving emancipation.[37]

This issue brings us to Habermas's well-known debate with his close friend Gadamer concerning the nature of hermeneutic praxis, as it was propounded in Gadamer's *Wahrheit und Methode* (*Truth and Method*). Two years after the publication of the second edition in 1965, Habermas issued a critical review in his book *Zur Logik der Sozialwissenschaften* (*On Logic of the Social Sciences*).[38] Habermas's critique initiated what would become an extended debate with Gadamer about the nature of sound hermeneutic practice. The details of this debate were published in the academic journal *Philosophische Rundschau*.[39]

At the outset of summarizing this debate, it should be noted that there were many points of agreement between Habermas and Gadamer. For example, both agreed that human communication should not be understood theoretically in terms of isolated propositions (contra early Wittgenstein) but rather practically in terms of actual usages of language in real social and material settings. Habermas and Gadamer also opposed the Enlightenment ideal of rationality, which was based on the concept of the rational sovereign subject. Furthermore, they were both also highly critical of any attempt to construct *objective* history; in their view, history is always a construct produced by historians. On this point, Habermas argued that history is always bound up with the transcendental framework of the interpreter. In the act of interpretation, the historian's transcendental framework is not extinguished but rather is put to work by coordinating historical facts into what appears to be a continual narrative of historical process. On this basis, Habermas calls into question the objectivity of historical accounts of influence and development

[36] Jürgen Habermas, *The Philosophical Discourse of Modernity: Twelve Lectures,* trans. Frederick Lawrence (Cambridge, MA: MIT Press, 1987 [1985]), 126–27.

[37] Cf. Jürgen Habermas, "The Entwinement of Myth and Enlightenment: Max Horkheimer and Theodor Adorno," in Habermas, *The Philosophical Discourse of Modernity: Twelve Lectures,* 106–30.

[38] Published with the title "Zur Logik der Sozialwissenschaften," in a special issue of *Philosophische Rundschau* (Tubingen: Suhrkamp Verlag, 1971), 188–251.

[39] In 1971 Habermas subsequently expanded his first review. The article, "Zu Gadamers 'Warheit und Methode,'" later appeared in a volume edited by Karl-Otto Apel, *Hermeneutik und Ideologiekritik,* 45–56. However, in all English translations of this review, Habermas's original review (1967) is combined with his expansion of this review (1971) into a single, five-section article, "A Review of Gadamer's *Truth and Method.*" Jürgen Habermas, "A Review of Gadamer's *Truth and Method*" [1967/1971], in *The Hermeneutic Tradition from Ast to Ricoeur,* ed. Gayle L. Ormiston and Alan D. Schrift (Albany: State University of New York Press, 1990), 220–41.

over time.[40] Having noted their points of agreement, we can now summarize the three main points of Habermas's critique of Gadamer, namely Gadamer's deferral to tradition, his concept of the historically effected consciousness, and his concept of interpretation as dialogue.

Gadamer's Deferral to Tradition

As previously noted, Gadamer viewed tradition positively, as an essential element of the horizon of every interpreter. In contrast, Habermas considers the effective history of tradition to be a possible carrier of ideology. For example, in the past the ideologies of religious fundamentalism, racism, colonialism, patriotism, sexism, and heterosexism have all been promoted by appealing to tradition. Each of these "-isms" has its own tradition, which can be cast as a narrative. As Homi Bhabha observes, the "narrative of (a) tradition" can function ideologically as a tool to exploit, oppress, and dominate others. Through the recitation of such narratives of traditionalism (such as white supremacy, Western supremacy, etc.), a dominant group can cover up the conflict and struggle of the past and substitute its own version of history, which invariably naturalizes its own ideology. Such narratives of traditionalism often present the past as a time of harmony and conformity, when no one questioned or resisted the good common sense of the dominant group: the implied logic of such narratives is "things have always been this way, and nobody has ever complained until now." In other words, those who question, struggle, and resist oppressiveness and exploitation in the present are the *real* problem. In his famous book *The Location of Culture,* Homi Bhabha observes:

The narrative of traditionalism is usually an unconscious strategy on the part of the commentator which serves the institutional purpose of undermining critique and safeguarding the status quo. It is part of the rhetoric of domination. It is an assertion of a monolithic, metaphysical past (which is never unitary), the repetition of which negates our awareness of culture-as-political-struggle in the past, and undermines contemporary struggle.[41]

In Habermas's view, in cases where a tradition does not exist, it can easily be invented, as it was by Nazism in its concept of the "Aryan race," a supposedly master race from which the German people had descended. Of course, it was on the basis of this same logic that the Nazis attempted to protect the purity of the Aryan bloodline by implementing the so-called Final Solution, the Shoah (Holocaust).[42] Thus, Habermas argues that the high value that Gadamer places on tradition causes him to *overlook the ideological component of the narrative of tradition.* Moreover, Gadamer's concept of the "universality" of hermeneutics does not provide any

---

[40] Habermas, "A Review of Gadamer's *Truth and Method*," 224.
[41] Homi Bhabha, *The Location of Culture* (London: Routledge, 1994), 35.
[42] On the use of this term, see Chapter 11.

means by which the effective history of tradition, as an oppressive force, can be critiqued for its ideological content.

Gadamer's Concept of the Historically Effected Consciousness

Habermas is also suspicious of Gadamer's concept of the historically effected consciousness. As previously discussed, Althusser argued that human consciousness is structured in such a way that it can easily be interpellated, or called, into ideology. For his part, Habermas asserts Gadamer's "historically effected consciousness" can be *filled out* with various locally and culturally specific ideologies, as evidenced in the rise of fascist ideologies in Europe during the early twentieth century. In other words, the content of one's historically effected consciousness is not just naturally "there." In many important ways, it is *delivered* to us from the outside through a process of socialization and mass education.

Of course, this process of becoming a "subject of ideology" almost always includes educational induction into a socially shared tradition. In part, children and young adults develop their phenomenological horizons of meaning through contact with authority figures such as teachers, experts in legal matters and social policy, ministers of the church, and university professors. This close connection between ideology and mass education helps to explain why some of the most violent dictatorships in world history have arisen in countries with the highest levels of formal education. Through the use of mass education, authorities can instill ideology in the historically effected consciousnesses of the masses. By facilitating the internalization of ideology in an underclass, an overclass can oppress and exploit them without the use of direct force.[43] In effect, those oppressed by the system become self-monitoring. Gadamer's phenomenological theorization of tradition lacks the capacity to address this critical problem.

Gadamer's Conception of Interpretation as Dialogue

Whereas Gadamer's concept of interpretation as dialogue requires a respectful listening to tradition, Habermas argues that his dialogic model does not provide an objective basis by which to critique and resist the oppressive prejudices inscribed within tradition. For example, the very act of entering into dialogue with religious tradition, or a tradition of interpreting a particular biblical text, could function as the decisive event whereby the oppressive prejudices of tradition or text reassert themselves again in the present. Furthermore, any apparent *consensus* on the authority or veracity of a religious tradition or textual interpretation in the present may be the result of the coercion of some people as well as

---

[43] Jürgen Habermas, *On Logic of the Social Sciences*, trans. Sherry Weber Nicholsen and Jerry A. Stark (Cambridge: Polity Press, 1988 [1967]), 169.

the exclusion of others: "Force can in any case acquire permanence only through the objective semblance of an unforced pseudo-communicative agreement."[44]

Moreover, it is a truism that *the denial of ideology is always part of the use of ideology*. By denying their use of ideology, a dominating group (such as those who opposed the ordination of women) can actually disguise its own use of ideology (e.g., a sexist theological anthropology) and mask its pursuit of its own self-interest (the oppression of women). This often takes the form of making its own ideology appear to be necessary, and even the natural order of things.

The denial of difference is another common ideological weapon: by arguing that "*you* people (e.g., a minority of another religion, culture, nationality, or gender) are *just like us*," a minority's own religious, cultural, ethnic, or sexual differences are *denied*. For example, this ideology of the *denial of difference* is operative in the well-intending, liberal Canadian Protestant Christianity, which often addresses the "problem" of religious pluralism by denying the critical *differences* between Christians, Jains, Muslims, Zoroastrians, Buddhists, Taoists, Jews, Hindus, and so forth. In the assertion that "you all are just like us," it denies the important intrinsic differences between people of different and theoretically unreconcilable faiths. The same point could be made with respect to attempts of a dominant ethnic group in a Christian church, denomination, or seminary, to come to terms with the differences posed by minority ethnic groups by arguing that "we are really *all the same* in Jesus Christ." This pointed theological claim *masks ideological content*, for, by denying difference, the minority groups themselves are incorporated into the whole and thereby denied their unique voice and perspective. In the same way, Gadamer's appeal to an idealized Western tradition is also potentially oppressive. By appealing to a homogenized, dehistoricized "tradition," and by denying the use of ideology in doing so, power holders in religious denominations and society at large can easily naturalize the status quo, thereby legitimizing their own self-interests and protecting their own social advantages and influence. For this reason, Habermas argues that the "power of reflection" must always include *the right to reject the authority of tradition*.

In reply to Habermas, Gadamer countered that the authority of tradition is not absolute. The effective history of tradition accrues from our free, ongoing dialogue with tradition. He argues that we are not compelled to accept the truth claims of tradition; in a very real way, we *are* the tradition. But Habermas counters this point, stating that our historical experience of ideology contradicts Gadamer's assertion.[45] Therefore, to ignore the hidden operations of ideology in the form of tradition (as Gadamer seems to do) is to risk becoming a subject of ideology, alienated both from our material environments and ourselves. In essence, Habermas

---

[44] Habermas, "The Hermeneutic Claim to Universality" [1971], in Ormiston and Schrift, *The Hermeneutic Tradition from Ast to Ricoeur*, 245–72, esp. 269.

[45] Ibid., 267.

challenged Gadamer's liberal conservatism because it is predisposed to trust and assent to, rather than critique, the authority of tradition. By virtue of Gadamer's impassioned desire to dialogue with tradition, rather than critique tradition, he has imposed a limit on human reason, as well as a limit on the power to resist injustice. In Habermas's view, we must retain the capacity to critique the ideologically saturated discourses that perpetuate the practices of oppression, exploitation, and marginalization in the contemporary world.

Gadamer	Habermas
Effective history of tradition and historically effected consciousness	Suspicion of tradition as a carrier of ideology and the necessity of rational critique
Fusion of phenomenological horizons	Necessity of critiquing the framework of knowledge with self-reflective methodology
Historicization of human understanding as a creative appropriation of tradition	Tradition submitted to reason as communicative action

Thus, even though Gadamer's program of hermeneutics has universal applicability, and indeed can be deemed to be "true" in a phenomenological sense, his related concepts of the "historically effected consciousness" and "dialogue with tradition" do not leave sufficient space for critiquing religious tradition as a carrier of ideology. In particular, his model of dialogue with religious tradition lacks the capacity to address the real threats posed by ideologically saturated discourses on the rights and well-being of women, LGBTQ communities, and people of other faiths.[46] In contrast, Habermas developed an alternative hermeneutics that is rooted in a *pragmatic* concern for justice, human flourishing, and an appropriate ecological attitude toward the environment.

LOCUTIONARY AND ILLOCUTIONARY SPEECH ACTS

As previously noted, Habermas was critical of the theoretical limitations imposed by Saussure's and Wittgenstein's respective philosophies of language. Saussure's theory of "language" (*langue*) emphasized the importance of the *structure* of language over any actual manifestation of this structure in real human "communication" (*parole*). Saussure conceived of the structure of language as if it was an

---

[46] LGBTQ is a commonly used acronym referring collectively to the lesbian, gay, bisexual, transgender, and queer community.

iceberg, the great majority of which remains hidden beneath the surface of the water. By privileging the hidden dimension of language over actual instances of human communication, Saussure's theory inadvertently lost sight of sociolinguistics and how language is employed strategically in real material contexts. Similarly, in his early writings, Wittgenstein considered the primary function of sentences to be the stating of propositions. He then attempted to purify the meaning of human speech utterances and treat them ahistorically, as ideal propositions, independent of their material contexts.[47] Thus, Wittgenstein also bracketed out the material environment of human communication in order to expose the abstract structure that makes all propositions possible. In conceiving of language as a set of ahistorical rules, both Saussure and Wittgenstein overlooked the *strategic* dimension of language as it is used as a communicative tool.

J. L. Austin (1911–60) criticized Wittgenstein's theorization of language, arguing that human communication involves more than the syntactical linking together of words to form propositions.[48] In most instances of human communication, there is a connection between language and its material context. Austin famously argued that the basic structure of language involves a "locutionary" aspect: a speaker says something with a purpose (intentionality) to an addressee about something, with the intention of trying to reach a common understanding. According to Austin, when one performs such a locutionary speech act, one usually performs an "illocutionary" speech act at the same time. An illocutionary speech act is formulated with the "design," "intention," or "purpose" of producing an effect on the addressee.[49] Thus, the illocutionary dimension of speech acts belongs to language's component of "manifestation" (see Chapter 1). Andrew Cohen identifies five categories of speech acts based on the purposes assigned to them:[50]

Representatives	*Directives*	*Expressives*	*Commissives*	*Declaratives*
Assertions	Suggestions	Apologies	Promises	Decrees
Claims	Requests	Complaints	Threats	Declarations
Reports	Commands	Thanks	Offers	

The term "illocutionary" concerns the *forceful* intent of the speaker. For example, if I were to make the statement to a student in my class, "The classroom door is open," it is highly probable that the student would not only comprehend the

[47] In his later writings, Wittgenstein understood language, selfhood, and community as provisional constructions, which are informed by particular language games and are connected to distinct sociocultural forms of life.

[48] Austin, *How to Do Things with Words*, 2nd ed. (Oxford: Clarendon Press, 1975).

[49] Habermas, *Theory of Communicative Action,* trans. Thomas McCarthy, 2 vols. (Boston: Beacon Press, 1984–89 [1981]), I, 289–90.

[50] Andrew Cohen, "Speech Acts," in *Sociolinguistics and Language Teaching*, ed. S. L. McKay and N. H. Hornberger (Cambridge: Cambridge University Press, 1996), 383–420.

locutionary content of this statement ("Yes, the door *is* open") but also experience the illocutionary force of my statement as a pressure to stand up and close the door. Similarly, my wife's statement to me as I am stepping out the front door, "It is going to rain today," conveys the illocutionary force, "Take an umbrella with you when you leave for work."[51] Even in her simple act of asking a question such as "Are you wearing *that* to work?" she can perform an illocutionary act. By virtue of all its implied "shoulds" and "oughts," speech and texts have the power to convey illocutionary force to stimulate people into various kinds of responses and actions. Indeed, even the act of asking a question obliges the addressee to do something in response, if only to answer the question. According to Habermas, this is the "teleological" orientation of statements.[52]

In practice, the effect upon the addressee may differ from that which was intended and expected by the speaker. *Perlocutionary* force views a speech act at the level of its actual psychological effect on the addressee rather than from the perspective of the intending speaker. For example, one might experience the perlocutionary force of a particular speech act as frightening or disappointing, even though this may not have been the original illocutionary intent of the speaker.

All biblical texts possess an additional illocutionary dimension as well, and (by extension) a perlocutionary dimension, beyond their locutionary content. These are nonsemiotic networks of forces, which are woven through the semiotic dimension of the text. Such illocutionary forces constitute the virtual "unsaid" of every biblical text. They are implied, imperatival forces. When a biblical text is viewed only as a *semiotic* medium, which stores information, which is later recovered through its translation and interpretation into English, these nonsemiotic, noninformational, illocutionary forces are overlooked.

Because these illocutionary forces cannot be separated out from the semiotic content, the unwary reader can become subject to these forces in the very act of interpreting a text's locutionary statements.[53] When experienced by the contemporary reader-interpreter as perlocutionary forces, these illocutionary forces have the potential of playing themselves out in people's lives, for good or ill. This fact – what Rudolf Bultmann referred to as the "problem of the past" – bestows upon the act of biblical interpretation a potentially dangerous character. Biblical

---

51 Habermas, "The Hermeneutic Claim to Universality," 245–72, esp. 248.
52 Habermas, *Theory of Communicative Action*, I, 289.
53 For example, Deleuze and Guattari argue that a literary text is not primarily a semiotic medium for the storage and retrieval of information. Fundamentally, a text is a noninformational and nondiscursive expression of differential forces, because signifying structures are generated by nonsignifying processes. The key text for understanding texts in terms of their constituting forces is Gilles Deleuze's *Nietzsche and Philosophy*, trans. Hugh Tomlinson (New York: Columbia University Press, 1983 [1962]); cf. Gilles Deleuze and Félix Guattari, *Kafka: Toward a Minor Literature*, trans. Dana Polan (Minneapolis: University of Minnesota Press, 1986 [1975]), 26; Brian Massumi, *A User's Guide to Capitalism and Schizophrenia: Deviations from Deleuze and Guattari*, Swerve Edition (Cambridge, MA: MIT Press, 1992), 41–45.

interpretation can facilitate the unleashing of a text's ancient illocutionary forces, which can alienate some readers from themselves, from others, and from their real material contexts.

For example, according to the Gospel of Matthew, the Jewish chief priests and elders persuaded the Jews to request Pontius Pilate to release Barabbas and to crucify Jesus (Matt 27:20–23). When Pilate declared himself innocent of Jesus' blood, the Jewish throng shouted in reply, according to Matthew's Gospel, "Let his blood be on us and our children" (Matt 27:25). Because the Gospel of Matthew was probably written by a Jewish community living in the late first century (ca. 75–85), well more than a generation after Jesus' death, it is very unlikely that this story is not based on an actual historical event in the life of Jesus of Nazareth. At the time of the composition of the Gospel of Matthew, severe tensions had arisen between the Matthean synagogue, a community of Jews who believed that Jesus was the Messiah, and other Jewish synagogues, which did not. Many Jews probably accused the Matthean Jews of being a deviant Jewish group. The Matthean text "Let his blood be on us and our children" is consistent with this hypothesis of a rising level of hostility between these two Jewish groups. By accusing their fellow Jews of bringing the destruction of the Temple upon themselves by crucifying Jesus, they released an illocutionary force on them, in an attempt to shame them into correct (messianic) belief.

In the twelfth century, Pope Innocent II's interpretation of this same accusation ("Let his blood be on us and our children") rendered him a subject of the same illocutionary forces, albeit experienced differently. This text fortified his own desire to promote the oppression of medieval Jews:

[I]t is not displeasing to God, but is rather acceptable to him, that dispersed Jewry should live among and serve Catholic kings and Christian princes.... But they should be oppressed by the servitude of which they rendered themselves deserving when they raised sacrilegious hands against Him who had come to confer true liberty, and *called His blood upon themselves and their children.*[54]

Pope Innocent II's act of interpreting Matthew 27:25 unleashed the text's hidden illocutionary forces upon twelfth-century European Christians, who then set about persecuting their Jewish countrymen. Examples such as this help us appreciate Habermas's attempt to address the strategic purposes of language. Owing to the hidden nature of the illocutionary forces within biblical texts, even disinterested and well-intended biblical interpreters, including preachers, scholars, and leaders of bible study groups, can become complicit in perpetuating forces of oppression and intolerance lying dormant within the texts themselves. For this reason, we must always be critically reflective about illocutionary and perlocutionary dimensions of biblical and theological texts.

---

[54] As quoted by Solomon Grayzel in *The Church and the Jews in the XIIIth Century* (New York: Hermon Press, 1966), 53 (emphasis added).

HABERMAS'S UNIVERSAL PRAGMATICS

Habermas argues that language exists *only as communicated*. In *The Theory of Communicative Action,* he employed the speech-act theory of J. L. Austin to describe discourse: by definition, a discourse is a communication addressed to someone in particular (i.e., it is locutionary). This is what makes it communication. He also made the qualitative distinction between communicative action "oriented to mutual understanding" (locutionary discourse) and the "instrumental use of language" (illocutionary discourse). Through an illocutionary speech act, a "speaker *performs an action* in saying something."[55] In other words, most speech acts are intended to achieve strategic effects. They are not purely informational: "These effects ensue whenever a speaker acts with an orientation to success, and thereby instrumentalizes speech acts for the purposes that are only contingently related to the meaning of what is said."[56] Such strategic speech includes insincere speech acts and manipulative communication such as ideology.

Habermas considers locutionary speech acts to be the primary form of speech because all illocutionary speech must simultaneously pursue locutionary aims as well, for if a shared understanding of something is not achieved first, then the intended persuasive effect will not be realized either: "If the hearer failed to understand what the speaker was saying, a strategically acting speaker would not be able to bring the hearer, by means of communicative acts, to behave in the desired way."[57] Thus, in Habermas's view, illocutionary speech is secondary to locutionary speech: "The use of language with an orientation to reaching understanding is the original mode of language use, upon which indirect understanding ... and the instrumental use of language in general, are parasitic,"[58] which is why Habermas concludes language to be essentially "communicative action" that is "oriented to mutual understanding," a premise that is important for his theory of communicative action.[59]

HABERMAS'S THEORY OF COMMUNICATIVE ACTION

The traditional, Western concept of truth is based on the *individual,* rational subject, who, through the exercise of reason, distinguishes between what is true and what is false. But Habermas observes that human beings are essentially *social* in nature. This observation leads him to ask, What role do *communities* have in discerning what is true? This question opened the door for Habermas *to resituate the*

---

[55] Habermas, *Theory of Communicative Action,* I, 389 (emphasis added).
[56] Ibid., 289.
[57] Ibid., 293.
[58] Ibid., 288.
[59] Jürgen Habermas, *Communication and the Evolution of Society,* trans. T. McCarthy (Boston: Beacon Press, 1979 [1976]), 1, 26–65 (emphasis added).

use of reason in communities as a shared communitarian practice. In so doing, he replaced the traditional, subject-centered concept of reason with a practice of reason that is carried out by the entire community through dialogue. This innovation transformed the exercise of reason into an *intersubjective process*, whose ultimate aim is mutual betterment.

Habermas emphasizes that to live together in a society, peaceably and justly, always requires negotiation and the coordination of effort. Whereas Heidegger's phenomenology focused on the ontological structure of each individual Da-sein, Habermas's theory of communicative action concentrates on *communality*. But Habermas is not constructing any sort of metaphysics or ontology, or making any explicit claims about the true essence of human society. For him, it is simply a self-evident fact that human beings tend to be social in nature and that the sociality of human life requires communication and negotiation.

Habermas calls this intersubjective communicative process "universal pragmatics." By "universal" he means that it is a form of communication that can be applied to all aspects of living together in society. By "pragmatics," he means that this communication is oriented toward truths that are practical, or useful, in terms of human wellness and justice. This emphasis on the pragmatic dimension of truth helps to explain why Habermas also refers to his approach to communication as "communicative *action*": it is a communicative practice that is oriented to action, not just improved understanding.

What, then, are the universal conditions for screening out distortions in communication (ideology) and achieving mutual understanding (*Verständigung*) that lead to transformational action? In simplest terms, Habermas argues that, for a speaker's statement to be deemed to be "true," it must satisfy the three following "validity claims":

1. *Evaluative criterion*: The speaker must make a statement about something in the world that is meaningful, reasonable, truthful, and sensible from the perspective of the community addressed.

2. *Expressive criterion*: The speaker must be *sincere* and *trustworthy* in expressing his, or her, true intentions, free of deceit, misrepresentation, or distortion. In other words, the speaker must be sincere.

3. *Normative criterion*: The speaker must also perform a speech act that is justifiable and appropriate with respect to the specific context.

These three criteria can be employed to establish or refute the implied truth claim of any speech act. A speaker must demonstrate the reasonableness of a speech act, prove his own trustworthiness, and also provide justification for it.

Here is a simple example: consider a statement made by a minister ordained in the Pentecostal-charismatic church. In the course of his interpretation of Genesis 3:5 and 1 Timothy 2:11–12, the minister states that the Bible teaches that ordained ministry is "specifically reserved for men." He argues that since Eve caused humankind's fall from grace, every woman carries the curse of Eve's sin and is thereby disqualified from ordained ministry. In reply, a group might contest the validity of the minister's statement "ordained ministry is specifically reserved for men" by employing Habermas's three criteria for validity, as follows:

1. *Evaluative criterion*: Concerning the *reasonableness* of the minister's speech act, it could be argued that this is an *unreasonable* statement. By virtue of Christian baptism, there is no longer any discrimination between male and female (Gal 3:28). *All* who are baptized in Christ have "put on Christ," irrespective of gender. Baptism implies a fundamental openness to ordained ministry to all who are called by God. Therefore, every baptized woman shares fully in Christ's mission, which includes ordained ministry. Therefore, the minister's statement fails the evaluative criterion.

2. *Expressive criterion*: Concerning the *trustworthiness* of this statement, it could be argued that the minister is not trustworthy. His real intention is to maintain women in a subordinate position in both his church and in the Pentecostal denomination as a whole. He also desires to garner for himself the reputation within Pentecostalism of someone who defends of the authority of the "literal" meaning of scripture. Therefore, this statement fails the expressive criterion of trustworthiness.

3. *Normative criterion*: Finally, the group might also observe that the New Testament is situated within an ancient culture that considered women to be inferior to men, physically, intellectually and emotionally. The Hellenistic world, which is reflected in the New Testament, also considered women to be incomplete and defective human beings. Because our modern cultural assumptions about women have radically changed, biblical passages that are imbued with first-century cultural presuppositions about women are no longer relevant. The minister's statement is not justifiable and therefore fails the normative criterion.

By means of these three criteria of validity, Habermas maintains that groups of people can reach a consensus on many controversial issues, despite differences in the participants' initial positions, because universal pragmatics provides a method of testing the validity of individual statements, and because all members of a group posit, at least as one possible outcome, the achievement of a consensus. In actual practice, Habermas's precondition for a speech situation may be difficult to satisfy. In the first place, Habermas imagines that the dialogical partners will all have a shared subjective experience with respect to social background and cultural orientation. On this point, Habermas redefined Wilhelm Dilthey's "life world" (*Lebenswelt*), a life formed by communal existence with others in a specific place and time, as a kind of public forum for communication. This "life world" consists of overlapping social, cultural, and personal dimensions, which together facilitate open interaction and dialogue. However, one could imagine

many real social contexts, especially in multicultural societies where this requirement would be impossible to fulfill.[60] Second, for this practice to be successful, all
participants must enter into the dialogue with a willingness to listen, as well as to
speak. In other words, as a matter of principle, each participant has not only the
right to try to convince others but also the corresponding obligation to be open
to being convinced *by* others. It is easy to list issues presently under debate in the
church, where participants are not willing to listen or engage in an open-ended
dialogue. Moreover, according to Habermas's model, all participants are expected
to communicate rationally, sincerely, and honestly. By way of analogy, Habermas
cites the practice of psychotherapy, which, to be successful, requires that patients
have a *sincere intention* to talk about and resolve their problems. Once again, this
requirement may be impossible to achieve: Habermas's ideal speech situation
also requires that all participants have the intention of ridding themselves of self-
deception.[61] Clearly, this model of communicative action can break down at many
different levels if the participants are unwilling or unable to satisfy these starting
requirements. Despite these shortcomings, Habermas's theory of universal pragmatics does underscore the need for communities to engage in a dialogical process
as a means of overcoming systematically distorted communication that may conceal a speaker's, or power group's, self-interest.

In terms of biblical interpretation, universal pragmatics would require that the
present sense-event of a biblical text can never be asserted by the "monological
self-certainty" of an isolated interpreter (whether a preacher, priest, TV evan-
gelist, scholar, or religious zealot), or even by one dominant group in a church
or denomination. The practice of universal pragmatics in biblical interpretation
would require that the textual present sense-event always be *negotiated* through
reasonable and sincere dialogue within a community of faith, whose ultimate goal
is to achieve an unforced consensus. In the opinion of Habermas, once such a consensus of the community has been achieved, it can be regarded as "true." After all,
this is a *consensus* theory of truth.[62]

There is much to applaud in Habermas's analysis of ideology, his emphasis on
critique, and his resituation of human reason as a shared communitarian practice. As important as his critique of Gadamer is, Habermas's own theory has
also attracted its critics. Most notable among these are Edward Said and Michel

---

[60] J. Habermas, "Communicative versus Subject-Centered Reason," in *The Philosophical Discourse of Modernity*, trans. Frederick G. Lawrence (Cambridge, MA: MIT Press, 1990), 298.

[61] Stanley Rosen, *Hermeneutics as Politics* (Cambridge: Oxford University Press, 1987), 11–16; Thomas McCarthy, "Reflection on Rationalization in the Theory of Communicative Action," in *Habermas and Modernity*, ed. Richard J. Bernstein (Cambridge, MA: MIT Press, 1994).

[62] "The prejudgmental structure of understanding not only prohibits us from questioning that factu-ally established consensus which underlies our misunderstanding and incomprehension, but makes such an understanding appear senseless." (Habermas, "The Hermeneutic Claim to Universality," 266).

Foucault, who have argued that Habermas has not sufficiently accounted for the relationship of power to knowledge. According to Foucault, power and knowledge are never external to one another: they operate in a mutually generative manner. Neither can be reduced to the other – hence, his neologism "power/knowledge."[63] According to Foucault, "Truth," as a *system* for production of knowledge, "is linked in a circular relation with the *systems* of power which produce it, and to effects of power which it [truth] induces and which extend it."[64] Edward Said similarly observes that the widespread belief "that 'true' knowledge is fundamentally non-political ... obscures the highly if obscurely organized political circumstances obtaining when knowledge is produced."[65] For his part, Foucault warns that we are often "unaware of" what he terms "the prodigious machinery of the will to truth, with its vocation of exclusion" of knowledge.[66] Indeed, if a biblical scholar were to assert that such and such a fact about Jesus is "true," people would be unlikely to ask why this particular "truth," and not some other "truth," is being asserted at this time and in this context by this scholar. Foucault argues that the "discovery" of "truth" always covers up the will-to-truth that made the discovery possible. The will-to-truth is always hidden, or "masked," by truth itself.[67]

Biblical interpreters may lack an awareness of the "machinery of the will to truth" in the church and in society at large, with the result that their interpretations become co-opted by those who promote intolerance and discrimination. This is not to imply that the power, which accompanies "truth," is only held in the hands of a privileged minority. According to Foucault, in the realm of power, there is no "them" versus "us." With the exception of the poorest and most oppressed people of the planet, most people (and all professional biblical interpreters) are located within regimes of power. In his celebrated book *The Open Society and Its Enemies,* Karl Popper has argued that the most dangerous people are those who believe themselves to have emerged from Plato's cave. Believing themselves to have contemplated eternal Truth directly, they now think they have the corresponding duty to return to the cave to *compel* all others to believe as they do.[68] The history of

[63] Michel Foucault, *Discipline and Punish* (New York: Pantheon, 1977), 27–28.

[64] Michel Foucault, "Truth and Power," in *Power/Knowledge: Selected Interviews & Other Writings, 1972–1977,* ed. Colin Gordon (New York: Pantheon, 1972), 109–33, esp. 133. For example, the prison system employed its power to produce knowledge by authorizing the close observation and study of prisoners; this knowledge, in time, was employed to increase the power of the prison system by justifying the incarceration of prisoners and providing data for the construction of better prisons.

[65] Edward Said, *Orientalism* (New York: Vintage Books, 1978), 10.

[66] Michel Foucault, "The Order of Discourse," included at the end of *The Archaeology of Knowledge* (New York: Tavistok Publications/Pantheon, 1972 [1969]), 215–37, esp. 220.

[67] On this point, Michel Foucault remarks that modern "power is tolerable only on the condition that it mask a substantial part of itself, even to those immediately involved. Its success is proportional to its ability to hide its own mechanism"; cf. Michel Foucault, *The History of Sexuality,* vol. 1: *An Introduction* (New York: Pantheon, 1978; Vintage Books, 1990), 86.

[68] Karl Popper, *The Open Society and Its Enemies,* 2 vols. (London: G. Routledge, 1945).

Western civilization attests to the "ruinous complicity" of such objectifications of truth with the forces of intolerance, oppression, and exploitation.[69] Even though there is no way for professional biblical interpreters to step outside of an institution's regimes of power, living *within* a regime of power does not necessarily entail replicating an institution's oppressive strategies of power and the practices of oppression produced by them. The biblical interpreter often has the choice of opening up alternative, unexplored domains of present sense-events, which lay outside the hierarchical binarisms of the dominant regime of power. From this perspective, the task of the post-historical interpreter is not to establish a hermeneutic perspective that is outside of "knowledge/power" but rather to *expose* the key axes of power associated with race, gender, color or ethnicity, and status (and the never ending "etceteras") and then to *exploit* the unpredictable configurations that their overlapping inadvertently creates (see Chapter 12).

CONCLUSION

Karl Marx argued that all human truths arise from existing material, politico-economic conditions. By implication, theory (and we would include the theory of biblical interpretation) is inseparable from practice of living in the world today. Therefore, the primary task of hermeneutics is not to understand biblical texts but rather to engage them within a broader strategy of transforming society. Habermas is likewise committed to such transformative knowledge, which is why he locates the practice of rationality not in the "monological self-certainty" of the individual but rather in the communicative practices of communities as a whole. Within this model, rationality is not deemed to be a property of an individual expert but rather a function carried out by a community as a whole. *Such communicative action involves searching out new kinds of community and new ways of living together, whose conditions of possibility have not yet been fully established.* As Gianni Vattimo observes, such searching will always involve striving for *collective* interpretations and constructing *shared* paradigms. In other words, "It always comes down to a question of belonging."[70]

For his part, Gadamer is not opposed to Habermas's concept of reason as communicative action. In fact, he even argues that what is "reasonable" emerges primarily in the course of dialogue. But, as we have seen, Gadamer privileged dialogue *with tradition* over dialogue with others. Moreover, in contrast to Habermas, Gadamer failed to provide any precise criteria whereby the validity of the truth claims of tradition can be tested, beyond that of mere hermeneutical self-reflection. This explains why Gadamer tended to defer to the authority of tradition, whereas

---

[69] Rancière, *Aesthetics*, 2.
[70] Gianni Vattimo, *A Farewell to Truth*, trans. William McCuaig (New York: Columbia University Press, 2011 [2009]), xxxv.

Habermas insists that tradition be subordinated to the reasoned critique of the community. While Gadamer holds out the hope of a fresh appropriation of tradition by a community of faith, Habermas's theory of communicative action defends the corresponding *need* of communities to resist ideologies that would obstruct the creation of more just and humane societies. In contrast to Gadamer's emphasis on understanding the other, the goal of Habermas's collective rationality is morally guided, collective, transformational *action* within one's community. As such, Habermas's theory of universal pragmatics provides us with some basic principles and insight – albeit imperfect ones – which can help us to identify and resist ideological strategies, presented in the guise of religious tradition, that would obstruct efforts in bringing about a more just, tolerant, and ecologically responsible world.

10

The Hermeneutics of Recollection and Suspicion: Paul Ricoeur

Of all the philosophers summarized in this book, the writings of Paul Ricoeur (1913–2005) are perhaps the most difficult to compress into a single chapter. Though Ricoeur is best known for his hermeneutical theory, his long career is characterized by such a great diversity of approaches, including phenomenology, structuralism, and narratology. This chapter deals with Ricoeur's earlier writings, particularly his mediation in the debate between Gadamer and Habermas, and his reflections on the meaning of symbols and the legacy of Sigmund Freud.

Paul Ricoeur began his academic career as a member of the Protestant faculty of theology at the University of Strasbourg. Like Gadamer and Emmanuel Levinas, his academic career began with a commitment to phenomenology as expounded by Husserl and Heidegger. But, on the basis of the logic that "I am" is prior to "I think," Ricoeur revised Husserl's phenomenology in the direction of Heidegger's existentialism.[1] Ricoeur's thought extended well beyond the framework of Heideggerian phenomenology and explored diverse themes such as hermeneutics, theology, biblical criticism, literary theory, Freudian psychoanalysis, and historiography. In 1956 Ricoeur took up a position at the Sorbonne, Paris, where he wrote many of his early works including *Fallible Man* (1960), *The Symbolism of Evil* (1960), and *Freud and Philosophy: An Essay on Interpretation* (1965). In 1970 Ricoeur accepted an academic position at the Divinity School of the University of Chicago, where he taught for many years. Within the field of biblical studies, Ricoeur is best known for articulating a "hermeneutics of suspicion." He famously argued that a hermeneutics of the restoration of meaning must be counterbalanced by a hermeneutics of the suspicion of meaning.[2]

The central issue of Ricoeur's early hermeneutical thought was the symbolic function of language. He studied the linguistic dimension of religious symbols and their importance for a reaffirmation of Christian understanding. He argued

---

[1]   In his early writings, Ricoeur understood the goal of the hermeneutics to be that of creating "a world in front of the text, a world that opens up new possibilities of being." He developed this theory on the basis of Division Two of Heidegger's *Being and Time*, trans. John Macquarrie and Edward Robinson (New York: Harper & Row, 1962 [1927]), §§ 45–83, 274ff.

[2]   Paul Ricoeur, *Freud and Philosophy: An Essay on Interpretation* (New Haven: Yale University Press, 1970 [1965]), 32–33; Paul Ricoeur, *Hermeneutics and the Human Sciences: Essays on Language, Action and Interpretation*, trans. John B. Thompson (Cambridge: Cambridge University Press, 1981), 63–100.

that individuals do not create the religious symbols of religious faith. Instead, they are something that human beings *receive* rather than make; they are the work of culture and formed within language, which then gives rise to thought, providing us "something to think about."[3] According to Ricoeur, symbols actually have a "double intention." A symbol has a literal meaning with reference to the world. For example, the literal meaning of the resurrection would be the raising of Jesus. However, built into this so-called first intention is a *second* intention that can lead those who contemplate it into its deeper meaning, such as emancipation. Specifically, religious symbols reenact the religious consciousness of human fault, culpability, and guilt, and other such boundary situations. Ricoeur believed that a reaffirmation of faith is possible through contemplation on this second intention of religious symbols.

RICOEUR'S THREE MASTERS OF SUSPICION

In previous chapters we have discussed the legacy of Nietzsche (Chapters 3–5) and Marx (Chapter 9) in twentieth-century thought. This chapter considers the corresponding impact of Sigmund Freud's psychoanalytic paradigm, as it subsequently was developed in the writings of Ricoeur. As previously noted, the writings of Nietzsche, Freud, and Marx have had an incalculable impression on contemporary thought and culture and our horizons of meaning. Their respective explorations of the will-to-power, human desire, and ideology have *called into question the epistemic status of all forms of objectifying knowledge*, including those associated with biblical studies. We can discern the continuing influence of the writings of Nietzsche, Freud, and Marx in such movements as poststructuralism, psychotherapy, feminism, critical theory, neopragmatism, gender studies, New Historicism, and postcolonial criticism, to name a few. In a very real sense, these three are the founding fathers of twentieth-century thought.

This explains why French and German theory in the 1960s produced a kind of composite construct of Nietzsche, Freud, and Marx, known by the acronym "NFM." This so-called NFM construct first appeared in the writings of Michel Foucault, who grouped them together as "masters of suspicion" in his famous essay of 1964 entitled "Nietzsche, Freud, Marx."[4] According to Foucault, Nietzsche's *Birth of Tragedy*, Marx's *Capital*, and Freud's *Interpretation of Dreams* caused three "inexhaustible wounds," the last of which was Freud's discovery of the unconscious as the basis of consciousness.[5] It is largely on account of the writings of Nietzsche, Freud,

---

3   Paul Ricoeur, *The Symbolism of Evil*, trans. Emerson Buchanan (Boston: Beacon Press, 1967), 348, cf. 14–18. Ricoeur distinguishes three dimensions of religious symbols: cosmic symbols, psychic symbols, and poetic symbols.
4   Michel Foucault, "Nietzsche, Freud, Marx," in *Transforming the Hermeneutic Context,* ed. Gayle L. Ormiston and Alan D. Schrift (Albany: State University of New York Press, 1990), 59–67.
5   Ibid., 59–61.

and Marx that postmodernity has *placed the idea of the suspicion and destruction of literal meaning at the very heart of the redefinition of critical thinking.*

The year following the publication of Foucault's article on the NFM construct, Ricoeur discussed the same NFM construct in his book *Freud and Philosophy* (1965), in which he dubbed them the three "masters of suspicion." By terming them "masters of suspicion," he was implying that all three had approached culture and texts suspiciously, as distorted communication that conceals a hidden message. In Ricoeur's estimation, all three looked upon the contents of human consciousness as, in some sense, *false* with respect to hidden "will-to-power" (Nietzsche), libidinal desire (Freud), and class interest (Marx), respectively.[6] Moreover, each in his own unique way attempted to transcend such false consciousness through interpretation and critique. Through critique, each attempted to unmask, demystify, and expose the *real* over and against the *apparent* by approaching society, culture, and texts suspiciously. In so doing, each, in his own way, demonstrated that language – including religious language – often does not say exactly what it means; language often transmits a different meaning beyond its literal meaning. For example, Marx argued that political, religious, and legal language conceals the "ideology" of the ruling class, whose purpose is to make its own self-interests appear to be just common wisdom and a widely held truth. From a Marxist perspective, such "common wisdom" is ideologically crafted with the intention of instilling in the proletariat a false consciousness of itself and of its relation to the world (see Chapter 9).[7]

For his part, Nietzsche explored the will-to-power (*der Wille zur Macht*), a hidden force operating within all human beings.[8] Though this will-to-power is sometimes expressed positively in the form of creative achievements, it can also be expressed negatively as *ressentiment,* which is a mixture of blame, resentment, and hostility that redirects or reassigns the guilt of an offense or transgression toward an innocent person. In essence, *ressentiment* is manifested by the blaming of others for one's own failings or, conversely, by falsely blaming oneself for wrongs in society, of which one is largely innocent. In the latter case, *ressentiment* turns the violence of the world inward upon the self, in the form of a bad conscience, false

---

6   Ricoeur, *Freud and Philosophy*, 32.
7   Marx's analysis of religion led him to the conclusion that while religion appeared to be concerned with the lofty issues of transcendence and personal salvation, in reality its true function was to provide a "flight from the reality of inhumane working conditions" and to make "the misery of life more endurable." Religion in this way served as "the opium of the masses"; Karl Marx, "Contribution to the Critique of Hegel's Philosophy of Right," in *Early Writings*, trans. and ed. T. B. Bottomore (New York: McGraw-Hill, 1964) 44.
8   Friedrich Nietzsche, *The Will to Power*, trans. Walter Kaufmann and R. J. Hollingdale (New York: Vintage Books, 1967); according to Gilles Deleuze, the will-to-power is "the element from which derive both the quantitative difference of related forces and the quality that devolves into each force in this relation," which is to say, it is "the principle of the synthesis of forces"; Gilles Deleuze, *Nietzsche and Philosophy,* trans. Hugh Tomlinson (New York: Columbia University Press, 1983 [1962]), 46.

guilt, and self-condemnation.[9] In either case, *ressentiment* results in a covering up of the true causes of an offense or transgression. Thus, the expression *ressentiment* in language is another form of distorted or false communication, which conceals a hidden message. Freud likewise argued that dreams are also forms of communication that conceal a hidden message as well: he believed that beneath the literal meaning of dreams is concealed another meaning, requiring interpretation, which is at odds with its literal meaning.

Ricoeur insists that Nietzsche, Freud, and Marx were more than masters of suspicion: through their "three convergent procedures of *demystification*," they also *revealed new truths*.[10] By calling our attention to distortions of meaning, they made possible the discovery of new truths, which had been previously suppressed, by creating new modes of interpretation. In Ricoeur's view, Nietzsche, Freud, and Marx "clear the horizon for a more authentic word, for a new reign of Truth, not only by means of a 'destructive' critique, but also by the *invention of an art of interpreting*."[11] This prompted Ricoeur to call for an "extreme iconoclasm" with respect to the interpretive tradition.[12]

Within the field of biblical studies, fewer than expected have answered this call to extreme iconoclasm. Nonetheless, despite our temerity, the "new reign of Truth," which was ushered in by the writings of Nietzsche, Freud, and Marx, has thrown the field of critical theory into turmoil, and hermeneutics along with it. As a result, as Ricoeur observes, the field of hermeneutics is now "at variance with itself."[13] Scholars' traditional preoccupation with the semantic meaning of biblical texts has caused them to overlook their concealed or suppressed meanings of texts, which may be at variance with their semantic meaning. With the discipline of hermeneutics being now at variance with itself, what is most apparent, says Ricoeur, is a *conflict of interpretations*, with no secure point of reference by which these conflicts can be resolved or adjudicated. In order to address this state of affairs, Ricoeur developed a new strategy in contrast to that of his previous "hermeneutics of recollection or retrieval": namely, a hermeneutics of suspicion.

Although Ricoeur is best known in the field of biblical studies for his articulation of this hermeneutics of suspicion, we should never lose sight of the fact that Ricoeur's hermeneutics of suspicion has a *dual focus*: it concerns the interpreter as well as the text. In Ricoeur's view, biblical scholars should also consider *themselves*, as well as the biblical

---

[9]   Cf. Friedrich Nietzsche, *On the Genealogy of Morals, Ecce Homo*, trans. Walter Kaufmann and R. J. Hollingdale (New York: Vintage Books, 1967), 5–10, 36–39 (I, 10), 40–42 (I, 11), 44–45 (I, 13), 54 (I, 16), 73–76 (II, 11), 86–87 (II, 17), 124 (III, 14). Nietzsche adopted this French term because no equivalent German term exists.

[10] Ricoeur, *Freud and Philosophy*, 34 (emphasis added).

[11] Ibid., 33 (emphasis added).

[12] "In our time we have not finished doing away with idols and we have barely begun to listen to symbols. It may be that this situation, in its apparent distress, is instructive: it may be that extreme iconoclasm belongs to the restoration of meaning" (ibid., 27).

[13] Ibid., 26–27.

texts they interpret, with suspicion, for biblical interpreters (like people in general) are, to one extent or another, alienated from their material environments and from themselves. Our everyday understanding of ourselves and the world routinely covers up this self-alienation, seeking out comfort and distraction instead. Thus, the hermeneutics of suspicion must be directed toward biblical interpreters and texts alike.[14]

LESSONS LEARNED FROM FREUD

Whenever one asks the question, What does this biblical text mean? there is human *desire*. The truth of this simple observation is perhaps more fearful to biblical interpreters than any other. For this reason, it is also the most ignored truth. In fact, in view of the growing appreciation of the human unconscious as the basis of consciousness and desire, it is remarkable that much of mainline biblical studies continues to disregard the role of the unconscious and libidinal desire in biblical interpretation. Nonetheless, the influx of new scholars in the 1960s, 1970s, and 1980s who do not belong to the all-white, male peer group of the discipline has succeeded in unsettling the discipline to some extent by bringing alternative perspectives from the so-called margins to the task of biblical interpretation.

As a starting point for appreciating changing attitudes toward human desire, we can consider a few of the key concepts of Sigmund Freud's psychoanalytic paradigm. Freud's theory is often divided into two streams. First, there is the *"energetic* Freud," who analyzed libidinal human desire,[15] and its investment in the material world.[16] (Libidinal desire can be defined as the energy behind all life-producing

---

[14]   Ricoeur's hermeneutics of suspicion has become a fundamental hallmark of modern biblical interpretation. Carolyn Osiek writes, "Today's preunderstanding requires analysis of how power is used. If the paschal mystery is about deliverance from death to life, then without the *hermeneutic of suspicion*, we risk being diminished, not by the text but by earlier pre-understandings that are not yet open to a wider and more inclusive way of living and loving. Just as historical criticism asked the hard analytical questions a century ago and was suspect by many for that reason, so too does the hermeneutic of suspicion today ask the critical questions of our time, and is suspect on the part of many for the same reasons" ("Catholic or catholic? Biblical Scholarship at the Center," *JBL* 125 [2006]: 5–22, esp. 20).

[15]   When Freud looks at civilization, he sees two fundamental principles at work, the life-drive (*Eros*) and the death-drive (*Thanatos*). The life-drive (libido/Eros) is the energy for survival, sex, and creation. The death-drive is related to the human desire to separate itself from the external world. According to Freud, the human mind is at constant battle or tension between its desire to flourish and to destroy itself; S. Freud, *Civilization and Its Discontents*, trans. James Strachey (New York: Norton, 2005 [1930]), 71–77.

[16]   In simplest terms, Freud argued that within the family triangle – father, mother, child – the child experiences an "oedipal" desire that arises from not having what it wants. To obtain its object of desire, its mother, the child transgresses the law of the father, ultimately hoping to replace father. The desire to transgress the law of the father and the attendant feelings of resentment eventually give way to a sense of guilt and the desire to seek the father's forgiveness. According to Freud, this apparent desire for the father's forgiveness is false because it conceals a deeper desire to one day possess the father's power to control and power to punish. Thus, oedipal desire is characterized by a double lack – lack of the mother and lack of the power of the father.

impulses [Eros] and life-destroying impulses [Thanatos], beyond those of desires connected with bare survival.) Second, there is the "*linguistic* Freud," who studied the unconscious by analyzing dreams, whose language and symbols are often fugitive and vaguely menacing. Freud argued that dreams employ two main mechanisms to disguise forbidden desires, namely condensation and displacement.[17]

Freudian psychoanalysis of dreams is regressive in the sense that it moves backward from conscious meaning (e.g., the literal content of dreams) into the unconscious, which is the realm of libidinal desire. Since the unconscious is, by definition, inaccessible to the consciousness, it cannot be observed or analyzed directly but only as it is expressed as desire in the coded language of dreams. Freud's classic definition of the unconscious is as follows:

It is essential to abandon the overvaluation of the property of being conscious before it becomes possible to form any correct view of the origin of what is mental…. The unconscious must be assumed to be the general basis of psychical life. The unconscious is the larger sphere, which includes within it the smaller sphere of the conscious. Everything conscious has an unconscious preliminary stage; whereas what is unconscious may remain at that stage and nevertheless claim to be regarded as having the full value of a psychical process. The unconscious is the true psychical reality; in its innermost nature it is as much unknown to us as the reality of the external world, and it is as incompletely presented by the data of consciousness as is the external world by the communications of our sense organs.[18]

Freud established the concept of the human self as that which is constituted primarily by the unconscious. In opposition to the modern Western notion of the autonomous self as volitional subject and author of meaning through the exercise of consciousness, rationality, free will, and self-reflection, Freud argued that the unconscious is the true source of meaning. In Freud's view, human actions, beliefs, thoughts, and the concept of self are all shaped by the desires and drives of the unconscious.[19]

---

[17] Condensation: the combination into a *single image* of many objects and ideas that do not appear together in any "real" experience, or the condensation of a complex meaning into a simpler one. Displacement is displacement of the meaning of one image or symbol onto something associated linearly with it. Displacement corresponds to the mechanism of *metonymy* in language, where one thing is replaced by something corresponding to it. An example of metonymy is when you evoke an image of a whole thing by naming a part of it: when you say "the crown" when you mean the king or royalty; or you say "twenty sails" when you mean twenty ships.

[18] Sigmund Freud, *The Interpretation of Dreams*, trans. Joyce Crick (Oxford: Oxford University Press, 1999 [1900]), VII, F.

[19] Deleuze and Guattari argue that the human unconscious consists of all that has been *left behind* in the process of the oedipal overcoding process. In other words, the unconscious is a storehouse of one's personalized redundancy of discarded possible "I's." This storehouse of the virtual potential of the individual person can be released by disrupting the analogical process of eliminating possible "I's," which had previously curtailed potential. These unused "I's," which are stored in the unconscious, can thus be reclaimed and filled with fresh intensity.

While it is now widely recognized that many of Freud's theories are now considered to be false, or at least problematic, one of his basic insights continues to be relevant.[20] For example, even if few people would recognize themselves in the classical formation of Freud's Oedipus complex, all people, to one degree or another, are insecure about their capacity for intimacy with others and are anxious about being under the power of others. The criticism that Freud's theories are not scientific misconstrues the essence of psychoanalysis. According to Ricoeur, Freud's theory should not be read through the epistemological lenses of the sciences. Psychoanalysis is not an *observational* discipline: it is a *hermeneutic* practice in the sense that the *language of psychoanalysis itself has an irreducible role in the very constitution of meaning.*[21] Therefore, psychoanalytic concepts should be judged "according to their status as conditions of the possibility of analytic experience, in so far as the latter operates in the field of speech."[22] As Richard Rorty observes, Freud actually invented his own "language game" in order to create the possibility of a *redescription* of what it means to be human. Freud's language of desire does not replace previous vocabularies of desire but instead adds a new language of description that is capable of achieving its own unique purposes: psychoanalytic conceptual language makes possible psychoanalytic meaning.

Despite the fact that Freud's thematic focus on family dynamics obscures the contributions of other factors to the formation of neurosis (see Chapter 12), the "energetic Freud" has nonetheless provided a new language with which to speak of the phenomena of the "sublimation" of the libidinal desire.[23] Similarly, the "linguistic Freud" has provided a new language with which to speak of the repression of libidinal energy in the unconscious.[24] Harold Bloom argues that Freud was as much a "myth maker" as he was a metaphysician: "[M]ore even than Proust, his was the mythopoeic mind of our age, as much our theologian and our moral philosophy as he was our psychologist and our prime maker of fictions."[25] Because Freud does not provide a scientific analysis of human desire, there is no need to literalize

---

[20] Cf. Peter D. Kramer, *Freud: Inventor of the Modern Mind* (New York: HarperCollins, 2006). For example, Judith Butler reappropriates the Freudian conceptual vocabulary of desire in order to problematize Freud's concept of gender as category of essence, without adopting the Freudian paradigm as a totalizing theory; cf. Judith Butler, "Imitation and Gender Insubordination," in *The Lesbian and Gay Studies Reader,* ed. Henry Abelove (London: Routledge, 1993), 307–20.

[21] Paul Ricoeur, *The Conflict of Interpretation: Essays in Hermeneutics,* trans. Willis Domingo (Evanston, IL: Northwestern University Press, 1974 [1969]), 263.

[22] Ricoeur, *Freud and Philosophy,* 375.

[23] The term "sublimation" refers to the redirection of libidinal energy, which cannot be fulfilled, into more productive activities.

[24] Repression: desires (whether sublimated or not) that cannot be fulfilled must be repressed into a particular place in the mind, which Freud labels the unconscious. The unconscious is the realm of repressed desires. It is the place where prohibited desires, and things your conscious mind does not want to know, are stored.

[25] Harold Bloom, *Agon: Toward a Theory of Revisionism* (Oxford: Oxford University Press, 1982), 43–44.

his theory as if it were a set of epistemological facts.[26] Instead, we should treat his psychoanalytic language as a "mixed discourse" in the sense that it includes both locutionary and illocutionary statements. Through the invention of new concepts, Freud provided his patients with the possibility of weaving together the fragmentary and idiosyncratic narratives of their lives in such a way as to break free from some of their determinism through a fresh act of renarration.[27] From this vantage point, Freud teaches the biblical interpreters one important truth: by changing our vocabulary of analysis of signs, hermeneutic interpretation can redefine its own purposes and find new significances and insights. Thus, Ricoeur argued that Freud's categories of analysis can help biblical interpreters recover an *authentic* hermeneutic practice.[28] In *Freud and Philosophy* (1965), he actually situated his own hermeneutics within the field of Freudian psychoanalysis and its appreciation of the *interpretive character of truth*. In effect, Ricoeur transposed Freud's psychoanalytic theory of the language into a *literary* theory of textual meaning.

Ricoeur divided Freud's ontology of desire into three cycles. The first cycle is concerned with "linguistic Freud's" analysis of dreams and neuroses; it deals with libidinal desire as expressed, repressed, and sublimated. In the second cycle, Ricoeur discussed the application of Freud's ideas in the sphere of human culture, and Freud's articulation of the *ego, id,* and *superego,* most notably appearing in *Moses and Monotheism*.[29] In the third cycle, Ricoeur addressed Freud's theory of *Eros* (creative desire), *Thanatos* (death instinct), and *Ananke* (relations based on the need to work together to survive). In Ricoeur's view, all three cycles share one central theme, namely, human desire as expressed, sublimated, and repressed, whether it is the desire to create or to destroy, to live or to die.

RICOEUR'S THREE MAPPINGS OF THE SELF

Ricoeur maintains that if one is going to *become* who one truly is, one must first *know* who one truly is. To this end, he combines Freud's ontology of desire with two other competing ontologisms: a "teleological" ontology and an "eschatological" ontology. By "ontology," Ricoeur means a study of the hidden structure of human existence. Ricoeur termed his Freudian ontology an "archaeology of the subject," which is a study of self as ruled by unconscious desire.[30] "Archaeology"

---

[26] Cf. Richard Rorty, "Freud and Moral Reflection," in *Pragmatism's Freud,* ed. William Kerrigan and Joseph Smith (Baltimore: Johns Hopkins University Press, 1986).

[27] Richard Rorty, *Contingency, Irony, and Solidarity* (Cambridge: Cambridge University Press, 1989), 33.

[28] Similarly, the Catholic biblical scholar Carolyn Osiek comments that a modern understanding of "the dynamics of unconscious forces" has the potential to give expanded meanings to biblical symbols and to our relationship with the biblical text; see Osiek, "Catholic or catholic?" 22.

[29] Sigmund Freud, *Moses and Monotheism,* trans. Katherine Jones (London: Hogarth Press, 1939).

[30] Paul Ricoeur, *The Conflict of Interpretations,* ed. Don Ihde, trans. Willis Domingo et al. (Evanston, IL: Northwestern University Press, 1974), 263.

roots the origin of meaning *regressively* in the unconscious (not in the intending subject), which is one dimension of language's component of "manifestation" (cf. Chapter 1).

Ricoeur balanced this regressive, Freudian, archaeological ontology with a "teleological" ontology that is oriented toward the future. By teleological ontology, he means a study of humanity that is progressive in the Hegelian sense. Ricoeur's third, "eschatological" ontology is founded on a phenomenology of religion. It studies human beings as they interpret themselves through the signs of the sacred and abandon themselves in utter dependence upon the Sacred.[31] This "eschatological" analysis shifts meaning beyond the self, beyond the body of the interpreter, and even beyond the progress of humanity, situating it in a relation of utter dependence on God.[32]

Ricoeur's eschatological ontology serves a mediating function between the *regressive* "archaeological" ontology and the *progressive* "teleological" ontology.[33] It serves to protect Ricoeur's model from being purely regressive or progressive, introducing an eschatological moment between them.[34] Because each of these ontologies is grounded in an *irreducible* modality of the *dependent* self, no single approach excludes the other. Each constitutes a complementary but conflicting perspective on the biblical interpreter. Ricoeur brings these three ontologies into relation with one another by combining them within Heidegger's hermeneutic circle to form what he terms an "ontology of understanding."[35] By means of this hermeneutic circle, one can catch sight of oneself in the very act of interpreting a biblical text archaeologically, teleologically, and eschatologically, through various rotations of the circle.

Ricoeur's three ontologies really represent three different *mappings* of the person of the interpreter. In contrast to images, a map is not a passive registration of the world. A map is really a theorization of the real, as opposed to an imitation of the real.[36] This is why it is possible to create so many different types of maps (e.g., political maps, road maps, physical maps, topographic maps, climate maps, resource maps, geological maps, population density maps). Maps can be experimented with and even be brought into interaction with other maps.[37] Thus, Ricoeur's three ontological maps can be brought into interaction with each other, as different ways of theorizing the interpreting subject. By combining his three ontological maps into a

---

[31] As articulated by Mircea Eliade (1907–86) and Gerardus Van der Leeuw (1890–1950).

[32] Ricoeur, *Freud and Philosophy*, 54–55, 133–34, 376–91, 422–29, 439–43.

[33] Ricoeur, *Conflict of Interpretations*, 12–22; Ricoeur, *Freud and Philosophy*, 344–52.

[34] Ricoeur, *Freud and Philosophy*, 459–93, 524–31.

[35] Ricoeur, *Conflict of Interpretations*, 19.

[36] Gilles Deleuze and Félix Guattari, *A Thousand Plateaus: Capitalism and Schizophrenia*, trans. Brian Massumi (Minneapolis: University of Minnesota Press, 1987 [1980]), 12–13.

[37] B. H. McLean, "The Exteriority of Biblical Meaning and the Plentitude of Desire: An Exploration of Deleuze's Non-metaphysical Hermeneutics of Kafka," *Neotestamentica: Journal of the New Testament Society of South Africa* 43/1 (2009): 93–122.

hermeneutic circle, he created a multicentric dynamic space, which recognizes the connections between his three maps. In so doing, he has subverted the exclusive right of any single theorization of the interpreter to function as a totalizing system. For this reason, Ricoeur's ontology of understanding opens up opportunities for liberation from the self-delusion and the falsehoods that stem from the adherence to any single theorization of the biblical interpreter.[38]

RICOEUR'S MEDIATION BETWEEN GADAMER AND HABERMAS

In his essay entitled "Hermeneutics and the Critique of Ideology," Ricoeur intervened in the debate between Habermas and Gadamer.[39] This essay is not so much an exposition on the key points of their debate as it is a third perspective. According to Ricoeur, the contrasting approaches of Habermas and Gadamer illustrate Wilhelm Dilthey's well-known distinction between explanation and understanding (cf. Chapter 3). As previously discussed, Dilthey distinguished between "explanation" (*Erklärung*) and "understanding" (*Verstehung*) as two contrasting approaches to knowledge. He argued that, while the natural sciences are concerned with explanation (through the formulation of general laws and ascribing causal effects), the goal of the humanities (*Geisteswissenschaften*) is "understanding" (*Verstehung*), which seeks to arrive at a *shared understanding* of things. On the basis of this distinction, Ricoeur designated the opposing hermeneutical approaches of Habermas and Gadamer, respectively, as the "descending pathway" of *explanation* and the "ascending pathway" of *understanding*.[40] Ricoeur is suspicious of any hermeneutical theory that relies exclusively on either explanation or understanding.[41]

Ricoeur's position in this debate can be summarized according to the following topics: contextualization, anti-intentionalism, and decontextualizing and recontextualizing the text.

Contextualization: The Role of the Sense of a Text

The genius of historicism has always been its ability to call attention to historical difference and defend the otherness of the past. By interpreting a biblical text in terms of its own historical and cultural context, biblical studies have succeeded in

---

[38] "The ontology of understanding is implied in the methodology of interpretation, following the ineluctable 'hermeneutic circle' which Heidegger himself taught us to delineate"; Ricoeur, *Conflict of Interpretations*, 19.

[39] Ricoeur, *Hermeneutics and the Human Sciences*, 63–100.

[40] Paul Ricoeur, "Ethics and Culture: Habermas and Gadamer in Dialogue," *Philosophy Today* 17 (1973): 153–65.

[41] See Paul Ricoeur, "Explanation and Understanding: On Some Remarkable Connections among the Theory of the Text, Theory of Action, and Theory of History," in *The Philosophy of Paul Ricoeur: An Anthology of His Work*, ed. C. Reagan and D. Stewart (Boston: Beacon Press, 1978), 149–66.

disclosing the particularity of biblical texts in all their disconcerting strangeness and thereby *protecting* these texts from being assimilated to our own contemporary expectations of meaning. But historicism also has a negative side. Ricoeur recognized that the antiquarian mode of historical interpretation often appeals to the original historical "sense" of biblical texts as part of a strategy of *controlling their present-day significance*. In Ricoeur's view, biblical hermeneutics must resituate historical interpretation in a multidimensional conceptualization of biblical texts.

Anti-intentionalism

Both Ricoeur and Gadamer are "anti-intentionalists" in the sense that they defend the authority of biblical *texts* over and against the purported intentions of their historical authors. Once an author finishes writing a text, it is released from his control, a fact that is magnified with the passage of time. Consequently, a text's present sense-event is not determined solely by its author. Ricoeur faults Habermas for the error of intentionalism, that is, of restricting the meaning of a text to its original sense-event. In Ricoeur's view, by "identifying the problem of understanding with the problem of understanding another [i.e., the original author]," Habermas "thinks in too exclusive a sense, that the meaning of a transmission must be the meaning that other subjects have put there."[42]

It is a simple fact that most biblical texts conceal, to one extent or another, the actual authors who brought them into existence (see Chapter 2). This fact has necessitated the ongoing reconstruction of biblical authors by scholars. Most of the books of the Bible, including the canonical Gospels and some of the letters attributed to Paul, were written anonymously or pseudonymously. But even if the historical identity of biblical authors can be known with some certainty, Ricoeur still argues that it remains true that the "written text," once circulated, "becomes a *disembodied* voice, detached from the author and the author's situation."[43] Thus, despite the fact that the twenty-seven texts composing the New Testament were intended to be read by recipients of their authors' own generation, the Christian tradition has always maintained that these texts have *autonomy* in the sense that they are, at least potentially, addressed to whoever has the ability to read them. This is the implication of calling these texts "scripture." This autonomy of biblical texts creates an openness, which cannot be closed. The New Testament is "inspired" in the sense that addressees of these writings have become universalized by their inclusion in a canon, and the particularity of the intentions of their

---

[42] Roy J. Howard, *Three Faces of Hermeneutics: An Introduction to Current Theories of Understanding* (Berkeley: University of California Press, 1982), 169.

[43] Anthony Thistleton, *New Horizons in Hermeneutics: The Theory and Practice of Transforming Biblical Reading* (Grand Rapids, MI: Zondervan, 1992), 69.

authors have been subsumed within the intentions of God, which is why multiple interpretations of the Bible are not only possible but also inevitable and even necessary.

This universalizing of the reader (from the original intended recipients to any person who can read) is one of the most striking features of biblical textuality: with the passage of time, the historically and contextually situated texts of the Bible have become monumentalized by their inclusion in a canon and, as a result, are read, and reread, by each new generation of Christians. The end result is that the present sense-event of these *monumentalized* texts *always escapes the finite contexts and intentions of their historical authors.* The original historical sense of a text, as intended by a historical author, is a fleeting event that pertained only to its originally intended recipients. *But, by virtue of the text-reception complex, biblical texts always carry a latent reserve of virtual sense beyond their founding sense-event.* This latent reserve is awakened by the act of interpretation, *resulting in an enlargement of the text's fields of reference.*

Gérard Genette has analyzed the many ways in which texts can find themselves in new relationships — "obvious or concealed" — with other texts.[44] As an explanatory metaphor, he employs a concept derived from the palimpsest, which is a manuscript in which one text is superimposed on another in such a way that "does not quite conceal [the original text] but allows [it] to show through." A palimpsest illustrates graphically the virtual capacity of texts to *bricolage* "new circuits of meaning" onto old ones in such a way as to "make old things new."[45] Genette terms this phenomenon "open structuralism" (cf. Chapter 12).

Similarly, Umberto Eco conceives of a text as an "open" system, which unfolds when the reader's horizon of understanding engages with the text. By virtue of a text's intrinsic *openness*, Eco argues that it is also susceptible to multiple "performances,"[46] allowing biblical texts to have multiple meanings beyond those of the intentions of their historical authors. According to Ricoeur, it is this characteristic of biblical texts that makes their interpretation an open-ended and even unpredictable event: "The right of the reader and the right of the text converge in an important struggle that generates the whole dynamic of interpretation."[47] By virtue

---

[44] Gérard Genette, *Palimpsests: Literature in the Second Degree* (Lincoln: University of Nebraska Press, 1977 [1982]), 1.

[45] Ibid., 7, 394–95, 398–400. The French term *bricolage* is derived from the verb *bricoler.* In colloquial English it has the sense of "do-it-yourself." The term "bricolage" has been taken up by literary criticism to specify the practice of experimentally and creatively bringing texts into relation with other texts, beyond the reach of structuring effects of appeals to original historical context, a specific epistemology knowledge, or metaphysics of meaning.

[46] Umberto Eco, *The Open Work*, trans. Anna Cancogni (Cambridge, MA: Harvard University Press, 1989), 4, 6.

[47] Paul Ricoeur, *Interpretation Theory: Discourse and the Surplus of Meaning* (Fort Worth: Texas Christian Press, 1976), 32.

of this open-endedness of the present sense-event, biblical texts have the potential to reveal new significances.[48]

Decontextualizing and Recontextualizing the Text

Many of the cultural and contextual factors that have shaped biblical texts actually distance contemporary readers from their overt meanings. As previously discussed, Rudolph Bultmann argued that the Jewish apocalyptic and gnostic "mythical world picture" of early Christian proclamation is *unbelievable* to modern people (or at least it should be) (see Chapter 6).

Owing to the foreignness of this ancient mythical world picture, contemporary hermeneutical understanding requires that biblical texts be *decontextualized*. To "decontextualize" a text is to abstract it from its original web of interconnections to its social and cultural context, its original author and intended readers. Such decontextualization entails the enlargement of the three referential fields of the founding sense-event to include the world of the interpreter. As discussed in Chapter 1, decontextualization always remains an open possibility because every biblical text possesses a virtual potential to form new sense-events over time (cf. my discussion of "deterritorialization" in Chapter 12). The past two thousand years of Christian interpretation testify to the *normative* practice of decontextualizing the "sense" of biblical texts. Our own interpretation's acts of decontextualization constitute an extension of this illustrious history. All this is to say that a biblical text is not a "sealed package." All biblical texts must be repeatedly recontextualized within the "time of tradition" in order to "remain living" to people of faith.

We feel that interpretation has a history and that this history is a segment of tradition itself. Interpretation does not spring from nowhere; rather, one interprets in order to make explicit, to extend, and so to keep alive the tradition itself, inside which one always remains. It is in this sense that the time of interpretation belongs in some way to the time of tradition. But tradition, in return, even understood as the transmission of a *depositum*, remains a dead tradition if it is not the continual interpretation of this deposit: our "heritage" is not a sealed package we pass from hand to hand, without ever opening, but rather a treasure from which we draw by the handful and which by this very act is replenished. *Every tradition lives by grace of interpretation, and it is at this price that it continues, that is, remains living.*[49]

We know that a biblical text has participated in a present sense-event when a new generation discerns within it answers to questions that they are asking from within their own contexts and challenges. As such, biblical texts are not isolated

---

[48]   Mario J. Valdés (ed.), "Introduction: Ricoeur's Post-Structuralist Hermeneutics," in *A Ricoeur Reader: Reflection and Imagination* (Toronto: University of Toronto Press, 1991), 24–25.

[49]   Ricoeur, *Conflict of Interpretations*, 27 (emphasis added).

objects. In principle, they remain open to reinsertion into the horizons of meaning of every new generation.[50]

Ricoeur's Intervention in the Debate

For Ricoeur, the debate between Habermas and Gadamer illustrates the "conflict of interpretation" that has overtaken the field as a whole. On the one hand, Ricoeur agrees with Habermas that Gadamer's universal hermeneutics is excessively subjective. Owing to Gadamer's strong aversion to positivistic thinking, he has failed to incorporate into his hermeneutical theory any of the methodological advances in the human sciences. In contrast, Habermas's universal pragmatics *does* employ a method that allows for the detection of hidden, ideological content, which is to say, the "instrumental use of language," behind the semantic meaning of language. In an effort to clarify the nature of this conflict between Gadamer's ascending and Habermas's descending pathways, Ricoeur asks:

Is this gesture [of hermeneutics] an avowal of the historical conditions to which all human understanding is subsumed under the reign of finitude [i.e., Gadamer's horizons of the historically effected consciousness]? Or rather is it, in the last analysis, an act of defiance, a critical gesture, relentlessly repeated and indefinitely turned against "false consciousness," against the distortions of human communication that conceal the permanent exercise of domination and violence [i.e., as asserted by Habermas]?[51]

Summarized in this way, one might suppose that this conflict of interpretation can be condensed into the form of two opposing alternatives. But, in Ricoeur's view, it is not necessary to choose between Gadamer's hermeneutic understanding and Habermas's critical explanation. Instead, Ricoeur opens up a space in which these two alternatives can enter into a productive dialogue. By putting these two positions into dialogue, Ricoeur aims to preserve Gadamer's hermeneutics of hope, which looks for a more complete appropriation of textual present sense-event, while also retaining Habermas's hermeneutics of suspicion, which guards against the unguarded simplistic assimilation of past meanings. Ricoeur believes that only a hermeneutics of hope *and* suspicion can provide us a means of replaying, or counteractualizing, the founding sense-event of biblical texts, while remaining vigilant against forms of distorted communication.

Ricoeur puts these two approaches into dialogue with each other by resituating their debate within the Heideggerian tradition: he asks the Heideggerian question, "In the end, hermeneutics will say, from where do you [Habermas] speak when you appeal to self-reflection (*Selbstreflexion*), if it is not from the place you yourself have denounced as a non-place, the non-place of the transcendental subject?"[52]

---

[50] Heidegger, *Being and Time*, 30.
[51] Ricoeur, *Hermeneutics and the Human Sciences*, 99.
[52] Ibid.

For even Habermas's theory comes out of a tradition: "It is indeed from the basis of a tradition that you speak. This tradition is not perhaps the same as Gadamer's; it is perhaps that of the Enlightenment, whereas Gadamer's would be Romanticism. But it [ideological critique] is a tradition nonetheless, the tradition of emancipation rather than that of recollection."[53] In other words, even Habermas's "critique is also a tradition," which can be situated within a tradition and, therefore, can be situated within Gadamer's own hermeneutic understanding of tradition. In fact, Habermas's critique "plunges [us] into the most impressive tradition, that of liberating acts, of the Exodus and the Resurrection. Perhaps there would be no more interest in emancipation, no more anticipation of freedom, if the Exodus and the Resurrection were effaced from the memory of [hu]mankind.... If that is so, then nothing is more deceptive than the alleged antinomy between an ontology of prior understanding and an eschatology of freedom."[54]

On this basis, Ricoeur argues that the supposed dichotomy between the theories of Gadamer and Habermas is *false*: "We have encountered these false antinomies elsewhere: as if it were necessary to choose between [Gadamer's] reminiscence and [Habermas's] hope! In theological terms, eschatology is nothing without the recitation of acts of deliverance from the past."[55] In his view, hermeneutic interpretation requires *both* Gadamer's "avowal of the historical conditions to which all human understanding is subsumed" *and* Habermas's critical "act of defiance," which "relentlessly repeated and indefinitely turned against 'false consciousness,' against the distortions of human communication that conceal the permanent exercise of domination and violence."[56] As David Jaspers observes, this is a dialectical dialogue, in which both sides not only are needed but also carry a responsibility:

For Gadamer we must choose between truth or method. Ricoeur, on the other hand, suggests not an opposition, but a dialectical relationship ... between explanations (method) and understanding (truth) which enable us more adequately to describe the tension between the self and the other, and to remain responsible to ... explanatory methods.[57]

Because the respective approaches of Gadamer and Habermas can be brought together in a dialectical relationship, it is more productive to explore that interactive space *between* them rather than to choose one over the other. To this end, Ricoeur explores this space of interaction between these two approaches in terms of four themes, which, taken together, bring Gadamer and Habermas into dialogue.

---

[53] Ibid.
[54] Ibid.
[55] Ibid.
[56] Ibid., 63.
[57] David Jaspers, "The Limits of Formalism and the Theology of Hope: Ricoeur, Moltmann and Dostoyevsky," *Literature and Theology* 1 (1987): 1–10, esp. 4.

FOUR THEMES

Theme 1: Distanciation from the Text

Ricoeur's first theme takes up Gadamer's concept of distanciation as a strategy for emancipating the "sense" of a biblical text. Because a biblical text is a product of signification, denotation, and manifestation, whose overall effect is to *distance* the contemporary reader from biblical text (see Chapters 1 and 3), the task of traditional biblical interpretation has been to call attention to the many differences between the world of the text and our own world. This experience of the *historical peculiarity* of ancient texts also has the effect of estranging us from their worlds of meaning. When we experience a biblical text's historical otherness and recognize that it is not addressed to us, we also lose our childlike naiveté. To lose one's naiveté is to realize that *we cannot live, with authenticity, within the implied symbolic worldview of the biblical text.* As such, this experience of estrangement from the implied world of the text requires that we seek alternative ways to discover the significance of biblical texts, both "through and beyond (our) estrangement," and thereby achieve what Ricoeur terms a "second naiveté."[58]

Theme 2: Structural Analysis

As a way of correcting the subjectivity of Gadamer's hermeneutics, Ricoeur introduces a second moment, namely structural analysis.[59] Every biblical text presupposes an unconscious horizon of meaning, which *precedes* all semantic meaning. To study the structure of a text is to view it as "the product of perceptual structures which operate at an *unconscious* level rather than at a consciously artistic level."[60] To expose a text's structure, one must first suspend both the semantic meaning of a text (i.e., what the text literally seems to be saying) and any direct, or implied, textual reference to the material (or spiritual) world behind, or beyond, the text, and then focus on the *text's implied horizon of meaning.*[61] For example, the implied structure of 1Thessalonians 5 is the phenomenological horizon of Jewish apocalypticism. In each case, one must ask, What kind of symbolic world is assumed or implied by the text?

---

[58] Ricoeur, *Interpretation Theory*, 43–44; Ricoeur, *Symbolism of Evil*, 351, cf. 349.
[59] Ricoeur actually designates this as a "depth" semantic analysis. I have changed the term "depth semantic analysis" to "structural analysis" to help avoid confusion with Deleuze's terminology (cf. Chapter 12), which employs the terms "depth" and "structure" in the opposite way. Since both terms imply metaphorical thinking, they can be used differently, as long as the different usage is clearly specified.
[60] Susan Wittig, "A Theory of Multiple Meanings," in *Polyvalent Narration*, ed. J. D. Crossan, Semeia 9 (Decatur: Scholars Press, 1977), 82 (emphasis added).
[61] Roland Barthes, "Introduction to the Structural Analysis of Narratives," in *A Barthes Reader*, ed. Susan Sontag (New York: Hill and Wang, 1980), 251–95.

If a biblical text is conceived of as a game of chess (cf. Chapter 7), then its structure could be compared to the rules of the game of chess (i.e., the structure of the game that is invoked by every particular game of chess). Just as one could deduce over time the rules of the game of chess by observing the playing of many actual chess games, one can also determine the structure of a biblical text by carefully observing the "playing out" of the "rules" in individual texts of the same genre.

Structurality can also be explained using the analogy of an apartment. Imagine that you live in a high-rise apartment. You can think about your own apartment residence in terms of its unique characteristics, such as its decor, furniture, pictures, carpets, and dishes. But you could also think of your apartment not in terms of its uniqueness, and as a solitary dwelling, but rather in terms of its place within the structure of the whole high-rise apartment building. You can imagine how your own apartment fits within the structurality of the whole building (e.g., it is located on the fifth floor of a fifteen-story structure. It is on the west side of the structure. It is one of thirty one-bedroom apartments). Gaining this new perspective is the moment when you can conceptualize your apartment as one of many apartments, participating in a shared structure. In a similar way, *all* biblical texts possess their own structurality and can be conceptualized in terms of their participation in shared literary structures.

For example, a genre is an underlying structure of a text. When one writes a letter, one structures it in terms of an epistolary structure, with some variation on "Dear so-and-so, I hope you are well." Then you explain the purpose of writing: "I hope to see you ..." before closing with "Sincerely," etc. But if you were writing a fairy tale, you might begin with the words, "Once upon a time." Similarly, in movies, we are accustomed to recognizing identifiable genres such as romance, suspense thriller, horror, documentary, science fiction, western, and comedy. Individual movies are material instantiations of the genres to which they belong.

The Bible contains many different genres. In the Tanakh (Old Testament), we find such genres as historical epic, law, wisdom, psalms, prophecy, and the apocalyptic. The New Testament includes epistolary genre, apocalyptic genre, pronouncement stories, parables, healing stories, aretalogies, "sayings" gospels, and so forth. Each of these genres can be conceived of as a horizon of meaning (like the rules of the game of chess) that shapes or structures biblical texts in a particular way.

Another way to conceive of the structurality of a text is to examine its underlying semiotic structure. Language is structured according to a system of differential relations, which together construct an implicit metaphysics of reality (cf. Chapters 1, 7, and 12). Within this semiotic structure, there are no absolute terms: every linguistic sign has "negative value" in terms of its relation to other signifieds within the system as a whole. For example, in the semiotic binarism man-woman, the term "man" functions as the standard against which "woman" (whose etymology means "wife-man") is defined. Implicit within each binarism is the contrast between the same versus different, with different (e.g., woman) being subordinated to and defined in terms of the degrees of difference from the primary term (e.g., man): hence, "woman" is what is not "man" and is thus defined in relation to "man" as the dominant term. According to this schema, difference is measured in terms of *degrees of variation* from the primary term: "culture" is measured in terms of degrees of variation from "nature," "copy" from "original," "black-brown-yellow" from "white," "Eastern" from "Western," and so forth. In each case, the second term of each binarism (e.g., woman, culture, copy, black-brown-yellow, Eastern) is subordinated to and defined in terms of the primary term (man, nature, original, white, Western).[62] Taken as a whole, these binary couplets form an unspoken system of the metaphysical understanding of the world of the Western cultural order. In Christian texts, the dominant term of each binarism indicates what the Christian culture of the time valued most and how these concepts were interconnected with each other (cf. Chapter 12).

All human languages employ some kind of semiotic structure to represent the "real." This structure functions like a categorical framework, consisting of interrelated sets of coordinates, which form a kind of categorical grid of a given culture. By its very nature, this categorical framework functions as a classification system that reduces the natural hybridity of reality, including human existence, and imposes sameness upon difference. Language, as the constructor of the "real," has the power to deliver our human bodies over to networks of forces that are at work within a given culture at any given time, and at work within the literature of that culture (cf. Chapter 12). In the act of interpreting biblical texts, the interpreter encounters not only the text's semantic meaning but also the ancient binarisms and categorical grids that structure its overt meaning. This is why Ricoeur insists that the analysis of the meaning of a biblical text (theme 1) must be accompanied by a corresponding analysis of a text's structure (theme 2).[63]

---

[62] Derrida states, "The enterprise of returning 'strategically,' 'ideally,' to an origin or to a priority thought to be simple, intact, normal, pure, standard, self-identical, in order then to think in terms of derivation, complication, deterioration, accident, etc. All metaphysicians, from Plato to Rousseau, Descartes to Husserl, have proceeded in this way, conceiving good to be before evil, the positive before the negative, the pure before the impure, the simple before the complex, the essential before the accidental, the imitated before the imitation, etc. And this is not just one metaphysical gesture among others, it is the metaphysical exigency, that which has been the most constant, most profound and most potent"; *Limited Inc*, trans. Samuel Weber (Evanston, IL: Northwestern University Press, 1990), 136. Brian Massumi observes that each term within these binarism pairs functions as a *stereotyped* abstract limit. For example, no actual person ever fully coincides with the gender categories male or female; *A User's Guide to Capitalism and Schizophrenia: Deviations from Deleuze and Guattari* (Cambridge, MA: MIT Press, 1992), 87–88.

[63] Nancy F. Partner, "Making Up Lost Time: Writing on the Writing of History," *Speculum* 61/1 (1986): 90–117.

Theme 3: Critique of Ideology

Next, Ricoeur's hermeneutic theory turns its attention to Habermas's critique of ideology, in order to guard against any oppressive potentialities within a biblical text. Ricoeur agrees with Habermas that interpretation should not lose sight of the connection of texts with their material, historical contexts, especially in terms of illocutionary forces at work within them. Even biblical texts, which may appear, at first glance, to be purely informational, are always formulated so as to bring about particular effects on their intended readers (perlocutionary effects, which we may view positively or negatively). All ancient texts, including biblical texts, were written with a view to persuading its readers to believe, think, or act in a particular ways. Ricoeur's third theme provides the opportunity to explore especially the "ideological" dimension of texts (cf. Chapter 9).

Theme 4: Self-Understanding

Ricoeur's fourth theme returns to Gadamer's hermeneutic model, with its concern for self-understanding. Gadamer argued that when one engages in an *open* dialogue with a text, the central hermeneutical question is, Who am I and who are you? By implication, when seeking such self-understanding, one must in principle be open to having critiqued one's own false consciousness and self-alienation from the world. Thus, in the final analysis the ultimate goal of biblical interpretation, and of Ricoeur's first three themes, is *self-understanding and understanding one's neighbor, as mediated by the "matter of the text," in the light of the horizon of one's tradition.*[64]

Taken together, Ricoeur's four themes constitute what might be termed a "fusion of the horizons" of Gadamer's and Habermas's hermeneutical models. Through thoughtful reflection on a biblical text, as guided by these four themes, the text becomes the site where the horizons of Habermasian explanation and Gadamerian understanding come into dialectic contact. As previously noted, this fusion does not mean assimilation. One model is not diluted by the other. Rather, the "fusion of horizons" (enacted by the application of Ricoeur's four themes) makes it possible for us to see the respective horizons of Gadamer and Habermas at one and the same time. In so doing, we, as interpreters, recognize the necessity of allowing a creative tension to continue between them, whose precise nature will vary from text to text.

---

[64] Ricoeur, *Hermeneutics and the Human Sciences*, 94.

CONCLUSION

In Ricoeur's mediation of the Gadamer-Habermas debate, he protected the dialogic space between their different approaches. I believe that it is significant that the first and fourth of his four themes (namely, distanciation and self-understanding) reflect Gadamer's own hermeneutic orientation. Ricoeur begins and ends with Gadamer, moving through Habermas's theory in the third theme, the critique of ideology. This suggests that Ricoeur never gives up on a hermeneutics of hope and the possibility of replaying, or counteractualization of, the founding sense-event of biblical texts, even while he defends the necessity of a hermeneutics of suspicion. This feature of Ricoeur's thought is also apparent in his three ontologies of the interpreter, in which the regressive "archaeological" (Freudian) ontology and the progressive "teleological ontology" are mediated by an "eschatological" ontology of the Sacred, wherein interpreters abandon themselves to utter dependence upon the true G-d. Thus, far from being an obstacle to scripture's revelatory power, Ricoeur anticipates that a combined hermeneutics of understanding *and* critique has the potential to usher in a new reign of God's Truth.

11

Interpretation before the Face of the Other: Emmanuel Levinas

In the story of Belshazzar's feast (Dan 5:1–6:1), the king of Babylon committed the sacrilege of desecrating the vessels sacred to the Lord. Following this desecration, a mysterious hand appeared and wrote the cryptic Aramaic words *menē'*, *teqēl*, *perēs*. These words *literally* denote three weights, or monetary units – namely a mina, a shekel, and a half mina.[1] But, according to the prophet Daniel, the present sense-event of these three words is that the days of Belshazzar's reign have been "weighed" and found wanting.[2] My point is that Daniel's interpretation of these three Aramaic words extended well beyond their literal meaning. Though his story does not provide a model for contemporary hermeneutic practice, it does demonstrate that hermeneutics is often productive in its work, extending beyond the discovery of the semantic meaning of a text to an imagining of its latent reserve of "sense."

This concept of a latent reserve of "sense" brings us to the hermeneutic thought of Emmanuel Levinas, who distinguishes "between the plain meaning" of a biblical text and "the meaning to be deciphered," and between "the search for this meaning buried away and for a meaning even *deeper* than [the text] contains."[3] In his view, the scriptures consist of a unique "mode of being whereby the history of each piece of writing counts less than the lessons it contains, and where its inspiration is measured by what it inspires."[4]

LEVINAS AND THE PROBLEM OF HISTORICAL MEANING

Emmanuel Levinas (1906–95) was born of Jewish parents in Lithuania, where he received a traditional Jewish education. Throughout the course of his life, he remained a devout, observant Jew. Following World War II, he studied the Talmud

---

[1] Alexander A. Di Lella, *The Book of Daniel*, Anchor Bible (Garden City, NY: Doubleday, 1978), 185–91, esp. 190.

[2] *Menē'*: G-d has numbered the days of your reign and brought it to an end; *teqēl*: you have been weighed on the scales and been found wanting; *perēs*: your kingdom has been divided up and given to the Medes and the Persians (Dan 5:26–28).

[3] Emmanuel Levinas, *Beyond the Verse: Talmudic Readings and Lectures*, trans. Gary D. Mole (London: Continuum, 2007 [1982]), 130 (emphasis added).

[4] Ibid., 134.

under the enigmatic Jewish teacher known as "Monsieur Chouchani."[5] He later moved to the University of Freiburg, where he studied the phenomenology of Edmund Husserl and of Martin Heidegger. This explains why Levinas's early philosophy is so deeply rooted in the philosophical writings of the early Heidegger.[6] In many ways these formational experiences influenced the course of his thought throughout his life, for Levinas distinguished himself both as a phenomenologist and as a Talmudic commentator. This background also helps to explain Levinas's aversion to Western methods of biblical studies.

In many ways, the goals of biblical studies continue to be guided by the theoretical structure of nineteenth-century historicism, which has led to a crisis of nihilism (cf. Chapters 2 and 3). According to Levinas, by granting to each successive historical moment the right to call into question the values and truths of all prior historical moments, historicism actually "calls into question, relativizes and devalues every moment."[7] In his critique of the relativizing tendencies of historicism, Levinas counters:

Everything in history is not true history; everything does not count as history. Every moment counts, but everything is not a moment…. The West professes the historical relativity of values and their questioning, but perhaps it takes every moment seriously, calls them all historical too quickly, and leaves this history the right both to judge the values and to sink into relativity. Hence the incessant re-evaluation of values, an incessant collapse of values, an incessant genealogy of morals. A history without permanence or a history without holiness.[8]

Levinas does not contest the self-evident fact that biblical values are historically relative. However, he nonetheless argues that a permanence of holiness can be recovered through a sublimation of biblical values that elevates the possibilities lying latent within biblical texts, which is what Levinas means by "difficult wisdom." He speaks of "a difficult wisdom concerned with truths that correlate to virtues."[9] In contrast to nineteenth-century biblical historicism and Judaic studies (*Wissenschaft des Judentums*) of the German academy, the Rabbinic interpretive tradition carries biblical values forward, raises them up, and sublimates them to new ends. This "elevation" of meaning is not a result of an isolated act of a lone interpreter: the interpreter always works within an interpretive community

---

5   Chouchani taught a small number of distinguished Jewish students in the years following World War II. His influence on Levinas is most evident in the latter's famous series of Talmudic readings: cf. Levinas, *Beyond the Verse*; Emmanuel Levinas, *Nine Talmudic Readings*, trans. Annette Aronowicz (Bloomington: Indiana University Press, 1994); Emmanuel Levinas, *New Talmudic Readings*, trans. Richard A. Cohen (Pittsburgh, PA: Duquesne University Press, 1999 [1996]).

6   Especially Heidegger's *Being and Time* and his "Letter on Humanism" (cf. *Martin Heidegger: Pathmarks*, ed. William McNeill [Cambridge: Cambridge University Press, 1998], 239–76).

7   Levinas, *Beyond the Verse*, 17.

8   Ibid., 21.

9   Emmanuel Levinas, *Difficult Freedom: Essays on Judaism,* trans. Sean Hand (London: Athlone Press, 1990), 275.

and within an interpretive tradition.[10] For this reason, Jewish scholars – Levinas included – never interpret the Tanakh directly but rather as it has been received and interpreted through the "long lens" of the Mishna, Gemara, and Talmud.[11] Levinas's interpretation is always a "mediation of the Talmudic commentary."[12] He encounters the Bible through the voices of the Rabbis, and he understands his own act of interpretation as a way of serving those Rabbis, who are no longer able to speak.[13]

Levinas expounds this interpretive principle through his commentary on Exodus 25:30 (the "bread of Presence" or "Showbread"), as interpreted in *Tractate Menahoth* (99b–100a).[14] When the bread of Presence is replaced each Sabbath, a row of priests stands at the north side of the sanctuary, holding fresh replacement loaves, and facing an opposing row of priests on the south side, who will remove the old loaves. This weekly ritual of the replacement of the bread of Presence involves the temple priests in an intentional face-to-face interaction. According to Levinas, this is how the Talmud is written. It is a face-to-face encounter with the Rabbis of the past: it attributes every opinion to the specific Rabbi who made it. Every voice is named, "not only to stress the eventually subjective character of all truth, but also to avoid losing, in the universal, the marvel and the light of the personal, to avoid transforming the domain of truth into the realm of anonymity."[15] This perspective transforms contemporary exegesis into a series of "answers," or replies, to the voices of the past from "within the community of the living."[16] Here is enshrined the principle that the biblical interpreter always stands face-to-face with the interpreters of the past and is indebted to their voices. The role of interpretation is always carried out within the context of a community of faith: Levinas states that this faith community "is a small society whose interpersonal relations constitute" our "real presence" to one another.[17] Our participation in such an interpretive community also entails our participation in an interpretive tradition that includes multiple voices:

A multiplicity of irreducible people is necessary to the dimensions of meaning; the multiple meanings are multiple people. We can thus see the whole impact of the reference

[10] Levinas, *Beyond the Verse*, 24.
[11] Ibid., 130, 133.
[12] Annette Aronowicz, "The Little Man with the Burned Thighs: Levinas's Biblical Hermeneutic," in *Levinas and Biblical Studies*, ed. Tamara Cohn Eskenazi, Gary A. Phillips, and David Jobling, Semeia 43 (Atlanta: Society of Biblical Literature, 2003), 33–48, esp. 33.
[13] Ibid., 42.
[14] The Showbread, or bread of Presence, consisted of twelve loaves of bread laid in two rows on a table in the Holy Place before the Lord. The loaves were replaced each Sabbath by new loaves (Exod 25:30; Lev 24:5–9; 1 Sam 21:6).
[15] Emmanuel Levinas, *In the Time of the Nations*, trans. Michael B. Smith (London: Continuum, 1994), 6–7.
[16] Aronowicz, "The Little Man with the Burned Thighs," 41.
[17] Levinas, *Beyond the Verse*, 18–19.

made by the Revelation to exegesis, to the freedom of this exegesis, the participation of the person listening to the Word making itself heard, but also the possibility for the Word to travel down the ages to announce the same truth in different times.[18]

Thus Levinasian exegesis is not about the resuscitation of past meanings which have been "frozen" in texts. Interpreters and their communities are *internal* to the revelation of Scripture, not a complement to it.

HEIDEGGER'S BETRAYAL

Despite Levinas's affinity with Heideggerian phenomenology, he came to regret his association with Heidegger, owing to the latter's infamous accommodation to Nazism. In 1933 Heidegger was elected rector of the University of Freiburg, less than four months after Hitler was appointed chancellor of Germany. About three weeks later, Heidegger joined the National Socialist German Workers' Party (NSDAP). In his notorious inaugural address, entitled "The Self-Assertion of the German University," Heidegger stated that leaders must be "led by the relentless-ness of that spiritual mission that forces the destiny of the German people into the shape of its history."[19] Even though Heidegger's rectorship was disastrous, leading to his resignation almost a year later, he nonetheless remained a member of the Nazi party until the end of World War II, following which he was reprimanded by being dismissed from the University of Freiburg (though he was subsequently allowed to return in 1951).

Many scholars are at a loss to explain how such a preeminent philosophical thinker as Heidegger could have sympathized with the Nazi cause. Moreover, Heidegger's silence concerning the Shoah (Holocaust) in the decades following the war shocked and alienated many of his former colleagues.[20] A case in point is Paul Celan, one of the twentieth century's most celebrated poets. Celan, though a Jew and Holocaust survivor, was profoundly affected by Heidegger's philosophi-cal writings.[21] Celan deeply respected Heidegger. However, he believed that their continued friendship required that Heidegger be held accountable for his past actions.

---

[18] Ibid., 133–34.

[19] Martin Heidegger, "The Self-Assertion of the German University," in *Philosophical and Political Writings* (London: Continuum, 2003), 2–11.

[20] In his review of Victor Farias's *Heidegger et le nazisme,* Thomas Sheehan contrasts "Heidegger's stunning silence concerning the Holocaust" with Heidegger's readiness to criticize the impact of technology: "We have his statements about the six million unemployed at the beginning of the Nazi regime, but not a word about the six million who were dead at the end of it"; see Thomas Sheehan's review of V. Farias, "Heidegger and the Nazis," in the *New York Review of Books* 35/10 (June 16, 1988): 38–47.

[21] For his part, Heidegger was a professed admirer of Celan's poetry. In 1967 he attended a guest lec-ture given by Celan at the University of Freiburg, at which time he gave Celan a copy of *What Is Thinking?*

When Heidegger invited Celan to visit him at his famous work retreat (*die Hütte*) at Todtnauberg on 25 July 1967, Celan accepted the invitation and even signed Heidegger's guestbook. It was on this occasion that Celan asked Heidegger to explain his failure to alter his own remarks concerning the "greatness" of National Socialism, as reprinted in the 1953 edition of his *Introduction to Metaphysics*. Though we have no record of Heidegger's reply, we do know that, following his face-to-face meeting with Heidegger, Celan completed his best-known poem, "Death Fugue" (*Todesfuge*), which depicts, with nightmarish detail, life in a German concentration camp. The fact that this poem is named after Heidegger's own retreat in Todtnauberg suggests that Celan anticipated the possibility of a rapprochement with Heidegger.[22]

Heidegger's ambiguous relationship with Celan illustrates why there is ongoing debate concerning the degree to which Heidegger's existential philosophy was itself implicated in Heidegger's existential decision to associate himself with Nazism. Heidegger's sympathizers, relying on an immanent criticism of his philosophical works, bracket out the events of his political life.[23] But Heidegger's detractors, such as Victor Farias, Hugo Ott, Jürgen Habermas, and Theodor Adorno, argue that Heidegger's own political actions must be taken into consideration and that his engagement with Nazism was partly derived from his own philosophical conceptions.[24]

Heidegger's association with Nazism was more than a philosophical issue for Levinas. His extended family in Lithuania was among the nearly six million Jews who were systematically murdered in the Shoah.[25] His wife and daughter were spared, but only through the intervention of Levinas's close friend, the French literary theorist Maurice Blanchot, who – at great risk to himself – arranged to have them accommodated in a monastery. Even Levinas, by then a French citizen and soldier, was compelled to labor as a prisoner of war for a period of time.

Given the fact that Heidegger never asked for forgiveness for his affiliation with Nazism, and given his silence on the Shoah, Levinas never sought a reconciliation with him. Indeed, in his commentary on a Talmudic discussion of forgiveness, Levinas wrote, "One can forgive many Germans, but there are some Germans it

---

[22] Celan sent Heidegger the first copy of a limited bibliophile edition of *Todesfuge*. Heidegger responded with a letter of perfunctory thanks. Celan also wrote a second poem describing the meeting itself. Celan had a sense of persecution that haunted him throughout his life, which ended with his suicide in 1970.

[23] For example, Jacques Derrida, Philippe Lacoue-Labarthe, and Beda Allemann maintain that Heidegger *was* capable of criticism of the horrors of Nazism. They argue that his greatest failure was really his silence on the Shoah, not his membership in the NSDAP.

[24] Cf. Victor Farias, *Heidegger and Nazism* (Philadelphia: Temple University Press, 1989 [1987]); Jeff Collins, *Heidegger and the Nazis* (Duxford: Icon, 2000).

[25] The term Shoah (האוש), meaning "calamity," is the standard Hebrew term for the Holocaust. This term is preferred by the Jewish people over the term "holocaust," which is theologically offensive because a holocaust is a sacrifice that is *offered* to G-d. In the case of the Shoah, the lives of six million Jews were not offered but rather taken by violence.

is difficult to forgive. *It is difficult to forgive Heidegger.*[26] Thus, Levinas, who had appropriated much of Heidegger's early philosophical thought, nonetheless had an uneasy relationship with Heidegger himself. Levinas's movement away from Heidegger's ethically neutral ontology of being is highly significant because, for Levinas, ethics is *beyond* being: indeed, it is *"otherwise* than being."

THE FACE OF THE "OTHER"

In many respects, Levinas's thought both challenges and moves beyond Heideggerian phenomenology. In Chapter 5, we discussed how the ontological structure of Heidegger's concept of "understanding" (*Verstehen*) is prior to, and determinative of, *all* interpretation. Interpretation emerges out of the circular structure of interpretation of Da-sein's "being-in-the-world." In reply, Levinas contests the primacy that Heidegger grants to understanding, and he argues that there is more to life than is contained within Heidegger's phenomenological concept of "being-in-the-world."

In Levinas's view, there is a *pre*ontological, *ethical* relation between the "I" and the "other" (such as one's neighbor) that *precedes* the thematizing function of Da-sein's own fore-structure. It is this *pre*ontological ethical relation – not "understanding" – that is primordial. In other words, ethics precedes ontology. Every person has a preontological bond of responsibility to the "other" that *precludes* the formation of a subject-object relation.

Heidegger's "Da-sein" is primarily *ethically* accountable *to itself* with respect to whether it strives to live authentically and resolutely and, thereby, embodies the hermeneutic truth disclosed in Da-sein's own being. In contrast, in Levinas's view, the "I" is first and foremost an ethical "I." The self's recognition of the "other" carries with it an ethical responsibility that cannot be phenomenologically reduced to "understanding."

In his first magnum opus, *Totality and Infinity: An Essay on Exteriority,* Levinas argued that when one looks into the "face of the other," this face establishes an *ethical* responsibility that precedes one's own understanding, one's own fore-structure, and indeed any calculative or rational attempt to weigh one's ethical responsibility to the "other."[27] According to Levinas, the "other" can never be fully known or analyzed. The "other" is irreducible to a social or historical context.[28] Indeed, when one looks into the face of the "other," one does not merely see one person among many but a unique person. In this gaze, we experience the implicit call of another

---

[26] Levinas, *Nine Talmudic Readings,* 25.

[27] Emmanuel Levinas, *Totality and Infinity: An Essay on Exteriority,* trans. Alphonso Lingis (Pittsburgh, PA: Duquesne University Press, 1969 [1961]); see also Emmanuel Levinas, *Entre nous: On Thinking-of-the-Other* (New York: Columbia University Press, 1998), 4.

[28] Levinas, *Totality and Infinity,* 202–9; Levinas, *Entre nous,* 6; Levinas, *Collected Philosophical Papers,* trans. A. Lingis (The Hague: Martinus Nijhoff, 1987), 115–20.

human being, who is different from what we are, and who lives in the world differently than we do, and whose speechless face entreats us to justice, saying, "Do not kill me."[29]

Even though the face "speaks," this ethical speaking is a *wordless* event. Indeed, this event cannot be translated into human speech because the alterity of the "other" lies beyond the signification of being. Nonetheless, this *wordless* event has the power to disturb the comfort of our own subjectivity.[30] Levinas refers to this disturbing experience of the alterity of the "other" as "transcendence." Indeed, for Levinas, *"religious" experience is the experience of such transcendence.* In other words, religious experience is primarily the experience of an unequivocal responsibility to one's neighbor, the stranger, the guest, the exploited, and the downtrodden.[31]

At this point, I must caution to add that Levinas is not making the mundane point that, as human beings who live together communally, we are faced with the practical necessity of finding ways to coexist peacefully with one another. He is not merely invoking the golden rule as a way of achieving peaceful coexistence, nor is he appealing to ethics simply because it is desirable. Levinas is a philosopher, not a social worker. He is arguing that our exposure to the "other" in its radical alterity, and indeed to G-d, the ultimate other, always has the effect of dispossessing one from one's own subjecthood and calling into question one's own independence. In fact, it is this exposure to alterity that actually causes a breakdown of one's own sense of self-as-subject. Levinas refers to this breakdown of subjecthood as "subjectity" (*subjectité*). One's exposure to alterity, whether it be the alterity of one's neighbor or of G-d, breaks down the synthesized "I" and forces one to confront a reality that is more profound than the fragile synthesis of one's own self as a "subject."

In *Totality and Infinity* Levinas illustrates the alterity of the "other" using the Cartesian concept of infinity. He observes that the concept of infinity cannot be comprehended by the human mind: none of us is capable of thinking about actual "infinity." Whenever we attempt to do so, we are immediately struck by the dramatic *difference* between our own mundane and flawed conception of infinity and the reality (*ideatum*) of infinity itself, a reality that always overflows our own conceptualization of it.[32] In fact, the *difference* between our own conceptualization of infinity and the reality of infinity is so vast that there is no correspondence between them. This being the case, the *difference* we experience is *not* the qualitative difference between the reality of infinity (*ideatum*) and that of our imperfect idea of infinity, for in this experience of difference, the first pole of the comparison

[29] Levinas, *Totality and Infinity*, 47, 52, 197, 202–3; Levinas, *In the Time of the Nations*, 111; Levinas, *Entre nous*, 9.
[30] Levinas, *Totality and Infinity*, 66.
[31] Levinas, *Nine Talmudic Readings*, 15; Levinas, *Beyond Verse*, 5.
[32] Levinas, *Totality and Infinity*, 49, 51.

(i.e., the reality of infinity) *is totally absent*. Instead, the first pole of this comparison is constituted by the very idea of the difference itself.[33] In other words, one is struck by the dramatic unreality of the comparative process itself. This comparison is a *non*relation or, as Levinas describes it, an "an-archic" inflection of difference, which overflows our own theoretical knowledge.[34]

According to Levinas, the "other" is likewise *infinitely* different from oneself. The alterity of the "other," like the alterity of infinity, cannot be thought, or put into a statement or a proposition. It is "beyond what a human being can ... show itself as."[35] Alterity is transcendence.[36] Even though human existence is immersed in the *ethical signifying* of alterity, this signifying – the very "saying" of this ethical relation – cannot be translated into words.[37] Levinas conceives of the transcendence as the *irreducible gap* between the reality of alterity and our so very flawed sensible experience of it.

From this perspective, the task of hermeneutics is to bear witness to this unrepresentable gap. By analogy, Levinas remarks that "to think ... the Stranger, is hence not to think an object."[38] The face of the "other" is an "epiphany" that "involves a signifyingness of its own, independent of this meaning received from the world," and even prior to our own interpretive horizons, for "the other comes to us not merely out of context, but also without mediator; he [or she] signifies by himself [or herself]."[39] As such, the face of the "other" represents the alterity of the "other" that "*exceed[s] the idea of the other in me....* At each moment it destroys and overflows the plastic image it leaves in me, the idea existing to my own measure and to the measure of its *ideatum* – the adequate idea."[40]

ALTERITY IS ERASED BY LANGUAGE

As previously discussed, the goal of Heideggerian "interpretation" (*Auslegung*) is not the disclosure of things in the world but rather the disclosure of one's ontological horizon within which things meaningfully show up to Da-sein (see Chapter 5). Levinas describes this thematizing and conceptualizing function of Heideggerian "interpretation" as follows: "The relation to the other is ... accomplished only through a third term which I find in myself.... *Being and Time* has argued perhaps

---

[33] Ibid., 49.

[34] Krzysztof Ziarek, *Inflected Language: Toward a Hermeneutics of Nearness; Heidegger, Levinas, Stevens, Celan* (Albany: State University of New York Press, 1994), 92–93.

[35] Levinas, *Humanisme de l'autre homme* (Paris: L.G.F., 1987), 142.

[36] "The 'intentionality' of transcendence is unique in its kind; the difference between objectivity and transcendence will serve as a general guideline for all the analyses of this work"; Levinas, *Totality and Infinity*, 49.

[37] Ziarek, *Inflected Language*, 99.

[38] Levinas, *Totality and Infinity*, 49; Levinas refers to this overflowing of the face as "the secret of the face," or, more technically, as "apresentation."

[39] Levinas, *Collected Philosophical Papers*, 95.

[40] Levinas, *Totality and Infinity*, 50–51.

but one sole thesis: Being is inseparable from the comprehension of Being (which unfolds in time)."[41]

Levinas does not contest Heidegger's point: he acknowledges that human beings do interpret the things around them according to their own phenomenological horizons.[42] But he also argues that Da-sein's process of thematization and conceptualization, which lies at the heart of Heidegger's phenomenological circle, *always involves some measure of violence*. Just as the German term *Begriff*, meaning "concept," is based upon the verb *greifen*, meaning "to grasp," or "to take hold of," Levinas argues that "knowledge is the embodiment of *seizure*."[43] The predicating action of the verb "to be" (εἶναι), in conjunction with the nominalizing function of language, fabricates the illusory appearance of sameness and identity out of *primordial difference* (cf. Chapter 12). But, in actuality, *difference precedes such sameness*.

In Levinas's view, the formation of concepts within the Western discourse of human sciences – which includes biblical studies – always involves some measure of a violent and nonethical *grasping* of being, which deprives the "other" of its alterity. Discursive language (such as one encounters in the theological disciplines) invariably reduces the alterity of the "other" (and the alterity of the *absolutely* other, G-d), to categories of the same, by means of classification, thematization, anthropomorphism, and totalization. Levinas is even suspicious of the *concept* of "difference" itself, within Western discourse, because this concept always participates in the metaphysical binary opposition of "same" versus "different," within which *difference is always subordinated to and measured against the same*. Language is a failure, when it comes to respecting the primordial difference of the world. But despite this failure of language and language's practice of reducing difference to categories of the same, Levinas insists that language can nonetheless function as a way of accessing a type of meaning that lies beyond language.[44] Just as the "reality" (*ideatum*) of infinity leaves its "trace" in our human idea of infinity through our awareness of a *nonrelation*, Levinas argues that alterity, as "otherwise than being," likewise leaves its "trace" in human language.

How is meaning beyond language possible? Levinas explains: even though language erases alterity, *it is unable to erase its erasure of alterity because this erasure is unerasable*.[45] As a way of explaining this complex concept, consider

---

[41] Ibid., 44, 45.

[42] Levinas, *Collected Philosophical Papers*, 95.

[43] Ibid., 159–61. He remarks, "Heideggerian ontology, which subordinates the relationship with the Other to the relation with Being in general, remains under obedience to the anonymous, and leads inevitably to another power, to imperialist domination"; Levinas, *Totality and Infinity*, 46–47.

[44] Ziarek, *Inflected Language*, 91.

[45] Levinas proposes a distinction between Heidegger's "saying" (*logos*) and ethical (preoriginal) "saying" (*le dire*): "[T]he thematizing logos, the 'saying' stating a 'said' in monologue and dialogue and in the exchange of information, with all the cultural and historical dimensions it bears, proceeds from the pre-original 'saying'"; Levinas, *Otherwise Than Being*, trans. Alphonso Lingis (Dordrecht: Kluwer Academic Publishers, 1978), 198.

the example of the ancient practice known as *damnatio memoriae*, in which the names of emperors on ancient Roman and Greek public monuments were deliberately erased (chiseled off) from inscriptions. For example, hatred for the emperors Domitian, Commodus, and Elagabalus was so great that a posthumous censure was passed upon them by the Senate. Their memory was condemned and their names were *erased* from all public monuments. For instance, in a Greek inscription (fig. 11.1), the names of Roman emperors have been erased in lines 6 and 8 by the stonemason's chisel.[46] But by virtue of this erasure, the very *fact* of the erasure still remains visible, even hundreds of years later. One could say that, through this erasure, their names have left a lingering "trace."

By way of another example of such an erasure and trace, consider footprints on a sandy beach. A footprint in the sand preserves the trace of a person, once present, but now absent. As wave after wave washes up on the shore, the footprints are gradually erased, eventually making them unrecognizable as footprints. In scene 1 (fig. 11.2), you might interpret the footprints as a *sign of human presence*; but by scene 3, the same footprints seem to signify *human absence*, not human presence. These "traces" of human presence in the sand are signs of both presence and absence simultaneously.

The erasure of alterity is itself a trace of alterity. According to Levinas, this bestows upon the trace a "semantics of proximity."[47] We have access to the alterity of the "other" only through this trace, which is left behind, following language's erasure of the alterity of this "other."[48] The primary point is that this erasure of alterity is itself unerasable.

When language erases the alterity of the "other," the rational subject takes no notice of the trace of alterity. In fact, alterity *always* goes undetected by Western, rational thought.[49] In the Greek philosophic tradition, *logos* (λόγος), meaning "reason" or "explanation," was the route to knowledge. The Western tradition privileges the use of reason to explain, linguistically manipulate, and finally predict the interaction of things in the world.[50] But Western rationality is blind to the alterity of reality because the language of rationality always reduces difference to sameness. For this reason, when alterity leaves its trace in language, through its

---

[46] C. T. Newton, *The Collection of Ancient Greek Inscriptions in the British Museum* (Oxford: Clarendon Press, 1883), II, no. 176.

[47] This can be contrasted with his earlier position, where Levinas argues, in Heideggerian fashion, that language in its essence does not refer to particular beings, or to phenomenological sense-data, but it brings to light the illumination of the horizon within which beings are given; cf. Levinas, *Collected Philosophical Papers*.

[48] Ziarek, *Inflected Language*, 93.

[49] In Levinasian terminology, alterity is "non-allergic" ("allergic" is literally ἄλλος + ἔργος, "effect of the other").

[50] Compare Hegel's conflation of the real and the rational in his statement, "the real is rational and the rational is real"; cf. Richard Cohen, *Elevations: The Height of the Good in Rosenzweig and Levinas* (Chicago: University of Chicago Press, 1994), 300–4.

11.1. *Damnatio memoriae* of Domitian, Commodus,
and Elagabalus, British Museum, London

erasure, it encounters no resistance because it always goes undetected by Western reason. When the trace of alterity is left in language, language is neither "torn" nor disrupted. Therefore, there is need for a "reweaving" of language following the insertion of the trace.[51] Indeed, according to Levinas, in the eyes of Western rational thought, the trace always has the precarious status of a "maybe" (*peut-être*); the rational Western subject is prepared to admit only the *possibility* that "perhaps" language may have a meaning beyond that which is allowed by the Western rational understanding of being.[52] This "perhaps" explains why the trace is even beyond the grasp of Heidegger's ontological meaning: alterity is *otherwise than being*. It

---

[51] Ziarek, *Inflected Language*, 93, 96.
[52] Ibid., 79.

11.2. Three adjacent scenes of footprints in the sand

signifies an ethical relation that is beyond the reach of all the thematizing powers of language and understanding.

I am not implying that the trace possesses some kind of metaphysical essence or being. Levinas is not arguing that the alterity of the "other" is a truth or "form" belonging to a higher Platonic world. Alterity belongs to *this* world. The "other" always signifies its alterity *laterally*, from the place of one's neighbor. The signifying of alterity is not a function of the signifying structure language, nor does it emanate from a transcendental realm above our material world. It signifies laterally, calling us to an ethical responsibility that is *in this world and of this world*. Nonetheless, alterity remains beyond our powers of human signification, conceptualization, and deduction.[53]

THE SAYING AND THE SAID

As previously discussed, Heidegger's ethically neutral phenomenology located the disclosure of the meaning of the "other" within the phenomenological circle of Da-sein. In his first major philosophical work, *Totality and Infinity* (1961), Levinas attempted to move beyond the inherent limitations of Heidegger's phenomenological approach by analyzing our face-to-face relation with the "other," arguing that this face-to-face relation is *primordially* ethical. In other words, ethical responsibility and the concern for justice are not derivative features of Da-sein's own phenomenological understanding.

Levinas's second great work, *Otherwise Than Being or Beyond Essence* (1974), was written to explore this issue further. In this work, Levinas argues that one's face-to-face relation with the "other" *precedes* all phenomenological awareness. This is what Levinas means when he states that alterity is "otherwise than being" (*autrement qu'être*). In fact, he argues that our own "subjectivity" (i.e., one's sense of being a unified "self") is not ready-made but is actually *formed through our ethical subjected-ness to the "other."*[54] One could say that Da-sein's sense of itself as a "self" is *grounded* by this face-to-face encounter with alterity.

In *Otherwise Than Being or Beyond Essence,* Levinas developed this concept of preontological meaning further by distinguishing between what he refers to as "the said" (*le dit*) of the linguistic, thematizing signification of Western discourse (and traditional Western biblical scholarship) and the *pre*ontological ethical "saying" (*le dire*) of alterity. While it is true that "the said" (*le dit*) is constituted from within Da-sein's hermeneutic circle, "the said" always proceeds *from* "the saying" (*le dire*).[55] It is "the saying" that imparts the true meaning of otherness to "the said" and, as such, is comparable to the reality (*ideatum*) of infinity in the sense that "the saying" is alterity, which can neither be captured by language nor be grasped by rational thought. *Even though "the saying" of alterity is not "being," it can nonetheless signal itself within being through language as "the said."* Indeed,

---

[53] Ibid., 92.
[54] Emmanuel Levinas, *Autrement qu'être ou au-delà de l'essence*, Phaenomenologica 54 (The Hague: Martinus Nijhoff, 1974); trans. *Otherwise than Being or Beyond Essence*, esp. chap. 4.
[55] Levinas, *Otherwise than Being*, 198.

"the saying" (*le dire*) of alterity can signal itself *only* as "the said" (*le dit*), as in the case of real texts, such as biblical texts, composed of Greek and Hebrew linguistic signs. But when "the saying" (*le dire*) of alterity is thematized by language as the (textual) said, it is thereby *erased* and *survives only as a trace*, in the form of its own erasure.

Thus, Levinas has radicalized the Western understanding of language by employing it to convey *non*semantic meaning: the face of alterity signifies itself from beyond language, and beyond Da-sein's hermeneutic circle, and even beyond being itself, by inscribing itself into language's "thematizations," through the trace of its erasure.[56] The "saying" of the ethical call is "said" *in the silence of this unerasable erasure*. Its status as a "perhaps" prevents it from being objectified by the rational *logos* of the empirical, thematizing, rational subject.

The importance of this insight can hardly be overemphasized. Many new methods of biblical interpretation, such as feminist criticism and postcolonial criticism, have attempted to address the nihilism of traditional biblical studies by a *pragmatic* turn toward ethics. But because this ethical turn *is* merely pragmatic, it is groundless. As Richard Rorty has argued, any appeal to ethics that is based solely on pragmatism can be defended only in terms of its "desirability." As such, this strategy fails to address the philosophical problem of nihilism in biblical studies and, in fact, extends nihilism in new directions. In contrast, Levinas's ethics is not based on its pragmatic value. He does choose or champion particular ethical values as ultimate values. Instead, Levinasian ethics is grounded in the trace of the "other," apart from the volitional subject, and apart from a "will-to-ethics."

The problem of nihilism cannot be addressed by the *willful* subject because the *will*-to-knowledge is the root cause of nihilism (cf. Chapter 3). Nihilism can be addressed only by grasping the *conditions* under which knowledge is formed (namely, the subject-object binarism) and the *structure* by which such knowledge is legitimated (namely, the authorized disciplinary methods). Levinasian ethics of alterity not only grasps these conditions but also changes the structure of the legitimation of knowledge by grounding ethics in the alterity of the "other" and the "trace" of the "other" – outside the metaphysics of historicism and apart from the rational subject's will-to-knowledge. By so doing, Levinasian ethics does address the problem of nihilism, and thereby restores an ethical voice to biblical interpreters.

Levinas's concept of the alterity of the "other" as "otherwise than being" provides a basis for a mode of biblical hermeneutics that is in ethical solidarity with others in the struggle for justice and peace. His concept of the "gaze of the other" reconfigures scholarly accountability in an ethical direction; whereas in traditional biblical studies the interpreter is primarily accountable to the disciplinary methods of analysis and the guild, and whereas Heidegger's "Da-sein" is primarily accountable to its own virtual authenticity, Levinas's exegetical pathway takes an altogether different course.

---

[56] Ziarek, *Inflected Language*, 91.

As Richard Cohen observes, Levinasian biblical interpretation "requires a more extreme vigilance, an unremitting attention to the ethical alterity of the other."[57] In contrast to the normative model of the biblical interpreter, the Levinasian interpreter, first and foremost, has an *ethical* accountability to real, actual others. In the gaze of the "other," the biblical interpreter experiences an appeal to ethical responsibility that cannot be evaded by appealing either to the requirements of the traditional methods of biblical interpretation or to Da-sein's call to authenticity, much less to some supposed "literal" meaning of a biblical text. In simplest terms, Levinas argues that the starting point of all biblical exegesis is neither the subject-object binarism of the human sciences, nor the ontology of Da-sein, nor even Gadamer's historically effected consciousness and dialogue with tradition. Rather, the starting point is a *preontological relation,* which every biblical interpreter has to "the other," which of course includes the poor, the exploited, and the oppressed. *This preontological relation constitutes the primary precondition for all biblical studies.*

At this point, it should be noted, by way of clarification, that Levinas is *not* arguing that the content and focus of all biblical interpretation should be exclusively ethical in nature, nor is he attempting to dictate a specific set of ethical guidelines. Rather, Levinas is articulating an ethics of ethics. In other words, he is setting out the ontological preconditions for *any* set of ethical standards and for *any* ethically responsible interpretation of a biblical text. In effect, he is saying that when one sets out to interpret a given biblical text, one *always already finds oneself in a relation of ethical accountability to the "other."* This ethical relation ought to liberate the interpreter's powers of compassion, generosity, welcome, and hospitality.[58]

EXEGESIS AS PRAYER FOR THE OTHER

If exegesis is not limited to the disciplinary methodologies of biblical studies, from what then does it derive its coherence? Levinas would answer: from the gaze of the "other." For Levinas, exegesis constitutes a manner in which the self moves beyond itself *for* the other. In this regard, it is noteworthy that he refers to biblical interpretation as "prayer."[59] The exegesis of sacred texts has the structure of prayer in the sense that it is a movement of the self *for* the "other." It is this structure that transforms the "call" to exegesis into a call to *prayerful* exegesis, which, in turn, transforms exegesis into a form of religious observance, as a carrying out of the commandments of G-d.[60] Thus, the *coherence* of Levinas's exegetical practice is not

57 Richard Cohen, *Ethics, Exegesis and Philosophy: Interpretation after Levinas* (Cambridge: Cambridge University Press, 2004), 227.
58 Levinas, *Totality and Infinity,* 205.
59 Levinas, *Entre Nous,* 7.
60 Gerald L. Bruns, "The Hermeneutical Significance of Emmanuel Levinas's Talmudic Readings," in *The Idea of Biblical Interpretation: Essays in Honour of James L. Kugel,* ed. Hindy Najman and Judith Newman (Leiden: Brill, 2004), 545–65, esp. 556.

derived from an interrelated set of approved disciplinary methods: it is grounded in a prayerful, ethical relation to the "other," as a carrying out of the commandments of G-d.

Indeed, for Levinas, exegesis is a form of call or "election" that is shaped by one's ethical responsibility to the "other," irrespective of the diverse ways in which this call might be worked out in the actual practice of exegesis, which is why exegesis also requires a humility, which is reminiscent of the humility of Abraham, who confessed before G-d, "I am ashes and dust" (Gen 18:27).[61] Levinas sums up this calling with the phrase "in this moment, in this work, here am I" (En ce moment même dans cet ouvrage *me voici*). The phrase "here I am" could be more accurately translated, "*it is me*."[62] The gaze of the "other" turns the nominative "I" of the interpreter into the accusative "me" (*me voici*). Levinas's phrase *me voici* is an obvious allusion to the story of Moses and the burning bush: when Moses turned aside to look at the fiery bush, the Lord called out to him, saying, "Moses, Moses!" and he replied, "me voici" (here I am; Exod 3:4). Moses' reply reminds us that one is always a "me" before G-d. G-d disappears before the arrogance of the "I." It is also worthy of note that in the Septuagintal (Greek) version of Exodus 3:4, we find something very remarkable: Moses does not reply, "Behold me," but τί ἐστιν; meaning, "What is [this]?" The Greek translation has Moses speak with an Alexandrian accent. This Hellenized Moses asks the kind of question that a Greek would ask: "What is this?" The Greek inquires into the "being" of G-d, employing a form of the Greek verb "to be," the verb of predication that explains the nature, property, or characteristic of something. The Septuagintal version of Exodus 3:4 perfectly captures the attitude of the ontotheologian and the rationalist, who sets out to explain G-d's nature. The problem with the Greek λόγος (*logos*) is that it is too self-confident of its place in the world.[63] The god it creates is conceived in its own image; it is an illusory god created through human rationality, which always turns out to be an extension of religious primitivism.

But Moses did not ask "What is this?" but rather replied "Behold me." In response to this act of humility, God declared "I am the God of your father, the God of Abraham, the God of Isaac, and the God of Jacob.... I have surely seen the affliction of my people who are in Egypt, and have given heed to their cry because of their taskmasters, for I am aware of their sufferings" (Exod 3:4–5). This

---

[61] Levinas, *Beyond Verse*, 142; Levinas, *Nine Talmudic Readings*, 85, 87, 114–15.

[62] The actual Hebrew words (הִנֵּנִי) literally mean "Behold me." Thus the French translation "*me voici*" captures the meaning of the Hebrew much better than does the English. The Hebrew *accusative* pronoun is lost in the English translation because the English verb "to be" does not take a definite object, thus forcing the "English Moses" to say, "Here I am"; cf. Levinas, *Entre nous*, 7; Jacques Derrida, "En ce moment même dans cet ouvrage me voici," in *Textes pour Emmanuel Lévinas*, ed. François Laruelle (Paris: Jean-Michel Place Éditeur, 1980), 21–60.

[63] Richard Cohen, *Elevations: The Height of the Good in Rosenzweig and Levinas* (Chicago: University of Chicago Press, 1994), 300–4.

declaration serves as a reminder that the wisdom of God is an ethical wisdom, and therefore a difficult wisdom that can unsettle the very core of our being by drawing us into the suffering of God's people.

NEW STARTING POINTS FOR BIBLICAL EXEGESIS

In his article "On the Jewish Reading of Scriptures," Levinas asks, "How is it that a book is instituted as the Book of books?"[64] How does a collection of ancient texts become scripture? Levinas's answer is that the Bible is "sacred." Richard Cohen explains Levinas's understanding of the sacredness of the texts of scripture:

A text is not sacred because it is inviolable, but precisely because it transfigures, engages, and in this way, is "alive." The significance of a text – inseparable from exegesis – is neither a subjective projection, as if the self remained untouched and imposed itself on the text, nor an impossible literalism, as if the self again remained immaculately unmoved while discovering something outside itself, unmoved and unmovable in the text. Rather, significance itself is an existential enterprise, fraught with difficulties and dangers, but also rewards.[65]

The Bible is sacred because it continues to live, and it lives because it continuously engages human beings in their quest for significance. I have argued that this quest always involves the interpreter in movement of the self toward the "other" and that it always involves the tradition of interpretation as it is held by an interpretive community. To appreciate how this is worked out in practice, we must discuss two fundamental Levinasian concepts, namely, the "open determinacy" of biblical texts and the hermeneutics of solicitation and elevation.

The Open Determinacy of Biblical Texts

In a manner similar to Umberto Eco's concept of the "open work," Jacques Derrida's "dissemination," and Deleuze and Guattari's "rhizomatic" philosophy (cf. Chapter 12), Levinas is primarily interested in the *productive* dimension of textuality. He argues that biblical texts do not inherently possess multiple meanings; they *form* multiple meanings through the text-reception complex. This openness constitutes a text's "open determinacy." A text's "sense," which is grounded in the three components of language (denotation, manifestation, and signification), remains *open* through the text-reception complex to all that lies beyond.[66] Texts "coexist" in porous, open-ended systems.[67] Levinas terms this potential of biblical texts to

[64] Emmanuel Levinas, "On the Jewish Reading of Scriptures," in *The Postmodern Bible Reader*, ed. David Jobling, Tina Pippin, and Ronald Schleifer (Oxford: Blackwell, 2001), 319–32, esp. 327.
[65] Cohen, *Ethics, Exegesis and Philosophy*, 252.
[66] Levinas, *In the Time of the Nations*, 112.
[67] Bruns, "Hermeneutical Significance," 558.

form new relations of sense in the present, beyond the plain or literal meaning of a text, "open determinacy."[68] From this perspective, biblical interpretation can be imagined as a process of helping one text, from anywhere in the whole of scripture, to animate other texts "through correspondences and echoes."[69] In the words of Psalm 42:7, such interpretation could be said to take the form of "the deep calling unto the deep."

Hermeneutics of Solicitation and Elevation

The hermeneutics of solicitation is based on the concept of open determinacy. From this perspective, what matters is not "the explanation of a word" but rather "the association of one 'biblical landscape' with another, in order to extract, through this pairing, the secret scent of the first."[70] For Levinas, each detail of a biblical text is endowed with a rich surplus of meaning, or an open determinacy, beyond that which the text "wants to say." As such, the aim of interpretation is not merely to clarify, or explain, a text, but rather to explore these inexhaustible surpluses of meaning. A text

is capable of saying beyond what it *wants* to say; that it contains more that it contains, that perhaps an inexhaustible surplus of meaning remains locked in the syntactic structures of the sentence, in its word-groups, its actual words, phonemes and letters, in all this materiality of the saying which is potentially signifying all the time. Exegesis would come to free, in these signs a bewitched significance that smolders beneath the characters or coils up in all this literature of letters.[71]

Thus, Levinas distinguishes "between the plain meaning and the meaning to be deciphered, the search for this meaning buried away and for a meaning even deeper than it [the text] contains."[72] Finding this deeper meaning entails "soliciting" the text, and even "forcing" the text, *to say more than it says*. In Levinas's view, such solicitation may even take the form of anachronistic and anarchic linkings of one text to another. This "soliciting" of new significances embodies an ethical, outward, "concernful" movement toward the "other," which is, ultimately, an openness to G-d. In Levinas's own words, it requires that we translate the "inexhaustible richness and innumerable dimensions" of biblical texts, not into abstract concepts but into the concrete reality of our daily life:

In order to arrive at a meaning that would survive despite apparently antiquated language, however, we must first patiently accept – as we do the conventions of a fable or a theatrical production – the specifics of the text in its own world; we must wait until

---

[68] Levinas, *In the Time of the Nations*, 498.
[69] Levinas, *New Talmudic Readings*, 55.
[70] Ibid.
[71] Levinas, *Beyond the Verse*, 109.
[72] Ibid.

these details begin to free themselves from the anachronisms and local color on which the curtain rose.… This is the paradigmatic modality of Talmudic reflection: ideas, that may have been mere springboards, remain constantly in communication with or return to the examples, which are raised to the level of generalizations and are formalized in logical concepts.… Far from being the result of equivocation, this translates the inexhaustible richness and innumerable dimensions of the concrete into a reality more concrete than our daily life, in whose immediacy this abundance is forgotten amidst the quest for usefulness or the practical finality of events, behavior, and situations. Perhaps our Western ideas detach themselves prematurely from the sensible order: "the impatience of the concept" is more frequent than its "patient suffering." Talmudic thought constantly returns to the example out of which the concept is born and delays over it in order to let ideas germinate and be able to start out in different directions, seeking new results. The fresh meanings that rabbinic attention and imagination confer on the concrete content of experience are advantageous to concepts, which are never completely abstract.[73]

Levinas recognizes the risk of subjectivism, which is clearly attached to such a hermeneutics of solicitation. But, in his view, the risk of subjectivism "must be run by the truth."[74] In his view, this risk is worth taking owing to the "status of the Revelation: its word coming from elsewhere, from outside, and simultaneously dwelling in the person who receives it."[75] Levinas's desire to enrich mystery, rather than dispel it, is what grants to his biblical interpretation a sense of permanence and holiness.

In contrast to historicism, Levinas does not relativize biblical ethical values by plotting them on the taxonomic grid of the ancient Mediterranean worldview, nor does he analyze their change and development over time. Instead, he *elevates* biblical values in order that they might come to mean *all that they can mean*. Even though biblical values did change and develop over time, through the act of interpretation, they are *never allowed to fall in value*: "[T]he principle of their change is one of elevation, within changing contexts and challenges. The principle of the permanence of values in succession is their elevation."[76] This permanence of values is not a property of biblical texts themselves. What is permanent is their *continuity of elevation*. It is this continuity of elevation that sustains their permanence of holiness.

At this point, it should be obvious that, for Levinas, exegesis is not about historical explanation. For him, the "biblical past" is more than a mere chronicle of historical origins and developments of the people of Israel. According to Levinas, from the time of Abraham the Jewish covenant with G-d has involved the intersection

---

[73] Emmanuel Levinas, "The Jewish Understanding of Scripture," *Cross Currents* 44 (1994–95): 488–504, esp. 490.
[74] Levinas, *Beyond the Verse*, 132.
[75] Ibid., 131.
[76] Ibid., 19.

of two times, the diachronic time of human life and the synchronic time of the "immemorial" past.[77] Whereas countless events belong to the historical past of diachronic time, relatively few events belong to the immemorial past. The Jewish interpretive tradition elevates the immemorial biblical past, and, by this elevation, it becomes more than historical origins for their present. In fact, "immemorial" time erases its origins and hands on biblical stories as eternal paradigms.

Traditional Western biblical scholarship has no such appreciation for immemorial time. Levinas likens the work of Western biblical interpretations to the journey of Odysseus (Ulysses), who left his home on the island of Ithaca to embark on a journey, only to subsequently return to the sameness of his homeland. *The story of the Odyssey is the story of his return.* As such, Odysseus is the true father of traditional Western biblical studies, for biblical studies can also be conceived of as such an odyssey: they embark from their sanctioned methodologies to journey through the world of the biblical texts in order to *return again* to their own weary categories of sameness (e.g., sources, historical development, relativity, influence, genre, worldview). In each instance of such interpretation, the otherness of the biblical text is always reduced to Western categories of sameness within the totalizing function of each methodology. Within the practice of each of the sanctioned methodologies, there is always a return to some kind of origin.

In contrast, Levinas's conception of biblical interpretation is rooted in the journey of Abraham. If Odysseus is the father of traditional biblical studies, then *Abraham is the father of post-historical hermeneutics,* for Abraham was called to embark upon a journey *without the hope of return.* G-d commanded Abraham, "Go forth from your own country" (Gen 12:1). When Abraham answered G-d's call, there was no possibility for him to return home:

This commandment uproots Abraham from his native realm. It forbids him to believe that he can find himself by cultivating a nostalgia for his past. Abraham discovers his integrity as a man called to be a blessing to all families of the earth, only on the condition that he loses himself, that is, only on the condition that he gets rid of all that which, by keeping him prisoner of the past – words, images, possessions – would make impossible for him the going forward to the Promised Land. It is a land to which he none the less proceeds, day after day, for his entire humanity lies in his answer to the call he heard. But it is a land which he has no certainty of entering and settling.[78]

In apposition to the *Greek* journey of Odysseus, Levinas argues that the journey of Abraham is emblematic of Hebraic thinking of alterity. The journey of Abraham, the nomad, is not the binary opposite of that of Odysseus: it is not concerned with a thematizable destination. The journey of the nomad has no identifiable *telos.* It

---

[77] Cohen, *Ethics, Exegesis and Philosophy,* 252.
[78] Catherine Chalier, "Levinas and the Talmud," in *The Cambridge Companion to Levinas,* ed. Simon Critchley and Robert Bernasconi (Cambridge: Cambridge University Press, 2002), 100–18, esp. 106.

cannot even be conceptualized as a methodology. As such, Levinas's nomadic quest for a "meaning even deeper than the text contains" requires a mode of interpretation "which does not return to itself."[79] Indeed, it cannot, because it always disrupts the sameness of disciplinary methodologies and linearity of Western reasoning. I discuss nomadic thought in much greater detail in the next chapter. Suffice it to say that nomadic interpreters are fated to never return home because their erotic desire for a "fecundity" of present meaning compels them to continue the journey:

Eros ... no longer has the structure of the subject which from every adventure turns to its island, like Ulysses [Odysseus]. The "I" springs forth without returning, finds itself the self of another.... Its future does not fall back upon the past it ought to renew, it remains an absolute future by virtue of this subjectivity which consists not in bearing representations or powers but in transcending absolutely in fecundity.[80]

In the shadow of the science of Western biblical studies, Levinas's nomadic interpretation and erotic quest for a "fecundity" of present significance may seem idiosyncratic, if not unproductive. But if Heidegger demonstrated the importance of self-understanding, then Levinas exposes what is lost in such an undistracted quest for self-understanding: one's individual ethical responsibility to others before G-d, which precedes all biblical interpretation and all self-understanding. Levinasian hermeneutics protects the radical alterity of both our neighbor and G-d from our Odyssean compulsion toward the *reduction of difference to sameness*, which is inscribed in the analytical methods of Western biblical studies. Levinas's Talmudic lectures exemplify a style of interpretation characterized by an open-ended, Abrahamic movement that is deeply respectful of what we cannot ever fully know or grasp.

A turn toward such a Levinasian mode of hermeneutics would redraw the lines of accountability for biblical interpreters. Instead of being primarily accountable to a set of disciplinary methods, the interpreter would be *ethically* accountable to the "other," to one's neighbor and to G-d, within the context of one's faith community and religious tradition. This shifts us toward a form of interpretation that is motivated more by a quest for justice than by a search for explanation and final objectivity. Within such nomadic interpretation, the role of the traditional methods of interpretation can be recontextualized by the recognition that the interpretive choices we make always possess an ethical dimension. Interpreters of scripture possess the ethical responsibility, as well as the freedom, to choose how they will open up the significance of a biblical text. Interpreters must also be prepared to answer for their choices before the gaze of the "other." In essence, this accountability would require that we situate our individual freedom within the vocation for building justice and peace, a vocation that we share with all humanity.

---

[79] Levinas, *Beyond the Verse*, 140.
[80] Levinas, *Totality and Infinity*, 271.

12

The Embodied Interpreter: Deleuze and Guattari

To express is always to sing the glory of God … not only do plants and animals, orchids and wasps, sing or express themselves, but so do rocks and even rivers, every stratified thing on earth.[1]

René Descartes once likened the structure of philosophy to a tree: "Thus the whole of philosophy is like a tree: the roots are metaphysics, the trunk is physics, and the branches that issue from the trunk are all the other sciences."[2] Building on Descartes' insight, Gilles Deleuze and Félix Guattari have argued that Western humanist tradition in general is modeled on a treelike structure, or what they term an "arborescent" structure.[3] A tree organizes its parts according to a principle that arises out of its own interiority and self-sufficiency: it germinates from a solitary seed or acorn and shoots forth what will become its trunk. Its whole canopy of branches above is integrated downward into this trunk, and all of its roots below are similarly integrated upward into the same trunk.

Considered as a model of Western knowledge, the trunk of this arborescent structure represents human rationality. Rationality is the highest value in an arborescent structure because it is rationality that organizes and integrates all forms of knowledge into a unified, coherent system, according to the classical oppositional logic of Western metaphysics, such as essence versus existence, subject versus object, nature versus culture, necessary versus contingent, original versus copy, content versus form, and text versus interpretation.[4]

---

[1] Gilles Deleuze and Félix Guattari, *A Thousand Plateaus: Capitalism and Schizophrenia*, trans. Brian Massumi (Minneapolis: University of Minnesota Press, 1987 [1980]), 49; cf. 1; cf. B. H. Mclean, "Re-imagining New Testament Interpretation in Terms of Deleuzian Geophilosophy," *Neotestamentica: Journal of the New Testament Society of South Africa* 42/1 (2008): 51–71.

[2] This is a quotation of Descartes as quoted by Martin Heidegger in his essay "What Is Metaphysics?" in *Martin Heidegger: Pathmarks*, ed. William McNeill (Cambridge: Cambridge University Press, 1998), 239–76, esp. 277.

[3] Deleuze and Guattari, *A Thousand Plateaus*, 3–25.

[4] As a way of redressing the binarism logic of arborescent knowledge, a so-called fascicular model is sometimes substituted. In a fascicular root system, there is no single taproot. Instead, a system of secondary roots radiate out into a circle. While this model appears to overcome the binarism logic of the arborescent model, its circular unity creates its own totalizing system, with its own mode of self-sufficiency. Its circular logic turns back upon itself, thereby preserving a binary logic only in a different form; cf. ibid., 5–6.

However, according to Deleuze and Guattari, the structure of Western knowledge can alternatively be conceived of in terms of a "rhizomatic" structure. A "rhizome" is a kind of fungus or mushroom-like growth whose bodily substance lacks a central coordinating structure or clearly identifiable internal anatomical features. A rhizome has no trunk, center, or periphery. There are "only lines" of intensity that connect all parts of a rhizome together into a whole.[5] Below the ground, the roots of a rhizome intertwine and connect with other rhizomes *horizontally* in a somewhat disorganized manner, forming expanding "rhizomatic" networks.

Rhizomatic networks are real. In nature, there are many kinds of rhizomatic networks (fig. 12.1) beyond the mycological world of fungi and mushrooms. For instance, crabgrass forms another kind of rhizomatic network. In the realm of technology, the Internet or World Wide Web also forms a kind of rhizomatic network: it has no central coordinating system or center but only webs of interconnected networks, consisting of millions of servers, which are connected to billions of users around the globe. This ever-expanding network of thousands of millions of hubs would not be compromised by the removal of any single server because the Internet has no "trunk." *Any* part of this rhizomatic network could be considered as its middle depending on one's perspective.

Using the mathematical formula $n - 1$, Deleuze and Guattari explicate the concept of a rhizome, according to which the total number of its dimensions is represented by the letter "n" and the concept of a totalizing system is represented by the numeral "1." Hence the mathematical definition of a rhizome is $n - 1$. In other words, take the total number of dimensions of any rhizome (n) and then subtract every totalizing system (1) that would overcode it and restrict its growth. In terms of hermeneutics, the formula $n - 1$ expresses in mathematical terms the imperative to protect the total number of dimensions of a text (n) by subtracting (i.e., rejecting) every totalizing system, the chief of which is human rationality.[6]

The "arborescent" and the "rhizomatic" models can be applied not only to the structure of Western knowledge as a whole but also to the field of textual interpretation. According to Deleuze and Guattari, texts also possess the same two dimensions, an arborescent dimension, and a rhizomatic dimension. A text, considered in its arborescent dimension, is a "signifying totality." Its "sense" is a function of those factors that stabilize, limit, and totalize textual meaning, such as authorial intent and sociohistorical context (cf. Chapters 2 and 3). But the same text, considered in its rhizomatic dimension, consists of non-semantic, "asignifying particles," which rescue the text from being a mere semantic storage container. In its rhizomatic dimension, a text belongs to a rhizomatic network. As such, it lacks any totalizing structure that would control or constrain its "sense." Indeed, in its rhizomatic

---

5 Ibid., 8.
6 Ibid., 9.

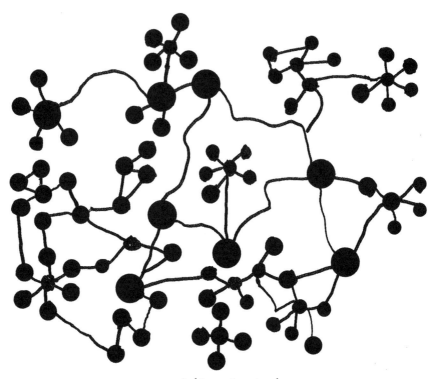

12.1. A rhizomatic network

dimension, a biblical text is antihegemonic, which is to say that it subverts the application of all such totalizing systems.

Employing a geological model, Deleuze and Guattari term entities that have become overcoded by such totalizing systems as "strata" and "territories." These *overcoded* regions exhibit predictable, domesticated, and stereotyped behaviors. For example, one could say that the application of the constructs of authorial intent and sociohistorical context in the interpretation of biblical texts "stratifies" or "territorializes" textual sense, resulting in stereotyped interpretations. But even within such "stratified" systems of thought (and these abound in biblical commentaries and journals), the potential still remains for the emergence of unexpected, asignifying events that can lead human understanding in new directions.

TEXTUAL DEPTH AND SURFACE

Trees grow downward, deep into the ground. In contrast to the *depth* of a tree, a rhizome's structure is flat. Rhizomes always grow *across the surface*. When viewed in terms of its surface dimension, a text is also flat. Its surface dimension is constituted by the flow of "asignifying particles," or intensities, between the text and other parts of the extended rhizomatic system. For example, I have previously explained how biblical texts possess a nonsemantic illocutionary dimension, nonsemiotic networks of forces, which are woven through the semiotic dimension of the text (cf. Chapter 9). These illocutionary forces constitute the virtual "unsaid" of every biblical text. They are implied imperatival forces. But when a biblical text is viewed only as a *semiotic* medium of information storage, which is later recovered through translation and interpretation into English, then these nonsemiotic, noninformational "asignifying particles" are overlooked. Such nonsemantic "asignifying particles" are forces that move across the surface of the rhizome, breaking down and disorganizing those arborescent forces that would stratify textual sense.[7]

Our eyes, which have been disciplined since the Enlightenment to perceive biblical texts in their arborescent depth, habitually overlook their dynamic surface dimension. Such blindness is lamentable because *the surface dimension of a text is always more important than its depth.* A biblical text in its depth dimension records only a one-time variation in a set of interrelated structures (i.e., that which I have previously termed the "founding sense-event"). But the same text, when passed down and interpreted from age to age, constitutes a "series" of present sense-events. Within this series, the flows of the "asignifying particles," or intensities, between the text and other structures within the rhizomatic network repeatedly form, strengthen, weaken, and rupture, over time. In the course of these surging and ebbing intensities, the "value" *relations* between them also change. That which is of critical importance to the biblical interpreter is not the absolute value of the strengthening and weakening of any particular asignifying intensity but rather the ongoing variation of the *relations* between these changing intensities over time. From this perspective, the present sense-event can be defined as a restructuring of the relations between "bodies" on the virtual surface of the rhizomatic system as a whole.

These "bodies" are of many different types and exist on many different levels. Of course, there are textual "bodies" and the "somatic bodies" of biblical interpreters; there are also institutional "bodies," such as universities and religious denominations; there are ideal "bodies," such as language, moral codes, and honor-shame codes; and there are virtual "bodies," such as relations of emotional investment. Owing to the complexity of the changing relations between the various flows that surge and ebb between these diverse "bodies," there is no privileged perspective, or totalizing methodology, which can permanently "stratify" or "territorialize" the "sense" of a text. Indeed, the surface dimension of texts actually facilitates a countermovement to that of "stratification" and "territorialization," namely "destratification" and "deterritorialization."[8] Textual sense is "destratified"

---

[7]   Ibid., 4, 9.
[8]   Ibid., 3, 4, 9.

and "deterritorialized" by the "lines of flight" that flow from the outside of the text along the *surface* of the rhizome to other "bodies" within the rhizomatic network.

HERMENEUTICS AS A HIGHER EMPIRICISM

What happens when an interpreter sets about to interpret a biblical text? At the outset of answering this question, we must avoid privileging the intentions and decisions of the historical authors of these texts and their present-day interpreters. We must also steer clear of the opposite strategy, which is the tendency to overstate the influence of the sociohistorical world behind a biblical text and the influence of a contemporary interpreter's own social location. Theories of downward causation by a transcendental subject (whether it be a historical author or a present-day interpreter) and theories of upward causation (by the sociohistorical world behind the text or the "social location" of the interpreter) are not the only – or even the primary – means by which textual sense-events actually come to pass. With respect to downward causation, the anthropocentric concept of a biblical author, who "puts" meaning into a text, and the analogous concept of the biblical interpreter, who subsequently rediscovers this same meaning, represent another form of "arborescent" thinking. Such thinking overestimates the place of the human beings (including human decisions and rationality) within the broader ecology of the sense-event.

Even though Heidegger's theorization of the hermeneutic act should not be reduced to such anthropocentrism, his concept of "Da-sein" is at least susceptible to the same critique: namely, Heideggerian ontology makes the lived body of the human being too large. Deleuze explains that "the phenomenological hypothesis" of Heidegger "is perhaps insufficient because it merely involves the lived body. But the lived body is a paltry thing compared to a more profound and almost unlivable Power [*Puissance*]."[9] Indeed, even Heidegger himself recognized the intrinsic anthropocentricity of his concept of "Da-sein" and abandoned the term after writing *Being and Time*. In the great, rhizomatic scheme of life, the lived human body of the biblical authors and interpreters is a "paltry thing" and matters much less than the romanticist tradition has supposed. While it is true that every sense-event *does* involve human agency, when viewed from the perspective of the rhizomatic network, sense-events actually arise from a restructuring of the virtual surface of the complex system *as a whole*, within which biblical authors and interpreters function only as *quasi causes* or "triggers."[10]

---

[9] Gilles Deleuze, *Francis Bacon: The Logic of Sensation,* trans. D. Smith (Minneapolis: University of Minnesota Press, 2003 [1981]), 39.

[10] Manuel DeLanda, *Intensive Science and Virtual Philosophy* (London: Continuum, 2002), 78–80.

All structures (including semiotic structures) are extended through time by means of a "series." A *novel* sense-event in a series is marked by the introduction of difference to the structure. Such difference is observable when the behavior of a system is drawn *out of line* from its previous behaviors ("attractors") and from what is normally expected, based on past performance.[11] The emergence of such novel behaviors within a structure is termed "diachronic emergence." For example, through diachronic emergence, difference can be introduced into a *signifying* system (which is projected through time as a "series") whereby the relations between signification, denotation, and manifestation, which contribute toward the formation of "sense," are drawn out of line from the "normal" behaviors. When this occurs, the signifying system can exhibit a novel, unexpected sense-event.

All this is to say that the sense-event of a biblical text is not merely an event "caused" by its original, historical author's intention, nor is it a function of the ancient sociohistorical world behind the text.[12] From the perspective of Deleuze's higher empiricism, such a sense-event arises from the *shifting* of the intensive relations themselves, which connect many different types of "bodies" together, within the whole rhizomatic network. *A present sense-event always emerges by virtue of a text's ongoing participation in the virtual surface of the whole of life.* It is never an autonomous event, nor is it tied to a single source or origin. A present sense-event can be defined as "a novel selection in ongoing and continuing series," which is continuously in variation over time.[13] From this perspective, biblical interpreters are not "meaning makers." They are "somatic bodies" that are destined to meaning within rhizomatic systems. The cognitive faculty of the scholar or interpreter does not function as a self-sufficient, authorizing source of meaning or knowledge because within the rhizome (*n*) all such totalizing functions (1) are excluded.

Indeed, as I have discussed in previous chapters, even our concepts of the "interpreter," "subject," "author," and "historian" *have their own histories*, which are rooted in traditions of the Enlightenment, romanticism, and humanism.[14] These concepts too belong to rhizomatic "structures," which change in time through series. In point of fact, as *embodied* interpreters, authors, and historians, we are all caught up in various kinds of structures, whether we are aware of them or not. For this reason, even when "we think we are speaking in our own name," we are actually producing the statements that are made possible by these very structures (cf. Chapter 7).[15] As such, we are really the midwives – not the mothers – of present sense-events.

---

[11] The term "attractor" refers to the long-term tendencies, shapes, or patterns of behavior of a real system.

[12] James Williams, *Gilles Deleuze's Logic of Sense: A Critical Introduction and Guide* (Edinburgh: Edinburgh University Press, 2008), 1–2.

[13] Ibid., 1–2.

[14] Cf. Gilles Deleuze and Félix Guattari, *What Is Philosophy?* trans. Hugh Tomlinson and Graham Burchell (New York: Columbia University Press, 1994 [1991]), 27.

[15] Deleuze, *Francis Bacon*, 36.

What is true of biblical interpreters is equally true of Deleuze and Guattari themselves. They did not theorize themselves as "authors" of their two books, *Anti-Oedipus* and *A Thousand Plateaus*. They rejected the label "authors" altogether. In their view, to describe their acts of writing as "authoring" would be to overlook the "working matters and the exteriority of their relations" to the wider rhizomatic network within which their books came to be.[16] Not only do they wish to reach the point "where one no longer says I." They want to reach the point "where it is no longer *of any importance* whether one says I" because each "I" has been rhizomatically "aided, inspired, multiplied":[17]

The two of us wrote *Anti-Oedipus* together. Since each one of us was several, there was already quite a crowd. Here we have made use of everything that came within range, what was closest as well as what was farthest away. We have assigned clever pseudonyms to prevent recognition. Why have we kept our own names? Out of habit, purely out of habit. To make ourselves unrecognizable in turn. To render imperceptible, not ourselves, but what makes us act, feel and think. Also because it's nice to talk like everybody else, to say that the sun rises when everybody knows it's only a figure of speech. To reach, not the point where one no longer says I, but the point where it is no longer of any importance whether one says I.[11] We are no longer ourselves. Each of us will know his own.[13] We have been aided, inspired, multiplied.[18]

If Heidegger's phenomenological concept of "Da-sein" renders the human being too large, then the opposite criticism could be made of theories of upward causation that understand the human being as being totally *determined* by cultural, social, and historical factors: such a theorization renders the human being *too small*. At the risk of oversimplifying the philosophy of Michel Foucault, it is fair to say that he comes close to rendering the human being as being utterly insignificant. Since Foucault deals with collective and largely unconscious structures of perception, individuals play almost no role in his work. In his so-called archaeological phase, he argued that the modern "[hu]man" is a mere discursive effect or "invention," generated by the intersection of the anonymous discursive practices of the disciplines of biology, linguistics, economics, anthropology, sociology, and so forth.[19]

---

[16] Deleuze and Guattari, *A Thousand Plateaus*, 3.

[17] Ibid.

[18] Ibid.

[19] This pairing of Heidegger with Foucault is not as far-fetched as it may seem. Though Foucault may seem to be antiphenomenological, this observation needs to be qualified. Foucault admits that he felt so close to Heidegger that he thought from within him and could not write about him: he confesses that "Heidegger has always been for me the essential philosopher.... My whole philosophical development was determined by my reading of Heidegger." Foucault recalls Heidegger's role in his own reading of Nietzsche: "I tried to read Nietzsche in the 50's, but Nietzsche by himself said nothing to me. Whereas Nietzsche and Heidegger – that was a philosophical shock!" Indeed, there is something strangely Heideggerian about Foucault's "analytic of finitude," and Heidegger, for his part, with his disavowal of "Da-sein," in the years following the publication of *Sein und Zeit*, and his shift toward "language" as the "House of being" (1947), makes a gesture that from the benefit of hindsight seems somewhat Foucaultian. All this is to say that Heidegger and Foucault are not as far apart as they may sometimes seem to be.

According to Foucault, his discovery of the discursive *invention* of modern "man" signals the "death of man," which he poetically described in the closing chapter of his celebrated *The Order of Things*:

As the archaeology of our thought easily shows, man is an invention of recent date. And one perhaps nearing its end. If those [discursive] arrangements were to disappear as they appeared … then one can certainly wager that man would be erased, like a face drawn in sand at the edge of the sea.[20]

With apologies to Foucault, perhaps the modern human being is not dead yet, but – like Monty Python's famous parrot – only "pining" for a more balanced appreciation of the place of human beings in the flow of life around them. The virtue of Deleuze and Guattari's higher empiricism is that it strikes a balance between theories of downward and upward causation. This conceptualization retains a place for embodied human beings as in the formation of sense-events, albeit a limited role as quasi causes. So if we are the midwives of meaning, then we are at least *indispensable* midwives.

At this point, it must be emphasized that Deleuze and Guattari are not advocating that we retreat into some kind of Dionysiac mysticism, or that we relax and celebrate the Joycean anarchy of a "chaosmos." Rather, in the face of the failure of traditional Western empiricism, they are attempting to advance what can be termed a "higher empiricism." In contrast to traditional empiricism, which (as we have previously discussed) is based on an obsolete, metaphysical view of the human being as a sovereign subject, Deleuze and Guattari's *higher empiricism* displaces human beings as the foundation of knowledge and reinstates them as *embodied* beings within a broader, nondeterministic, rhizomatic system. What Deleuze and Guattari have accomplished, in the view of Manuel DeLanda, is to create an "ontology *of the world*."[21] By situating sense-events in this vastly expanded ontology of the whole world, theorized as a complex, self-organizing structure, they have provided a theoretical apparatus by which to explain how biblical textual present sense-events actually occur.

This higher empiricism combines complexity theory with structuralism's concern for repeating structures (such as repeating configurations in textuality or social practices) in order to explain how new sense-events are possible within synchronic structures (cf. Chapter 7).[22] It is important to bear in mind that the concept of a "structure" does not imply uniformity within it. As previously noted,

---

[20] Michel Foucault, *The Order of Things* (New York: Pantheon, 1970 [1966]), 387.
[21] Manuel DeLanda and Peter Gaffney, "The Metaphysics of Science: An Interview with Manuel Delanda," in *The Force of the Virtual: Deleuze, Science, and Philosophy*, ed. Peter Gaffney (Minnesota: University of Minnesota Press, 2010), 325ff., esp. 328 (emphasis added).
[22] Cf. Félix Guattari, *Chaosophy: Texts and Interviews, 1972–1977*, ed. Sylvère Lotringer, trans. David L. Sweet and Chet Wiener (New York: Semiotext(e), 2009 [1996]); Elizabeth Grosz, *Chaos, Territory, Art: Deleuze and the Framing of the Earth* (New York: Columbia University Press, 2008).

Foucault has emphasized that discursive structures are *systems of dispersion*. In other words, they support difference and discontinuity and allow for points of diffraction. Structures can allow two or more incompatible statements to coexist on the same level. These points of diffraction might represent forks leading to different theoretical turns and developments.[23]

But undiluted structuralism is inadequate because it conceptualizes structures in static terms and therefore cannot account for the *diachronic* transformation in structures over long periods of time. The structure is traditionally deemed to be antonymous and closed off to being changed by human actions in the material world. On the other hand, the diachronic forms of analysis that dominate biblical studies (e.g., philology, historical positivism) fail to adequately account for the self-evident structurality of human society. A theory was needed to account for the fact that, while structures manifest short-term predictability, they also manifest *long-term unpredictability*. This is to say not that they are chaotic but rather that they display freedom, creativity, and novelty, in the form of a "series."[24] Deleuze and Guattari discovered a way to account for how (synchronic) structures unexpectedly and creatively change through time (diachronically), by introducing the concept of a "series." "Structures," which are by definition synchronic, are extended through time in a "series." As applied to biblical hermeneutics, a sense-event could be said to occur (diachronically) within a "series" (e.g., the historical development of an idea), even while that same series can equally be viewed from the perspective of the many structures in which it participates.[25]

A MULTIPLICITY

As a starting point for expanding on Deleuze and Guattari's "ontology of the world," let us consider the Deleuzian term "multiplicity." The concept of a "multiplicity" is derived from the French philosophy of Henri Bergson (1859–1941), who coined the term to describe entities that lack a fixed, internal unity and organization. A "multiplicity," being ever changing, cannot be adequately described by immobile concepts.

---

[23] According to *Archaeology of Knowledge*, one does not find diffractions everywhere the rules allow them because "authorities" limit the number of alternatives.

[24] Michel Foucault remarks, "The life of interpretation, on the contrary, is to believe that there is nothing but interpretations. It seems to me that one must understand well that which many of our contemporaries forget, *that hermeneutics and semiology are two ferocious enemies*. A hermeneutics that in fact winds itself around semiology, believing in the absolute existence of signs, gives up the violence, the incompleteness, the infinity of interpretations, so as to create a reign of terror where the mark rules and suspects language – we recognize here Marxism after Marx" ("Nietzsche, Freud, Marx," in *Transforming the Hermeneutic Context,* ed. Gayle L. Ormiston and Alan D. Schrift [Albany: State University of New York Press, 1990], 59–67, esp. 66–67).

[25] Williams, *Gilles Deleuze's Logic of Sense*, 1–2.

12.2. Fractals

A multiplicity consists of a coexistence of forces in flux, which belongs to a larger network of other multiplicities. Beyond this brief explanation, it is difficult to further define a "multiplicity" because *multiplicities are antirepresentational*: being mobile, they are actually characterized not by an essence but by the shifting nature of their *exterior relations* to other multiplicities in the rhizomatic field. These shifting relations facilitate their metamorphosis into something new.[26] As such, a multiplicity always has the uncertain status of being there and not being there, at one and the same time.

One of the best examples of a multiplicity is a fractal. Fractals are geometric figures formed by iterative processes (see fig. 12.2). To create a fractal, simply take any geometric figure (e.g., a line segment or a triangle) and repeatedly complicate its form in the same way, thereby creating increasingly more complex forms, each of which is different from, but related to, all prior forms in the series. A fractal *is* a fractal by virtue of its constantly evolving into a new shape. By implication, a fractal is incapable of being self-identical from one moment to the next. Only by *constant evolving* does it continue to retain its identity. To freeze it in one of its forms would be to "kill" it. Similarly, a multiplicity – like a fractal – continues to retain its identity as a multiplicity by engaging in a process of constant change.

A biblical text *is* a "multiplicity" by virtue of the fact that its surface dimension is characterized by shifting *exterior* relations to other multiplicities in the rhizomatic network. To understand a text-as-multiplicity is to focus on these *surface interactions* – the flows of intensity and rupture of flows – that occur between textual "bodies" and other "bodies" within the rhizomatic network. When viewed from this perspective, the "sense" of a biblical text cannot be limited to such filial constructs as authorial intent (downward causation) or sociohistorical context (upward causation) because the text's surface plane is repeatedly forming and unforming connections with other multiplicities.[27] In contrast to a text's open surface dimension, its depth dimension is a closed system, which, like any Newtonian

---

[26] Deleuze and Guattari, *A Thousand Plateaus*, 9.
[27] Umberto Eco, *The Open Work*, trans. Anna Cancogni (Cambridge, MA: Harvard University Press, 1989), 14–15.

system, possesses constant energy and matter. This is how biblical texts are traditionally conceptualized. To construe a biblical text as an ancient semantic container is to view it as a closed, predictable system, operating according to fixed linguistic and semiotic laws.

For example, the committee that recently produced *A New Translation of the Septuagint* (*NETS*) had to make a choice as to whether it would treat the Greek text of the Septuagint (LXX) as a closed or open system:[28] In Deleuzian terminology, its members had to decide whether they would grant primacy to the Septuagint as it was "aborescently" *produced* in conformity to its Hebrew exemplar or as it was "rhizomatically" *received* (in a series over time) by countless communities of Jews and Christians during the centuries that followed. Predictably, the committee members decided in favor of depth over surface, focusing on what they deemed to be "the most original character of this collection," namely its "interlinearity with," and "dependence on," its Hebrew exemplar.[29] This decision in favor of what they termed the "most original character" of the Septuagint was also a decision to treat the Septuagint as a closed system of meaning. This was simultaneously a decision against understanding the Septuagint as a multiplicity, which is to say, treating it as it was repeatedly received and reinterpreted "as Holy Writ" by contemporary Hellenistic Jews and Christians over the centuries that followed.[30] As a multiplicity, the "sense" of the Septuagint was never restricted by its Hebrew exemplar because its virtual surface *always remained open* to its oriented insertion into other multiplicities in the Jewish and Christian Hellenistic world, textual and otherwise.[31]

The members of the *NETS* committee are almost apologetic regarding the choice they made. They freely confess that they were well aware that most of the ancient Jews and Christians who read the Septuagint understood it as an "independent *self-sufficient* entity," apart from its Hebrew original.[32] Indeed, this was typically how the Septuagint *was* read by Christians and Jews, as an *open system of meaning*, independent of its Hebrew master.

For example, Paul's use of the Septuagint would be inexplicable on the basis of a Newtonian, closed-system model. His allegorical interpretation of the story of Sarah and Hagar (Gen 21:1–20; Gal 4:21–5:1), his *typological* interpretation of Adam (Gen 3:1–24; Rom 5:6–21), and his typological interpretation of the story of the idolatry of the Israelites (Exod 32:6; 1 Cor 10:1–15), not to mention his use of the concept of *recapitulation* (ἀνακεφαλαιοῦν) to interpret the giving of the Decalogue (Exod 20:13–17; cf. Rom 13:8–10), *all* unfold on the level of the virtual surface of the rhizome. In each of these cases, these Septuagintal texts functioned as multiplicities,

[28]   Albert Pietermas and Benjamin G. Wright (eds.), *A New Translation of the Septuagint: A New Translation of the Greek into Contemporary English* (New York: Oxford University Press, 2007).
[29]   Ibid., xv.
[30]   Ibid.
[31]   Eco, *The Open Work*, 14–15.
[32]   Pietermas and Wright, *New Translation of the Septuagint*, xvii.

becoming changed by their oriented insertion into the Pauline thought-world, thereby giving them the potential to communicate fresh significance in altered circumstances. In each of these examples, a "present (Pauline) sense-event" has released a "reserve" of the Septuagintal text's "potential happenings."[33]

The present sense-event of the Septuagint could be compared to Hagar, who, though once a slave to her Hebrew master, Abraham, was later granted freedom (Gen 21:12–21). Once released from her servitude, she was *free* to explore the boundless *exteriority* of the world beyond her master's tribe. The *NETS* committee, in treating the Septuagint as a kind of "interlinear" translation in "subservience" to the Hebrew original, in effect rescinded the Septuagint's freedom and reasserted its servitude to its Hebrew master. Even though the decision of the *NETS* committee is defensible in terms of the traditional "tree-logic" of the discipline of biblical studies, it remains true that their avoidance of the Septuagint's surface dimension caused them to overlook how the Septuagint, as an open system, historically functioned over time through a series.

A biblical interpreter is also a multiplicity, which is to say, a coexistence of forces that transmit intensities to other "bodies" within a rhizomatic network. Deleuze conveys in language the *virtual* mode of these forces through the use of verbal infinitives such as "to care," "to believe," "to fear," and "to love." On the other hand, to convey these forces, as they are *expressed* as flows on intensities, Deleuze employs their gerundive forms, such as "caring," "believing," "fearing," and "loving." In each case, what is most important for understanding the human somatic "body" is not the virtual (infinitival) forces themselves, or even their expressed (gerundive) intensities, but rather the *changing relationship between these various expressed intensities,* over time within the rhizomatic network. For example, the act of "caring" (as an expression of the virtual force "to care") is of lesser significance than the changing relation between "caring" and other expressed intensities, such as "believing," "fearing," and "loving," within the rhizomatic system, in contact with other multiplicities. From this perspective, the so-called text-reception complex could be redefined as the role of the interpreter-as-multiplicity in the disclosure of textual sense, within a changing set of "value" relations in the rhizomatic system as a whole.

A MACHINE

Deleuze and Guattari's terminology models the fluidity and mobility of the multiplicities they attempt to describe. New terminology is introduced in an unsystematic (rhizomatic) manner, without clear definitions, always putting the onus on the reader to assimilate the elastic connotations of their terminology. One of the most

---

[33] Deleuze, *Francis Bacon.*

important of these terms is the "machine." In the language of Deleuze, a "machine" is anything that connects with anything else in such a way as to produce some kind of flux or flow of intensities, or what they term "lines of flight, escape, or leakage" (*fuite*), whether these flows be physical, semiotic, intellectual, or emotional, leaving or entering the "machine." Deleuze and Guattari give the example of an infant's mouth suckling its mother's breast: the infant is a "mouth-machine" connected to a "breast-machine" by a *flow* of milk. Such flows are not permanent: connections form for a time and then rupture, when flows weaken and cease. When a child breastfeeds, the flow of milk is interrupted by longer cessations of flow, when the infant ceases to suckle. This important concept of *rupture* introduces dynamism, complexity, and intensity into the concept of the machine.

Contrary to what one might infer from the term "machine," the "flows" that occur between machines are in no way "mechanical." In other words, these flows do not occur in a deterministic way. Indeed, they cannot do so because (as noted previously) complex systems are not closed, Newtonian systems: as open systems, "machines" always possess the potential to manifest new, creative "events." In the case of human "machines," libidinal desire, the aleatory, and what Deleuze terms the "swerve" always prevent the flows of intensity from functioning in a deterministic manner.[34]

A Deleuzian "machine" cannot be defined further because "machines" also function as "war machines," which deterritorialize and reterritorialize all essentialist definitions. Machines actually function by *blurring*, not clarifying, individual identities and by mitigating the boundaries between discrete entities, such as the boundary between a suckling infant and its mother. (Of course, not even an infant distinguishes itself as a separate "self" until much later in its developmental process.)[35] Similarly, to conceive of an interpreter and a text as two "machines" is to understand them in terms of *their degrees of connectedness* rather than as nonrelational entities.

---

[34] While the term "aleatory" concerns the introduction of the *element of chance* into the creative process, Christians may also perceive the hand of God at work in the aleatory. The "swerve," or *clinamen*, is a spontaneous, unpredictable deviation from what is expected on the basis of the previous behavior of a system. (As Lucretius states, "Sometimes, at uncertain times and places, the eternal, universal fall of the atoms is disturbed by a very slight deviation – the *clinamen*. The resulting vortex gives rise to the world, to all natural things.") The "swerve" (or "clinamen" in Lucretius' terminology) is a term used by Epicurus in the atomistic doctrine to describe the unpredictable swerve of atoms. According to Lucretius, this indeterminacy of atomic movement provides the "free will which living things throughout the world have"; cf. Brad Inwood and L. P. Gerson (trans.), *The Epicurus Reader: Selected Writings and Testimonia*, introd. D. S. Hutchinson (Indianapolis: Hackett, 1994), 66; Gilles Deleuze, *Difference and Repetition*, trans. Paul Patton (New York: Columbia University Press, 1994 [1968]), 184).

[35] See my explanation in Chapter 11, n. 55; cf. Jacque Lacan, *Ecrits: A Selection*, trans. Bruce Fink (New York: Norton, 2002 [1966]), 3–9.

12.3. Bee and flowers

Deleuze and Guattari's best-known example of a flow between machines is that of the interaction between an orchid and a wasp (fig. 12.3). An orchid and a wasp, each conceived of as a "machine," participate in three successive syntheses:[36]

1. A connective synthesis of *production*
2. A disjunctive synthesis of *recording*
3. A conjunctive synthesis of *deterritorialization*

Out of the immanence of its desire, the wasp alights upon the orchid and forms a temporary connection with it. This connection enables a flow, or connective synthesis, when pollen on the anther of the orchid's flower is transferred to the legs of a wasp. This flow of pollen is a disjunctive synthesis or semiotic recording: from the perspective of the wasp, this transfer is a kind of "recording" of the orchid's identity onto the identity of the wasp, which constitutes an addition of surplus value to the wasp's identity. But that which is recorded onto the wasp's body is not the entire identity or code of the orchid but only a "fragment" of code. All the same, this transfer of a code-fragment transforms the wasp into an extension of the orchid's own reproductive system.

---

[36] Gilles Deleuze and Félix Guattari, *Anti-Oedipus: Capitalism and Schizophrenia* (Minneapolis: University of Minnesota Press, 1983 [1972]), 68–113.

From the perspective of the rhizome as a whole, within which both are included, both the orchid and the wasp constitute a heterogeneous series, which becomes joined together by the transfer, or "lines of flight," of code. In effect, the orchid has reterritorialized the wasp's identity, by bestowing upon it a fragment of its own identity.[37] But from the perspective of the wasp, it has been *de*territorialized by the same transfer, and its own identity has thereby become blurred. This obscuring of bodily boundaries is not an assimilation toward a single series: the wasp does not become an orchid, nor does the orchid become a wasp: "There is neither imitation nor resemblance [between them], only an exploding of two heterogeneous series on the line of flight composed by a common rhizome that can no longer be attributed to, or subjugated by, anything signifying."[38] Finally, in a conjunctive synthesis, the flow of intensity between these two heterogeneous series is ruptured by the flight of the wasp, which then carries the orchid's pollen away to other parts of the field.

In a manner comparable to Deleuze's orchid-machine/wasp-machine model, the text-reception complex constitutes a temporary "line of flight" between a "text-machine" and an "interpreter-machine," understood as two heterogeneous series. The flow of intensity between them temporarily disorganizes their individual boundaries. Each has become disorganized by the transfer of surplus "value" (code) from the text to the interpreter, resulting in the interpreter becoming *de*territorialized by the text, as a bearer of its surplus identity, just as the text has *re*territorialized its own identity onto that of the interpreter. In essence, both have participated in an aparallel evolution that obscures the distinction between them.[39] Finally, this transfer of intensities is ruptured by the ensuing "flight" of the interpreter, who carries these textual intensities to other texts and entities beyond the immediate reach of the text itself. Every act of biblical interpretation is the product of such a machine-like assemblage.[40]

ANALOGICAL THOUGHT

If the concept of a text and interpreter as "machines" seems like science fiction, it is because our arborified minds have been trained to essentialize things as isolated entities, rather than as mobile entities that enter into dynamic interconnections with other entities. Thinking ecologically does not come easily to us. As discussed

---

[37] Gilles Deleuze and Félix Guattari, *Kafka: Toward a Minor Literature*, trans. Dana Polan, introd. Réda Bensmaïa (Minneapolis: University of Minnesota Press, 1986 [1975]), 14, cf. 2; B. H. McLean, "The Exteriority of Biblical Meaning and the Plentitude of Desire: An Exploration of Deleuze's Non-metaphysical Hermeneutics of Kafka," *Neotestamentica: Journal of the New Testament Society of South Africa* 43/1 (2009): 93–122.

[38] Deleuze and Guattari, *A Thousand Plateaus*, 10.

[39] Ibid., 15.

[40] Deleuze, *Francis Bacon*, 37.

in Chapter 7, this arborific mode of thinking is largely an *effect* produced by the semiotic structure of language itself. Taken as a whole, the structure of language is twinned with the symbolic world of the dominant cultural order. Its binary logic and categorical grids construct a symbolizing structure that is mirrored in the cultural order. The resulting symbolic system organizes reality into the "Real" of human understanding. Language literalizes this dissimulation of reality as the "Real," making it appear to be the natural state of the world, with the result that we, who "live and work and have our being" in this structure fail to perceive this semiotic codification of reality.

Deleuze and Guattari term forms of thinking that naturalize language's codification of reality "analogic thought." For example, analogical thought is evident in the overcoding of our human bodies in terms of the "family" versus "society" semiotic binarism. Freudian and Lacanian forms of psychoanalysis have traditionally defined a child's attachment to society *negatively and subordinately* with reference to a child's primary attachment to its family, the dominant term in the family-society binarism. But in their book *Anti-Oedipus*, Deleuze and Guattari argue that this binarism traps the child within the family's "holy trinity" of father-mother-child, which shapes the child into a stereotyped child, with a corresponding reduction of its rhizomatic intensity, complexity, and potential. In Freud's opinion, "it all leads back to daddy." But Deleuze and Guattari argue that the "family versus society" binarism is not the primordial locus of childhood development. The "family versus society" binarism is a categorical grid which is superimposed onto the body of the child. Prior to this categorical overlay, the natural parameters of a child's life are much broader, consisting of its friends, toys, projects, and nonparental figures, all of which "deterritorialize" the family triangle.[41]

In passing, one might observe that there are traces of resistance to this family-society binarism even in the New Testament. When the Jesus of the Gospel of Mark is informed that his mother and brothers have arrived outside the house where he is teaching, he asks, "Who are my mother and brothers? … whoever does the will of God is my brother, sister and mother" (Mark 3:31–35). Jesus' statement reterritorializes the family by resituating it within an expanded social network of those who do God's will. In essence, Jesus' statement challenges the primacy of the family-society binarism of analogic thought.

Of course, the family-society binarism is only one of the many binarisms by which analogical thought delivers our somatic bodies over to the forces at work within Western culture and capitalism, and within patriarchy (both biblical and contemporary), and within the literatures produced by them. Though the binarisms differ, the final result of analogic overcoding is always the same: the creation of an appropriately *labeled body*, according to family status (as a father or mother; husband or wife; son or daughter), gender (as masculine or feminine; straight or

---

[41]   Deleuze and Guattari, *Kafka: Toward a Minor Literature*, 79.

gay), color (white or nonwhite), ethnicity (as Western or non-Western), and economic status (rich or poor).[42] For example, even though no actual person ever fully coincides with either pole of the "male-female" binarism, all persons are *gendered* to one extent or another by the inscription of this binarism on their bodies.[43]

According to Foucault, the body is the essential component for the operation of power relations in society. Power and knowledge are never external to one another. They operate in a mutually generative manner – neither can be reduced to the other, hence his neologism "power/knowledge."[44] Through power, knowledge structured according to the dominant cultural order is insinuated into the human body under the guise of improving the welfare of individuals and society as a whole. Thus the somatic body is a place where the minute and local practices of biopower are linked with larger-scale organizations of power body-molding techniques. Foucault warns that we are often "unaware of the prodigious machinery of the will to truth, with its vocation of exclusion" of knowledge.[45] Biopower employs a select variety of knowledges in order to remain relatively hidden. For example, *Discipline and Punish* analyzes "disciplinary power," which is centered on the body as an object to be manipulated; its basic goal: to produce useful and docile bodies.[46] The critical categories of analogic thought in the West, especially those of gender, color/race, ethnicity, and economic status, as well as the never-ending "etceteras" that must inevitably follow in such lists, make up the critical *axes of power and domination* shared by various forms of capitalism and patriarchy. Each of these binarisms constructs its own axis of power and domination. By naturalizing these binarisms, analogical thought simultaneously naturalizes the axes of power produced by them.

When these many axes are superimposed upon one another, they create a complex categorical grid, by which the individual forces attached to individual binarisms overlap and reinforce each another. Analogic thought then inscribes these forces upon our human bodies. The body, so inscribed, can be conceived of as an assemblage, constituted by the intersection of the critical binaries of the dominant social order, as enumerated earlier. Though the specifics of this process may vary from place to place, the final result is always the same: the construction of a body that is subject to power, with the corresponding reduction of its rhizomatic

---

42 In the secular Western world, the religion marker appears to be in flux, but moving toward a "secular/nonobservant versus religiously observant" binary. But, in the past, the normative Western binarism has always been Christian versus non-Christian (atheist/agnostic/Jewish/Muslim/Buddhist, etc.).

43 Brian Massumi, *A User's Guide to Capitalism and Schizophrenia: Deviations from Deleuze and Guattari*, Swerve Edition (Cambridge, MA: MIT Press, 1992), 87–88.

44 Foucault, *Discipline and Punish* (New York: Pantheon, 1977), 27–28.

45 Michel Foucault, "The Order of Discourse," included at the end of *The Archaeology of Knowledge* (New York: Tavistok Publications/Pantheon, 1972 [1969]), 215–37, esp. 220.

46 Foucault, *Discipline and Punish*, 25, 133–34.

intensity and complexity, by its insertion into a productive bio-social-political-technical assemblage.

If one were to follow the logic of these axes of power, then the most oppressed persons in Western society would be those whose bodies have been constructed on the basis of the *subordinate* term of the critical binarisms, especially with regard to gender, color/race, ethnicity, and economic status. For example, the analogic construction of a specific body, as a "black, unemployed, lesbian female, of Zulu ethnicity," would be to construct this unique human body, exhibiting its own originary difference, in one of the most oppressive ways possible (and even to invite moral judgment of her). On the other hand, the analogic construction of another specific body, in terms of the *same* axes of power, as a "white, employed, heterosexual male, of Anglo-Saxon descent," would be to construct *this* human body in a way that grants it automatic entitlement, privilege, and power in the same society. Of course, the former body could be discursively constructed in a number of other ways, such as a "ballet instructor," or as a "human rights activist," or as a "donor to Greenpeace," and the latter body could perhaps be constructed as a "football fan," or as a "member of a condominium board," or as a "hunter," but such descriptors occupy much lower places in the hierarchy of binarisms of analogic thought, compared to such critical binarisms as gender, color/race, economic status, and ethnicity.

It is worthy of note that the apostle Paul called into question the normative character of the fundamental binarisms of Hellenistic Judaism when he asserted that there is neither Jew nor Greek, freeman nor slave, male nor female for those who are "in Christ Jesus" (Gal 3:28). This text can be read as Paul's rejection (at least for those who are "in Christ") of three of the fundamental binarisms of Judaism, namely "Jewish" versus "Greek," "freeman" versus "slave," and "male" versus "female," as three overlapping axes of power. Once again, the discursive construction of a unique body within Hellenistic society in terms of the subordinate member of each binary, as a "Greek, female slave," would be to construct this body in a most oppressive way. Interestingly, Paul, whose constructed identity as "Jewish, male freeman" accorded him power and privilege within Hellenistic Judaism, was prepared to sacrifice this constructed identity for the sake of being "in" Christ.

In Philippians 3:4–7, Paul once again dismisses the categorical grid of Jewish subjectivity. Paul, whose identity had previously been shaped by the binarisms of "Hebrew" versus "Gentile," as "Pharisee" versus being a mere "Jew," and as "blameless" under the Torah versus being a "transgressor," now declares that he counts these binarisms of Jewish identity to be a "loss" (ζημίαν) (Phil 3:8). While being enmeshed within the Jewish system of analogical thought, Paul *did not perceive the rules of the game*. But following his revelatory experience, his eyes were opened, and he rejected the categorical grid of language/culture and the corresponding biopower that analogical thought exercised over his body. Though much more could be said on this point, it is clear that analogical thought's dissimulation of reality loses its secure character even in the pages of scripture.

NOMADIC THOUGHT

By its very nature, analogical thought reduces the diversity and intensity of human life, *imposing sameness upon originary difference.* According to Deleuze and Guattari, the opposing form of thought to analogical thought is "nomadic thought." Nomadic thought takes the *end point* of analogical thought as a starting point for unraveling its effects. For example, if we were to apply nomadic thought to the constructed body of the previously mentioned "black, unemployed, lesbian female, of Zulu ethnicity," we can trace her body back to its virtual, hyperdifferentiated body of rhizomatic intensity. This is not simply a matter of inviting her to freely *choose* to live a new, rhizomatic life because there is no place of unfettered freedom on earth that is beyond the reach of analogical thought and biopower. Because her constructed body is the result of the *inscription* of the axes of power of analogical thought upon it, *new possibilities for living can arise only from processes of reinscription upon the body, and especially by redirecting the process of inscription itself.* In this process of redirection, her personal agency is not exercised by simply choosing resolutely to step beyond the reach of analogical thought (which is impossible) but rather by creatively redirecting and misdirecting its processes of inscription upon her body *from within the system itself.*

This can only be accomplished if one first appreciates the weaknesses inherent in the system itself. When the axes of power of analogical thought overlap, they often reinforce one another (e.g., white + heterosexual + male + Western = entitlement + power + privilege). But at other points the overlapping of its axes in the hybridity of real life often inadvertently creates dissonance between them (e.g., Is white female > or < black male?). At such conflicting intersections, the logic of analogical thought becomes confused and disorganized. This phenomenon is particularly evident in multicultural settings that mix together people whose ancestral and traditional cultures and values presume non-Western axes of power with people whose culture is formed by Western axes of power. For example, one can imagine the confusion and dissonance within the British and Indian systems of analogical thought, when British traders in the early eighteenth century first established the East India Trading Company in Surat, Bombay, Madras, and Calcutta. This mercantile enterprise effected a superimposition of the British class system upon the heavily stratified Indian caste system, a structure that had no place to accommodate this imported system. This clash of systems created many conflicting intersections that had to be negotiated, especially with respect to gender, color or race, ethnicity, economic status, and religion. Similarly, the election of a new president of the United States, whose father was black and mother was white, has confused the analogical thought processes of white Americans, whose "white versus nonwhite" logic has no place for a person who belonged to both sides of this binarism. Though much more could be said, suffice it to say that through the confusion and disorganization of the axes of power, analogical thought has the potential to open up ways for biblical interpreters, especially those who are most oppressed by the reigning regime of knowledge, to regain some of their rhizomatic intensity.

THERE ARE NO METAPHORS

Within a literary framework, Deleuze and Guattari develop their theory of nomadic thought in their book *Kafka: Toward a Minor Literature*. As one might expect, they do not attempt to explicate the "inner" meaning of Kafka's prose in terms of the categories of analogical thought. They do not even interpret Kafka's stories in terms of their purported "metaphorical" meaning.[47] In fact, they reject the concept of a metaphor altogether.

The term "metaphor" is derived from the Greek word *metapherin* (μεταφέρειν), meaning "to transfer." A *conventional* metaphor is one that *transfers* meaning from one term (such as a noun, adjective, or verb) to another term in an established language game.[48] For example, metaphors can easily be formed using simple nouns (e.g., "She is not an *angel*," "George is a *snake* in the grass," "His home is a *prison*"). Of course, some key theological metaphors have also been formed from nouns, the paramount ones being "God is father" and "Christ is his son." These metaphors express, in theological terms, the interrelation between two persons of the Trinity and, by extension, the relation of God, through the Son, to those who are baptized in the name of the Trinity. Metaphors can also be formed from verbs (e.g., "the committee *shot down* her ideas," "Christ *redeemed* us from our sins") and from adjectives (e.g., "they had a *heated* argument"). Such conventional metaphors are readily understandable, owing to their frequent repetition in one's culture and religion over time. Through repetition, they often become literalized. They thereby take on a habitual meaning in a particular language game. For this reason, we are often unaware that a metaphor is even being used. For instance, if I were to tell my friend that I had just had a "*heated* argument" with my colleague, my meaning would be self-evident, and my supposed metaphor would go undetected. No explanation of the metaphorical use of the adjective "heated" would be required. Similarly, when we pray "Our Father, who art in

---

[47] Hayden White considers metaphor, metonymy, synecdoche, and irony to be the "archetypal plot of (all) discursive formations." Only within this endlessly expanding set of different orders and systems of relation do individual words and verses acquire their "meanings" (*Tropics of Discourse: Essays in Cultural Criticism* [Baltimore: Johns Hopkins University Press, 1978], 5).

[48] Cf. Donald Davidson, *Inquiries into Truth and Interpretation* (Oxford: Oxford University Press, 1984), 262; Richard Rorty, *Contingency, Irony, and Solidarity* (Cambridge: Cambridge University Press, 1989), 18–19.

heaven," the metaphor typically also goes undetected, which can give rise to the danger that one might literalize this *theological* metaphor as an actual state of affairs, supposing that God is not *like* a father with respect to Christ's identity but rather that God *is* a father. Here, there is a real danger that this metaphor might be literalized under the influence of analogical thought, as a way of sublimating one's own oedipal drives.[49] However, my primary point is that all conventional metaphors are really *dead* metaphors in the sense that they have become stereotyped usages, with a *fixed* content. A conventional metaphor is a cultural cliché, which is why they so often go undetected.

According to Deleuze and Guattari, one cannot escape such conventional metaphors by trying to renovate them in some way. For example, it would not be enough to pray to "Our *Mother,* who art in heaven." Not only does the construction of God as "Our Mother" perpetuate the same oedipal binarism; it is also amenable to being literalized the same oedipal way. Kafka actually set out to kill all conventional metaphors.[50] In his diaries, he writes that "metaphors are one of the things that make me despair of literature."[51] In contrast to conventional metaphors, Kafka employed what I term here "true metaphors."

A true metaphor has no established place in an existing language game. As such, it has no fixed meaning. For example, if I were to make the statement, "The world is an orange," my intended meaning would not be obvious. One might reply, "How is the world like an orange?" This is a true metaphor. Kafka's metaphors are also true metaphors. Kafka's metaphors never acquire a stereotyped meaning. They are neither literalizations of his interior guilt arising from his inner struggles with his own overbearing father nor religious symbols relating to Kafka's negative theology or Jewish mysticism. Indeed, at least according to Deleuze and Guattari, Kafka's metaphors do not hold within them any fixed meaning whatsoever because they are always unexpected.

According to Deleuze and Guattari, Kafka's metaphors result from cathexis, which is to say, from the release of his repressed mental and emotional energy. Kafka employed cathexis idiosyncratically to subvert analogical thought's

---

[49] Freud argued that a son experiences an oedipal desire within the family triangle. In rebellion against the father, the son transgresses the law of the father. But having committed the transgression, the child then experiences the attendant feelings of guilt and remorse for having disappointed his father and the accompanying desire to seek the father's forgiveness. When the theological metaphor of "God as Father" is literalized by analogical thought, men may neurotically transfer their feelings of guilt and their desire for forgiveness from their earthly father (whether living or deceased) to a heavenly "Father"; cf. Franz Kafka's *Dearest Father,* trans. Hannah Stokes and Richard Stokes (Surrey: Oneworld Classics, 2008 [1953]), in which he enlarges Oedipus to the point of absurdity (cf. Deleuze and Guattari, *Kafka: Toward a Minor Literature,* 2).

[50] Deleuze and Guattari, *Kafka: Toward a Minor Literature,* 22; Deleuze and Guattari argue that metaphors, symbols, and allegories are products of oedipal forces, which territorialize desire.

[51] Franz Kafka's *Diaries* (1921), as quoted in Deleuze and Guattari, *Kafka: Toward a Minor Literature,* 22.

construction of him as an authoring, intending subject.[52] This subversion of ana-logical thought allowed Kafka, in the very act of writing, to *disperse* his own authorial identity. His literary characters are not mimetic of his own authorial self. They do not represent persons in his sociocultural world. His literary char-acters are only abstract "figures of desire."[53] For example, the main character in *The Castle,* known simply as K, is a figure of a thwarted desire to establish a liaison with the castle. Similarly, K in Kafka's novel *The Trial,* animated by desire, walks from room to room and office to office seeking justice from the legal system. But wherever K "believed there was law, there is in fact desire and desire alone."[54] Similarly, Kafka's famous description of Gregor Samsa becoming a "monstrous bug" (*ungeheuren Ungeziefer*) in his story "The Metamorphosis" has no fixed content. Kafka's monstrous bug does not correspond metaphorically to a Jungian or Freudian archetype. In fact, the bug does not symbolize any one thing in Kafka's outer and inner world. In becoming an insect, Gregor Samsa is simply transformed by "becoming-animal" in opposition to the "great paranoid bureaucratic machines."[55] The metaphor of "becoming-beetle" is neither true nor false. It is just an extension of his general metaphor of "becoming-animal." Owing to Kafka's idiosyncratic use of metaphors, there is no single metaphor to be deciphered that would supply the interpretive key to unlock the meaning of his stories. In the end, all that matters is that his metaphors were meaningful to Kafka himself. We, as the interpreters of this story, can neither confirm nor con-tradict them. All we can do, as Richard Rorty vividly observes, is "savor" them or "spit (them) out."[56]

Thus, Kafka's narratives do not contain metaphors that secretly *represent* some-thing else. Like his "monstrous bug," which lacked an endoskeleton, his prose has no inside. In fact, his writings actually succeeded in deterritorializing the "form versus content" binarism of analogical thought.[57] Here we are reminded of Marshall McLuhan's famous dictum, "The medium is the message."[58] In Kafka's writings, there is no interiorized message that stabilizes the meaning of the literary medium. Kafka's medium actually subverts the metaphysics of interiority and of author intent. From the perspective of nomadic thought, "meaning" is found not

---

[52] "He [Kafka] knows that all the lines link him to a literary machine of expression for which he is simultaneously the gears, the mechanic, the operator, and the victim" (ibid., 58).

[53] Ibid., 28.

[54] Ibid., 49.

[55] Ibid., 34. Deleuze states, "To the inhumanness of the 'diabolical powers' there is the answer of becoming-animal: to become a beetle, to become a dog, to become an ape … rather than lowering one's head and remaining a bureaucrat, inspector, judge, or judged.… To become animal is to par-ticipate in movement, to stake out the path of escape in all its positivity" (ibid., 12–13).

[56] Rorty, *Contingency,* 18.

[57] Réda Bensmaïa, introduction to Deleuze and Guattari, *Kafka: Toward a Minor Literature,* xviii.

[58] Marshall McLuhan, *Understanding Media: The Extensions of Man,* introd. Lewis Lapham (Cambridge, MA: MIT Press, 1994 [1964]), 8.

in any single literary phrase, character, concept, or metaphor, but only in the totality of the literary *expression*. In short, Kafka's expressive medium *is* his message.
His nomadic way of thinking *is* his message. As a deterritorializing "machine,"
Kafka's nomadic thought belongs to a dynamic *open system*, with multiple connections to many other machines.

This is also true of biblical texts: considered in their surface dimension, there
is no need to distinguish between their outer "form" and inner "content," as analogical thought would dictate, because "there is no difference between what a
book talks about [i.e., its content or message] and how it is made [its form or
media]."[59] Rather than attempting to distinguish between the inner form and outer
content of a biblical text, we should literally say that a biblical text (in its surface
dimension) *is* a "machine." A biblical text is not *like* a machine: it *is* a machine. In
Anti-Oedipus (1972), Deleuze and Guattari, building on Franz Reuleaux's classic
definition of a "machine," insist that they employ the term machine "irrespective
of any metaphor."[60]

This concept of the Bible *as* (not "like") a literary machine can be explained
on the basis of our previous discussion of language and analogical thought (cf.
Chapters 1, 7, and 8). Because language actually constructs the "Real" (rather than
passively registering reality), and because the relationship between signifiers and
signifieds is *arbitrary*, there are no "proper words" for any one thing. There is no
natural or essential connection between words and things. As previously noted,
the concept (signified) associated with the English signifier "tree" can be denoted
by many other signifiers such as *arbre* (French), *Baum* (German), δένδρον
(Greek), and *ağaç* (Turkish). Because the relationship between morphemes
(words), concepts, and things is arbitrary and culturally constructed, then the
very concept of a metaphor can be said to be unnecessary: from the global perspective of Deleuze's "world ontology," all one needs to say is that human beings
employ "*inexact* words to designate" things "exactly."[61] Depending on one's point
of view, either all words or no words are metaphors. In the structure of language,
"*there are no metaphors*, only conjugations" of words in different "regimes of
signs."[62] Because there are no exact linguistic signs for any entity, then even the
linguistic signs such as "machine," "multiplicity," and "body" can have "different
meanings" when they enter "into a different syntax" or into a different "regime of

---

59 Deleuze and Guattari, *A Thousand Plateaus*, 4.
60 Deleuze and Guattari, *Anti-Oedipus*, 165–66, cf. 155, 299, 272. Reuleaux defined a machine as "a
    combination of resistant bodies so arranged that by their means the mechanical forces of nature
    can be compelled to do work accompanied by certain determinate motions"; Franz Reuleaux, *The
    Constructor: A Handbook of Machine Design*, trans. Henry Harrison Suplee (Philadelphia, 1893),
    viii.
61 Gilles Deleuze and Claire Parnet, *Dialogues*, rev. ed., trans. Hugh Tomlinson and Barbara Habberjam
    (New York: Columbia University Press, 2007 [1977]), 3 (emphasis added).
62 Ibid., 140 (emphasis added).

signs."[63] Therefore, from a global perspective, recourse to the concept of metaphor is an unnecessary detour.

To return to my earlier point, the Bible *is* "a little [literary] machine" by virtue of its demonstrated capacity to couple with other machines – literary and nonliterary, religious and secular, somatic and institutional, ethical and economic, political and aesthetic, biological and cultural, and so forth – allowing intensive asignifying forces to flow between them.[64] By implication, the interpretation of any Greek or Hebrew biblical text should "never be a scholarly exercise in search of what is signified," but rather an exploration of the "*productive* use of the literary machine … that extracts from the text its revolutionary force."[65] From this vantage point, a given biblical text, such as Joshua 2–19, 1 Samuel 17–30, and Luke 23–24, does not represent or denote something else (such as the conquest of Canaan, events in the life of King David, the crucifixion of Jesus). Each of these texts, as an assemblage, "has only itself, in connection with other assemblages."[66] From this nomadic point of view, Deleuze and Guattari would argue that we should not ask what the narrative of Jesus's death in Luke 23–24 means "as a signified," or "look for anything to understand it."[67] Instead, we should ask, With what does this narrative function, in connection with what other machines does it transmit its own intensities, and into which other multiplicities [are] its own (intensities) inserted and metamorphosed? These are indeed productive questions because a biblical text such as Luke 23–24 "exists only through the outside and on the outside."[68] On the textual surface, the Bible's "sense" is an event that is produced through the *exteriority* of its relations within the rhizomatic network as a whole.[69]

THE "BODY WITHOUT ORGANS" AND THE "ORGANISM"

In order to prevent the reduction of their philosophy to a formal set of definitions and yet another totalizing method, Deleuze and Guattari routinely shift from one neologism to another. Perhaps the best known of these neologisms is the term "body without organs" (*corps sans organes*), a term that was first coined by the French playwright Antonin Artaud (1896–1948). A "body without organs" (often abbreviated "BwO") refers to a body *outside of any determined state.*[70] In point of

---

[63] Ibid., 140, cf. 111, 117.

[64] Deleuze and Guattari, *A Thousand Plateaus*, 23.

[65] Deleuze and Guattari, *Anti-Oedipus,* 116 (emphasis added).

[66] Deleuze and Guattari, *A Thousand Plateaus*, 4.

[67] Ibid.

[68] Ibid.

[69] Cf. Massumi, *A User's Guide to Capitalism and Schizophrenia*, 10.

[70] Cf. Susan Sontag (ed.), *Antonin Artaud: Selected Writings*, trans. Helen Weaver (New York: Farrar, Straus and Giroux, 1976). Deleuze and Guattari subsequently theorized this term in "Plateau 6: November 28, 1947 – How Do You Make Yourself a Body without Organs?" in *A Thousand Plateaus*, 149–66.

fact, a "body without organs" *does* possess organs: the modifier "without organs" implies only that the *interconnections between* the organs of the body, on the one hand, and the connections *between* the body and its external environment, on the other, are more significant than any of the body's discrete organs viewed in isolation. From the perspective of these connections, a "body without organs" is more like a "deterritorialized" zone than it is an isolated life form.

The contrasting term to the BwO is the "organism." In contrast to the BwO, an "organism" has been "territorialized" by the forces of capitalism and patriarchy, which, together, have organized it into a productive bio-social-political-technical assemblage, with the purpose of extracting "useful labor" from it and redirecting its desires toward consumption, "useful labor" and "consumption" being the two primary values of capitalism. In contrast to this well-organized "organism," the BwO is a *disorganized* system, in the sense that it has de-organized the overcoding forces of capitalism and patriarchy.

Deleuze's "body with organs" actually erases the boundary between the natural human body and the culturally encoded body, which in itself is highly significant. The BwO also erases the boundary between the prediscursive and discursive "I." This is not to say that Deleuze is trying to reassert an ontologically original, unified, or prediscursive "self." He is not. But as a *deterritorialized* body, the BwO is simply no longer overcoded by these totalizing systems and is thereby free to live in the most desirous, intense, and generous way possible. Its identity is no longer defined in terms of the values of capitalism and patriarchy.

The BwO is a virtual field of creative life, whose engagement with the world is characterized by *productive desire*. In their ground-breaking book *Anti-Oedipus*, Deleuze and Guattari contest the primacy of human "desire as lack" as conceptualized by theories of desire rooted in capitalism and in the Freudian and Lacanian psychoanalytic paradigm. Whereas one experiences "desire-as-lack," when one is *excluded* from a set of relations (e.g., from the family triangle), one experiences "productive desire" when *included within* a set of relations.[71] In contrast to desire-as-lack (i.e., the forms of desire that are characteristic of capitalism and the oedipal complex), productive desire never covets an object, nor is it defined by any particular wants or needs. Instead, "productive desire" is outward-focused, generative, and creative.[72] Thus, in contrast to the grasping and acquiring person characterized by "desire-as-lack," the person with *productive* desire is characterized by plenitude, generosity, and conviviality. Such persons see the world as being pregnant with possibilities for new gestures of friendship and for fresh acts of solidarity with others. But such productive desire wanes when the BwO becomes "territorialized" into an "organism." When the BwO becomes "arborified," it loses its rhizomatic

---

[71] Deleuze and Parnet, *Dialogues*, 35.

[72] Alan D. Schrift, "Spinoza, Nietzsche, Deleuze: An Other Discourse of Desire," in *Philosophy of Desire*, ed. Hugh J. Silverman (New York: Routledge, 2000), 173–85; Dorothea Olkowski, "Deleuze and Guattari: Flows of Desire and the Body," in Silverman, *Philosophy of Desire*, 186–207.

intensity, "for it is always by rhizome that desire moves and produces. Whenever desire climbs a tree, internal repercussions trip it up and it falls to its death."[73]

If this focus on the human *body* seems out of place in this book on *biblical* interpretation, then two points must be emphasized. First, the human *body* is the site where biblical interpretation takes place (as a key dimension of the text-reception complex). Second, the human body has always occupied a very high place in orthodox Christian theology: after all, the centerpiece of the Christian faith is the *bodily* resurrection of Christ. According to the Gospel of Luke, the resurrected Jesus appeared to the disciples in *bodily* form (Luke 24:36–43). He showed them his physical wounds and even invited them to "handle" his flesh. Similarly, the Jesus of the Fourth Gospel commanded the doubting disciple, Thomas, to insert his fingers into his physical wounds: "Put your finger here, and see my hands; and put out your hand, and place it in my side" (John 20:24–28). Just as it is Jesus' physical body that is resurrected, so also it is the physical bodies of Christians that are "snatched up" at Christ's Parousia: Paul reassures the Thessalonian Christians that "we who are alive, who are left, shall be caught up (physically) … in the clouds to meet the Lord in the air" (1 Thess 4:17). Whatever one might make of these passages from an existential or even scientific perspective, it is clear that from a theological perspective, the human body has positive value: it is Christ's human "body" that is resurrected, and it is our human bodies that are saved, which helps to explain why Tertullian goes so far as to declare that anyone who denies the resurrection *of the flesh* is a heretic.[74] Putting aside the excesses of Tertullian's thought, it remains true, nonetheless, that any theory of biblical interpretation that overlooks, or demeans, the *physical* body of the interpreter must be inadequate. The interpreter is not a spirit or mind in a box. Biblical interpreters are fleshy bodies of meat, blood, bone, and sinew, which are always being subjected to and molded by real forces around and within them.

But like Heidegger's concept of "authenticity," the Deleuzian "body without organs" is more of a *desideratum* than an attainable state of being. Whereas each of us is unequivocally an "organism" (to one degree or another), which has been organized into a productive bio-social-political-technical assemblage, no one ever manages to fully become a body without organs. According to Antonin Artaud, the "body without organs" is actually *beyond the limit of real life*. A body lived with such pure intensity would be incapable of coping with the oppressive forces of everyday life.

For real people, the attainable goal is not that of becoming a BwO but rather is finding an *intermediate* way of living between these two poles, that of the BwO and that of the organism. Deleuze and Guattari term this intermediate state, the "schizo." The term "schizo" should *not* be confused with the psychiatric disorder

---

[73] Deleuze and Guattari, *A Thousand Plateaus*, 14.
[74] Earnest Evans (ed., trans.), *Tertullian's Treatise on the* Resurrection (London: SPCK, 1960), § 2; Earnest Evans (ed., trans.), *Tertullian on the Flesh of Christ* (London: SPCK, 1956), § 5.

"schizophrenia." Because both the BwO and pure organism are unlivable conditions (but for different reasons), the life of the "schizo" represents the ultimate
goal of achieving some kind of balanced embodied existence. Like other balanced
things on earth, including "plants and animals, orchids and wasps ... rocks and
even rivers," it is the "schizo" that always sings to "the glory of God."[75]

In his monograph *Francis Bacon: Logique de la sensation*, Deleuze states that
the contemporary painter Francis Bacon actually depicts the body of the "schizo"
in his paintings.[76] Francis Bacon's bodies do not have organs: they have meat and
bone, upon which operate the elementary forces of life, which stress, mold, and
deform them and generally dissipate their rhizomatic intensity and diminish
original difference. Though human bodies are unable to experience these forces
directly as physical sensations (owing to sensation's irreducibly *synthetic* character), human bodies *do* experience the "rhythms of sensation," arising from the
rising and falling intensity of these forces.[77]

The human "body" (including the embodied interpreter) can be theorized as a
sensitive, self-organizing system, with many different dimensions: physical, biological, chemical, emotional, social, economic, semiotic, cultural, existential, religious, ethical, and cognitive. On a day-to-day basis, this system passes through a
predictable repertoire of behaviors ("attractors") in response to various external
and internal forces.[78] Fluctuations in these forces trigger prepatterned, qualitative
changes in behavior ("bifurcation") to return the system to homeostasis.[79] In complexity theory, this phenomenon is termed *synchronic emergence*.[80]

According to Deleuze, the somatic body oscillates between two basic rhythms:
a rising rhythm and a falling rhythm. The "rising" rhythm is one of increasing

---

[75] Deleuze and Guattari, *A Thousand Plateaus*, 49; cf. 1; also cf. B. H. McLean, "Re-imagining New
Testament Interpretation in terms of Deleuzian Geophilosophy," *Neotestamentica: Journal of the
New Testament Society of South Africa* 42/1 (2008): 51–71.

[76] Gilles Deleuze, *Francis Bacon: Logique de la sensation* (Paris: Éditions de Seuil, 1981).

[77] "Thresholds" are the virtual limits of the degree that a system can change. Self-organizing systems
often oscillate between two thresholds. This normal range of behavior which is available to your
body is termed its "basin of attraction."

[78] The term "attractor" designates the long-term tendencies, shapes, or patterns of behavior in *real*
systems. There are various kinds of attractors including "point" attractors (stable or steady-state
systems), "loop" attractors (oscillating systems), and "strange/fractal" attractors (turbulent or chaotic systems). In terms of complexity theory, such normal fluctuation of a bodily system, between a
stereotyped set of repertoires, is termed "synchronic emergence." A "singularity" is the point where
the graph of the function changes direction as it reaches local minimum or maximum threshold.
This is a zone of sensitivity. A singularity is not an attractor but defines where attractors are found
by indicating the limits of basins of attraction. The layout of attractors in a phase state is defined by
the layout of singularities.

[79] The term "bifurcation" refers to a sudden qualitative change in a self-organizing system when the
parameter values of the system change.

[80] But fluctuations *beyond* tolerable thresholds can tax one's body's system beyond its recuperative
powers. This occurs when one's body lacks a behavior within its repertoire to cope with radically
altered parameters. This event can even lead a body toward its "death zone," where there are no fixed
patterns at all and only chaos reigns.

variation and amplitude. This rhythm is associated with productive desire, deterritorialization, and general resistance to those forces that would further transform it into an "organism." The corresponding "falling" rhythm is one of decreasing variation and amplitude. The falling rhythm is triggered by those forces that isolate and deform the body and dissipate its natural intensity. As noted earlier, though the body is incapable of experiencing these forces directly, it does experience the *sensation of the rhythm* of its rising and falling intensity or amplitude. According to Deleuze, this rhythm can be traced back to these forces by virtue of the fact that "for a sensation to exist, a force must be exerted on a body."[81]

In his paintings, Francis Bacon attempted to paint these two basic rhythms of sensation by employing the technique of isolation: he isolated his figures by painting them within the three *disconnected* panels of a triptych, by surrounding them with backgrounds of intense color, and by encircling them in ovals of color. His purpose in doing so was to *disrupt any possible narrative and to block representation*. In other words, this technique prevents Bacon's human figures from telling any story or representing any actual human beings.

This absence of narrative is most obvious in Bacon's famous triptychs, such as his four crucifixion triptychs.[82] In the case of his first crucifixion triptych, *Three Studies at the Base of a Crucifixion* (1944), Bacon painted an isolated body in each of the three triptych panels. By isolating these painted bodies, he eliminated the spectators needed to create a narrative relation between the panels. There is no narrative progression in the triptych panels from left to right, or from right to left, nor does the central panel have any kind of univocal role. Indeed, these panels are unable to tell any story because no one is present to witness what happens to Bacon's tortured figures. Only an "attendant" – who is not a spectator – is depicted in one panel. But since this "attendant" is not in a position to see anything, there is no witness to tell a story. The isolated figures in Bacon's paintings do not even represent actual people. Here, we are reminded of Kafka's use of cathexis to depict figures of desire. Similarly, Bacon's human figures are nonillustrative, as well as nonnarrative. One could even say that Bacon's aesthetic is really an "anti-aesthetic," which employs the technique of isolation to liberate his art from its traditional role of narration and representation.[83]

---

[81] Deleuze, *Francis Bacon*, 48.
[82] The four crucifixion triptychs are as follows: *Three Studies at the Base of a Crucifixion* (1944) (*Francis Bacon with Essays by Dawn Ades and Andrew Forge: The Tate Gallery* [London: Thames and Hudson, 1985], fig. 1); *Three Studies for a Crucifixion* (1962) (ibid., fig. 39); *Crucifixion* (1965), triptych (ibid., fig. 45); *The Second Version of "Triptych 1944"* (1988) (Luigi Ficacci, *Bacon 1909–1992* [Cologne: Taschen, 2003], 12–13, 18–19). Bacon also painted two crucifixion paintings: *Crucifixion* (1933) (Christophe Domino, *Francis Bacon: Painter of a Dark Vision* [New York: Harry Abrams, 1997], 23) and *Fragment of a Crucifixion* (1950).
[83] According to Artur Danto, in *The Abuse of Beauty: Aesthetics and the Concept of Art* (Chicago: Open Court, 2003), 19, Bacon's paintings belong to art after "end of art," which frees his crucifixion motif from the burden of its traditional cultural-religious significations to explore a fuller range of possibilities. This "anti-aesthetic" is comparable to that of Kafka and Proust.

Bacon terms the nonnarrative relation between the three panels simply "matters of fact."[84] Indeed, something "matter of fact" does happen to his painted figures, even though Bacon's paintings do not narrate a story or depict actual human beings.[85] By disrupting the possibility of narrative and representation, Bacon's paintings are thereby freed to reveal the invisible forces that act upon the body, especially as manifested by the two primary "rhythms of sensation," the rising and falling rhythms.[86] In one of the triptych panels, a figure is depicted in its *rising* rhythm, and in another panel a figure is displayed in its *falling* rhythm. These two figures *resonate* together.

Bacon particularly pitied the figure in its falling rhythm because it is the outer threshold of the falling rhythm – with all of its immobile waiting, spasms, and screams – that manifests the body's "convulsive pain and vulnerability."[87] Deleuze was also fascinated by this falling rhythm, particularly its motionless effort, which he likened to the main character, K, in Kafka's novel *The Trial*. K's search for justice entailed his prolonged walking from room to room, ad infinitum, in a search for that which cannot be found – justice.[88] Such prolonged walking, like the prolonged waiting of Bacon's figures, captures a kind of *immobility that saps human desire and intensity.* Bacon's paintings also depict the intense effort expended by the body in its immobile waiting, as so much meat and bone, convulsing in its vulnerability and pain.

In the case of his famous painting of the scream of Pope Innocent X (fig. 12.4), we again witness the intense effort of immobile waiting that triggers an internal spasm, expressed by the pope's scream.[89] Bacon manages to avoid all narrative elements in this painting by having the pope scream unseen, from behind a curtain. Being hidden from all possible witnesses, the only function of this painted figure "is to render visible" by a scream the "invisible forces" acting upon the body.[90] We, as viewers of this screaming figure, are moved with pity for the suffering body as so much meat and bone.[91]

DIACHRONIC EMERGENCE

Deleuze also took special interest in the *outer threshold* of the falling rhythm because it is at *this* point that the invisible forces put the body's homeostasis *at risk*

---

[84]   Deleuze, *Francis Bacon*, 7, 151, 154.
[85]   Ibid., 13.
[86]   Deleuze, *Francis Bacon*, 13.
[87]   Ibid., 21.
[88]   "To enter or leave the machine, to be in the machine, to walk around it, to approach it – these are all still components of the machine itself: these are states of desire, free of all interpretation." Deleuze and Guattari, *Kafka: Toward a Minor Literature*, 11.
[89]   Entitled *Study after Velázquez's Portrait of Pope Innocent X* (1953); cf. Deleuze, *Francis Bacon*, 15, 16, 52.
[90]   Deleuze, *Francis Bacon*, 51.
[91]   Forms of transversal emergence are a special interest of Deleuze and Guattari, *Anti-Oedipus* and *A Thousand Plateaus.*

12.4. Francis Bacon, *Study after Velázquez's Portrait of Pope Innocent X* (1953), Des Moines Art Center, Des Moines, Iowa (Bridgeman-Giraudon / Art Resource, NY)

and threaten to plunge it into its "death zone." But this outer threshold also harbors within it the potential for recovery through the emergence of an unexpected or novel rhythm, outside of the body's normal repertoire of behaviors. According to complexity theory, "diachronic emergence" occurs when the fluctuations in the external and internal forces that act upon the body, exceed its tolerable thresholds.

Sometimes, instead of continuing with one of its normal, synchronic repertoires of behavior, the body unexpectedly improvises a novel behavior that has never been part of its previous set of repertoires. In other words, the horizon of emergence for this novel behavior is one of pure, originary "difference." Somehow, the "body" (and there are many different types of "bodies"), as a complex, self-organizing system, manages to restructure its virtual realm so as to make a novel, unanticipated behavior possible. This restructuring is termed "diachronic emergence." From this perspective, the isolated and tortured bodies depicted in Francis Bacon's triptychs implicitly *point beyond their present condition* to the future possibility of their escape from their immobile waiting, spasms, and screams.

Diachronic emergence manifests not only a "body's" capacity (as a complex system) to adapt but also a "body without organs," to live a life of *originary* difference. Such difference is not a difference with respect to sameness. Whereas traditional Western philosophy subordinates the concept of "difference" to the concept of the "same" (i.e., difference is attributed to things that are deemed to be fundamentally the same), Deleuze's concept of originary "difference" cannot be measured in terms of degrees of variation from sameness. As he argues in his book *Difference and Repetition* (1968), this emergence of change posits pure difference as its horizon for transformation.[92]

Thus, Deleuze did not simply invert the "same versus different" binarism in favor of difference. Rather, he installed the concept of originary difference in its radical *singularity*, independent of the concept of the "same." The "body without organs" is a body characterized by originary difference, as is manifested by its capacity for diachronic emergence. As such, the BwO is not a flawed copy of a Platonic ideal but rather an originary manifestation of difference.[93] Such an expression of difference can be said to be "spiritual" in nature in the sense that it manifests the creative, immanent force of life itself within the body, which is the basis for Deleuze's "spirituality of the body." By virtue of this "spirit *of* the body," the human "organism" always retains its capacity to behave like a "body without organs," even after it has been "territorialized" by capitalism and patriarchy into productive bio-social-political-technical assemblages.

THE FORMATION OF LARGER BODIES: TRANSVERSAL EMERGENCE

The human body is only one kind of "body" among many, which exist on many different levels. Indeed, in Deleuzian philosophy, the term "body" can designate many different types of complex systems. When considered at different levels of

---

[92] Deleuze, *Difference and Repetition*, 28–30.
[93] Ibid., 41, cf. 299. Thus, Deleuze reinterprets simulacra as "those systems in which different relates to different by means of difference itself. What is essential is that we find in these systems no prior identity, no internal resemblance."

magnification, a single cell, a bodily organ, a university, a religious denomination, a city, a tribe, an ecosystem, or even a language or moral code can each be considered to be "a body." All such "bodies" are formed through a process termed "homeostratic transversal emergence."

Homeostratic transversal emergence occurs when larger "bodies" are formed by the combination of smaller bodies *of the same type or stratum*. For instance, that which one would consider to be a "body" from one perspective, such as a single cell, an individual human being, a tree, a word, or a text, can, from a higher or more general perspective, be conceived of as only one component in a larger "body," such as a bodily organ (in the case of a cell), a community (in the case of an individual), a forest (in the case of a tree), a text (in the case of a word), and an oeuvre or genre (in the case of a text). Single cells, human beings, trees, words, and texts, as well as many other entities, unite with themselves through homeostratic transversal emergence to form larger "bodies." Similarly, human bodies combine to form larger bodies such as families, churches, towns, universities, nations, and even sports teams.

In contrast to homeostratic transversal emergence, *heterostratic* transversal emergence refers to the formation of larger "bodies" through the combination of *dissimilar entities*. Bodies of different types also combine transversally to form larger complex "bodies." Heterostratic transversal emergence is particularly relevant to biblical interpretation because textual "sense" is neither a property of an isolated text (as a semantic container) nor a product of an isolated interpreter (as a meaning maker), but rather is always an event arising out of *heterostratic* transversal emergence.

When viewed from the perspective of Deleuze's global ontology, the text-reception complex belongs to a larger assemblage, in which different types of bodies – textual, somatic, social, semiotic, cultural, religious, and so forth – combine transversally to form the larger bodies in which the present sense-event occurs. Within this larger body, smaller bodies of different types, in multiple registers, exchange flows.[94] Thus,

---

[94] By way of a simple example, consider the reproductive process of a potato plant, as a "body," that participates in a transversal emergence with dissimilar entities to form more complex assemblages or "bodies." The flowers of a potato plant are cross-pollinated "transversally"; the flowers produced by these hybrid plants are cross-pollinated, transversally, by the pollen produced by the other forty or more varieties of potatoes growing in the same region and transported by the agents of wind and flying insects. (Thus, a potato plant's method of propagation does not display a purity of origins but rather a radical hybridity.) A potato "body" is also joined "transversally" to the sun, through flows of warmth from the sun, and to the soil, through flows of nutrients. There are also nonmaterial intensive flows between potato "bodies" and types of bodies, such as farming equipment "bodies," farming-family "bodies," the somatic "bodies" of seasonal workers, produce regulatory bodies (provincial licensing systems), and commercial bodies such as inspecting agencies, storage facilities, trucking companies, and the food service industry. In terms of semantic "bodies," potatoes "transversally" connect to "bodies" of agricultural and scientific journals, farm-reporting newspapers, and even "bodies" of maritime literature, which include potato farming in its narratives. Thus, the humble potato participates in heterostratic transversal emergence to form many complex systems.

the present sense-event, which we might anthropocentrically theorize at the level of the intentional author, or volitional interpreter, can also be theorized at the level of a much larger assemblage, within which they are both situated.

CONCLUSION

How might one briefly summarize rhizomatic hermeneutics? First of all, rhizomatic hermeneutics begins with the recognition that the founding sense-event of a biblical text is always aided, encoded, and multiplied by the circular movement of the three components of language – namely, signification, denotation, and manifestation – and the fourth dimension of sense. But the depth dimension of a text's founding sense-event is only a record of a one-time variation in a structure, which stretches through time as a "series." For this reason, a text's depth dimension is of lesser importance than its surface dimension because the surface is where the sense-event is replayed and counteractualized in a "series" over time. Once the biblical interpreter has entered this circle of language through the text-reception complex, signification loses its primacy because the three components are not hierarchically arranged. For a present sense-event to occur, the post-historical interpreter must contemplate all three components and especially their *interdependence*.

Second (as strange as it may seem to say), the ideal body of the biblical interpreter is that of the "schizo," which is to say part "body without organs" – flooded with productive desire – and part "organism," sufficiently territorialized to cope with the demands of the Real, as constructed by the axes of power and domination of capitalism and patriarchy, and capitalism's chief values, "useful work" and "consumption." The "schizo-interpreter" neither receives the "founding" biblical "sense event," as a piece of semantic code, frozen and passed on through time, nor creates a new "sense-event" ex nihilo. The embodied "schizo-interpreter" and text find themselves combined with similar bodies (homeostratically) and with *dissimilar* bodies (heterostratically) in the formation of larger assemblages. In the case of heterostratic transversal emergence, the interpreter and text – as two dissimilar "bodies" – are transversally linked, both to each other as "orchid and wasp" and to other kinds of "bodies," to form an expanded rhizomatic network. The resulting present sense-event is constituted by a novel selection, at a given place and time, of new relations of intensity across the surface of the entire rhizomatic network. While such selections are often predictable and stereotypical, arising as they do from synchronic emergence, the heterostratic system is not deterministic: owing to an unpredictable event, termed *diachronic emergence*, new present sense-events can occur, which open up unexplored possibilities of meaning and living.

In the case of both the synchronic and the diachronic emergences of sense-events, textual meaning always accrues from the intense *surface* relations across the rhizomatic network. Thus, a basic principle of rhizomatic hermeneutics is that biblical texts function "only through the outside and on the outside."[95] Therefore, we, as "nomadic" interpreters, need not ask what a biblical text means (as if it were a semantic container), or look for a historical author or historical content by which to restrict its meaning (as if it were a mere residue of vanished authorial presence). Rather the nomadic interpreter, abounding in productive desire, seeks out all that the text functions with, and all that it transmits its own intensities to. Such a hermeneutic strategy transforms textual interpretation from an archaeological dig into an exploration of how both the text and interpreter actually function within a unified, pulsating world ontology.

---

[95] Deleuze and Guattari, *A Thousand Plateaus*, 4.

Conclusion: Post-historical Interpretation

❧

Despite their canonical status as "scripture," the sixty-six books that compose the Bible are, in many respects, profoundly human documents – a fact that has been elaborated upon time and again over the past four centuries with the advance of historical methods of interpretation. Thanks to historical analysis, our knowledge of the original sociohistorical contexts of the Jewish and Christian scriptures is unsurpassed compared to that of previous generations. Without doubt, this historical perspective has made an irreplaceable contribution to our understanding of the original sense of biblical texts. Given its remarkable contribution to the discipline, it is not surprising that the historically guided analysis, as well as epistemology of Enlightenment that sustains it, has come to dominate the discipline of biblical studies in our own era.

The most striking indicator of this dominance is the renaming of the discipline of New Testament Studies as "Christian origins" in universities across North America over the past twenty years. This simple substitution of "Christian origins" for "New Testament studies" signals the profound transformation of the discipline from one that was traditionally concerned with the New Testament's theological meaning into a present-day quest for Christianity's lost historical beginnings and a mapping out of its subsequent developments over time. The disciplinary field now known as "Christian origins" has become a subset of the West's long-standing antiquarian interest in ancient cultures and civilizations. This present state of affairs may seem relatively harmless, but is this where the discipline had promised to take us?

If one were to take one step backward and survey the legacy of post-Enlightenment rationality from a global perspective, I would suggest that we can see little evidence of the benefits that were intended to accompany the application of Enlightenment rationality, with the notable exception of the fields of science, medicine, and technology. (But since even the notable accomplishments in these fields have generally been reserved for the rich and the people of the north, those living on the margins may remain somewhat skeptical about these "advances.") Indeed, even as long as fifty years ago, Max Horkheimer and Theodor Adorno warned that the Enlightenment program, which had promised *liberation* to humanity, was itself another *myth*: far from liberating humanity, the unchecked use of rationality has actually functioned to mold human beings into "human resources" for the rape of the environment and the exploitation of the two-thirds world in the pursuit of profit and power.

In the 1970s, Jean-François Lyotard famously defined the term "postmodern" as an "incredulity" of the "metanarrative" that has legitimated this Enlightenment paradigm of the progress of knowledge. The Enlightenment has traditionally been viewed as the era when human rationality overthrew religious myth and superstition and liberated Western civilization from ignorance, installing humanity as master of its own destiny. Implicitly, if not explicitly, this metanarrative continues to dominate much of Western culture, including the academic discipline of biblical studies. But with the benefit of hindsight, it is now obvious that the forms of knowledge produced by Enlightenment empiricism have often functioned in tandem with strategies of power and oppression in a mutually generative manner. In fact, it could be argued that much of what is deemed to be "knowledge" derives its coherence not from its transcendental foundation in some kind of universal Truth but rather from the concrete strategies of power it has made possible.

Given the fact that historicism was itself a child of the Enlightenment paradigm, it is not surprising that both historicism and its heir, historical positivism, have failed to produce many of their promised benefits. Not only has the application of historicism in the discipline of biblical studies failed to provide a secure historical and reasoned foundation for Christian faith (as was originally hoped) but, by drawing attention to the rootedness of the biblical texts in their respective sociohistorical contexts, historicism and historical positivism have inadvertently severed the connection between biblical texts and ourselves in the present. With the realization that the intended recipients of biblical texts were *contemporaneous* with their historical authors, and that these people shared mythical beliefs, ancient worldviews, and cultural assumptions that are strikingly different from our own, it could no longer be maintained – at least from a historical perspective – that biblical texts are in any way addressed to the modern reader or contemporary church. This post-Enlightenment understanding of biblical texts helps to explain why Albert Schweitzer concluded his famous *Quest of the Historical Jesus* in 1906 by stating that through the application of a "historical treatment ... the historical Jesus will be to our time *a stranger and an enigma*."[1]

Indeed, if biblical studies has succeeded in anything, it has succeeded in *defamiliarizing* present-day readers of scripture with the biblical text. The scripture they thought they knew so well now seems strange and enigmatic. There can be no doubt that such a "defamiliarization" was needed. But the legacy of historicism has not all been positive. One of the results of the "critical distancing of the (biblical) text in the historical approach," as Edgar McKnight observes, has been the

---

[1] Albert Schweitzer, *Quest of the Historical Jesus: A Critical Study of Its Progress from Reimarus to Wrede*, trans. W. Montgomery et al. (Minneapolis: Fortress, 2001 [1906]), 478 (emphasis added).

transformation of "biblical writings into museum pieces without contemporary relevance."[2]

Though traditional biblical scholars continue to argue that the intent of the original historical authors of scripture constitutes the "true" meaning of biblical texts, their use of the adjective "true" generally does not imply "truth," as understood within a correspondence theory of truth. Indeed, the majority of such interpreters would freely acknowledge that this "true" meaning may actually be *false* in historical, geographic, medical, botanical, scientific, or astronomical terms.

In this book, I have argued that historicism's discovery of the historical and cultural *contingency* of all biblical beliefs, values, and ethics has brought about a crisis of nihilism from which the discipline has yet to recover. As Thomas Reynolds explains, when "all human events, traditions, and texts are historical, subject to the limiting conditions of time and space … there is no fixed and final center of truth that lies outside the contingency and flux of historical life. Everything human is caught up in process."[3] As a result, we who stand at the beginning of a new century have the dubious privilege of seeing Nietzsche's prediction fulfilled: as he predicted, when early Christianity is analyzed into "completely historical" knowledge, and is "resolved … into pure knowledge," it "ceases to live" and is thereby "annihilated" by the historicizing process itself.[4]

In point of fact, historicism ceased to "serve life" more than a century ago, a fact that is made abundantly clear from the title of Ernst Troeltsch's famous essay "The Crisis of Historicism" (1922).[5] Troeltsch, a one-time defender of historicism, argued that the relativism of historicism actually "shakes all eternal truths."[6] Over the decades, following Troeltsch's warning, many scholars have come to feel this crisis of nihilism most acutely. In a very real way, we still live in this time of crisis. Whether individual biblical scholars in their professional lives are capable of experiencing this crisis is beside the point: it is this very crisis of historical meaning that constitutes *the* dominant theme of postmodernity. Biblical studies' unwitting surrender to nihilism constitutes just one more witness to its pervasiveness in society at large.

I have argued in Chapter 3 that historicism is not just a historical method of analysis. It is also a form of metaphysical thinking that is based on this subject-object epistemological model of the Enlightenment. As such, the crisis of nihilism

2   Edgar McKnight, *Postmodern Uses of the Bible: The Emergence of Reader-Oriented Criticism* (Nashville: Abingdon Press, 1988), 14.
3   Thomas E. Reynolds, *The Broken Whole: Philosophical Steps toward a Theology of Global Solidarity* (Albany: State University of New York Press, 2006), 19.
4   Friedrich Nietzsche, *On the Advantage and Disadvantage of History for Life,* trans. Peter Preuss (Indianapolis: Hackett, 1980 [1874]), 39, 40 (§ 7).
5   Ernst Troeltsch, "Die Krisis des Historismus," *Die neue Rundschau* 33 (1922): 572–90; cf. Ernst Troeltsch, *Der Historismus und seine Probleme, Gesammelte Schriften* 3 (Aalen: J. C. B. Mohr [Paul Siebeck), 1961 [1922]).
6   Troeltsch, "Die Krisis des Historismus," 573.

is rooted in a still deeper crisis: a crisis of the rational, sovereign subject. In fact, the metaphysics of the sovereign subject *is* nihilism proper. By establishing human rationality as the final arbiter for what counts as knowledge, the subject-object model of the post-Enlightenment era has made all knowledge (including knowledge of biblical texts) dependent upon the perspective of the knowing subject. As Gianni Vattimo observes, this model of knowledge "places humanity in the centre of the universe and makes it the master of Being."[7] But because this model makes *all knowledge a form of human interpretation*, which is dependent on, and limited by, the perspective of the historical subject, it can never establish a permanent foundation for truth outside of the inquiring subject's own historicality. For this reason, the historical reconstruction of the life of the historical Jesus and early Christianities actually *dissolves* the very meaning of objective truth and makes all historical knowledge of early Christianity dependent upon the perspectives of the very scholars who create such knowledge. Whether we realize it or not, it is this death of the sovereign subject that makes us postmodern people. According to Gianni Vattimo, *the actual meaning of our own age is the death of the sovereign subject.*[8] The continued avoidance of this crisis of subjecthood can only deepen it further. But, in positive terms, this same crisis has also brought us to a *point of decision* about "the use and abuse of history," to borrow a phrase from Nietzsche.

This book has laid down some principles that are intended to help the biblical interpreters recover from this crisis by providing a framework that would allow them to think outside the subject-object epistemological model. We began this undertaking in Chapter 5, with a consideration of Heidegger's existential phenomenology, which demonstrated that the metaphysics of the sovereign subject is false. Because human consciousness is not a passive registration of things in the world (including biblical texts), and since understanding is always mediated by one's phenomenological horizon, interpreters can never stand apart from the phenomenon they are interpreting. Every meaningful statement about biblical texts must be grounded in something unthought and unthinkable, an unconscious horizon, or "fore-structure," that resists representation. In Heidegger's terminology, the biblical interpreter is "Da-sein," a phenomenological space or "clearing" of understanding, care, and temporality. Perhaps Heidegger's greatest contribution to hermeneutics lies in his recognition that we can grasp the meaning of a biblical text only by appropriating it from within our own historical lives. Our understanding of biblical texts is *always* mediated by our horizons of meaning, which include our own *relation* to the texts being interpreted. I have termed this relation the "text-reception complex."

---

7 Gianni Vattimo, *The End of Modernity*, trans. Jon R. Snyder (Baltimore: Johns Hopkins University Press, 1991 [1985]), 32.
8 Ibid., 145–63.

Because the biblical interpreter can never be a "subject," the Bible can never function as an "object" of scientific inquiry. In other words, *the concept of objective biblical meaning is another myth*, along with the myth of the sovereign subject. Over the past two centuries, historicism and historical positivism have perpetuated these two myths. In so doing, they have kept alive a form of thought that alienates us both from our own authenticity and from the past.

Our renunciation of these two myths can function as a point of departure for a renewed, *post-historical* mode of hermeneutics. The concept of a *post-historical* mode of hermeneutics in no way implies a rejection of historical inquiry. Historical analysis continues to serve a vital role within the overall practice of biblical interpretation: its genius has always been its ability to disclose the disconcerting uniqueness of historically situated biblical texts and persons. Historical analysis has a necessary role in subverting all strategic appeals to "objective" truth and all attempts to ground Christian ethics, faith, and theology upon bare historical facts. By shedding light on the historical particularity of the historical Jesus and Paul and early Christian communities, historical analysis still has the potential to contribute to strategies of resisting totalizing theological discourses (past and present) and the various forms of intolerance, misunderstanding, and oppression that they can produce.

However, such historically based strategies of resistance always fall short of addressing the crisis of nihilism, owing to the limitations inherent in historicism's own epistemology of the autonomous subject, as well as the limitations of human language, owing to the principle of linguistic relativity. With the rediscovery of Saussure's semiotic theory in the late 1950s and 1960s, and the ensuing "linguistic turn" of Western philosophy, came the recognition that language is more than a tool of human communication: it also codifies reality and structures what is thinkable. The principle of linguistic relativity, the Sapir-Whorf hypothesis, states that the structures of language influence the ways in which humans linguistically conceptualize the world. Our recognition of the effect of linguistic relativity empties the interpretive space of biblical studies of such traditional concepts as the grand narrative of disciplinary progress and the concept of noncontextual truth.

Those who truly desire to recover from nihilism, must first reject two of the primary concepts of the Enlightenment, their acceptance of themselves as autonomous subjects, and their tacit acceptance of language as a transparent tool for the communication of knowledge. (One can escape from nihilism only by rejecting the primary concepts of the Enlightenment, which constituted nihilism's root cause.) The rejection of these two concepts opens up an opportunity to explore our own historically effected consciousness.

In the view of Hans-Georg Gadamer, this discovery of our own "historically effected consciousness" is "very likely the most important *revolution* among those we have undergone since the beginning of the modern epoch," whose "*spiritual* magnitude probably surpasses what we recognize in the application of natural science."[9] Similarly, Julia Kristeva considers the "decentering of the speaking subject" to be a fundamental "theoretical *breakthrough*" that must never be lost sight of.[10] This recovery of our own "historically effected consciousness" is important because the very factors that preclude our objective knowledge of the Bible also supply the necessary conditions for an existential understanding of its meaning in the present.[11] The experience of the contingent nature of our own perceptual world can lead to a liberating form of consciousness that recognizes that interpretation can never be solely oriented toward recovering past meanings, because authentic biblical interpretation is always informed by one's own spirituality.

According to Michel Foucault, one of the primary truths of this "spirituality" is that the truth about ourselves "is only given ... at a price that brings the subject's being into play.... It follows that from this point of view there can be no truth without a conversion or a transformation of the subject."[12] In contrast to the antiquarian impulse to discover historical facts, the sighting of a present sense-event is always connected with one's spirituality in the sense that it always concerns self-discovery, the care of the self, personal transformation, the care of others, and one's meaningful engagement with the world. Thus, in Gadamer's view, the primary goal of hermeneutics is not the mere elucidation of the textual "said" but rather the discernment of "practical knowledge" (*phronesis*), or the textual "saying," for those who live in the present. This spiritual orientation transforms biblical interpretation from a procedure guided by a set of authorized methodologies into an open-ended quest that entails risk, personal transformation, and the quest for liberation and justice. By implication, in the very act of interpreting a biblical text, the lives of interpreters, and the communities to which they are connected, are at stake.[13]

Given the nature of the spirituality that informs post-historical interpretation, what then is the appropriate epistemological structure for a renewed practice of biblical interpretation? If historical positivism is defined as an epistemological structure that is based on the metaphysics of the sovereign subject, then *it can also be defined in terms of what escapes its own epistemological structure.* It is because the discursive conditions of traditional biblical studies have no primordial unity,

---

[9] Hans-Georg Gadamer, "The Problem of Historical Consciousness," in *Interpretive Social Science: A Reader,* ed. Paul Rabinow and William A. Sullivan (Berkeley: University of California Press, 1979), 109 (emphasis added).

[10] Julia Kristeva, "Psychoanalysis and the Polis," in *Transforming the Hermeneutic Context,* ed. Gayle L. Ormiston and Alan D. Schrift (Albany: State University of New York Press, 1990), 89–105, esp. 89 (emphasis added).

[11] Bultmann states that "Historicism has also the merit itself of showing the way in which it is to be overcome"; R. Bultmann, *History and Eschatology: The Presence of Eternity; The Gifford Lectures, 1955* (New York: Harper & Brothers, 1957), 143.

[12] Michel Foucault, *The Hermeneutics of the Subject: Lectures at the Collège de France, 1981–1982,* ed. F. Gross, trans. Graham Bruchell (New York: Palgrave Macmillan, 2005), 15.

[13] Foucault, *Hermeneutics of the Subject,* xxiv.

or fixity, that its procedures can be reappropriated to achieve new ends. On this basis, we can ask, What lies beyond the reach of its epistemological structure? *For, if biblical texts mean only what they are capable of meaning within the epistemological structure of historical positivism, then it is also true that new meaning, which lies beyond the epistemological structure of historical positivism, can be found by altering the conditions for the creation of knowledge.* This insight is the starting point for all forms of post-historical hermeneutical inquiry.

At the outset of all post-historical interpretation, the interpreter must respect the traditional requirement to engage in an open-ended dialogue with the biblical text. We cannot simply leap into past meanings. Interpretation always requires a true dialogue, which will always move beyond the founding sense-event of a text to a fresh experience of the text from within one's own present possibilities. In this dialogue, interpreters always stand within a living tradition, whose effective history is woven into their own historically effected consciousnesses. This *effective history* guides the questions we ask of the text and what we find to be meaningful.

By implication, the present sense-event of the Bible is not a fixed semantic content, frozen in time and silently awaiting rediscovery. Rather, it is a sense-event that changes over time according to how it is read within different traditions, by different interpreting communities, and in different sociohistorical contexts. In this dialogue, biblical texts, the effective history of the interpretive tradition, and our own socially shared horizons of meaning recombine into new wisdom for the present.

Because the interpretive tradition has a role to play in our own acts of interpretation, we must also be on guard against any ideological prejudices that may be inscribed within it or within the interpretive traditions that arise from it. Owing to the hidden nature of ideology, even the well-intended biblical scholars can become complicit in reawakening ideological forces in texts and the interpretive tradition. Such forces can then reassert themselves in the very act of interpretation. Worse still, not-so-well-intended interpreters may even appeal to the "tradition" of interpretation to rationalize the status quo and legitimate one group's self-interest and advantage over another. As such, whether inadvertently or intentionally, the process of "interpretation as dialogue" is fraught with the possibility of reenabling oppressive forces within texts and the interpretive tradition to reassert themselves in the present situation.

Recognizing this danger, Jürgen Habermas has argued that his good friend Gadamer had not adequately provided a means whereby the truth claims of texts and the interpretive tradition can be tested for their ideological content. To address this deficiency, he reintroduced the Enlightenment's emancipatory theme of *reasoned critique*, arguing that the "power of reflection" must always include the possibility of critiquing the authority of tradition. But in order to avoid the Enlightenment's metaphysics of the sovereign subject, Habermas *resituated the practice of reason within communities*, thereby transforming it into a *shared communicative practice.*

Habermas's three validity claims of "universal pragmatics" – the evaluative, expressive, and normative criteria – can be employed (at least experimentally) to establish or refute the implied validity ("truth") claims of any given biblical interpretation: those who interpret a text in a particular way must be able to demonstrate to their respective communities the reasonableness of their interpretation, their own trustworthiness, and the contextual justification for the appropriateness of their interpretation. In this way, as Gianni Vattimo states, *the "truth" is always rooted in "social sharing."*[14] The ultimate goal of such "social sharing" is not self-understanding but morally guided, collective, transformational action in society. As such, Habermas's theory of universal pragmatics gives to *communities* the means to resist ideologies that are presented in the guise of hallowed tradition, which, if left unopposed, would obstruct the creation of a more just, tolerant, and ecologically responsible society.

The opposing theories of Gadamer's hermeneutics of restoration and Habermas's collective rationality do not require us to choose between them. Paul Ricoeur has argued that there is no need to make a choice.[15] In fact, he is suspicious of any hermeneutical practice that relies exclusively on one or the other, arguing that the alleged dichotomy between them is actually false. Ricoeur's intervention in this debate opened up a productive space of interaction between these two approaches by observing that reasoned critique also comes out of an interpretive tradition – namely, the tradition of the Enlightenment. As such, even Habermas's reclamation of the role of reason itself represents *an interpretive tradition,* and it can therefore be situated within Gadamer's own hermeneutic model, which requires ongoing dialogue with the interpretive tradition. Ricoeur's intervention in this classical debate reminds us of the necessity of balancing dialogue with the interpretive tradition with a corresponding critique of any ideological tendencies within it.[16]

Emmanuel Levinas, for his part, revealed what was overlooked by Gadamer and Ricoeur: namely our *preontological relation to the other.* In his view, the starting point of all biblical interpretation is neither the biblical text, nor the tradition of interpretation, nor even one's historically effected consciousness, but rather the "gaze of the other." When we look into the face of the other, we do not see merely one person among many: we see a unique person, whose speechless face entreats us to justice. In this gaze, we experience the implicit call of the alterity of another human being, who is different from us, who lives in the world differently and sees the world differently.[17] This gaze summons the biblical interpreter to an ethical

---

[14] Gianni Vattimo, *A Farewell to Truth,* trans. William McCuaig (New York: Columbia University Press, 2011 [2009]), xxxiv.

[15] Paul Ricoeur, "Ethics and Culture: Habermas and Gadamer in Dialogue," *Philosophy Today* 17 (1973): 153–65.

[16] Paul Ricoeur, *Hermeneutics and the Human Sciences: Essays on Language, Action and Interpretation,* trans. John B. Thompson (Cambridge: Cambridge University Press, 1981), 63.

[17] Emmanuel Levinas, *Totality and Infinity: An Essay on Exteriority,* trans. Alphonso Lingis (Pittsburgh, PA: Duquesne University Press, 1969 [1961]), 52; Emmanuel Levinas, *In the Time of Nations,* trans. Michael B. Smith (London: Continuum, 2007 [1988]), 112.

responsibility, which cannot be evaded by appealing to the original intent of a biblical author, or to the original historical context of a text, or even to Heidegger's phenomenological circle or Gadamer's interpretive tradition. Ethical responsibility cannot be evaded by any such appeal because alterity is "otherwise than being." It signifies an ethical demand that is beyond the reach of history, human understanding, and reason. It is this preontological relation that constitutes the *primary precondition* for all biblical interpretation.

The importance of Levinas's insight can hardly be overemphasized. Previous attempts to address the crisis of nihilism by means of a pragmatic turn toward ethics failed because this ethical turn was merely pragmatic: *if the logic of nihilism is one of overcoming past knowledge through an act of human will, then any attempt to willfully overcome nihilism by pragmatically turning to ethics can only extend nihilism further.* In contrast, by grounding ethics in the alterity of the other – apart from the metaphysics of the sovereign, rational subject – and indeed, apart from "being," Levinas succeeded in answering the challenge of nihilism. *No act of will is required by human beings because ethics is "otherwise than being."* Levinas has not only restored to biblical studies an ethical voice. He has also established the ethics of the other as the final arbiter of the truth of any biblical interpretation. *Any interpretation of scripture that fails to respect the alterity of the "other" should be rejected.*

As we have seen, Levinas works out his ethics through a hermeneutics of "solicitation" and "elevation," by which biblical values and morals are continually elevated in order that they may come to mean all that they can mean. Despite the fact that biblical values and morals *were* historically relative and did change over time (even during what might be called the "biblical" period), the contemporary interpreter should never allow them to fall in value. Levinas enunciates this principle, noting that "the principle of their change is one of elevation, within changing contexts and challenges. The principle of the permanence of values in succession is *their elevation*."[18] By implication, the permanence of the "holiness" of biblical values is a property of the *continuity* of their elevation within the interpretive tradition itself, before the face of the other. It is this continuity of elevation that sustains their permanence of holiness and their revelatory power.

With this ontological foundation of ethics in place, bracketed by Gadamer's hope and Habermas's reasoned critique, and informed by an appreciation of linguistic relativity, our exploration of a post-historical mode of interpretation was at last freed to explore a fully *embodied* expression of hermeneutics, as expounded by Gilles Deleuze and Félix Guattari. With full appreciation of one's decentered subjectivity and of the relativity of language, one does not automatically find oneself in a higher, methodological realm, beyond the discursive field of traditional

---

[18]   Emmanuel Levinas, *Beyond the Verse: Talmudic Readings and Lectures*, trans. Gary D. Mole (London: Continuum, 2007 [1982]), 19.

biblical studies. However, a Deleuzian "higher empiricism" can reposition biblical interpreters in an expanded interpretive field. From the vantage point of this
"higher empiricism," we can perceive that a biblical text has two different dimensions, a *depth* dimension as a "signifying totality" and a *surface* dimension as
"asignifying particles." Traditional strategies of interpretation, which have always
focused on textual *depth*, have overlooked a text's potential to form new "surface"
relations within a wider ecology of meaning. By virtue of their *surface* dimension,
biblical texts always retain this virtual capacity to "reterritorialize" themselves and
thereby release their reserves of potential happenings. A biblical text *is* a little literary "machine" that couples with other "machines" – people, languages, faiths, histories, cultures, literatures, and societies – thereby becoming part of an extended
rhizomatic system through the flows of intensities between them. A present sense-
event is one that awakens a text's *latent reserve of "sense" through an enlargement
of its fields of reference.* Therefore, owing to this redundancy of a text's outsides,
biblical interpretation does not involve asking the tired question, What did this
text mean? Rather, it asks, With what does this text function, and into what other
"bodies" are this text's own intensities inserted? From this perspective, each interaction between a biblical text and an interpreter becomes a kind of replaying or
counteractualizing of the text's founding sense-event. The interpreter, like a desirous "wasp," facilitates energetic connections between texts and the rhizomatic
world beyond them, thereby liberating their *latent reserve* of "sayings."

 The rhizomatic space of biblical interpretation changes our role, as interpreters,
from that of creating knowledge to "associating" things together. Such "associating" can perform a vital hermeneutic role because this is the very means by which
biblical interpreters both discover and enact the potentialities inherent in biblical
texts. In other words, the realization that our thought has been shaped by the very
language we employ to create thought has the positive effect of transforming us
into *active agents*, who are empowered to enact associations between things. For
the interpreter-as-wasp, what matters most is not the consumption of the text's
original "sense" but the possibility of journeying over the erotic surface of the rhizome in widely different registers – religious, social, ethical, sexual, economic, and
material – to enact a present sense-event. This present sense-event both reveals
and creates ways in which a biblical text is meaningfully situated within the wider
ecology of life.

 These many principles of post-historical interpretation, as summarized earlier,
share one thing in common: they all conceive of hermeneutics as a practice that is
accountable to others, within an expanded ecology of life. In this expanded hermeneutic ecology, post-historical interpreters will continue to ask historically guided
questions, as well as other kinds of questions, but the answers to these questions
will not lead them down the pathway of nihilism and self-alienation because their
inquiry remains grounded in an ethics of alterity rather than in a metaphysics of
subjecthood.

Such post-historical interpreters remain "pious" in the sense that they value the Christian interpretive tradition, with which they are always recollectively and hopefully engaged. But, at the same time, they are also critically reflective about its reappropriation in the present moment. As pious *and* critical, the interpreter meditates on how the possibilities for existence that are offered up by biblical texts can be replayed or counteractualized in the present, before the gaze of the other. Indeed, in all these ways, historically, ethically, piously, recollectively, critically – and especially, desirously – the vocation of the post-historical interpreter is always to embody the present sense-event as revelation in our ever shortening "now time."

But how could *we*, through our own acts of biblical interpretation, possibly embody biblical revelation in *our* now time? Surely we are too timid and too rooted in the mundanity of our academic guilds to do so. After all, *we* still speak of the sun "rising" and "setting," when we *know for certain* that it is the earth that moves around the sun. And we quaintly seek out the historical truth of the Bible, when we know – on an existential level – that the sovereign subject who discovers such historical truth is a myth, which we ourselves have created. The first step toward embodying such revelation must be to abandon our youthful attachments to such myths, and our nostalgia to turn back the clock on the discipline of biblical studies, and then to dare to embrace the nomadic thought of a post-historical mode of interpretation.

Perhaps the lives of the great nomads of immemorial time, Abraham, Hagar, Sarah, and their daughters and sons, can shed light on the way of nomadic thinking. For if Odysseus is the true father of traditional biblical interpretation (because his life was guided by a nostalgia for his home and a desire to *return* to the comforts of the familiar), then Abraham is the father of the nomadic interpretation. After all, Abraham had to put aside all such nostalgia for his past in order to embark upon a journey *with no possibility of return*. Similarly, a hermeneutic practice characterized by nomadic thinking must likewise be prepared to let go of the comfortable and familiar, and make a commitment to a journey that has no known destination.

The lives of the great nomads remind us that this journey is no mere academic or intellectual exercise. G-d's holy nomads were fully embodied people, who faced real uncertainty, threats, and dangers in their wilderness wandering. Similarly, we wander in a complicated land, characterized by extreme wealth alongside desperate poverty, unspoiled natural beauty next to environmental degradation, and acts of solidarity in friendship alongside acts of human exploitation. For guidance on such a perilous journey in such a complicated land, we, as nomadic interpreters, can still open the pages of scripture and read again the sacred stories of the *Lord of the Nomads*, "I Am Who I Am," the One in whom Abraham and Moses put their trust. Following the example of these holy nomads, we too can respond to G-d's call to "Go forth from" our "own country" and journey toward a new land, which we as yet cannot imagine.

Index